Confronting Trauma & Toxicity:

Tools for Transformative Leaders, Workplace Warriors, and Community Builders to Foster Resilience and Meaningful Lives

PETTIS PERRY

Library of Congress Control Number: 2025911008

ISBN: 979-8-999042-40-8 (Hardcover)
ISBN: 979-8-999042-41-5 (Paperback)
ISBN: 979-8-999042-42-2 (eBook)

Illustrations: Pettis Perry
Cover design: Regan Robertson
Book design: Melissa Vail Coffman

About the Cover

Like the book itself, the cover of *Confronting Trauma & Toxicity* emerged through a collaborative, community-rooted process. It began with a concept by Ashleigh Bostic, daughter of my late friend and Alpha Phi Alpha Fraternity, Inc. brother, Peter F. Bostic. Her vision inspired nearly a dozen iterations, each refined through reflection and dialogue, culminating in the image you now hold.

The photos on the back cover mark pivotal moments in my life. The first, from 2011, captures a joyful return to Self after surviving a wrongful termination in 1998 and a year of homelessness in 2008–2009—sustained only by the generosity of friends who took me in. The second, from 2015, was taken during a prolonged period of adversity under toxic leadership in a hostile workplace.

The ethereal figure on the front, rising from the earth into light, symbolizes my journey from trauma to transcendence. The light represents the Source of all things, known by many names—a metaphor for resilience, healing, and hope.

This cover, like the message within, was shaped by a global community. Hundreds of people—many I've never met—shared insights online and in person that helped shape this project. Each voice mattered.

I am deeply grateful for every contribution. Their support and yours have been a profound blessing.

Disclosures Emergency Support

Should you become triggered or agitated by case examples, personal stories, content, or data, PLEASE seek professional help to explore why such feelings exist. If you find yourself with hard-to-reconcile and persistent intrusive thoughts that make you uncomfortable or cause you to consider harming yourself or others, PLEASE reach out to the National Suicide and Crisis Hotline (dial 988) in the United States or local support centers in your area.

For information about the genetics of suicide and other suicide research, see the American Foundation for the Prevention of Suicide (AFSP.org). Research Connections Retrieved from https://afsp.org/our-work/research/research-connections/

Trauma-informed Communities Fund

As part of my support to build trauma-informed communities, I am contributing 7% of net sales from this book and other revenue generating projects to a fund held by an investment company for that purpose. My goal is to raise $7,000,000 for the fund that will support trauma research, trauma prevention, and post-trauma growth and wellness programs and services.

Contents

L-R; Rose (mom), brother Frederick Douglass (lap),
brother Richard Rizzo (c), Pettis (dad), me (lap) c 1953.
Image printed with permission from People's World *magazine*

Dedication

This resource guide is dedicated to the Manosia-Rizzo-Perry family and to my Sicilian, African, Choctaw, and Creek ancestors I do not know. I have done my very best to represent our family well. To my parents, Pettis and Rose, you gave me the power of free will and with it the power of agency, personal ownership, and responsibility that comes with such power. You did not let me slack on becoming the best version of myself I could become. To my brothers, Richard and Frederick Douglass, and their families, thank you for the many contributions you've made to my life helping me become who I am today.

To my son, Matthew, you have always been the brightest light in my life. You are my constant teacher, giving me the strength to endure hardship and uphold my dignity in the face of tremendous trauma and toxicity. You are the meaningfulness in my life that fills me with continuous joy. You've increased my capacity to love through Jennifer and Liam. To my daughter-in-law, Jennifer, who has allowed me to be me, even when it might not have made sense, you accepted my son as your life partner and brought our family lines together. I love and appreciate you for standing by me as I shed the skin of my past. Thank you for bringing my (our) grandson, Liam, into this world. I am doing my very best, as my parents did before me to help create a better world for you and him—*it's always about the children*, as mom would say. I love you all deeply and live to serve you and humanity as I was trained to do.

To my favorite professor ever, Dr. Robert Lamp, the only teacher who expressed his belief in me, defended me against naysayers, and for the first time told me I was one of the best students in my doctoral program during my time at the University of San Francisco. Dr. Lamp, you walked the talk of a transformative leader. You were my no-nonsense teacher and mentor who fully embraced the best Jesuit teaching practices. You taught me systems thinking; how to embrace conflict as a positive source of energy to effectuate change; and how to understand the subtleties between leadership, group dynamics, and goal behavior performance. I hope this guide makes you proud of the time you took to shape my thinking.

To the stories of the biblical figures Jesus, Moses, and Job that have profoundly influenced my life: Jesus, the teacher who sacrificed his life for the sake of humanity and who suffered the ultimate price for daring to challenge the thinking of those he encountered. You taught me to be prepared for the storms and the great cost that would result from whatever actions I took challenging the status quo. Moses, the eternal guide who leads others to experiences he will not share. You taught me that when we are called to lead, it is about the mission and not about being rewarded for the work in fulfilling your purpose. Last but certainly not least, Job, endured immense suffering to demonstrate his unwavering faith. You taught me that my commitment to my faith includes a path that will bring me great harm to test my faith, yet I must endure to fulfill my life purpose.

Your stories, and those of countless others before me, have reinforced the importance of commitment to purpose. You illustrate that challenging the status quo carries a weighty burden and exacts a toll on loved ones, highlighting the price to be paid.

To my childhood friends Charles Clay, Robert Lett, and John Brown and their families, thank you for providing me with the few safe havens I experienced during that phase of my life. Without you all, I am not sure what would have become of me. Your families accepted me without knowing just how wounded and broken I was. When I was with you, my pain was elsewhere.

To Sgt. Kent Waldoch and his family, thank you for rescuing me from being without a home for the first time in my life. You all gave me a place to heal, transform, and move on with my life.

To my fraternal brothers in Alpha Phi Alpha Fraternity, Inc., my consulting partner for many decades, Brother Michael F. Lange, and Brother Peter F. Bostic, for the many days and nights we spent working on improving YMCA's and other organizations serving inner-city communities throughout California. Brother LeRoy Titus, you provided leadership to the YMCA's Serving Disadvantage Communities (YSDAC) working group, the YMCA's Career Development Program (CDP), and founded the Weingart YMCA serving south-central Los Angeles, and you still found time to mentor me. Each of you, and your families shaped my life in profound ways, leading to my growth and development as a practitioner.

To my brave contributors who weathered your personal storms to help others despite the anxiety and suffering you've encountered along your paths, thank you for having the courage to challenge yourselves so that you might become even better versions of yourselves by sharing your personal stories.

To my friends and colleagues across the country who have made positive contributions to my life and supported me at the most critical times in my life, thank you.

To those I've harmed, I am deeply sorry for the pain I caused you. Be at peace knowing that in harming you, I also harmed myself.

To my enemies and others who've brought me great harm, you have all been my teachers. Despite the pain you have caused me, you have taught me valuable lessons of who and what not to become, the endurance required to still be standing when all is said and done, and in the end, it is up to me in the face of adversity whether my star continues to rise!

To all of you I say, *my head is bloodied, but unbowed*! This guide, *Confronting Trauma & Toxicity: Tools for Transformative Leaders, Workplace Warriors, and Community Builders to Foster Resilience and Meaningful Lives* would not be possible without each of your contributions.

Acknowledgments

I wish to thank my sister-in-law, Valerie Haynes Perry, who initially edited this manuscript. I also thank my neighbor, Gregory Houlton, owner of Alegra Marketing Print Mail of Warsaw, Indiana who has supported me in the marketing and distribution of the guide. I am deeply indebted to him and his team for their support and friendship.

Special acknowledgment is given to Marlo Lynn Cooley, who became my best friend. Her undying love for God greatly influenced my soul's development. Her rich friendship, unwavering support, and spiritual magic during the five months of my transition from the darkness of my past into the light of my future gave me five of the best months of my life.

There are too many others to name who offered advice, counsel, and additional support to help me get to the finish line. I could not have done this project without your support and guidance. Thank you!

To the contributors who braved their circumstances to submit their personal story accounts, thank you for your courage and willingness to contribute:

Dr. Janine Crifasi

Dr. Lucy J. Crowder

Dr. Alan Faingold

Dr. Karen Linyard

Dr. Peterson Mirville

Dr. Ann M. Morgan

Frederick Douglass Perry (brother)

René Pratt

Lara Raggon

Dawn DePalma Ross

Heather Timmons

Foreword

"You can't judge a book by looking at the cover"
— Bo Diddley (Willie Dixon, 1962)

How many of the people with whom you are acquainted do you know completely; every aspect of them? Do you know how their experiences shaped their thoughts and behaviors, why they chose their life path, and what drives them to achieve or prevents them from achieving their goals? What can we know about someone after our initial introduction when we tend to judge them immediately by observing their external cues and then classifying them in our minds by "stereotyping" them into discrete groups—men, women, and children have certain characteristics and roles regardless of where they are from? But is this true?

Stereotyping is the act of assigning generalized and oversimplified beliefs or assumptions about a group of people based on characteristics such as race, gender, or occupation, without considering individual differences. Stereotyping is a common human behavior that makes it easier for us to distinguish friends from foes, but in doing so we attribute characteristics associated with specific individuals to entire groups of people. The associated bias and over-generalizations can result in interpersonal and intergroup conflicts because we perceive and expect what we have learned or heard about a single person to be attributed to an entire group of people, rather than seeking to understand someone as an individual with unique characteristics and ways of being.

Underneath the aspects we perceive, everyone has complex differences influenced by their life experiences. The photo of an iceberg below illustrates unseen deep personal attributes, making it impossible to know exactly what is happening in an individual's world. Learning a person's hidden attributes is essential for establishing understanding, building connections, relationship development, and understanding what makes them who they are.

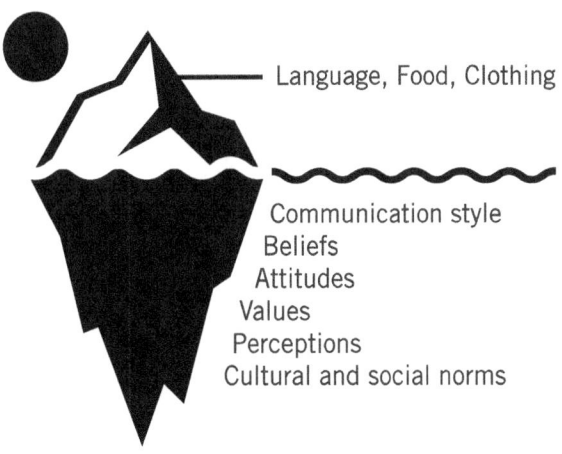

Language, Food, Clothing

Communication style
Beliefs
Attitudes
Values
Perceptions
Cultural and social norms

My first encounter with Dr. Pettis Perry was as a Walden University Master's student attending his online course about Leading Vibrant and Diverse Teams. I will always remember when he posted his course survival guide on May 9, 2011. I know the date because I still have the 15-page PowerPoint presentation in my documents. I saved it because I wanted to become an online instructor. His guide was easily the best example of inspirational and aspirational course direction I had seen in online education and remains so today. Dr. Perry was very responsive to all the students in the class and our group gained substantial knowledge because of his leadership acumen, agility, and wisdom. I met him face-to-face at the 2012 Walden University Master of Leadership graduation ceremony: An extremely social, happy, and knowledgeable professor who was kind enough to spend time with my colleagues and I to discuss our future goals. In *"Confronting Trauma & Toxicity: Tools for Transformative Leaders, Workplace Warriors, and Community Builders to Foster Resilience and Meaningful Lives"* Dr. Perry takes readers on a journey of hope, survival, and resilience about coping with adverse situations. He explains the impact of trauma and toxicity in the workplace and elsewhere by helping you understand how trauma and toxic environments affect individual well-being and organizational productivity. You will also learn about the long-lasting psychological effects of trauma, including Complex PTSD (CPTSD), and how it manifests in everyday interactions. The exploration of the connection between trauma and behavior illustrates how unresolved trauma influences workplace behaviors, which often leads to cycles of toxicity that affect leadership and group dynamics. Understanding group dynamics and power structures is essential because the impact of group dynamics, social identity theory, and toxic leadership can perpetuate harmful environments.

The existing trauma in any person's life may not be discovered during the hiring process. Trauma from personal life often migrates into the workplace and vice versa, creating a complex interplay that can perpetuate harm. Dr. Perry provides actionable advice for employees and leaders on navigating, surviving, and transforming toxic environments into healthier and more productive ones by offering real-life examples and stories from personal experiences illustrated through case studies. He shares practical strategies for building resilience in the face of workplace toxicity and overcoming trauma to foster personal and professional growth. He also presents pathways to healing and personal growth and outlines how individuals can move from trauma toward healing and post-traumatic growth, emphasizing the importance of personal reflection and professional help.

Dr. Perry showcases his leadership expertise as he skillfully emphasizes leaders' roles in shaping workplace culture and fostering inclusivity and fairness by examining how they create either a toxic or healthy organizational culture, provides insights into how leadership behaviors can harm or heal, and highlights how transformative leadership can challenge toxic systems, promote equity, and foster inclusive work environments.

Dr. Perry was the first instructor to recommend that I enroll in a Doctorate program. Following his advice, I earned my Ed.D. in 2019. We are colleagues and friends, and I am honored to be a contributor to his literary work. Although I know some of his hidden values, I learned much more about his passion for leadership and having a positive impact on the lives of others after reading "*Confronting Trauma & Toxicity: Tools for Transformative Leaders, Workplace Warriors, and Community Builders to Foster Resilience and Meaningful Lives.*" Now you can begin (or continue) your journey of hope, survival, and resilience as you create more meaning in your life with the help of this powerful resource guide!

Alan Faingold Ed.D.

Preface

Trauma and toxicity in our workplaces and groups are pervasive. However, instead of focusing solely on their negative aspects, I choose to show how they can be transformed into opportunities for creating a meaningful life. The way I see it, ignoring this approach would mean succumbing to the harm they cause, rather than showcasing my accomplishments despite these persistent obstacles. It also seems to me that despite whatever we face, the objective is to create the most meaningful life possible for as long as we have to live—at least that's my desire and part of my belief system.

"*Confronting Trauma & Toxicity: Tools for Transformative Leaders, Workplace Warriors, and Community Builders to Foster Resilience and Meaningful Lives*" is the culmination of my training, education, personal, and professional experiences during my long career. As a social scientist, educator, and practitioner, I have spent my career empowering others, navigating the complexities of trauma, and confronting toxic environments in organizations and personal relationships. This is a story of healing and leaders who have done what they could to create transformative changes in their toxic workplace environments.

The belief that trauma, while inevitable, does not have to define us, is central to this guide. From an early age, I learned that life is shaped by challenges and our choices in response to them. My parents and mentors instilled in me the values of service, resilience, and the pursuit of excellence—principles that have guided my journey. This guide draws from these experiences and aims to support human service professionals, leaders, parents, and anyone striving to create a more meaningful life for themselves despite the obstacles they encounter.

Throughout my career, I have served in various capacities, from working as a volunteer to becoming the Executive Director/CEO of the largest statewide YMCA program in the country, as well as a leadership and organizational effectiveness educator and consultant. Each role brought unique challenges, triumphs, and lessons. However, it was my personal experiences with trauma and workplace toxicity that became the impetus for and truly shaped the message of this book. These experiences, while painful, became the foundation of my understanding of human experience, and my resilience and growth.

"*Confronting Trauma & Toxicity: Tools for Transformative Leaders, Workplace Warriors, and Community Builders to Foster Resilience and Meaningful Lives*" symbolizes not only my journey through trauma and toxicity but also my commitment to helping others by sharing the insights I've gained. It is a guide for transformative leaders and individuals, aiming to foster resilience, healing, and purpose as they navigate and transform their own environments.

A key component of this guide is the personal stories shared by individuals who, like me, have faced trauma and toxicity in their workplace environments. These stories illustrate the deep emotional and psychological toll that toxic environments can have, but they also highlight the resilience and strength that emerge in the process of overcoming adversity.

The contributions of people like Janine Crifasi and Frederick Douglass Perry underscore how toxic leadership, manipulation, and discrimination can cause lasting harm. Their experiences with abusive bosses, racial bias, and systemic discrimination reveal the insidious nature of toxicity in the workplace. Others, like Lucy J. Crowder, share how poor leadership can result in betrayal, sabotage, and quiet firings, which leave lasting scars. Yet, each story is also a testament to the power of resilience, personal growth, and the capacity for healing.

Through these personal accounts, we see how people find strength through self-reflection, therapy, and the pursuit of personal development. Whether through mentorship, faith, or practices like Taekwondo, as in Peterson Mirville's story, individuals find ways to reclaim control of their lives and carve out new paths forward. Ann M. Morgan reflects on the transformative power of supportive leadership, contrasting her positive experiences with earlier toxic workplaces and demonstrating the profound impact that leadership and culture can have on individual well-being.

These stories are central to the message of this guide. They show that while trauma and toxicity are unfortunately common, they do not have to be permanent conditions. Instead, with the right tools, support, and mindset, we can transform these difficult experiences into opportunities for growth and meaning.

In sharing these experiences and the lessons I've learned, I hope this guide provides practical strategies, reflections, and inspiration to help others on their journey. It is my belief that we can transform our lives by facing the trauma and toxicity that surrounds us and choosing to create a life filled with purpose, compassion, and resilience.

This guide is not only a resource for understanding the signs of trauma and toxicity but also a call to action. It offers practical solutions for leaders, supervisors, and individuals who seek to foster healthier, more supportive environments. Through these personal stories and professional insights, this guide serves as a roadmap for turning trauma into growth and for building meaningful lives in the workplace and beyond.

You are invited to walk with me through these pages, explore your own journey, and find meaning in the experiences that shape your life. Together, we can create a world where workplaces, homes, and communities are kinder, healthier, and more supportive for all. May this guide become a useful resource for you as you pursue your version of creating a meaningful life for yourself.

Life

Life, filled with twists and turns
Yielding excitement
Beauty
Purpose Love
Betrayal
Pain
Obstacles
Interference
Resilience
Never knowing
First a loss, then a win
Lessons in both
Committed to what I yearn to find
A search for acceptance
A belief in me
A lifelong journey
No trepidation
Abundant faith
I know I'll find it one day
That's life!

This poem is dedicated to Laurel Smith, LICSW, of Washington state who supported me for many years at a time when I was under vicious attacks from highly toxic people.

Principle 1: *Life's unpredictability underscores the importance of resilience and stamina for navigating challenges and seizing growth opportunities, so be a long-distance runner.*

CHAPTER 1

Experiences Shape Behaviors

Welcome

Hello, fellow traveler, and welcome! Our paths have crossed because of the many choices we've made on our journeys, and I'm grateful to have you here. This guide serves as a comprehensive resource for anyone—whether you're a professional, parent, student, or simply someone interested in personal growth—seeking to create a meaningful life despite trauma and toxicity in the workplace and elsewhere. It delves into how our psychological development, shaped by life experiences, influences behaviors that affect our future. For example, you might continue buying a product you loved as a child, feel fear due to a past injury, or recall a cherished memory when a familiar scent fills the air.

For me it's eating strawberries, falling on roller skates while wearing shorts skating down a sloped driveway, and the smell of garlic particularly when making spaghetti sauce. Strawberries were my favorite childhood fruit and remain so in adulthood. Even though I was allergic to them, I ate them anyway and eliminated the allergy over the years. Falling on skates and ripping the skin from my ankle to my thigh, promotes a fear when I'm on skates and whenever I begin thinking about learning to ski. Whenever my mom made spaghetti sauce you could smell it a block away. Today, whenever I smell that combination, my mouth begins to water.

Each of these are examples of how isolated experiences produce long-term positive and negative impacts that can last a lifetime. Wherever I go and whatever I do, whenever I encounter strawberries, skates, and spaghetti sauce I'm reminded of events that passed long ago. What I've found is that the more intense the feelings about events the more they tend to linger and reappear periodically (or frequently) as life continues. This is true whether they are negative or positive experiences—these experiences become precursors to future feelings and behaviors.

Without a doubt, navigating life is tough because of the physical and psychological wounds (*trauma)* we encounter over the course of our lifetimes. The American Psychological Association (A.P.A.) tells us that the term *trauma* is derived from the Greek word for *wound* resulting from overt exposure to traumatic events, also suggesting that trauma has become an epidemic, which is confirmed by the data (DSM-5, 2013). *Trauma* describes the overt exposure to physical, psychological, social, and environmental events producing wounds that impact us sufficiently to generate lasting effects, but it lives in the mind.

Trauma produces aftereffects that filter perspectives, trigger biological responses, and have more than three dozen potential aftereffects associated with emotional, mental, behavioral, and physical aftereffects that can work independently or collectively, causing us to act in ways that become hard to explain without professional help. The aftereffects of trauma exposure can become a significant part of these experiences, affecting individuals who then carry it into their homes, workplaces, public spaces, and social groups, often producing toxicity without realizing it. Toxicity is an outgrowth of trauma, and it refers to harmful behaviors, attitudes, or environments that negatively affect people's well-being, health, or performance. In the workplace, and as is the case in our homes, it can include things like bullying, manipulation, disrespect, or creating a hostile atmosphere, leading to stress and damage to both individuals and the organization.

Taking Ownership

We are all products of our environments and contributors to the environments in which we live. In my case, I have never known life without trauma. However, through writing this resource guide, I've come to better understand the pervasive impact of the trauma and toxicity I encountered both inside and outside the work environment. Because of my circumstances, I've had to find ways to pursue my dreams in the face of continuous attempts made by others to thwart my efforts. Despite the myriad negative people and events, encountered along the way, my life has been meaningful and fulfilling, nonetheless. One of my secrets has been to find ways of converting my pain into fuel for accomplishing my life goals, and producing this guide is one tangible example of how I am able to do this.

Still, the harm I might have caused others haunts me, and while the weight of good I may have done outweighs the bad when looking from the audience's perspective, for those I harmed it pales in comparison to the weight of the burden caused by me and carried forward by them. I know from personal experience this is true. From personal experience what it shall become for them is up to each person, as it has been for me. I am truly sorry and intimately understand your pain as my humanness shows through.

As crazy as it sounds, *life* exists solely in our minds through a process of perspective shaping how we interpret our experiences (existence). For as long as we live, we are in the process of always becoming the next version of ourselves. Therefore, taking ownership of who we are at any given moment is critically important if the goal is to make the most of what life has to offer.

The easiest thing in the world to do is to blame others for our failures. The hardest is making the inward journey to confront the demons that haunt us. But it is through the inward journey that we come to understand the richness that life has to offer us. We cannot achieve our potential if we continuously lay blame at the feet of others and only accept credit for whatever success we might have. Taking personal ownership is the first step towards maximizing your potential and creating a more meaningful life.

Life with Complex Posttraumatic Stress Disorder (CPTSD)

Of all the projects I have undertaken, this one has been the most challenging. Living with complex post-traumatic stress disorder (CPTSD), writing about it, and dealing with the aftermath of a four-car collision early in the writing process significantly increased the difficulty of completing this project. CPTSD is a psychological condition that occurs in response to prolonged, repeated exposure to traumatic events, often involving abuse, neglect, or captivity. Unlike traditional PTSD, which can result from a single seismic traumatic event, C-PTSD is characterized by additional symptoms such as difficulties with emotional regulation, negative self-perception, relationship challenges, and a persistent feeling of helplessness. It is commonly associated with trauma that occurs in interpersonal situations where the victim feels trapped, such as ongoing abuse or exploitation.

This guide offers stories to show how our lives are interconnected and how we all must navigate our journeys—pursuing our goals while supporting those we care about, even in the face of challenges, harm, or danger. Creating this guide has forced me to relive my life in many unique ways. Workplace and homeplace trauma and toxicity have filled about 75% of my life, which explains why I live with CPTSD. This condition complicates life, especially in work, politics, and social environments that are themselves filled with traumatized people spreading their toxicity through bias-laden behaviors, hate-filled rhetoric, and disparate treatment of various socially categorized groups. All of these factors combined make interpersonal and intergroup interactions more difficult.

Professional and Personal Perspectives

The lens through which I view the world—as a parent, practitioner, educator, consultant, and social scientist—is leadership and organizational effectiveness. Thus, this guide is written as a primer on trauma, toxicity, and organizational dynamics for a broad audience including professionals across sectors and industries, parents (family dynamics), and anyone interested in improving their life skills. While workplaces are the primary setting discussed, the dynamics occurring in work environments are similar to those in our homes and social groups.

This guide uniquely weaves theoretical research from various disciplines to help explain workplace dynamics, using real-life examples and personal stories as case studies. My goal is to share with you what I've learned about life, leadership, organizational effectiveness, trauma, and toxicity by drawing from my own lived experiences as an *everyday Joe* confronting real-time responses to seismic traumatic events.

The trauma in my last job with a large university was so pervasive that I got physically sick twice on my way to national faculty meetings and was unable to leave my room. When I was able to show up to the company's social events and meals, after showing my face and making the rounds to ensure people saw me, I would lose myself in the crowd. Quietly making my exit, I would eat alone at my own expense just to avoid people. At home, the trauma carried over, making it difficult for me to even be around people in social gatherings for more than a few minutes. Today, when I go to events, I still find myself experiencing extreme sensory overload and having to leave in order to escape what I am feeling—something I will continue working to resolve.

My Dye was Cast at Birth

Being born into a family of activists shaped my life's purpose and equipped me for the journey through adulthood. My upbringing instilled a deep commitment to serving others, which I've pursued professionally as a transformative executive leader, organizational effectiveness educator, and consultant. Thanks to my parents who were exemplary role models, I learned early on to challenge harmful status-quo conditions that hinder positive social change, intellectual growth, and personal freedoms of choice. This narrative also highlights the challenges faced by those who dare to speak the truth to power, even when done with love and a desire to improve conditions for all, without malice towards anyone.

Despite my considerable challenges, I have accomplished what many around me—coaches, teachers, counselors, supervisors, and even some family members—considered impossible, deeming my cause hopeless and foolish. However, here I am, proving them wrong and showing how perseverance can overcome even the most daunting obstacles.

Having spent much of my career in toxic environments, and with Smith (2016) finding that over half of the U.S. workforce report trauma at work, I feel compelled to speak out about my professional observations and experiences, gathered over nearly six decades in the field and the rest from lifelong lessons. This guide explores how trauma breeds toxicity and how this toxicity, in turn, perpetuates more trauma. I discuss the transmission of trauma between home and workplace, using research, data, and real-life personal stories to highlight the effects of trauma and toxicity on individuals.

Furthermore, my aim is to promote finding ways to create a meaningful life. I provide strategies for navigating through trauma toward a state of posttraumatic wellness and growth. The journey to recovery is deeply personal, as each individual has their unique path to follow throughout their lifetime, or said another way, the time they have for life.

Serving humanity with a total commitment to changing lives for the better when conditions are dire and appear insurmountable is the life I trained for in childhood, and in the end, I chose this path for myself. Watching my father on the national stage fighting for human rights, I also witnessed the treatment he received when he was imprisoned for his beliefs. Living through the assassinations of John F. Kennedy, Malcolm X, Martin Luther King, Jr., and Bobby Kennedy taught me that danger waits for the transformative spirit who comes along to bring about change. However, I consciously chose to walk headlong and headstrong into the storm.

With the advantage of hindsight, I know the things I have done through my life's work are precisely why I was born. It's obvious but worth saying that had I not had the toxicity and trauma at work and in my personal experiences, I would not have become the person I am today and could not have produced this project in this way. Moreover, it is also important for me to acknowledge that if the people who harmed me had supported me instead, there is no telling what else I might have accomplished that could have helped humanity. This exemplifies how life experiences often become precursors for future behaviors, including the paths and work people choose to do, as well as how they treat others.

What I need to make very clear is this: I do not advocate looking for trauma so we can learn about it or grow from it, as one client suggested. The truth is that no matter which path is selected, it will undoubtedly include trauma, so learn about it, understand it, and be prepared to embrace it so you can figure out how to navigate once it happens—because at some point, it will.

The Optimist Creed

The first service group I joined was an Optimist Club, which cultivates a healthy attitude for enduring whatever life throws our way. The Optimist Creed, written by Christian Larson and originally published under the title *Promise Yourself* in 1912, was adopted as the organization's official creed in 1922.

> Optimist Creed: To think only of the best, to work only for the best, and to expect only the best. To be just as enthusiastic about the success of others as you are about your own. To forget the past mistakes and press on to the greater achievements of the future. (Source: rb.gy/mjxn9h)

This creed gives me a concrete starting point to shape a better version of myself, and in many ways, it has brought me to this moment with you. It embodies what James Redfield, author of *The Celestine Prophecy* (1993), describes as "discovering the keys to life." Each key is a lesson that leads to finding the next important lesson (key) necessary to complete the journey. Consequently, my quest has been to grasp and gather truths and seemingly disparate pearls of wisdom that, upon reflection today, reveal their interconnectedness as part of a unified whole.

Leader Behaviors Impact Outcomes

After 15 consecutive years of working in highly toxic environments and now nearing the end of my career, I finally have time to collect my thoughts and make sense of my life. I am also at a point where I can now speak freely about my experiences, unencumbered by internal organizational threats because of my beliefs about the harm being caused to employees by toxic supervisors and other leaders. One of my realizations is that no matter how hard someone might try to do the right thing for their organization by bringing issues to the forefront for leader consideration, the messenger matters in terms of whether or not they will be heard by leaders. That is, the leader's perception of the messenger shapes both how the message is perceived as well as the treatment the messenger receives.

Leadership is a social dynamic that only occurs in groups and therefore it does not occur in a vacuum or in isolation from others. However, from my experience, there are many more leaders who fail to fully understand or grasp how their behaviors (subtle or otherwise) impact their followers. The tendency for most leaders is to see problems as belonging to others rather than exploring how their failures as leaders may have produced the problems they see. For example, poor communication from the leader can produce poor systems design, confusion, fear, or anger.

Everyone has their own idea of what leadership means, shaped by personal mental models. These mental models are the frameworks or thought patterns we rely on to make sense of how leadership and the world around us function. They shape how we interpret information, solve problems, and make decisions. These models are based on our experiences, beliefs, and knowledge, and they help us simplify complex situations by providing a mental blueprint for navigating them. However, they can also limit our thinking if we rely too heavily on outdated or inaccurate models.

Consequently, we also bring our personal implicit biases about leaders and what work means to any group we join, as does the leader. This is supported by implicit leadership theory (ILT) (Billsbury & O'Callahan, 2024). Therefore, we can also logically conclude that what a person believes going into a group also influences how they behave in the group, and it shapes their perceptions of the behaviors they see in the group. Any fore knowledge of any of the individuals within the group also tempers interpersonal interactions.

When talking about a leader's role in their group, we also have to consider how their behaviors shape the conditions within the group. For example, an autocratic leader will cause certain behaviors to emerge that are quite different than the behaviors emerging from a more participative leader. According to Billsbury and O'Callahan (2024), this occurs because of the leader's social construction of leadership perceptions. They found ". . . an individual's values, interests, and preferences will affect which voices are listened to [by the leader] and which voices have the most impact" (p.4).

These dynamics help to explain why I had so much difficulty getting promoted in an organization led by a self-described *Redneck* who ultimately became president of our organization. I may have literally been the only person of color who was willing to give him the benefit of the doubt in terms of initially setting aside my feelings about his self-identification when he first introduced himself as a dean in the college where I worked. Over the years, I was always respectful, but I challenged his thinking around key organizational decisions that maximized profits over the welfare of employees and students because I was a good soldier trying to support an organization I loved.

He also fully supported my highly toxic supervisor who was summarily fired after a 360-degree performance review was conducted of all supervisors in our college. In the end, I was targeted as a difficult employee and was passed over for promotions more than a dozen times. Once he became president, he refused to interview me three times for a position I helped to create and was eminently qualified to serve. His decision to not hire me, instead hiring two other people who failed, killed the diversity initiatives we worked so hard to create.

This is a key point in how leader behaviors can undermine the success of their organizations when they allow their personal feelings about an individual to get in the way of better judgment. Had the president met with me to discuss any concerns he might have had; I am highly confident that we could have come to an understanding that would have served his interests and those of our organization more fully. However, he could not get past his implicit biases informed by his misperceptions of the supervisor he supported. That supervisor was stealing my work by calling it his own and forcing me to do many of his tasks in order to present them as his work. Most importantly, that supervisor lacked the support of many of those reporting directly to him. However, rather than even considering that his perceptions of the supervisor might have been wrong, the president chose to target me, instead.

Internalizing Lessons

"Confronting Trauma & Toxicity: Tools for Transformative Leaders, Workplace Warriors, and Community Builders to Foster Resilience and Meaningful Lives" was written with you in mind. I've aimed to create something I wish I had much earlier in life, something that could have helped me better understand the behavioral and mental health dynamics that come with navigating life's obstacles.

Life is filled with ironies. Some early life experiences may very well show up later in some form or manner. Working as a part-time janitor at my local YMCA and working for a janitorial company where I learned how to buff floors came in handy as an executive director with responsibilities for cleaning and maintaining facilities. The more impactful irony though, was studying YMCA attrition as my dissertation topic and then several years later finding myself in a wrongful termination lawsuit with the organization I loved.

What you choose to do with the insights from our time together is entirely up to you. I can only share the lessons I've gained from my experiences, just as my teachers did for me. Our ability as a species to learn from each other allows us to grow and evolve, both individually and collectively. This exchange of knowledge is what makes life exciting and beautiful—it is the foundation of our authentic diversity and strength, and it fuels our evolution. However, there's still a lot of challenging work ahead.

Nothing about my path indicates what will happen to you on yours as each one is separate. Even if we were life partners or twins, there would be lots for us to share, but in the end, life is a solitary journey that we each must navigate alone—even in the midst of loved ones. We see this most poignantly when we lose someone we love. So, please do not measure yourself against me. Your life is your life, and this is a process of sharing, understanding, growth, finding happiness, and sustaining the capacity for resiliency in response to trauma and toxicity. It is only a competition with yourself if you make it one. Perhaps you like challenging yourself (as I sometimes do) to see what the best version of yourself might become. Should you do so, just remember you are playing a game with yourself.

Goals for Using this Guide

Today, our civilization is currently experiencing unprecedented turmoil. The World Health Organization (W.H.O.) (2017) found in a study of twenty-four countries, including the U.S., that:

> Trauma exposure is common throughout the world, unequally distrib-
> uted, and differential across trauma types with respect to PTSD risk.
> Although a substantial minority of PTSD cases remits within months
> after onset, the mean symptom duration is considerably longer than
> previously recognized. [Reportedly,] 70.4% of respondents experi-
> enced lifetime traumas, with exposure averaging 3.2 traumas per capita
> . . . .[Further,] the broad category of intimate partner sexual violence
> accounted for nearly 42.7% of all persons with PTSD. Prior trauma his-
> tory predicted both future trauma exposure and future PTSD risk.

My goal with this guide is to offer a comprehensive resource that explores various human behavior topics, highlighting leadership's pervasive influence and vital role in various contexts. It underscores the significance of understanding and responsibly exercising leadership, recognizing its profound impact on the behaviors of individuals and groups.

Leadership can be defined as the ability to inspire, influence, and guide individuals or groups toward achieving a common goal or vision (Stogdill, 1950 as cited in Stogdill, 1974). It involves taking responsibility, making decisions, and creating an environment where others feel motivated, supported, and empowered to contribute their best efforts. Effective leadership is characterized by qualities such as vision, communication, integrity, empathy, and the capacity to adapt to changing circumstances while fostering collaboration and growth. Ultimately, leadership is about positively impacting people and processes to create meaningful outcomes.

Using this definition, we can see that leadership is a behavior that goes well beyond a position. It can come from positional authority but also emerges when leadership comes from followers exercising their power to move group members towards an action. For example, a low-level employee taking the initiative to solve a problem that a group adopts, a child influencing a parent to take some sort of action they would not have initiated on their own, or standing up against a bully.

This guide contains data points and theories that help explain trauma and toxic behaviors. It also contains stories to illustrate the impacts of toxic behaviors on the lives of real people, thereby demonstrating the application of theory in practice. As a result, anyone interested in effective leadership, group dynamics, organizational behavior, becoming a better parent, or looking for ways to change their conditions can find ideas and resources within these pages to help them. As you read this guide, please keep an open mind and lean into it rather than shy away from any discomfort you might feel from the materials presented here. Your discomfort may very well be a key, that if explored, may lead to a happier and more fulfilling life.

I wish you peace and love while pursuing a well-lived, happy, and meaningful life.

Navigating Trauma

Living with CPTSD (complex post-traumatic stress disorder) deepens my purpose, driving me to enlighten others about trauma and the potential for growth, resilience, and wisdom that can emerge from even the most painful experiences—those we wish we could erase but leave indelible marks on us. Trauma is inevitable—as inescapable as death—and we are all challenged to prepare ourselves for life's future trials. However, our level of preparedness dramatically influences how we perceive and respond to it. My exploration of the Dark Nights of the Soul (see Chapter 8) revealed a poignant truth: Escaping one traumatic event only brings us closer to the next.

Surviving trauma often leaves us with broken pieces of ourselves and visible or invisible scars. However, understanding these experiences provides profound insight into our behaviors and fosters empathy, enhancing our ability to comprehend others' pain when their trauma surfaces. Trauma-informed communities offer invaluable opportunities for building relationships and uniting around shared experiences, especially during large-scale traumatic events like climate disasters, mass shootings, threats to democracy fueled by notions of White supremacy, and the erosion of individual freedoms.

Imagine a world with less fear and division, where misunderstandings and disputes do not escalate into violence. My seven-year journey researching trauma has not only helped me better understand my own reactions and emotions but has also empowered me to share this knowledge widely. Like Johnny Appleseed spreading seeds, I aim to disseminate information about trauma, its effects, and coping strategies, helping to lighten others' burdens and guide them out of darkness, serving as a beacon toward safer grounds. It is also a reminder that sometimes we are called to stand amidst the storm to light the way for others to find safe harbors.

Acknowledging the inherent pain of existence can transform our communities. By recognizing our shared experiences of suffering, we can forge deep connections with others, even with strangers, united in our collective endurance. This guide is the embodiment of that vision—*my why*—born from a lifetime of personal trauma and professional engagement in human services, organizational effectiveness, and leadership education. Standing on the shoulders of those who came before me, I now share my insights, connecting the dots of my journey to assist others in navigating theirs.

Contributor Lara Raggon illustrates the lingering impacts of trauma from toxic work environments by emphasizing how toxic work environments can leave lasting psychological scars, even after one has left the environment. She discusses how trauma can manifest in many ways, such as anxiety, mistrust, and difficulty in fully engaging in new, healthier environments. Lara demonstrates how the psychological toll of working under a toxic leader affected her well-being, relationships, and overall quality of life, showing the deep and enduring impact of such experiences. She also offers insights into the ongoing process of healing from the trauma experienced in a toxic work environment, which for her includes self-reflection, seeking professional help, and gradually rebuilding confidence and emotional stability. Lara highlights the importance of recognizing and addressing the residual effects of trauma, as well as the positive changes in her life since leaving the toxic workplace. The focus on healing underscores the possibility of recovery and personal growth after enduring a harmful work environment.

Root Cause Analysis

At what point should we shift from merely addressing symptoms to tackling the root causes? Consider the issues of housing insecurity, homelessness, and crime, which are often symptoms of deeper problems such as poverty, inadequate mental and general healthcare, outdated education systems, values that put profits before people, and entrenched beliefs among policymakers about the limitations of marginalized communities. When these factors intersect with the mental models of influential individuals and the disproportionate political influence of a small, uninformed group, the result is a system where a minority sets the rules, while the majority remains disadvantaged.

Throughout my career, I've observed these dynamics at play. For example, the militarization of police in the United States began to take shape in the 1960s and 1970s, particularly in response to civil unrest and increasing concerns over crime. Two significant events accelerated this process: The Civil Rights Movement and the War on Drugs. The Civil Rights Movement was a direct response to Jim Crow segregation, historic numbers of lynchings, police brutality, and Urban Riots of the 1960s that saw protests and civil disturbances grow in cities across the U.S. In response, the government started providing local police with more military-grade equipment to control crowds and address violent confrontations. The 1965 Watts riots in Los Angeles, the emergence of the Black Panther Party in 1966 in Oakland, California, and the unrest following Dr. Martin Luther King Jr.'s assassination in 1968 were key moments that led to this shift.

The War on Drugs (1980s) led to furthering the militarization of police under President Ronald Reagan. Reagan defunded highly successful criminal diversion programs to redirect those resources into hiring more police. In 1981, the Military Cooperation with Civilian Law Enforcement Agencies Act allowed military forces to assist local police in drug enforcement efforts, opening the door for law enforcement to acquire surplus military equipment. The establishment of Special Weapons and Tactics (SWAT) teams during this time also contributed to the militarized approach. This process continued to expand through federal programs like the 1033 Program in the 1990s, which enabled the transfer of military equipment such as armored vehicles and weapons to local police departments, solidifying the militarization trend seen today.

The result of these initiatives means the increased militarization of the police has had significant and lasting effects on the relationship between law enforcement and the communities they serve, especially with marginalized and minority populations. The use of military-grade equipment and aggressive tactics has contributed to a growing perception of police as occupiers, rather than protectors, particularly in high-crime areas and during protests. This shift strained trust between law enforcement and the public.

President Reagan's shifting of resources from successful criminal diversion programs focusing on prevention and rehabilitation and redirecting them to fund increased policing efforts led to a rise in arrests and a growing prison population, but it did little to address the underlying causes of crime, such as poverty and lack of opportunity. The War on Drugs and police militarization disproportionately impacted Black and Brown communities, leading to higher incarceration rates and further inflaming tensions between these communities and law enforcement.

Overall, these decisions changed the context in which the police forces are more heavily militarized, a public that is increasingly distrustful of law enforcement, and a reduction in programs that could address the root causes of crime, leaving these deeper social issues unresolved and illustrating how leader perceptions of problems shape their behaviors and ultimately the behaviors of their followers.

In leadership, *contextual* refers to understanding and adapting leadership styles and strategies based on specific circumstances, environments, or cultures. There is no universal approach to leadership; instead, effective leaders tailor their actions to fit factors like organizational culture, social norms, economic conditions, and the unique characteristics of team members. This flexibility allows leaders to adjust behaviors—whether adopting a directive stance during crises or fostering collaboration for innovation.

To be an effective leader in the twenty-first century, cultural sensitivity is crucial but lacking in most leaders and therefore enhancing communication and collaboration by respecting diverse backgrounds is made nearly impossible. Leaders must maintain situational awareness and have the skills to balance external market dynamics and internal team factors such as the needs of diverse groups. However, the U.S. Supreme Court significantly weakened affirmative action in college admissions on June 29, 2023, in the case of Students for Fair Admissions v. Harvard. The ruling effectively ended the consideration of race as a factor in college admissions, declaring that the race-conscious admissions policies at Harvard University and the University of North Carolina were unconstitutional. The Court ruled that these policies violated the Equal Protection Clause of the 14th Amendment. This decision marked a major shift away from decades of precedent that allowed limited use of race in college admissions to promote diversity, and along with it, teaching students today to bridge differences is being made more difficult at a time when it is needed most.

Since the Supreme Court's ruling in Students for Fair Admissions v. Harvard, corporate affirmative action programs have also come under heightened scrutiny, even though the decision directly addressed higher education. Consequently, this ruling triggered broader legal and political challenges to race-conscious practices in corporate America.

Following the decision, some companies have faced lawsuits targeting their diversity, equity, and inclusion (DEI) initiatives, with claims that certain hiring and promotion practices unfairly favor underrepresented minorities. In response, many businesses have reassessed and modified their DEI strategies, shifting away from explicitly race-based criteria to focus on concepts like *diversity of thought* and socioeconomic background. Companies are emphasizing skills-based hiring to continue promoting diversity without relying on race.

As a result, some organizations have scaled back their public commitments to racial diversity and adopted more cautious language to avoid legal risks. Meanwhile, state-level actions have varied, with more conservative states restricting affirmative action in other areas, while progressive states continue to defend race-conscious programs where possible. Despite these changes, many companies remain dedicated to fostering inclusive workplaces. They are focusing on developing inclusive cultures through mentorship, training, and sponsorship programs that support underrepresented groups without directly using race as a factor. The ruling has also sparked wider discussions about equity, prompting businesses to explore how they can support disadvantaged groups through socioeconomic diversity initiatives.

Therefore, while the ruling directly impacted higher education, it has also led companies to adapt their diversity efforts, reframing them to navigate the new legal environment illustrating how external political and market factors impact internal organizational behaviors. Ronald Heifetz and Marty Linsky (2002) emphasize this adaptive approach in *Leadership on the Line*, noting how influential leaders navigate challenges by embracing conflicts as opportunities for growth. Similarly, as described by Hersey and Blanchard (1985), situational leadership underscores the need for leaders to adjust their styles based on their team members' specific needs and readiness.

The Data

Staglin (2021), writing for Forbes Magazine, calls for a change in workforce treatment, citing research indicating that "... *trauma is widespread among employees beyond ... [the] high-risk/high-stress jobs [that] can impact workers in any industry for a multitude of reasons that often go overlooked or ignored.*"

Prevalence of Trauma

The prevalence of trauma in the workplace and society writ large cannot be overstated. More than half (53%) of working Americans have experienced a seismic traumatic event while on the job, with less than half (46%) of those saying their employer offered any support to help them grieve, cope, or recover in the aftermath of their events (Smith, 2016). Nearly seventy percent (69.9%) of medical students report bullying, which is then carried over into the professions when you discuss the issue with practicing medical professionals (Leisy & Ahmad, 2016).

In a study sponsored by the American Psychological Association (APA), Kilpatrick et al. (2013) analyzed nearly 3,000 U.S. adults (N = 2,953) and found that exposure to multiple traumatic events was common, with approximately 90% (89.7%) of participants reporting multiple traumatic stressors. This repeated exposure significantly increased the likelihood of developing post-traumatic stress disorder (PTSD), highlighting the cumulative effect of trauma. The study also revealed that PTSD prevalence was higher among women than men, and the risk of PTSD rose with the number of traumatic events experienced.

Tedeschi et al. (2018) further support this finding, noting that traumatic stress events tend to accumulate over time, leading to greater psychological impact. These studies emphasize the need for a comprehensive approach to addressing trauma due to its compounding effects and widespread occurrence. Moreover, according to the U.S. Centers for Disease Control (C.D.C.) (n.d.):

> . . . suicide rates increased approximately 36% between 2000–2023 . . . In 2021, an estimated 12.3 million American adults seriously thought about suicide, 3.5 million planned a suicide attempt, and 1.7 million attempted suicides . . . Suicide was responsible for 48,183 deaths in 2021 . . . [and] is the second leading cause of death for people ages 10-14 and 20-34.

Traumatic Event (T.E.) Exposure

Benjet et al. (2023) highlight in a global study that traumatic event (T.E.) exposure does not occur randomly in the population. The rate and type of T.E.s vary according to country of residence, sociodemographic characteristics, and history of prior T.E. exposure. This means most people experience trauma exposures shaped by their life circumstances, painting a nuanced picture rather than identifying a particular group of vulnerable individuals.

Adverse Childhood Experience (A.C.E.)

Furthermore, Swedo et al. (2023) found that nearly two-thirds (63.9%) of U.S. adults have experienced at least one adverse childhood experience (A.C.E.), defined as preventable, potentially traumatic events that occur among persons under 18 years of age and are associated with numerous adverse outcomes.

In other words, the data show that our life circumstances at birth and during childhood significantly influence our likelihood of experiencing increased numbers and types of traumatic events during our lifetimes. This connection becomes evident when considering how poverty increases exposure to adverse life events, such as how food and housing insecurities lead to differential health outcomes and poorer educational achievements than those of peers in more affluent communities.

Violence Project Findings

Fox (2021), reporting on Violence Project findings, illustrated that the number one issue for mass shootings is employment related. In other words, mass shootings happen more frequently in the workplace (31%) than anywhere else, with maybe as much as 70% of mass shootings being linked to employment issues like terminations, with nearly a quarter (23%) of them stemming from interpersonal conflicts and more than ten percent (13%) of them such as economic and legal issues. The Violence Project (2021) identified that "... most *of the shooters had been fired or were in trouble at work. They had an identifiable grievance, and they had studied the actions of past shooters, seeking validation.*"

Mass Shootings

Active shooter drills exist in every school and many workplaces. Between January 1 and December 31, 2023, there were 656 mass shootings in the United States, averaging nearly two per day (1.8/day) (Mass Shooting Tracker, December 31, 2023). In 2023, more than 40,000 people were killed in gun violence in the United States, according to Kiara Alfonseca of A.B.C. News. Of the 656 recorded mass shootings reported in 2023, 346 were school-affiliated mass shootings. Further, Smart and Schell (2021) reported in a Rand Corporation study that "... *domestic violence represents a risk factor for perpetrating a mass shooting . . . [with] nearly two-thirds (61%) of mass shooters having been previously engaged in the criminal justice system with almost one-third (31%) with suspected domestic violence in their backgrounds.*"

There is more evidence of the interplay between trauma, work, and social groups (including families), demonstrating that their dynamics feed each other. According to the National Coalition Against Domestic Violence (NCADV, n.d.), almost sixty percent (59.1%) of mass shootings between 2014 and 2019 were related to domestic violence. In nearly seventy percent (68%) of mass shooting cases, the shooter had a history of domestic violence or killed a family member or intimate partner. We must recognize the trauma left in the wake of violent events that traumatize whole communities. We must realize that we cannot harm others without harming ourselves.

Moving Beyond the Data

We must come to grips with the fact that, in no uncertain terms, trauma migrates from the home into the workplace and from the workplace into our homes. Trauma poses an existential threat confronting all of us today, and its impacts undercut interpersonal and intergroup relationships. The more sources of trauma and aftereffects, the more complex the trauma becomes. As will be shown, trauma shapes our personalities, and our personalities govern or at least influence our behaviors. Therefore, the more our trauma becomes acute, the more potential there is for it to become negatively impactful to ourselves and others—often at the most inopportune times.

Understanding trauma presents a significant challenge because its impacts often remain hidden until prompted by therapy or a moment of profound self-reflection. To truly grasp its roots, we must peel back the layers of defense we have constructed around ourselves. By identifying and naming the root cause of our trauma, we can effectively address it, reducing its lingering effects on our lives. The journey through our pain is arduous, but it holds the potential for immense growth and wisdom, helping us emerge as improved versions of ourselves. Moreover, this journey reminds us that we are not isolated in our experiences; countless others share the aftereffects of trauma, providing us with opportunities for a sense of shared understanding, resilience, and solidarity.

As we awaken each day, we are who we are at that moment, but there is no guarantee that we will be the same person when we go to bed at night. Whether by our creation or luck, something can completely derail our plans, not just for the day but for the rest of our lifetimes. After all, events happen, and they can positively or negatively transform life instantly, causing destiny to turn on a dime. Doing what we can to understand the fuller extent of life can facilitate resiliency occurring more quickly should the moment come when needed.

When Trauma Occurs

When trauma occurs, it does not simply evaporate into thin air. While the data are transparent about calculating in numeric terms the extent of many of the problems in the workplace, they do not account for the actual toll of trauma on the individuals who were harmed in the workplace. For example, consider Smith's (2016) findings of more than 53% of working Americans experiencing a traumatic event while on the job. Looking at the U.S. Bureau of Labor Statistics (B.L.S.) employment data for 2023, we see roughly 160,000,000 people in the workforce.

Suppose we use Smith's findings of 53% of the workforce as our factor. In that case, we can extrapolate that nearly eighty-five million (84.8 million) employees experienced at least one traumatic event on the job during 2023 and took their trauma into their homes. Depending on their previous life experiences and individual circumstances, that traumatic event may not be their first trauma and, therefore, may have added to the impacts of previous traumatic events felt and expressed inside the home. Since trauma is additive, it can compound, making treatments more complex. Logically, trauma may shape behaviors, and when that happens, trauma can then be carried back into their households, where it may at some point reveal itself as toxicity and then impact family members in a variety of ways.

Living in Dangerous Times

We also live in dangerous times, likely the deadliest in history, and we do so with the capability of wiping out civilization in an apocalyptic manner with the push of a single button. Currently, the Geneva Academy is monitoring 110 armed conflicts around the world, enveloping a quarter of the world's population—some 2 billion people. Globally, democracies are being threatened by both the far-right and the far-left political fringes in their populations, each extreme being as bad as the other because their dogmas lead to totalitarian rule that would leave most of the world's population out of any democratic decision-making practices.

Rather than fomenting peace, some leaders are fomenting violence by promoting and perpetuating fear and distrust of groups unlike their own. That fear is then used to stoke the idea that there is a need for self-protection against those groups and the government and of fear that their guns will be taken away. By stoking fear through *othering* (the process of demonizing others who are unlike us), leaders raise anxiety levels for all groups, producing trauma, triggering those already traumatized, and further aggravating an entire society that is already thoroughly traumatized.

Impact of Leader Words and Behaviors

There is ample evidence to illustrate how leader words and behaviors shape the behaviors of their followers. Political rhetoric on fear, insecurity, and gun control increases weapons purchases. Using a simple Google search, on June 13, 2024, as of 2018, the United States had an estimated 393.3 million guns owned by civilians, which is more than the country's population of about 330 million. The U.S. has more guns than 24 countries, with the highest civilian gun ownership combined. Additionally, the number of guns owned by U.S. adults has been increasing for years, with one study finding that the number increased from 265 million in 2015 to 326 million in 2019. (Source: https://rb.gy/ftoggl)

Further, according to ammo.com (June 13, 2024):

- Gun ownership in America increased 28% from 1994 to 2023.

- Based on NICS background data and manufacturing records, it is estimated that there are 393 million civilian-owned firearms in the U.S., but only 6.06 million firearms are registered in America (NFA registrations and states with permits to purchase).

- Estimates show that 82,880,000 people own at least one firearm in 2023.

- 43% of households have at least one firearm in 2023.

- Women's firearm ownership has increased by 177.8% since 1993.

- Hispanics are the fastest-growing demographic of gun owners, with a 33% increase in ownership between 2017 and 2023.

- Gun ownership declined by 22% in the 18-29 age group between 2017 and 2023.

- 1 out of 20 adults in the U.S. purchased a firearm for the first time during the pandemic.

(Source: rb.gy/eq8u73)

If this is not alarming enough by itself, factor in that democracy in the United States rests on the blade's edge. We have yet to see what happens when the country celebrates its 250th anniversary in a few years and whether its people will celebrate democracy or be in a fight to get it back. When some Supreme Court Justics talk about a society in which factions can only coexist at best, rather than having one in which inclusion and multiculturalism are embraced, we can predict a problem on the horizon that could likely combust into violence.

Further, rather than bringing people together in healthy ways of living, such self-fulfilling prophecies lead to assumptions about how to construct a society within which singular consistency of thought is the only statutory option as was the case with Jim Crow; legalized segregation; book banning to limit knowledge; pushing theocracy into politics; and controlling individual rights making inclusion impossible (e.g., the dismemberment of Affirmative Action programs and initiatives to preserve segregated ways of living).

Coexistence vs. Inclusive Societies

Several dynamics can emerge when people from different groups coexist without deeper interaction. When consciously choosing to coexist rather than considering inclusive societies, individuals wall themselves off from different groups they do not like. We can only coexist without deeper interaction and the intention to bridge our differences rather than exaggerate them. Patterns of coexistence, especially when lacking meaningful interaction, can lead to several outcomes:

1. It can lead to superficial tolerance. Coexistence may foster basic tolerance, but without deeper engagement, it often remains surface-level. This can create an environment where people coexist without truly accepting or understanding one another, leading to limited opportunities for genuine inclusion or advancement.

2. It can result in isolation and segregation. When groups coexist without interaction, they tend to remain isolated, leading to segregated communities. This separation reinforces stereotypes, biases, and misunderstandings, further dividing people based on race, class, or culture.

3. It can produce missed opportunities for Innovation. Diverse groups that fail to collaborate miss out on the potential for creative problem-solving and innovation. Research shows that collaboration among diverse perspectives leads to better outcomes, but without engagement, these benefits are lost.

4. It can create a lack of empathy and understanding which is prevalent in the United States and elsewhere. Coexisting without meaningful interaction prevents people from understanding each other's experiences and struggles, reducing empathy. This lack of connection can lead to harmful decision-making and perpetuate social inequities.

5. It can result in stagnation of social progress as various groups fight for dominance. Without the exchange of ideas and cultural blending, social progress slows. Coexistence without interaction creates a stagnant society, where isolation prevents the integration necessary for a more equitable and inclusive community.

6. It can foster entrenched power imbalances when influential groups isolate themselves from others, by often maintaining power and limiting their understanding of the challenges faced by marginalized groups. This perpetuates elitism and systemic inequalities, further widening the gap between those with privilege and those without.

Consequently, coexistence without meaningful interaction can lead to shallow relationships, isolation, missed opportunities for growth, and perpetuate social inequities, slowing progress toward a more integrated and harmonious society. But it doesn't have to be that way. By fostering deeper interaction through dialogue, shared experiences, and collaborative efforts can transform mere coexistence into meaningful inclusion and unity. Breaking down barriers between groups is critical for fostering healthier, more productive environments and reducing the hate-filled rhetoric in society.

For society to progress, we must address the harm caused by those who believe in superiority, segregation, and unequal treatment, as well as the myth of individualism in a world where people rely on each other for nearly everything they cannot do alone. Our interdependence is essential for a functioning society. However, when we divide and vilify one another by categorizing each other into different social groups, we do so at the risk of creating ongoing interpersonal and intergroup conflicts.

My Compass Point

Much of what I understand about leading and managing nonprofit organizations comes from nearly thirty years of professional YMCA experience that included executive leadership roles and roles on the national training faculty. But I also have fond memories of participating in YMCA activities and camps as a child, thanks to my mom who even worked in a resident camp kitchen so her children could benefit from the experiences. My favorite counselor was a man without feet or hands; I'm guessing caused by birth defects but do not know for certain. He would pick me up in the pool and throw me, which I absolutely loved. I can see him in my mind's eye at this moment and my memory of him has a profound impact on my feelings about people living with what we call disabilities.

In my mid-twenties, I came to a crossroads with what I thought were two great career opportunities: One was a football coaching position at Chabot College in Hayward California (coaching was one of my childhood dream jobs), and the other was a YMCA executive leader role in Oakland, California. Going into coaching would have meant becoming an educator, and the other was moving into recreation and human services. I knew one day I would become an educator, but that would not occur for another twenty-five years.

As I thought about my choices at that moment, I felt my path would lead me beyond the football field to do more serious work in the impoverished communities I opted to serve. On the day of our football team's end-of-season banquet, I decided to take my first executive role for a small-branch YMCA in East Oakland, California, that struggled financially. Once appointed, I immediately met with my new supervisor the corporate VP for Operations, who happened to be White, to ask him for advice on working with my board members. Referring to Black people he responded with, "I don't know how to work with you people," (meaning Black people) as though Black people are any different than White or other people.

My question was not about working with Black people, it was about working with *people* on my newly adopted Board of Directors. Though I had several years of program director experience, this was my first executive role requiring me to recruit, train, and lead board members living in my service area. Great executive directors have dynamic boards that set policies for the work being done by their organizations. So, who was on the board and how well the board functioned was of primary concern, because they also provided leadership during fundraising campaigns. Generally speaking, the stronger the board, the greater the executive director's capacity to provide impactful leadership.

The YMCA raises billions of dollars annually, using low-income, largely minority communities such as Oakland, Berkeley, Hayward, San Leandro, and Alameda, California, as their case statements for donations. Despite this, my supervisor at the time failed to offer guidance to a young executive director due to perceived racial differences, illustrating how past experiences and ingrained biases shape future behaviors. This lack of support, rooted in the corporate VP of Operations' willful ignorance, remains a painful reminder of how racial biases influence leadership interactions and decisions, becoming precursors to future discriminatory practices.

Today, the YMCA of the USA (Y-USA) generates approximately $7 billion annually, supporting critical services in over 10,000 communities across the U.S. Despite this impressive reach, my experience with willful ignorance in leadership persisted throughout my YMCA career and later in my academic roles. For example, a university president, who openly identified himself as a Redneck, blocked my advancement over more than a dozen years, refusing to promote me—even for positions I helped create. His decisions ultimately led to the collapse of a major diversity and inclusion initiative, reflecting a broader pattern where racial biases and leadership failures hinder both individual progress and organizational success.

Contributor Karen Linyard discusses the impact of toxic leadership on her career progression and well-being. She shares how a toxic manager deliberately hindered her career advancement by refusing to promote her for reasons unrelated to skills or performance. In her case, her manager's decision was based on maintaining the status quo rather than recognizing merit, leading to feelings of disappointment, and hurt. Her toxic work environment was characterized by a lack of respect and support from her manager, which produced lasting negative impacts on her emotional and mental well-being, which is what happens at the hands of toxic leaders.

Willful Ignorance is a Choice

We live in a time when information is everywhere—at our fingertips in books, articles, podcasts, and digital devices of every kind. In 2025, there's little excuse for ignorance, unless it stems from a simple lack of exposure. Ignorance, by definition, is the absence of knowledge, understanding, or awareness about something. It's not the same as stupidity. Ignorance can be unintentional—maybe you just haven't learned something yet—or it can be deliberate, where a person chooses not to know or refuses to acknowledge facts that are readily available.

Stupidity, on the other hand, runs deeper. It's marked by an unwillingness or inability to apply knowledge effectively, even when the information is right there. It often results in poor judgment, reckless decisions, and actions that defy common sense. Where ignorance can be cured with education and curiosity, stupidity resists both.

What troubles me most is when ignorance becomes willful—when people actively avoid learning or cling to falsehoods in the face of truth. That kind of chosen ignorance, especially when weaponized, drives many of the divisions we see in our country and across the globe. The problem isn't that we don't know, it's that too many people simply don't want to challenge their deeply held belief systems: And that's what keeps us from healing, from learning, and from building something better together.

Although the racial composition of the United States is rapidly changing, race as a construct has historically been found to underlie many of the most significant problems, we face at this moment. The United States is projected to become a majority-minority country by 2045. This means that by then, no single racial or ethnic group will make up more than 50% of the population. The shift is primarily driven by the growing Hispanic, Asian, and multiracial populations, along with a steady decline in the non-Hispanic White population as a percentage of the total. The U.S. Census Bureau's projections show that by mid-century, the country will be much more racially and ethnically diverse. Anyone seriously studying the population shifts understands that the demographic shifts are fueling much of the domestic violence we see today.

Over the years, I have had many White leaders tell me how much they don't know about communities other than their own, and they do nothing to change those dynamics. For example, a few of them told me that only non-Whites can teach others about diversity—tragic statements at best in the United States, and I am guessing elsewhere. This makes it possible for those demographically in the White population to choose whether to learn about non-White communities if they want to. We can see the backlash this produces in the current attacks on "wokeness" and DEI in places like Florida and elsewhere. The efforts to wipe history clean of the contributions of all non-White citizens is a deliberate and willful attempt to remain ignorant of the harm being done to all members of our society.

However, non-Whites in the population must learn how to live in at least a bi-cultural state if they want to successfully navigate societal norms. That is, we must learn to navigate the norms defining our own cultures as well as those defined by "the dominant White largely Judeo-Christian culture." Those refusing to embrace multiculturalism are really missing out on the richness of what has always made America great. In the process they impede our collective ability to maximize our true potential. They make it much more difficult for members of marginalized groups to succeed because of artificial barriers established to make things easier for some and more difficult for others. Their selfishness and desire to isolate as well as insulate themselves from the rest of us makes life more difficult for everyone.

Nonetheless, these ugly realities still make me angry today. In the United States, we can all choose willful ignorance by segregating ourselves in our own communities and away from others, or we can embrace members of other groups to become more well-rounded about the lives lived by those unlike ourselves and become more enriched in meaningful ways in the process. Such a shift would embrace a true multicultural society in which all people have the opportunity to become the best versions of themselves.

Choosing the YMCA as a career, set my life's compass point and cast my future. That choice led to wonderful experiences living in service to others and to highly traumatic experiences because of willful ignorance about living in a multicultural society. That ignorance, combined with an unwillingness to accept differences between socially categorized groups, has been a source of great trauma for me. My path has taught me that anyone who chooses willful ignorance (and it is a choice) creates traumatic experiences for others while protecting the ego of the individual who chooses ignorance over learning new ways of being. This willful ignorance becomes one of the many sources of trauma for large segments of the population.

The North Star

Life is a solitary journey for each of us to navigate as best we can, but no one can live our lives for us. Consciously or not, we all must choose a direction to travel in during our lifetime. Metaphorically for me, the North Star serves a practical function in guiding travelers. Its historical symbolism of pointing toward freedom for those traveling the Underground Railroad was as much a part of my family's bedtime tales as *The Little Engine That Could*. Because of my reverence for the North Star, I approach everything in my life with great intention, staying the course no matter how difficult the journey becomes. This guiding principle shapes my work and the specific jobs I choose to hold, which serve as building blocks for accomplishing my life's mission and vision:

> **Life Mission:** *To improve individual and organizational performance.*

> **Life Vision:** *To foster kinder, gentler, and healthier organizations and communities by promoting positive social change, social justice, and peace.*

The best I can do is to serve humanity in whatever way I can, striving to become a consummate professional, and working every day to become the best version of myself when facing obstacles placed in my way. Borrowing from the Blackfoot way of life, I work every day to prove my worthiness to be part of the communities to which I belong; those I choose to adopt; and to those that adopt me.

Childhood, Adolescence, and Rage

My family is exceptionally well-read and at one point we had a library with about three thousand books. My father was of African, Choctaw, and Creek descent. He had about fifteen months of formal education, so he taught himself how to read and write. My mom, a daughter of Sicilian immigrants, graduated high school at a time when only about a third of the U.S. population did so. Together they took away any excuses for ignorance and stupidity from their three children—who in their own ways carried on as activists to improve fairness and improved quality of life for those with whom they worked.

My compass point has not strayed far from the direction of my childhood aspirations. As a child, I wanted nothing more than to be accepted for my character and the goodness I tried to share wherever I went. However, as I grew older, maintaining that goodness became increasingly difficult due to successive traumatic events. By the time I was fifteen, I lived in a state of rage. Today, looking back on my life, which I am required to do for this story, I can see how childhood and adolescence locked me into the path I chose to travel, and how trauma and toxic environments have been the majority norms in my life.

Adolescence marks the beginning of the transition from childhood to adulthood and is characterized by significant physical, emotional, and cognitive changes. During early adolescence, individuals experience puberty, develop more complex thinking abilities, form a stronger sense of identity, and seek greater independence. These years are crucial in shaping a person's future personality, values, and behaviors.

In my case, by the time I was fifteen, I had been physically assaulted more than a half dozen times; verbally assaulted and threatened more times than I am able to count; and my father passed away. A year after my father died, I was ripped from the home I loved in Altadena and relocated 500 miles to the north to an equally toxic environment in Berkeley, but one I hated because it was filthy, and produced even more harm through a lack of not being accepted for reasons I cannot explain since it was so diverse.

My upbringing was marked by the unwavering dedication of my parents to provide for our family's needs, ensuring we had food, clothing, and shelter despite the challenges we faced. Living in what could be termed middle-class communities, my parents exemplified remarkable qualities; my father's courage and lifelong sacrifices for civil and human rights were matched only by my mother's creativity, intuition, and inner strength. They were a dynamic power couple who committed everything they had to challenge misogyny, bigotry, White supremacy, and class warfare as issues bringing harm to people. Their profound influence instilled in me a deep sense of purpose and a recognition of the sacrifices often required along the solitary path I now tread.

No matter what else might have happened as a child, my parents incubated my mind in a rich environment committed to stimulating deep thought, maximal learning, and leadership development from phenomenal role models. The pearls of wisdom and training made sense as I got older, and I continue to pass them along to my son, my students, and now to you.

Another saving grace is that my parents filled my head with stories of courage, persistence, tenacity, and devoting my life to something significant beyond myself that would better humanity. My father taught me to stand up for what I believe in. One day, I insisted that I could become anything I wanted, and he insisted I couldn't. The back-and-forth exchange escalated into a "Yes, I can," "No, you can't," argument.

He challenged me to move to the nearby San Gabriel mountains. I responded with, "You give me enough men and equipment, and I will!" When I asserted myself in the argument at fourteen, he went ballistic in a way I had never seen before—likely, in his eyes—as a last-ditch effort to save my life. He perceived my determination to create the life I wanted as being uppity, a trait that many African American parents fear in their strong-willed children because it could get them killed. Nevertheless, I was demonstrating what he taught me, which was to stand up for my beliefs. At that moment, I expressed a belief in myself and my ability to achieve the goals I set for myself.

It was on that day that I became a man. I stood up to the most powerful person I knew and survived. That day also became a precursor that enabled me to respect but not fear power, and I found what was worth fighting for and if necessary, dying for: Equality and fairness in the face of White supremacy and discrimination.

As I think back to those moments today, I realize that our argument came at a time when I was nearing my threshold of rage because of all the other dynamics of integrating into a segregated community. A few months later, my father would pass away while on a trip, never giving us a chance to resolve what happened. Losing my hero on top of everything else that I was enduring was the last straw, pushing me into a state of rage.

My Dad and Mom

My dad was a no-nonsense, courageous man who grew up in rural Alabama at the end of the nineteenth and beginning of the twentieth centuries. He knew the harm and pain caused by segregation and maltreatment based solely on race. At the age of fifteen, he had to flee the South after hitting a White man in the head with a 2x4 piece of lumber after he called my dad a *nigger*. My dad promised the uncle who raised him that he would do that if a White man ever called him that name. The family story is that after witnessing a White man call a Black man that name, he made that promise to his uncle who also happened to be the Sherriff. Once it happened my father had to leave home to avoid being lynched by the Ku Klux Klan, establishing his life path from then on.

This incident was so deeply embedded in my father's psyche that he passed it along to me when I was a teenager. He said I was never to fight unless I was called the *N-word*. Once that happened, he said, "All bets are off," and I was instructed to pick up a 2x4 piece of lumber and use it to defend myself. The problem was that when it happened it was usually while playing sports or when being outnumbered without any lumber in sight, so I didn't have any way to defend myself.

Meanwhile, my mother taught me to see with my ears and to hear with my eyes. She taught me to make life about helping children because they are our future and to ensure that any children of my own were exposed to the breadth of wonders that life offers each of us. She encouraged me to be a rising star, not a shooting star and I continue to rise by fulfilling my life purpose every day. Together my dad and mom taught me to be courageous, to fight for what was right, to only fight to protect myself and others from harm, to always search for the light in my darkest moments, and to become the best version of myself that I could become. Simply put, I could not have had better role models, teachers, and parents, and I am who I am today, because of them.

Today, I am able to explain how a fun-loving child navigated his life from his earliest traumatic event at the age of two to his most recent traumatic events decades later. I have lived long enough to make better sense of things I thought I fully understood. Finally, I can now explain how two neural hijacks earlier in my life could have derailed my life entirely, if not shortened my life because of my early childhood trauma producing my rage.

Attitude

Our attitude matters because it shapes how we perceive and respond to the world around us. It influences our interactions, our resilience in the face of challenges, and our well-being. An optimistic attitude can enhance our ability to cope with stress, improve our relationships, and increase our chances of success in various endeavors. For instance, when faced with adversity, a positive attitude can help us see opportunities for growth and learning rather than as insurmountable obstacles. This mindset fosters resilience, allowing us to recover from setbacks more quickly and continue pursuing our goals with renewed energy and determination. Research shows that individuals with positive attitudes are more likely to experience better mental and physical health, as their outlook influences their behavior and stress levels (Fredrickson, 2001).

Moreover, our attitude impacts our interactions with others. A positive attitude can make us more approachable and likable, leading to stronger and more supportive relationships. Conversely, a negative attitude can create barriers, making it harder to connect with others and receive the support we need (Carnegie, 1936). In the workplace, a constructive attitude can improve our performance and job satisfaction. It helps us stay motivated, embrace challenges, and work collaboratively with colleagues. Employers often value a positive attitude as it contributes to a more productive and harmonious work environment (Luthans & Youssef, 2007).

Our attitude is a powerful tool that shapes our life outcomes. By cultivating a positive and resilient mindset, we can better navigate life's complexities, build meaningful relationships, and achieve our aspirations. Creating something meaningful in our lives requires deliberate effort and energy. Life is a journey where we are both the sculptor and the sculpture. This process reveals how we see ourselves and our legacy. On social media, everyone shows who they are through what they choose to post. We define our in-groups by aligning with those who share our views and our out-groups by opposing or ignoring those who don't. This behavior reflects how we share insights and information within our circles. Therefore, recognizing the power of our attitude and the intentionality behind our actions, we can shape our lives and the connections we build with others.

The Power of Optimism and Mindset

Today, as an educator and consultant, I remain fully committed to my students, clients, and followers. This project is supported by data collected from reputable organizations and transdisciplinary experts, incorporating leadership and organizational effectiveness research and theories from various disciplines. The information in this guide has been collected through academic and professional research and observations made in the field during my capacity as an executive leader, consultant, and educator.

This project presents personal stories from my workplace experiences and those shared by others, highlighting the human impact of the harm prevalent in many organizations. These narratives aim to provide a more authentic and less sanitized view than typical presentations. The materials include summaries of research studies, data from reputable organizations, established and emerging theoretical models, and real-life case studies. These are presented as informational rather than prescriptive, recognizing the need for targeted assessments and analysis before making specific recommendations.

Included are stories of some of the most meaningful moments in my life, which may seem fantastical but are authentic to the best of my understanding and recollection. While discussing trauma and toxicity is challenging, my goal is to create a positive narrative of someone who, despite the odds, found pathways to success where the leaders who were my predecessors failed. This project demonstrates how I continue to overcome obstacles to make positive social change and create a meaningful life for myself and others—this guide is one such example.

If you are a novice to trauma, this guide could serve as a crash course, allowing you to understand, manage, and grow from the myriad difficulties encountered while aging over the lifespan. You will know this difference if you listen to your heart and gut without letting your head interfere and tell you otherwise. Leave the head for planning and decision-making to change circumstances for the better and to gather additional information to aid decision-making.

Multiple Brains

Grant Soosalu and Marvin Oka (2012) developed a concept of multiple brains, detailed in their book, *mBraining: Using Your Multiple Brains to Do Cool Stuff*. The multiple-brain concept integrates neuroscience, cognitive science, and behavioral modeling findings. It proposes that humans possess three main types of brains:

- Head-Brain

- Heart-Brain

- Gut-Brain

Each brain has its own functions, processing capabilities, and ways of understanding the world. Soosalu and Oka assert that the *Head-Brain* is responsible for cognitive perception, thinking, and logic. It involves in analyzing, planning, and problem-solving. The *Heart-Brain* is associated with emotions, values, and relational processing. It plays a role in compassion, empathy, and emotional intelligence. The *Gut-Brain* is linked to intuition, identity, and self-preservation. It involves instinctual responses, *gut feelings*, and managing our core sense of Self.

When we are at our best, all three brains work together to inform our decisions and decisionmaking processes. mBraining suggests individuals can enhance their decision-making, leadership, creativity, and overall well-being by aligning and integrating these three brains. The approach emphasizes the importance of coherence and communication between these neural networks to achieve a balanced and harmonious life.

In the spirit of full disclosure, I choose to be the eternal optimist in addition to subscribing to mBraining as part of my practice of living my life more fully. It is in my DNA. It is what drives me to keep going under the most arduous circumstances. It has given me the strength to complete this *traveler's guide*.

Perspectives and Mindsets

We often encounter seemingly unrelated events that ultimately connect to something more significant, which in turn connects to something new, and so forth. It is akin to ascending a path where you can look back from a higher vantage point and see the entire journey more clearly. A life well lived depends on perspectives and perspectives depend on mindsets.

A person with a *fixed mindset* may believe that intelligence and growth are limited, hindering their potential for development. Shifting to a *growth mindset* can be transformative. However, the latter may be more challenging for some due to rigid thinking; a reluctance to confront *cognitive dissonance* (the mental conflict between opposing ideas that challenges long-held beliefs); low tolerance for ambiguity; and limited resilience in the face of failure and difficulty.

A Growth Mindset

One of the beautiful aspects of being human is our capacity to adapt to the conditions within which we find ourselves. This is particularly true if we adopt what Stanford University professor, Carol Dweck (2006), describes as a *growth mindset*. According to Dweck:

> This growth mindset is based on the belief that your basic qualities are things you can cultivate through your efforts, your strategies, and help from others. Although people may differ in every way—in their initial talents and aptitudes, interests, or temperaments—everyone can change and grow through application and experience.

A Fixed Mindset

In contrast, those with a fixed mindset see abilities as static, believing intelligence and growth are inherently limited. This mindset can stifle potential and prevent beneficial development. Overcoming this requires confronting cognitive dissonance, embracing ambiguity, and cultivating resilience from failure and difficulty.

The Three A's of Life

There is an old saying that Attitude determines Altitude, which is true. However, my late consulting partner, Michael F. Lange, and I expanded on this idea with the Three A's of Life:

Attitude + Aptitude + Application = Altitude

Living in the aftermath of trauma and retaining sufficient equilibrium to function well in society can be difficult, but it is certainly doable with the right mindset and desire to live psychologically well. How we engage with our life experiences makes all the difference in our perspectives and, ultimately, the outcomes we achieve throughout our lifetimes. A proper mindset can shift our perspective from hopeless to hopeful and impossible to possible.

Fueling motivation and enthusiasm is essential for sustained effort and engagement in tasks. A positive *attitude*—encompassing one's outlook, mindset, and resilience—is essential for fueling motivation and enthusiasm, helping individuals bounce back from setbacks, persist through difficulties, and view challenges as opportunities to learn and grow, thereby ensuring sustained effort and task engagement.

Aptitude refers to the natural abilities and talents that an individual possesses. These innate qualities influence how easily a person can learn and excel in specific areas. Critical aspects of aptitude include natural skills determined by genetics that provide individuals with an early advantage in academics, arts, athletics, or technical domains. Higher aptitude is often viewed as an advantage because it correlates with the ability to quickly and effectively grasp new concepts, enhancing one's capacity to solve complex problems and think critically. But, as with most things, where a person begins does not determine where they end.

Application, on the other hand, is the consistent effort and disciplined practice an individual puts into developing their skills and achieving their goals. Regardless of one's attitude or aptitude, success is primarily determined by persistent effort over time, which is crucial for mastering any skill and achieving long-term objectives. Regular, focused practice refines abilities and improves performance. Effective application involves setting clear, achievable goals and creating action plans to achieve them.

The interplay of attitude, aptitude, and application creates a powerful synergy that propels individuals toward higher levels of success (altitude) when they engage in the process seriously. When these three factors are aligned, they generate a combined impact that enhances outcomes for those adapting to the Three A's of Life. For example:

> **Attitude + Aptitude:** A positive attitude can enhance the effectiveness of natural aptitude, encouraging individuals to push their limits and leverage their talents.

> **Aptitude + Application:** High aptitude without diligent application may leave natural talents underdeveloped and unutilized.

> **Attitude + Application:** A growth-oriented attitude drives individuals to apply themselves consistently, embrace challenges, and learn from failures.

The Role of Adversity

Ultimately, how far a person can go depends on their ability to maintain a positive attitude, leverage their natural aptitudes, and apply themselves diligently. Individuals can achieve remarkable success and reach their full potential by cultivating a resilient mindset, honing their innate talents, and committing to a disciplined effort. The combination of attitude, aptitude, and application uniquely contributes to success, and their interplay can profoundly impact an individual's achievements.

It is important to note here that substantial effort is often applied by power structures to destroy positive attitudes by fostering environments of control, fear, and inequality, which serves to maintain the status quo and consolidate power. Power structures often use tactics such as control and manipulation; fear and intimidation; and fostering inequality and oppression to manipulate stakeholder behaviors.

By controlling information, resources, and opportunities, power structures manipulate individuals, suppressing dissent and promoting compliance. This manipulation erodes trust and diminishes motivation and enthusiasm (Foucault, 1975). Power structures may use fear and intimidation to keep individuals in line, creating a culture of anxiety and stress. This atmosphere stifles creativity and initiative, leading to a negative outlook and reduced resilience (Freire, 1970). By sustaining inequality and systemic oppression, power structures ensure that certain groups remain marginalized and disadvantaged. This systemic disenfranchisement fosters feelings of helplessness and diminishes hope, undermining positive attitudes (Marx, 1867). These methods serve to reinforce the dominance of those in power by preventing the development of a critical and empowered populace, ultimately ensuring the continued dominance of the existing power hierarchy (Gramsci, 1971).

Adversity and Trauma

Adversity refers to difficult or unpleasant situations that present challenges or hardships. It can involve a wide range of experiences, from personal struggles such as illness or loss to broader issues like economic hardship or natural disasters. Facing adversity often requires resilience and determination. While it can be a source of stress, it also offers opportunities for growth and learning. Overcoming adversity can lead to developing new skills, increased strength, and a deeper understanding of one's capacities and values.

The link between adversity and trauma lies in the manner in which adverse experiences can precipitate traumatic responses in individuals. Adversity encompasses a broad spectrum of challenging circumstances or events that individuals may encounter throughout their lives. These can range from significant life stressors such as loss, abuse, or natural disasters to more commonplace challenges like financial difficulties or interpersonal conflicts. When individuals are confronted with adverse situations that exceed their coping mechanisms or resilience capacities, they may experience psychological distress or disruption.

Trauma, on the other hand, refers to the psychological and emotional response to distressing or disturbing events that exceed an individual's ability to cope. Traumatic experiences often involve a perceived threat to one's physical or psychological well-being, resulting in feelings of helplessness, fear, or horror. While not all adverse experiences lead to trauma, certain types of adversity, particularly those involving significant threat or harm, have a higher likelihood of precipitating traumatic responses.

The relationship between adversity and trauma is complex and multifaceted. Adverse experiences can serve as precursors to trauma by exposing individuals to situations that challenge their sense of safety, stability, or predictability. Additionally, repeated exposure to adversity over time, especially during critical periods of development, can increase the risk of trauma and exacerbate its long-term effects. Furthermore, the subjective nature of adversity and trauma underscores the importance of individual differences in how people perceive and respond to challenging situations. Factors such as prior experiences, coping strategies, social support networks, and resilience levels all play crucial roles in determining the likelihood and severity of traumatic reactions to adversity.

From a leadership perspective, adversity and trauma can function as situations and contexts depending on the specific circumstances and how they are perceived and addressed by leaders and their teams. Adversity as a situation means that adversity can be viewed as a specific situation or event that poses a challenge, obstacle, or difficulty to individuals or groups. For example, an organization facing a financial downturn, a team encountering a significant project setback, or a leader dealing with a crisis within the organization all represent adversity as a situational challenge that needs to be addressed.

Trauma as a context means that trauma often represents a broader context or environment that encompasses past experiences, events, or conditions that have caused significant distress or harm to individuals or groups. Trauma can influence perceptions, behaviors, and reactions to current situations and challenges. For instance, employees who have experienced trauma in their personal lives or within the organization may carry those experiences into their current work environment, shaping their responses to adversity and influencing team dynamics.

However, it's important to note that these distinctions are not always clear-cut, and the line between situation and context can sometimes blur. Adversity and trauma can interact and overlap, with past traumatic experiences influencing how individuals perceive and respond to current adversities. Effective leadership involves recognizing both the situational challenges and the broader contextual factors at play and addressing them in a way that supports individuals and teams in overcoming obstacles and building resilience. This perspective aligns with leaders' key responsibilities to remove obstacles to performance.

Understanding the link between adversity and trauma is essential for informing prevention, intervention, and treatment efforts aimed at mitigating the negative impact of adverse experiences on employee or member well-being. By recognizing the interconnectedness of these phenomena, mental health and other professionals (educators, trainers, coaches, mentors, and leaders) can develop more comprehensive approaches to supporting individuals who have experienced adversity and addressing the underlying trauma that may result from such experiences. As successful as I've been over the length of my career, the information outlined in these pages would have substantially increased my capacity to become an even more effective leader.

Adversity and Wellness

For those of us who experience adversity as children, as odd as it seems, we may have an advantage because of the survival skills we had to develop early on in our lifetimes. Those who escape adversity in childhood may have a more difficult time adjusting to adversity later in life but their freedom from childhood adversity may offer them opportunities to become more fully developed and therefore better able to understand and reconcile the adversity they encounter when it does arise.

However, too much adversity during childhood could produce additional unintended consequences such as greater susceptibility to PTSD with greater exposure to trauma at an early age. In my case, adversity became a personal challenge for me to overcome. In the act of continuously having to overcome greater obstacles than my counterparts, I developed greater skills and accomplished things they failed at, and it gave me a great sense of purpose and meaning. What I did not realize though at the time was that living to a different standard and watching my peers get recognized when I outperformed them eventually took its toll on me over time.

Divine Timing and Trust

Danielle Koepke (n.d.) speaks of *Divine Timing and Trust*, emphasizing the transformative power of adversity, suggesting that our most painful struggles can lead to significant personal growth and that apparent curses can become blessings in disguise. It speaks to the resilience and hope that individuals must maintain, even in the face of overwhelming challenges, reinforcing the idea that perseverance is critical to overcoming life's difficulties. Our perspectives reflect everything we think we know at any given moment. Koepke perfectly captures the wisdom that can come from adversity through a change in perspective about the role of adversity and the persistence required to overcome it as part of the rite of passage to fulfillment:

> If I have learned anything from life, the darkest times can sometimes lead us to the brightest places. I have learned that the most toxic people can teach us the most important lessons, that our most painful struggles can give us the most necessary growth, and that the most heartbreaking losses of friendship and love can make room for the most wonderful people. What seems like a curse at the moment can be a blessing, and what seems like the end of the road is just the discovery that we are destined to walk a different path. I have learned that there is always hope, no matter how difficult things seem. Moreover, I have learned that we cannot give up no matter how helpless we feel or how horrible things seem. We have to move on. Even when it is scary and all our strength seems to be gone, we must keep getting up and moving forward because whatever we are fighting for at the moment will pass, and we will get through it. We have come this far. We can get through whatever comes next.

You can learn more about Danielle Koepke in The Minds Journal and Inspiring and Positive Quotes.

The point is this: Adversity is our teacher, and our perceptions about adversity shape our outcomes. In other words, if we run from adversity, there will be one outcome, but if we lean into adversity, there will be a different outcome. Our outcomes are also determined by the *willpower* we have to overcome whatever adversity is before us. The magnitude of adversity is relative to its nature and type, context, and the person's constitution, including the pre-event behavioral precursors of the person and the resilience capacity of the person post-event. Depending on perspective, adversity may seem like hell when going through it, but it is our path to personal fulfillment. Everyone who has ever achieved anything significant for themselves knows this to be true. Those who try to circumvent or cheat the system at some point may find themselves running into a ditch because of their arrogance to think they are more potent than nature rather than *being part of nature* and its universal laws governing everything.

Contributor Frederick Douglass Perry's story illustrates the themes of resilience, perseverance, and leadership in the face of adversity, particularly racial discrimination in the workplace. Despite facing exclusion, hostility, and being passed over for opportunities due to his race, Perry chose to respond by mastering his craft, excelling in his work, and remaining committed to professional excellence. His determination to overcome bias, gain the respect of colleagues, and break barriers created a more inclusive environment for future workers.

F. D. Perry's journey also highlights the importance of mentorship and advocacy. As he advanced in his career, he took on leadership roles within unions and the broader entertainment industry, working to promote diversity and inclusion. His efforts not only helped him succeed personally but also contributed to systemic changes that supported underrepresented groups. In the end, his story demonstrates how adapting to challenges and staying focused on personal and professional growth can lead to overcoming even deeply entrenched obstacles. Perry's journey from exclusion to leadership reflects the power of determination, advocacy, and the ability to turn adversity into meaningful change. This theme highlights the triumph of resilience over the obstacles posed by prejudice and bias.

Life as Navigating the Storm

Navigating anywhere requires the decision to take the first step, and the first step requires a commitment to a different way of being. It is also necessary to have the courage to confront whatever obstacles are known and the willingness to face uncertainty. Then there is the matter of quieting the mind from manufacturing intrusive thoughts about *imagined what-ifs*. This navigation requires the motivation and sustained commitment to create a different future than the one that appears inevitable based on the information available at the time.

Anyone with significant trauma knows that it is a beast to battle, and battling *the trauma beast* requires courage, support, and often professional guidance. It is a journey through treacherous psychological terrain, confronting painful memories and challenging deeply ingrained fears. Healing does not mean *the beast* is completely vanquished; it means learning to live despite its presence, reducing its power and control, and finding moments of peace and joy in its shadow to create a quality life for ourselves.

The Toxic Triangle

Toxic workplace behaviors result because they can emerge in the culture, fester, and spread through leader-follower exchanges. Toxic behaviors are possible when senior leaders model or tolerate such conduct as part of the culture. Our legal and political systems are case examples of how these dynamics in the public sphere are replicated in the dynamics we see in our workplaces, families, and other social groups.

Edmonds (2021) makes it clear that toxicity in the workplace arises from a toxic triangle of destructive leaders, susceptible followers, and conducive environments in which leaders ". . . feed off their followers as much as their followers feed off of them" (pp.69-70). Toxic behaviors last for as long as the people being impacted by them allow them to happen, so in many ways, they enable them to occur (Edmonds, 2021). Our hostile political environment offers plenty of real-time examples to illustrate how this works in the notable case of one of the major political parties subverting political and legal systems to protect a former president; change rules to block and then appoint justices; and support efforts that undermine democracy in the United States.

Group dynamics are observable and measurable, so we can track the toxicity by the number of events and the suffering inflicted by the number of people harmed, assess the shifts in cultures resulting in changes in behaviors by analyzing actions taken, and measure the psychological well-being of individual members and groups. Therefore, since the dynamics are observable and measurable, we can find the path to changing them assuming we have the willpower to do so.

Ultimately, the world you experience exists entirely in your mind, as it does for all of us. This is a difficult truth to fully grasp—at least, it has been for me. The storms we face, whether they bring turmoil, fear, and discomfort or love, joy, and excitement, all reside within our minds. Our perception of life is shaped by our experiences and how we interpret them, which in turn influences our actions and behaviors. Therefore, living a successful life requires defining what success means to you, charting a course, navigating the inevitable challenges, and maintaining the willpower to pursue your goals until they are achieved.

Navigating Life with Purpose and Resilience

Time is a precious gift because it is finite and non-renewable, meaning it cannot be recovered once spent. Since time is an irreplaceable resource, we have to make wise choices about how we use it, never knowing whether some decision we make may be the last one. My dear friend and colleague, Jill Cody, hosts the biweekly *Be Bold America* radio show on KSQD 90.7FM, serving Santa Cruz and the California Central Coast. Periodically, Jill reminds me that everyone has the same twenty-four hours daily. However, how we use that time shapes the degree of richness of our lives.

Having known Jill for over twenty years, co-hosting her show for two years was a great honor and joy. It allowed me to interview some of my heroes, including Dr.

Jane Elliott, former Alabama Governor Don Siegelman, and syndicated talk show host, Thom Hartman. These brilliant guests and many others discussed crucial topics about sustaining and improving our democracy. My time with the show was invaluable, allowing me to connect critical insights to the complexities of the world framed in various contexts and now informing many of the things presented in this guide.

Life: Filled with Peaks and Valleys

My earlier teachings emphasized that life seems like a linear journey, but it is really about navigating a series of peaks and valleys until the end of life (see Figure 1-1 Below: Life is a Process of Always Becoming).

LIFE IS A PROCESS OF ALWAYS BECOMING

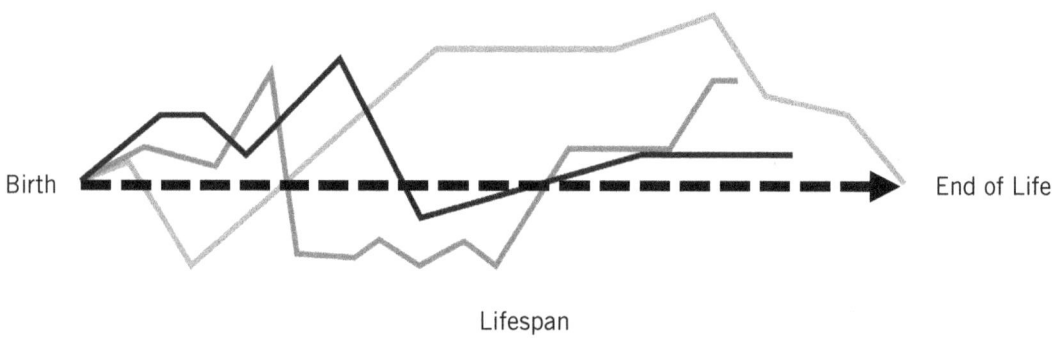

Birth   End of Life

Lifespan

My perspective has since shifted. I now understand that while life involves highs and lows, for those grappling with trauma, it feels more like running through a gauntlet. Traumatic events strike like punches and body blows, amplifying the highs and deepening the lows along this seemingly straight path toward life's end. Practically, this means that as we traverse our inevitable peaks and valleys, we endure hits and carry with us the bruises inflicted by others (and ourselves) trying to hinder our progress. When trauma is severe enough, it becomes a constant daily burden. But the trials and adversity encountered along the life path serve to strengthen our constitution, build our resilience, and help us appreciate our lives more fully.

This shift in thinking may seem insignificant to some, but it deepens my understanding of how minor changes in perspective can help diminish or maximize the value of positive and negative experiences. For example, a person with a negative mindset might miss out on beneficial opportunities because they are looking for what's wrong rather than right with an opportunity. Or, if they are experiencing something negative, they may exaggerate or magnify the problem, driving them towards mentally dark places. On the other hand, a person with a positive mindset might be able to find opportunities in what appear to be negative circumstances at first glance. For example, a person buying a fixer-upper home might see the increased value of their purchase by making improvements.

Mindsets and Multiple Truths

It is also essential to realize that in the same way, mindsets about trauma can amplify relatively minor issues into major problems (an inopportune sprained ankle) or even make it feel like it's the end of the world. In other words, mindset and perceptions of daily events can shape our behaviors in response to our trauma, producing unrecognizable or unexplainable emotional responses to our experiences.

Life is complex and multidimensional, meaning multiple truths can coexist. We have various roles and responsibilities in our families, jobs, careers, schools, and social groups, each requiring attention and balance. Stressors in one area can affect our behavior in others. For example, a failing marriage can impact performance at work or school, and a traumatic event in the workplace or academic setting can affect behaviors at home. In cases where both home and work produce trauma, the individual does not have a safe space to recover and heal, thereby increasing the stress on all of the body's survival mechanisms.

Today, my life's journey is an intricate mosaic woven with the threads of professional practice, academic scholarship, and thirst for lifelong personal growth. From the bustling arenas of organizational leadership to the corridors of academia, my path has been guided by a relentless pursuit of understanding human behavior and the impacts of leadership on group dynamics, a commitment to excellence in the work I choose to do, and an unwavering belief in the transformative power of leadership to effectuate positive social change.

In Pursuit of Happiness

Fundamentally, the pursuit of happiness is a choice. Happiness is a complex and multifaceted emotional state characterized by feelings of contentment, joy, and fulfillment. It often involves experiencing positive emotions, a sense of purpose, and overall life satisfaction. Various factors, including relationships, achievements, personal values, and life circumstances, can influence happiness. It is not a constant state but rather it can fluctuate based on different aspects of one's life and experiences. *Happiness* is a deeply personal and subjective experience, varying wildly from person to person.

Pursuing happiness is a worthy goal. Life is indeed what we make it given whatever genetic tools we are born with and cards we are dealt at birth by our circumstances. I have always pursued happiness. As a child, I did not care about anything other than *exploring ways to be happy,* not realizing that my thirst for exploring would one day lead to pioneering.

My parents stimulated broad and deep thinking, my desire for service, and my appreciation for diversity in all its forms, and they instilled a passion for lifelong learning, which has served me well in my pursuit of personal happiness. Consequently, during periods of deep despair when I was being accused of things that just were not true or otherwise being attacked, I focused on my accomplishments however small or inconsequential they might seem to the outside world. By focusing on what my mom called the "silver lining" I've always found some happiness in my accomplishments even during my darkest moments no matter how I was treated

For example, when I was passed over twice as a YMCA manager of the year, despite outperforming my peers in every metric used to determine the top performer, I focused on the successes my team and I accomplished. For example, in one case we generated the largest financial surpluses of any corporate branch operating unit, built programs that were better and had more participants than the city government programs that were less expensive because of their tax subsidies, built the largest and best childcare system that led to being offered every city operated childcare center to manage. My teams eliminated large deficits, brought high-quality programs and services to underserved as well as marginalized groups, and solved problems where others failed. By keeping happiness as my goal, I found joy in simple moments of pleasure stolen from negative events like my team earning the corporate trophy for fundraising excellence even though I was not recognized as manager of the year. If your definition of happiness (joy, bliss, etc.) is not your prime objective in life, I encourage you to rethink your priorities, at least as you read this story.

Search for the Silver Lining

One simple, yet exceptionally important lesson I learned from my mother is to *continually search for the silver lining* no matter how dark the times appear. This lesson is a sober reminder that we all experience dark times at some point and how we work through them is critically important to achieving and sustaining good mental health. It is also a reminder that whatever life is and becomes is up to each of us. You can be a maker or a taker. You can choose to be a failure, mediocre, or excellent. You can choose to be happy in the face of circumstances or wallow in the circumstances and be consumed by them. The approach we take to life matters. Life is about choices and personal ownership, even under the direst circumstances. So, learn from the moment by seeking the lesson found only in the silver lining at the edges of the darkness.

Perception is Reality

A second simple but important lesson I have learned since childhood is that each experience is unique unto itself and, at the same time part of a larger, ever-changing tapestry that appears as an image in the mind of what life is like for us—our individuated perception of reality. More simply, how we perceive life through our experiences and how we each interpret them is unique. A workgroup with five members and the same experience will each interpret their individual experience differently. It is also true that two workgroups in an organization with different leaders may experience the organization differently because we perceive the organization by the treatment and relationship we have with supervisors. Consider the implications of this for families and our social groups.

My parents filled my head with stories of courage, persistence, tenacity, and commitment to purpose. Those stories contributed to my ability to pursue happiness despite overwhelming obstacles, setbacks, trials, temptations, and disappointments. Happiness holds a unique meaning for each of us, but what remains valid for all is that happiness lives solely in our minds and is expressed through our emotions, feelings, and behaviors.

As someone who has never known life without trauma, I've had to find ways to set my pain aside so that I could find glimmers of hope, enjoyment, happiness, and moments of peace. My way of doing that was to literally search for the hope and possibilities in what were the silver linings amidst the storms I encountered on a near daily basis. I literally learned how to take my pain and use it as fuel to achieve my goals and dreams.

Emotions and Feelings

Generally speaking, *emotions* are immediate, automatic responses involving physiological changes, while *feelings* are the subjective interpretation and conscious experience of those emotions, shaped by personal context and reflection. Emotions and feelings are closely related but are distinct concepts in psychology:

1. Both emotions and feelings are integral to human experience and influence each other. Emotions often lead to feelings, and feelings can trigger emotions.

2. Both are subjective experiences, varying from person to person based on individual perceptions and contexts.

3. Both emotions and feelings can significantly influence a person's behavior, decision-making, and interactions with others.

Regarding differences, emotions are complex psychological states that involve physiological arousal, expressive behaviors, and conscious experience. They are often automatic responses to stimuli. Feelings, on the other hand, are the conscious awareness and interpretation of emotions. They are the mental associations and reactions to emotions. Emotions tend to be more immediate and short-lived, arising in response to specific events or situations, while feelings can be longer-lasting as they involve reflection and cognitive processing of emotions.

Emotions are typically considered more primal and instinctual, often involving the limbic system in the brain, while feelings are shaped by personal experiences, beliefs, and memories, involving higher cognitive processes in the brain. Emotions can often be observed through physical expressions such as facial expressions, and body language, and physiological responses such as heart rate and sweating. Feelings are internal experiences and are not directly observable by others. They are expressed through verbal communication and introspection.

Behaviors

Functionally, *behaviors* are the actions or reactions of individuals, groups, or organisms in response to external or internal stimuli. These actions can range from simple reflexes to complex decisions and can be observed directly or indirectly. Behaviors can be voluntary or involuntary, overt (observable) or covert (not directly observable), and are influenced by genetic, psychological, social, and environmental factors. Essentially, behaviors represent how individuals or groups interact with their environment and express their internal states and processes.

Genetics plays a significant role in shaping our emotions, feelings, and behaviors by influencing the biological systems that govern these aspects of human experience. For emotions, genes impact the production and regulation of neurotransmitters like serotonin, dopamine, and norepinephrine, which are critical for emotional regulation. Variations in these genes can affect our mood and emotional responses. Additionally, genetic factors contribute to the development and functioning of brain regions such as the amygdala, prefrontal cortex, and hippocampus, which are involved in processing emotions. Differences in these brain regions can impact how we react emotionally to stimuli.

When it comes to feelings, genetic predispositions determine how sensitive we are to emotional stimuli, shaping the intensity of our feelings in response to various emotions. Genes also influence cognitive functions such as attention, memory, and interpretation, which affect how feelings are generated and experienced based on emotional events.

Behaviors are influenced by genetics through their impact on temperament and personality. Genetic factors contribute to fundamental aspects of temperament, such as introversion or extroversion, impulsivity, and risk-taking tendencies. These traits influence behavior patterns and responses to environmental stimuli. Furthermore, certain genes are associated with predispositions to specific behaviors, such as aggression, altruism, or social engagement. While these behavioral tendencies have a genetic basis, they can be modified by environmental factors such as the conditions within which a child is reared, the conditions within which domestic relationships exist, or the consequences of various prolonged treatment practices in the workplace or social groups.

The body's stress response system, regulated by genes, also plays a crucial role in shaping behavior under challenging conditions. Genetic differences in how the hypothalamic-pituitary-adrenal (HPA) axis functions can affect individuals' coping with stress and adversity, influencing their behavioral outcomes. Although genetics provide a foundational blueprint for emotions, feelings, and behaviors, environmental factors significantly influence their expression. This interaction, known as gene-environment interplay, means that while a person may have a genetic predisposition for high emotional reactivity, supportive relationships, and positive experiences can mitigate adverse emotional responses.

Genetics influence brain function, neurotransmitter systems, and personality traits, shaping the biological foundations of our emotions, feelings, and behaviors. However, the environment plays a crucial role in shaping how these genetic predispositions are expressed and experienced throughout life. Therefore, to understand the dynamics related to trauma and toxicity in the workplace, we have to recognize the interrelationships between multiple facets of what it means to be human biologically, psychologically, spiritually, socially, and environmentally.

In hindsight, when I became the executive leader of a forty-two-year-old nonprofit organization with a stable, no-growth culture, I experienced strong resistance to growth for eight years because many of the leaders had participated in the organization as youth. They wanted to preserve what they knew through their experiences, which also meant not expanding the excellent program to new areas, including urban areas. At the time, had I understood Trauma Theory, Conservation of Resources Theory, and System Preservation Theory, which suggests that individuals will preserve the status quo, I would have been better equipped to effectively navigate the complex challenges I encountered, even when it is contrary to their self-interest. What I did well was to avoid forcing immediate changes. Instead, I promised everyone that I would take a year to evaluate things, and if, in the end, as a group, we could not do better, I would bring that message back to the Board.

Between July and March of my first year, I gathered extensive information and insights. During our Spring leadership meeting, I presented a film by futurist Joel Barker that highlighted how innovation is often obstructed. This film helped key leaders realize how their actions were hindering the organization from achieving the goals and objectives set by the Board of Directors. From that day forward we were able to grow the organization despite continued resistance and we accomplished more than most thought possible.

Commitment to Purpose

My parents instilled in me an unwavering commitment to purpose, no matter the cost. Their activism meant that my childhood was anything but ordinary. My father was imprisoned for his beliefs, and I suspect his life was ultimately cut short because of his work. Though I cannot prove it, I believe he was murdered, but with his cremation, the truth was lost. My mother, in her tireless effort to provide for my brothers and me, worked herself to the point of exhaustion, ensuring we always had a roof over our heads and food on the table. It wasn't until I became a father myself that I truly grasped the depth of her exhaustion and sacrifice.

When I began this writing project, I had no idea how long it would take, how much effort it would demand, or how deeply it would trigger the trauma I had buried. Nor did I anticipate that I would experience even more trauma during the process. Yet, through it all, one thing remained certain—I was driven by an unshakable need to finish, to create something that could help others. From the moment I started, I knew that no matter what, I would see it through.

Throughout the writing process, I've uncovered deeper truths about myself, my trauma, and the events that have shaped my life and career. Now, as I near finishing this work, I find myself with a rare opportunity to pause, reflect, and chart the next phase of my journey. Along the way, I've gained clarity on how seemingly isolated incidents in my life were interconnected. I can now see a path forward, one that leads me toward becoming an author and speaker on the topics that matter most to me.

What is clearer than ever is that while we may not be able to prevent trauma from entering our lives, how we respond to it determines our trajectory. With the benefit of hindsight, I can see how the lessons from my childhood, like the importance of doing a job well, prepared me for the varied roles I've taken on throughout my career. It wasn't just about completing tasks but about doing them with excellence, no matter how mundane they seemed at the time.

These experiences taught me the value of humility and perseverance, even in the face of injustice. I learned that hard work might not always be rewarded and that others might take credit for what you've accomplished. This was a lesson I first encountered as a teenager working at a local car wash, where older coworkers often stole my tips—a behavior I saw repeated throughout my career. Yet, my father's words, "Any job worth doing is a job worth doing well," have grounded me throughout my life, shaping my character and keeping me humble.

As I reconcile decades of personal and professional trauma, I see how my story aligns with the broader theme of overcoming adversity caused by trauma and toxicity in the workplace. My experiences, combined with my training, offer a unique perspective on how to navigate these challenges. This journey has allowed me to connect the dots between my past and the work I now feel called to do, offering insights that I hope will resonate with others who face similar struggles.

Changing the Status Quo

Anyone seriously intent on improving organizational effectiveness should prepare themselves for the blowback they will receive due to their efforts to change the status quo. Depending on the nature of the change (type, size), existing culture, climate, systems, available resources, and leadership, commitment to purpose either fosters, obstructs, or blocks change initiatives. Experienced leaders and consultants generally know what needs to be done or can figure it out. Leadership willpower, a high tolerance for ambiguity, and trust and belief in their employees make or break the effort.

Personal Timeline

In 2000, I developed a comprehensive life plan that included a mission statement, vision statement, goals, and objectives to prepare for teaching a class on creating a meaningful life. During my first year, I noticed that some students, particularly females, exhibited signs of trauma while completing an exercise using Figure 1-1: Life is a Process of

Always Becoming. When distress was evident, I escorted these students to the counseling center for additional help. Although it was a simple exercise, it unintentionally provoked strong emotional responses in some students.

In 2016, after settling in my new home, I reviewed all my college transcripts together. This exercise revealed a clear, coherent direction from start to finish in my educational pursuits. My education turned out to be much more synchronized than I initially thought. It has consistently supported the work I love most, and this work has become the foundation of my teaching.

By 2018, when I started integrating discussions about trauma into my life's work, I reviewed my life plan. I was on track with my original goals, demonstrating that the system I designed for an undergraduate class nearly two decades earlier was an effective tool for proactively planning a life on purpose. This experience affirmed the viability of my approach and its potential to help others plan and achieve their life aspirations.

In 2018, my path as a graduate school professor of leadership took an unexpected turn toward trauma education work. My shift was sparked by a conversation with a student telling me of her uncle, who was tragically shot and killed the night before. Although this was a tragic enough story, she was my seventh student in ten years, sharing a similar story. This one, though, finally triggered my trauma and caused me to act and do something about it.

The event in 2018 resonated deeply with me because it reminded me of a harrowing experience when I witnessed the murder of a neighbor, a moment of violence that has stayed with me: The killer locked eyes with me, leaving an indelible mark on my psyche that I quickly could have died that day, and I was defenseless to stop it. That moment also caused me to think about a previous class I taught when I asked a group of about fifty undergraduate students how many knew someone who was shot, and about three-quarters of them raised their hands.

Within a week or so after the student communicated with me, another student reached out to tell me of his struggles completing coursework because, in addition to going to graduate school, he was also performing as his aunt's primary caregiver and working a full-time job. This story added another layer to my growing awareness of the personal and systemic challenges students and others face today. I thought about my mom, who passed away much too young from cancer when I was in my mid-thirties. Looking at her and engaging with her, you would never have known she was ill. It was surreal. I also know what it was like to be a single parent while working full-time and being a full-time student. I know exhaustion, and what I learned later from my trauma research, what my caretaker student was describing to me, is called compassion fatigue or secondary traumatic stress (STS.).

At the same time, these personal student encounters coincided with a significant professional disappointment: Being passed over for a director of diversity position at the university where I was working. It was my twelfth or thirteenth time being passed over for positions I was qualified to hold. This time, however, this particular role I helped to create and for which I was eminently qualified was given to someone else, not once but twice to outsiders not involved in our work, highlighting a continued pattern of being overlooked for promotional opportunities despite my significant contributions and effective university-wide leadership, particularly in leadership and diversity initiatives. It is the one job I have coveted most, but it has always eluded me.

However, hiring someone else had more significant implications for the organization. On an organizational level, the absence of effective senior leadership meant that the critical work our working group was engaged in on behalf of the Board of Directors for three years was undermined and became neglected, leading to lost projects that could have significantly furthered the organization's mission, goals, and vision. Ironically, this is the president who introduced himself as a Redneck when he was first hired, so I am not surprised that he undermined our diversity initiatives by, among other things, refusing to interview the person who implemented the major Diversity and Inclusion Working Group initiatives—me.

The president's interference and neglect directly contradicted the aspirations of the Board of Directors, who had been keen on advancing diversity and inclusion efforts. In the end, rather than developing the robust program we were going to accomplish, it fragmented into the recesses of various isolated academic programs. He effectively killed the initiative that had begun three years earlier. The outcome is predictable when personalities override the interests of the organization and the collective whole.

These examples illustrate how stakeholder personalities and interactions converge in our workplaces and how the experiences and belief systems of the actors involved temper interpersonal relationships and the outcomes for entire organizations. How interpersonal and intergroup relationships intertwine and become a fabric stretching across the boundary between what happens at work and how those interactions connect to events outside work and vice versa is observable to the trained eye. We cannot separate the two because, in many ways, the only thing that separates these two distinct worlds is the threshold we cross in our minds as we go between the two worlds—the world inside work and the world outside work. This guide illuminates these dynamics, offering insights and perspectives that can help others navigate the complexities of trauma and adversity in their personal and professional lives.

Creating Your Own Balance

The chapter "Experiences Shape Behaviors" highlights how life experiences, especially trauma, play a significant role in shaping individual behaviors and future outcomes. The chapter begins by emphasizing resilience, comparing life to a long-distance run, and illustrates how early experiences—whether positive or negative—create lasting impacts. It provides personal anecdotes, like my relationship with strawberries and their fear of skating, to explain how emotions tied to experiences influence behavior.

A key theme is the pervasive impact of trauma. The chapter discusses trauma's psychological, physical, and emotional aftereffects, which can manifest in toxic behaviors in various environments, especially the workplace. It also touches on the importance of taking ownership of one's experiences and behaviors, advocating for personal responsibility rather than blaming others for failures. The chapter emphasizes that trauma and toxicity are part of life, but individuals can convert pain into a source of motivation.

The chapter also explores living with Complex Post-Traumatic Stress Disorder (CPTSD), explaining how prolonged exposure to traumatic events leads to difficulties in emotional regulation and relationships. Despite these challenges, I emphasize personal growth and resilience.

Professionally, the chapter addresses how leadership behaviors—especially toxic leadership—affect organizational and group dynamics. It stresses the need for leaders to be aware of their influence on others and how implicit biases and past experiences shape their decisions. The chapter closes with a call to understand trauma's broader societal effects and how healing from toxic environments is possible, advocating for a compassionate approach to leadership that promotes resilience and personal development.

DEMYSTIFYING TRAUMA

Principle 2: *Whether we like it or not,
we are all part of each other's story.*

CHAPTER 2

Creating Trauma-informed Communities

The Field of Traumatology

Traumatology is the study of trauma, its effects, and the methods of treatment or healing from traumatic experiences. It encompasses a multidisciplinary social science approach, drawing on insights from multiple social sciences. *Traumatologists* examine how trauma affects individuals and communities, exploring both the immediate and long-term consequences of exposure to traumatic events.

The field of traumatology covers a wide range of traumatic experiences, including but not limited to:

- Personal experiences of violence or abuse (physical, sexual, emotional)

- Natural disasters (earthquakes, floods, hurricanes)

- War and conflict

- Accidents and injuries

- Witnessing traumatic events

- Workplace trauma, including bullying, harassment, and other forms of toxicity

Traumatology is concerned with identifying the symptoms and disorders that can arise from trauma, such as acute stress disorder, post-traumatic stress disorder (PTSD), and complex PTSD (CPTSD). It also explores resilience factors and coping mechanisms that help individuals recover from trauma, as well as prevention strategies to minimize the impact of future traumatic events.

The goal is to help individuals process their traumatic experiences, reduce symptoms of trauma, and support those affected in rebuilding a sense of safety and trust. In terms of treatment, traumatology promotes a variety of therapeutic approaches tailored to the needs of trauma survivors. Among others, these may include the following:

- Cognitive-behavioral therapy (CBT)

- Eye movement desensitization and reprocessing (EMDR)

- Accelerated resolution therapy (ART)

- Narrative therapy

- Somatic experiencing

As a field, traumatology emphasizes the importance of a compassionate, trauma-informed approach in all areas of care and support, recognizing the widespread impact of trauma on individuals' lives, and the need for sensitive and effective interventions.

The time has come to demystify and destigmatize trauma and to create trauma-informed communities. Surviving life is tough, and our time is not guaranteed. Traumatized people are the majority of the population in many countries, and we try to sweep trauma and its aftereffects under the rug. When a violent outbreak such as a mass shooting occurs, we point our fingers at the shooter, suggesting the shooter had a mental health problem, as though the shooter lived in a vacuum and without the influence of others around them. However, mass shooters are embedded within our workplaces and social communities (Fox et al., 2021; The Violence Project (2021); Smart and Schell (2021); The National Safety Council (2019); National Coalition Against Domestic Violence (n.d,).

Representing What Others Fear

My trauma is my precursor for my life's work, which in part is to help others find a path towards healing. My life has been devoted to helping people precisely because so many have harmed me over my lifetime. As I've tried to understand why that has been the case, I can only conclude that I represent what other people fear.

A few years ago, speaking with my high school best friend, John Brown, we were reminiscing about our experiences, and he said, "I don't know why Coach didn't like you. The guys were jealous of you. The teachers, I don't know, man, what it was." Whatever it is that I project is misunderstood and has resulted in half a dozen physical assaults and multiple workplace traumatic events inflicted by supervisors.

The Last-Straw Job

In what now appears to be my final full-time job as an employee, I was initially hired by one of the two most wonderful supervisors in my career. However, I ended up being supervised by two highly toxic individuals, spending 70% of my time under their direction. Because there wasn't any way to provide performance feedback about their supervision, there wasn't a system for me or others to alert the supervisor for toxic supervisor #1 that he was having issues. It would not have mattered anyway because, in the first instance, his supervisor supported him and thought I was a difficult employee. In fact, my supervisor was stealing my work and claiming it as his own (a clear academic integrity violation that should have resulted in disciplinary action). Among other things, he assigned me to write the five-year academic program review without providing release-time from other responsibilities.

In the second instance, toxic supervisor #2 was friends with the first one. So, when he became my supervisor the first thing out of his mouth was, "wasn't he (my former toxic supervisor) a great guy?" attempting to get me to agree with him that my abuser was a "great guy." The best response I could muster was, "I have a different opinion about that." From that point forward, he never asked another question, but instead, opted to continuously accuse me of things that were patently false.

Poor Leadership Produces Performance Problems

One day, a senior administrator conducted a 360-degree performance review to obtain feedback about the performance of supervisors in our college. The feedback was so negative about toxic supervisor #1 that he was summarily fired within a few days, and, in the process, I became targeted and unpromotable.

Although performance reviews are intended to foster employee growth and development, many organizations do not utilize them effectively or at all, resulting in unnecessary harm to employees, avoidable attrition, and terminations. Throughout my career, I only had one opportunity to provide feedback about a supervisor during my final full-time employment position spanning over a dozen years. Moreover, the prevalent leadership styles employed were Autocratic and Laissez-faire, where leaders allowed supervisors to operate with minimal oversight, resulting in a lack of effective leadership. Consequently, supervisors, whether good, poor, or toxic leaders, could behave in ways that go unchecked.

During my tenure in that role, I was expected to maintain a positive attitude and perform my job managing classroom behaviors despite encountering relentless workplace trauma and toxicity. Because the supervisor was incompetent, there wasn't any consideration given to supporting students experiencing trauma or addressing toxic student behaviors that unfairly blamed faculty members for student-related issues. One particularly toxic student was able to graduate with a Master of Science in Leadership degree without demonstrating any leadership competence, as the university failed to challenge his toxic behaviors and did not protect faculty members from his ruthless and aggressive behaviors.

Problems that are not addressed appropriately only fester, grow, and become more damaging. This student wrote a disparaging letter attacking a faculty member's qualifications, and the supervisor's failure to act led to the faculty member's removal and their workload being transferred to me, resulting in overwork and abuse of power by the supervisor. This was a blatant failure of his leadership as my supervisor and program director.

Despite being given release time to complete a significant departmental project, the supervisor refused to pay a different part-time faculty member to take the classroom teaching responsibilities. Instead, I was forced to take on additional responsibilities, reflecting an abusive action by the supervisor. His decisions only protected and enabled the student to commit more harm, enabling him to go on to harm other faculty in the future, made faculty impotent to manage his destructive behaviors in the classroom, and facilitated actual harm to multiple faculty members in their workplace.

Poor Leadership Produces Poor Outcomes

Organizations of all types exist to serve some purpose; therefore, whatever purpose they serve impacts all stakeholder groups. What sets them apart are the leaders and cultures created by those leaders. I can attest to my experiences, which include that there are many more poorly led organizations than great ones, with lots of mediocre, underperforming ones in the middle. More than half the workforce is being harmed, so we cannot pretend there isn't a problem with how stakeholders are treated. We also know that trauma experienced in the workplace travels into our homes, exacerbating whatever situation exists in the household. We must own that trauma is a fact of life, and therefore, it impacts all of us in ways most of us do not understand.

Consequently, we must find solutions within our workplaces and social communities by changing how we treat people in our society because that treatment has future impacts that carry over into every aspect of our lives with deleterious effects for us all. Consider as examples active shooter drills being carried out in all of our schools and in many of our organizations, the impacts that mass shooting events have on entire communities, and the continuous bombardment of mass shooting news has on our psyches.

Growing up during the height of the Cold War, we used to have nuclear explosion drills as though hiding under a desk would save us, but no bombs were being dropped in the United States to make the exercise real. Today, active shooter drills are done because of the real possibility that an active shooter will emerge in some public space. Consequently, we are preparing people for a potential actual occurrence and thereby raising everyone's anxiety levels.

The impact of mass shootings and other violent events in our society extends far beyond the immediate victims and their families. It affects entire communities and can have a profound psychological impact on individuals who are not directly involved. This is why it is essential to seek solutions within our workplaces and social communities, addressing the root causes of such violence and promoting trauma-informed communities with cultures of safety, support, and inclusivity.

Active shooter drills in schools and organizations can be a necessary precaution. Still, they also highlight the prevalence of violence in our society. They can have a traumatic impact on individuals who are already experiencing anxiety or other mental health issues. Similarly, the constant bombardment of mass shooting news can contribute to a general sense of fear and helplessness, further exacerbating mental health challenges. Therefore, it is essential to approach these issues with sensitivity and awareness, recognizing their impact on individuals and communities.

By changing how we treat people in our society, we can work towards preventing violence and promoting a culture of safety and support. This includes addressing issues such as mental health, social isolation, and access to firearms. We can create a healthier and safer society by promoting inclusivity, empathy, and understanding.

Trauma and Toxicity

To appreciate the interplay between trauma and toxicity, we must distinguish between the two terms. From the perspective of someone experiencing both trauma and toxicity, *trauma* is omnipresent but contained within the individual. When there is a trauma-induced behavior (*toxicity*) such as anger or a burst of rage as an outward expression of internal pain and suffering in a manner that impacts others, then we are describing how toxicity manifests in the environment. We see this occurring in the explanation for violent crimes such as mass shootings, bullying, and other forms of abuse and harmful behaviors.

Tedeschi, Shakespeare-Finch, Taku, and Calhoun (2018) remind us that trauma is a highly stressful (seismic) and challenging life-altering event. What constitutes a traumatic event may change over time for a given individual and may differ across cultures, and whether an event is traumatic is in the eye of the beholder. It's not the event itself that defines trauma but its effects on our *schemas* (mental models), thereby exposing them to reconstruction and providing opportunities for transformative learning to take place.

While trauma is like a specific injury to our physical or emotional well-being caused by intense events, toxicity is more about being in a harmful environment that continuously affects us in negative ways. Healing from trauma often involves processing painful memories and working through the emotional aftermath, whereas dealing with toxicity usually requires changing the environment or leaving the toxic situation to protect our well-being. Both require awareness and action to move toward healing and healthier living.

Toxicity is more like being in an environment filled with noxious air that brings out Dr. Hyde if inhaled too long. It refers to situations or relationships that are consistently harmful and drain our energy, make us feel bad, keep us in a state of stress or unhappiness, and thwart fulfillment. It's not about a single event or a series of events but rather about being in a harmful setting that affects our well-being regularly. This could be a toxic relationship where you're constantly put down, a workplace that leaves you feeling undervalued and stressed, or any other environment where negativity prevails and seems to contaminate your life.

It's also important to recognize that trauma can produce toxic people, and toxic people can produce trauma. We will have a robust discussion about trauma (what it is, its key characteristics, and its potential aftereffects), the impact of toxic leaders on workplace cultures and climates, their role in fomenting workplace violence, and the need for creating trauma-informed communities. We'll also discuss whether we are who we are by nature or nurture. That is, are we born to become who we are with certain genetic predispositions (genetic traits—the nature argument), or do we become who we are because of our experiences (the nurture argument)?

Contributor Heather Timmons also speaks about the impact of toxic leadership on professional and personal well-being in the medical profession. She reflects on the profound effects of working under a toxic leader, JD, and how her initial excitement and optimism about a new job quickly deteriorated due to JD's defensive, dismissive, and manipulative behavior. The toxic work environment, characterized by a lack of trust, emotional manipulation, and the undermining of professional growth, led to significant stress, anxiety, and ultimately a loss of trust in the leader. She also emphasizes the lingering effects of this toxic relationship, which necessitated a journey of self-reflection and healing to move past the trauma that is the silver lining in the darkest of moments. Despite the challenging experience with JD, Heather focused on personal growth, resilience, and the lessons learned from the situation using the experience as a catalyst for self-improvement and pursuing a master's degree in leadership to better understand relationships and effective leadership. Her narrative underscores the importance of reclaiming one's power, changing negative thought patterns, and using difficult experiences as learning opportunities. Her journey from hurt and anger to acceptance and understanding demonstrates the potential for growth even in the face of adversity.

Trauma is exceptionally complex, and therefore, information about any of the things discussed here should be explored with a professionally licensed mental health worker to better understand any personal implications. But, when triggered by trauma, a person may exhibit any one or combination of more than three dozen aftereffects depending on threat type, their previous training, psychodynamics, constitution, context, and situation. Someone living with previous trauma may have benefited from what they learned from their previous trauma, but they also now carry the burden of a second trauma to contend with as they continue living.

Trauma can also lead to toxic behaviors that become normalized within individuals or entire families, influencing how they interact with their various social groups. Once ingrained, this toxicity can trigger a person's deepest emotional struggles, causing internal torment until they either seek therapy to regain control or express that pain outwardly, potentially traumatizing others. Since we are all interconnected, our actions inevitably affect one another so the sooner we understand this, the sooner we can work toward creating better futures for everyone.

Changing our lens to see trauma exhibited through behaviors that impact others—generally in some inappropriate, uncomfortable, or harmful way—opens the door for us to respond to trauma differently. From the perspective of someone who lives with trauma and then enters a toxic environment, it can feel like high levels of sensory over-load, and when it is bad enough, it can produce a fight-or-flight sensation. Whether it becomes a fight or flight response behavior, is mainly due to personal circumstances, precursor events, and an individual's cost-benefit analysis when they contemplate their circumstances.

The Convergence of Trauma and Toxicity

It's important to recognize that trauma can produce toxic people and toxic people can produce trauma impacting others when trauma and toxicity converge in a person with position and influence. Toxic people who rise to leadership positions expand their capacities to negatively impact workplace cultures and climates with the further poten-tial of fomenting workplace violence as when poor leader-member relationships push employees to retaliate with changes to their goal behaviors and sometimes workplace violence, highlighting the need for creating trauma-informed communities.

On the other hand, trauma can also produce toxic behaviors adopted as behavioral norms expressed by individuals or entire families as they intermix with their various groups. However, the toxicity expressed by someone already living with trauma may cause them to find themselves in the throes of having their worst demons triggered, tormenting them until they regain control of them through therapy or expressing them outwardly to traumatize others. We are all connected in one way or another and there-fore, our shared exeriences make an impact on all of our lives The sooner we accept this, the sooner we can work together to create better futures for all of us.

Changing our lens to see trauma exhibited through behaviors that impact others, in some inappropriate, uncomfortable, or negative way, opens the door for us to respond to trauma differently. From the perspective of someone who lives with trauma and who then enters a toxic environment, it can feel like elevated levels of sensory overload, and when it is bad enough, it can produce a fight-or-flight sensation. Whether it becomes a fight or flight response behavior is due to personal circumstances, precursor events, and an individual's cost-benefit analysis when they contemplate their circumstances.

Trauma and Toxicity Produce Real Impacts

As a high school sophomore, I mentally snapped and attacked a teammate one day after football practice. I tried to punch his head through the high school gym concrete floor because he wouldn't leave me alone after multiple attempts to get him to stop what he was doing. During the incident, I was in such a rage and so intensely hyper-focused on hitting him harder each time his head bounced off the floor that everything else appeared blacked out except my target, his face, and his head.

Within a fraction of a second, I went from being upset at what someone was doing to me, trying to avoid escalation, to completely out of control until someone grabbed me from behind and pulled me off him. At that moment, I came back to my senses and could hear him screaming, get this crazy motherfucker off me! His words and the images from that outburst of rage remain vivid in my memory—a lesson I learned a decade later from a reading assignment by the Brazilian Educator Paulo Freire, who discussed the harm done to the perpetrator of the harm in his book, *The Pedagogy of the Oppressed*.

Once the incident was over, I nonchalantly finished getting dressed as though it had been just another day at school and then left for home. I felt nothing. I wasn't angry, upset, or afraid of expulsion. I felt nothing, a complete void. I had fully dissociated myself from what happened. There were witnesses to everything that happened, so their statements must have exonerated me of any fault for starting the incident because I never heard anything more about it. Ironically, he was the same person who punched me in the stomach in the first hour on my first day in a new school midway through my fifth-grade year after my family moved from Los Angeles to Altadena, California.

A decade later, I exploded once again in rage when a female friend, who was like the sister I never had, told me about a guy who had been bothering her. I didn't like the person anyway, so I approached him, and as soon as he opened his mouth to explain, I exploded. Before I knew it, I had him over my head and was about to throw him off a second-floor balcony like a sack of potatoes when the memory of the gym incident came to mind, along with the voice of my spirit guide whispering in my ears, "If you do that, you are going to San Quentin" so I put him down without taking further action.

By *spirit guide* I mean the inner voice (non-physical entity) we all have that offers us direction, guidance, support, and wisdom during our life journey. Often considered a guardian or mentor, spirit guides are thought to help individuals navigate challenges, make decisions, and achieve personal growth, typically in a spiritual or metaphysical context.

Overcoming Internal Mental Obstacles

W. Timothy Gallwey (1974) describes experiencing the inner voice we all have in his book, *The Inner Game of Tennis*, where he discusses how the key to improving tennis performance lies in overcoming internal mental obstacles. He emphasizes the importance of quieting the mind, focusing on the present moment, and trusting one's natural abilities, rather than overthinking and self-criticism. Gallwey introduces techniques for achieving a state of relaxed concentration and peak performance by balancing the mind and body, which can be done in real-time even when playing a fast-paced game such as tennis.

My destiny would have changed that day had it not been for the previous incident in the gym. I had the advantage of a decade to think about that day, what I had done, and what was becoming of me because of my capacity for rage, which happened pretty frequently by that point. I'm blessed to have lived long enough to learn that while anger and rage are useful in violent combat and competitions, they can turn a potentially extraordinary destiny on a dime by capturing its owner in a moment of bad decision-making. I know, I've been there.

Growing up, I observed in myself that when I am headed to the point of rage, I go from any outward signs of anger to absolute quiet before the storm. This epiphany was a badly needed insight to help me monitor my temper, allowing me to leave when the calm arrives rather than waiting too long until the storm overcomes my sensibilities.

Impacts of Trauma

Trauma is a response to a deeply distressing or disturbing event that overwhelms an individual's ability to cope, causes feelings of helplessness, and diminishes their sense of Self and their ability to feel the full range of emotions and experiences. Trauma can result from an event, series of events, or set of circumstances that is experienced by an individual as physically or emotionally harmful or life-threatening, and that has lasting adverse effects on the individual's functioning and mental, physical, social, emotional, or spiritual well-being.

Since trauma is additive, it can compound, making treatments more complex. Logically, trauma may shape behaviors, and when that happens, the trauma is then carried back into households, where it may at some point reveal itself and then impact family members in a variety of ways. For anyone who has experienced seismic trauma, The nexus between trauma in the work environment and the home environment cannot be overstated, and the impacts cannot be understated, as Kristina C.'s story outlined in a personal correspondence to me illustrates:

> I recently left the job I had been in for ten years due to my boss being fired and them placing all the work on me to complete since I was the one who had been there the longest. Beyond being promised raises frequently if I got additional education, I was given more work instead of any additional pay, so I quit. I had no plan to quit, but my mental health was highly affected; I cashed out my retirement and searched for a job for three months before being offered to be a middle school teacher at a charter school. At first, I thought it would be an easy transition, but teaching middle school students with extreme emotional regulation problems has been increasingly difficult to juggle with life and school. The school was more of a backburner [issue so I was slow to respond], and when I tried to get back in, I was locked out, and it took a while for me to get a reply from the IT assistant. (Personal Correspondence December 12, 2023).

This story also illustrates how psychodynamics in our environments matter. Kristina C.'s story does not tell the potential long-term social, psychological, economic, and behavioral impacts there might be on her because of her experiences and the resulting decisions she has had to make for herself. For example, cashing out her retirement means Kristina has lost that money as well as its earnings forever, reducing the amount of money she might have available when she retires or is unable to work near the end of her life. The ways Kristina was treated by a former employer may also impact how she views work for the rest of her life and how she treats people in the future. Only she can determine what the experience and its consequences mean to her.

Addressing Workplace Trauma

To adequately address trauma in the workplace requires self-regulation to avoid undesirable explosive behaviors that can produce negative employer repercussions. Self-regulation refers to the ability to manage and control one's emotions, thoughts, and behaviors in response to external demands or challenges. It involves staying focused, managing impulses, and making thoughtful decisions, even in stressful or difficult situations, to achieve long-term goals.

Self-regulation becomes more difficult when our trauma is triggered, or at least our lives are made more complex when we exist in environments where others are also experiencing self-regulation problems. We see this dynamic at work in how peer pressure can distort decision-making, and even more starkly in cases of "mob mentality," where the collective force of a group can compel otherwise self-governed individuals to engage in behaviors they would scarcely recognize as their own. Remembering the Kilpatrick et al. (2013) study can be very instructive, more than ten years downstream for those of us who are now carrying more psychological burdens because of the pandemic, its aftermath, and the tribalism that has gotten much worse in that timeframe. Tragically, the ongoing demonization of various marginalized groups creates conditions in which there is an increased likelihood that things will get much worse before they get better. We are part of the culture we are in, and we shape it as much as it shapes us. It's part of being human and why it is so essential for us to choose our friends and our environment well whenever possible.

The impact of workplace trauma can be profound, affecting not only the mental health and well-being of employees but also their goal behaviors, productivity, and the collective health of the organization, which can be measured by monitoring employee goal behaviors. Addressing workplace trauma involves:

- Creating a supportive and responsive environment

- Providing access to mental health resources

- Fostering open and respectful communication

- Ensuring policies are in place to prevent and address traumatic events and their aftermath

The Nature of Trauma

The nature of traumatic experiences is highly individualized, which means that what may be traumatic for one person may not be for another. This is partly due to individual differences in past experiences, capacity for resilience, and available support systems. Traumatic experiences can vary widely, including but not limited to physical violence, accidents, natural disasters, war, abuse, and neglect. The impact of trauma can be immediate or delayed, and it can have a ripple effect on various aspects of a person's life. Traumatic events can include, but are not limited to:

- **Physical or Sexual Abuse**: Experiences of violence, such as physical or sexual abuse, assault, or domestic violence.

- **Emotional Abuse and Neglect**: Experiences of emotional abuse, neglect, or significant abandonment.

- **Accidents and Natural Disasters**: Serious accidents and natural disasters like earthquakes, floods, hurricanes, or other catastrophes.

- **War and Conflict**: Experiences related to war, conflict, terrorism, or displacement as a refugee.

- **Severe Illness or Injury**: Life-threatening illness, severe injury, or medical trauma.

- **Loss and Grief**: The sudden or traumatic loss of a loved one.

- **Witnessing Violence or Trauma**: Witnessing acts of violence, death, or serious accidents.

- **Chronic Stress and Adversity**: Prolonged exposure to highly stressful situations, such as living in poverty, community violence, or being in a toxic home or work environment.

Table 2-1 identifies the types of aftereffects that might result from traumatic event experiences.

EMOTIONAL AFTEREFFECTS TO TRAUMA	MENTAL AFTEREFFECTS TO TRAUMA	BEHAVIORAL AFTEREFFECTS TO TRAUMA	PHYSICAL AFTEREFFECTS TO TRAUMA
• Feeling alone	• Loss of concentration	• Withdrawal from others	• Aches and pains
• Feeling afraid	• Disorientation and	• Impulsive behavior	• Fatigue and tiredness
• Anger and frustration	confusion	• Aggression	• Racing heart
• Mood swings	• Memory loss	• Crying	• Nausea and vomiting
• Difficulty sleeping	• Obsessive thoughts	• Arguing with loved ones	• Shakiness and
• Feeling sad	• Distractibility	• Increased sleeping	trembling
• Feeling hopeless	• Indecisiveness	• Changes in appetite	• Headaches
• Helplessness	• Thoughts about death	• Being easily startled	• Numbness and tingling
• Feeling numb	and dying	• Increased drug or	• Diarrhea
• Anxiety and panic	• Racing thoughts	alcohol use	• Hot flashes
• Nightmares	• Anxiety and panic		
• Lack of confidence	• Nightmares		
	• Lack of confidence		

Table 2-1: Potential Aftereffects of Traumatic Experiences
(*Source: Tedeschi & Moore, 2016*)

In my case, before undergoing accelerated resolution therapy (ART), when any of the triggers became activated, it caused me to cycle my trauma from the earliest event through the most recent event before being able to move on with my day. This happened once or twice on a good day and six to ten times on a bad day. Having to navigate a highly toxic work environment while living with CPTSD forced me back into therapy as a direct result of the harm being caused by my two toxic supervisors producing increased frequencies of traumatic events. This resulted in increased frequencies and durations of trauma cycling. It's easy to see how traumatic events can produce aftereffects that work independently or in concert to produce the aftereffect experiences.

Studying Psychology and Social Psychology

With the prevalence of trauma today, leadership training should include courses in psychology and social psychology so leaders can learn about human behavior and their own behaviors more specifically. This is not to suggest that an untrained person can diagnose another person's mental state. Still, awareness of the various types of aftereffects can help us all better recognize them in ourselves. That awareness can also help us to be more empathetic when we see aftereffects emerge in others as they often do through changes in behaviors. For example, symptoms observable through changes in behaviors may include anxiety, depression, increased absenteeism, decreased job performance, and a breakdown in team dynamics.

The Grief Model

The grief model, often called the *Five Stages of Grief,* was introduced by Elisabeth Kübler-Ross in her 1969 book *On Death and Dying.* This model outlines a series of emotional stages that people typically experience when faced with significant loss, such as the death of a loved one. The five stages are:

1. **Denial:** This initial stage involves shock and disbelief. Individuals may struggle to accept the reality of the loss, often feeling numb or in a state of denial.

2. **Anger:** As denial fades, it's replaced by feelings of frustration and anger. Individuals may direct their anger towards themselves, others, or the situation.

3. **Bargaining:** In this stage, people may attempt to negotiate or make deals, often with a higher power, in hopes of reversing or minimizing the loss. This can involve *what-if* or *if-only* statements.

4. **Depression:** Deep sadness and despair are common during this stage. Individuals may feel overwhelmed by the weight of the loss and may withdraw from daily activities.

5. **Acceptance:** The final stage of grieving is marked by a sense of coming to terms with the loss. While not necessarily a state of happiness, it involves finding a way to move forward and adjust to life without a loved one.

Once we've accepted that we have to live with a *new reality* of whatever was produced by the trauma event, we are able to move on with our lives. **Figure 2-1 Moving on From Grief** illustrates the process we go through when overcoming grief to get to the point of acceptance, giving us the ability to move on.

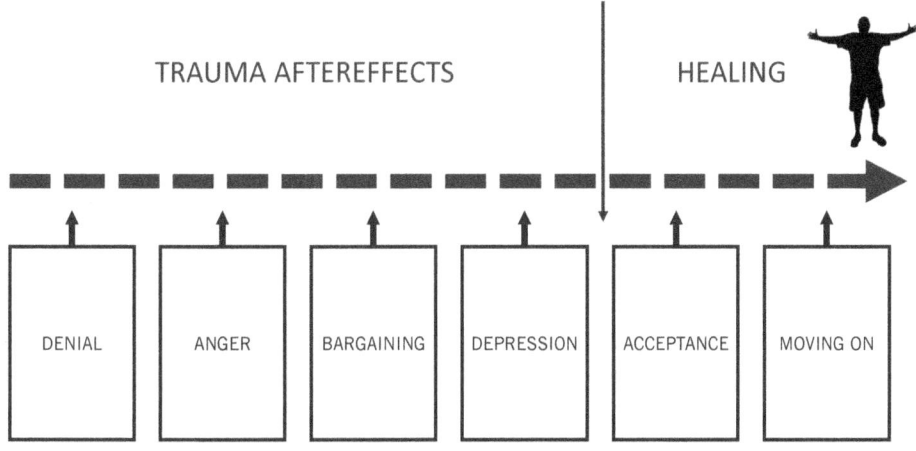

TRAUMA AFTEREFFECTS   HEALING

| DENIAL | ANGER | BARGAINING | DEPRESSION | ACCEPTANCE | MOVING ON |

Figure 2-1: Moving on from Grief

What I've learned working through my trauma is that it's important to remember that not everyone experiences these stages in a linear fashion. Some may revisit certain stages multiple times. The model is a framework for understanding that overcoming grief is a complex process with outcomes based on the individual nature of each person who has been harmed and goes through the grieving process.

Intrusive Ruminations

There is a difference between intrusive ruminations and intrusive thoughts, though they are related concepts. *Intrusive thoughts* are unwanted, involuntary thoughts, images, or ideas that can be distressing or disturbing. They often pop into the mind without warning and can be about anything, including fears, worries, or irrational ideas. These thoughts are common and can happen to anyone, though they are particularly prevalent in conditions like obsessive-compulsive disorder (OCD), anxiety disorders, and PTSD.

Intrusive ruminations, on the other hand, are a specific type of intrusive thought that involves repetitive, persistent thinking about distressing topics. Unlike fleeting intrusive thoughts, ruminations tend to linger and revolve around specific themes, often related to personal worries or past experiences. Ruminations are characterized by a loop of negative thinking that is difficult to break and can lead to feelings of hopelessness and increased anxiety or depression. While both intrusive thoughts and intrusive ruminations are unwelcome and distressing, intrusive ruminations are more repetitive and persistent, often focusing on specific worries or past events. Intrusive thoughts can be more random and varied.

If you have ever been in love, you may have experienced intrusive thoughts during periods when you could not stop thinking about the object of your affection. Intrusive ruminations are persistent. If distressing thoughts repeatedly invade a person's mind, they can cause significant emotional turmoil. These thoughts can be triggered and exacerbated by various factors, including high levels of stress and anxiety.

For instance, someone facing chronic work stress might repeatedly worry about job performance, leading to intrusive thoughts that are difficult to shake. In my case, as the toxicity increased, I began cycling through all of my traumatic events, beginning at the age of two, and recalling each event several times before I could move on with whatever I was doing. As the toxicity mounted, I became overwhelmed by stress, becoming fixated on negative thoughts, perpetuating a cycle of anxiety and rumination.

Past Trauma

Past trauma also plays a significant role in the occurrence of intrusive ruminations. Experiences of trauma can leave deep psychological scars, making it difficult for the mind to process these events fully. This can result in recurrent intrusive thoughts as the brain attempts to make sense of the traumatic experiences. For example, a person who has survived a car accident may constantly relive the incident through intrusive memories and thoughts.

Cognitive Patterns

Specific cognitive patterns, such as a tendency to overanalyze situations or focus excessively on problems, can contribute to the development of intrusive ruminations. Individuals who habitually dwell on negative aspects of their lives may find themselves trapped in a loop of repetitive, distressing thoughts. These cognitive tendencies are often associated with various mental health disorders, including depression, post-traumatic stress disorder (PTSD), and obsessive-compulsive disorder (OCD). These conditions involve cognitive and emotional dysregulation, making individuals more susceptible to persistent negative thoughts. For instance, a person with OCD might experience intrusive thoughts about contamination or harm, leading to compulsive behaviors aimed at alleviating these fears.

Understanding Underlying Causes

Biological factors, such as genetic predispositions and neurobiological differences, also influence the tendency to experience intrusive ruminations. Some individuals may be more biologically inclined to ruminate due to inherited traits or neurochemical imbalances that affect how their brains process stress and negative emotions.

Understanding these underlying causes can help in developing effective strategies for managing and reducing intrusive ruminations, such as cognitive-behavioral therapy (CBT), mindfulness practices, and, in some cases, medication. CBT is particularly effective in helping individuals identify and challenge negative thought patterns. Techniques from CBT can teach people how to redirect their thinking and reduce the impact of ruminative thoughts. Mindfulness and meditation practices are also beneficial, promoting present-moment awareness and helping to break the cycle of repetitive thinking. In some cases, medication such as antidepressants may be prescribed to help manage the symptoms associated with these intrusive thoughts.

Constant preoccupation with distressing thoughts can impair cognitive functioning, affecting concentration, decision-making, and the ability to engage fully in daily activities. This can lead to decreased productivity and a decline in quality of life. Managing intrusive ruminations involves recognizing these thoughts for what they are and employing effective strategies to regain control over the mental landscape and improve overall well-being.

Vicarious Trauma

Vicarious trauma is a psychological phenomenon experienced by professionals often working directly with trauma survivors, such as therapists, social workers, emergency responders, and healthcare providers. It occurs when a person is indirectly exposed to traumatic events through hearing about or witnessing the aftermath of these events in others. This exposure can lead to changes in the helper's inner experience, manifesting in symptoms similar to those of post-traumatic stress disorder (PTSD), including increased anxiety, hypervigilance, intrusive thoughts, and difficulties with emotional regulation.

Vicarious trauma can significantly impact a professional's worldview, sense of safety, feelings of trust, and levels of empathy. It can also affect personal relationships and professional efficacy. Unlike *burnout*, which results from chronic workplace stress and can affect anyone in any profession, vicarious trauma arises explicitly from exposure to the traumatic experiences of others and empathetic engagement with those individuals.

Professionals are encouraged to engage in self-care practices, seek supervision and support, establish healthy work-life boundaries, and possibly participate in professional therapy or counseling to manage and mitigate the effects of vicarious trauma. Awareness and acknowledgment of vicarious trauma within helping professions have led to the development of organizational strategies aimed at supporting staff, including training on trauma-informed care, promoting resilience, and providing resources for coping with the emotional demands of their work. This can occur in professions such as social work, counseling, healthcare, law enforcement, and emergency response, where professionals are exposed to the trauma stories and experiences of others.

Secondary Traumatic Stress (STS)

Secondary traumatic stress (STS) is closely related to the concept of vicarious trauma. It refers to the emotional duress and symptoms experienced by individuals as a result of indirect exposure to traumatic events through their work with trauma survivors. The symptoms of secondary traumatic stress mirror those of post-traumatic stress disorder (PTSD) and can include:

- Intrusive thoughts or imagery related to the trauma stories heard

- Avoidance of reminders of the trauma

- Adverse changes in mood and beliefs (e.g., feeling hopeless about the world or having a diminished sense of personal accomplishment)

- Hyperarousal symptoms (e.g., being easily startled, feeling on edge)

Like vicarious trauma, secondary traumatic stress results from the empathetic engagement with traumatized individuals and the cumulative effect of being exposed to their traumatic experiences. It is essential to differentiate STS from burnout, though they can co-occur. *Burnout* is characterized by emotional exhaustion, depersonalization, and reduced personal accomplishment that can occur due to chronic work stress, not necessarily linked to trauma exposure.

Table 2-2 illustrates the similarities and differences between the sources of trauma, which are closely related and separated primarily by the relationship to the individual being harmed. It should also be noted that teachers are now being considered in the same category as first responders, as many of them have to intervene in traumatic events in the course of their jobs. Prevention and management strategies for secondary traumatic stress are similar to those for vicarious trauma.

VICARIOUS TRAUMA	SECONDARY TRAUMATIC STRESS (STS)	SECONDARY TRAUMATIC STRESS (STS)	VICARIOUS TRAUMA & STS

▪ Vicarious traumatization — a process of [cognitive] change resulting from [chronic] empathic professional engagement with trauma survivors (Pearlman, 1999, p. 52)
▪ Cognitive changes could include:
  o Alterations in one's sense of self
  o Changes in world views about key issues such as safety, trust, and control
  o Changes in spiritual beliefs
  o Cognitive shifts in beliefs and thinking that occur in professional workers in their direct practice with victims of trauma
	▪ STS—knowing about a traumatizing event experienced by a significant other and the stress resulting from helping or wanting to help a traumatized or suffering person [or client]
	▪ STS results from engaging in an empathic relationship with an individual suffering from a traumatic experience
	▪ STS results from bearing witness to the intense or horrific experiences of that particular person's trauma
	▪ STS symptoms mirror the symptoms of post-traumatic stress disorder (PTSD) experienced by the primary trauma victim of trauma
		▪ Experiencing STS may include a full range of PTSD symptoms
		▪ Feeling anxious or on edge
		▪ Intrusive thoughts and memories of event
		▪ Difficulty sleeping or having nightmares associated with client trauma
		▪ Feeling angry or irritable
		▪ Poor concentration or memory loss
		▪ Difficulty concentrating
		▪ Being startled easily
		▪ Feeling disconnected from work or relationships
		▪ Hypervigilant about surroundings
		▪ Avoiding tasks or things that trigger unpleasant memories, thoughts, or feelings
			▪ Similar defining features, however:
			▪ Vicarious trauma results from chronic direct professional practice with trauma populations
			▪ STS results from engaging in an empathic relationship with a significant other suffering from a traumatic experience

Tedeschi & Moore, 2016	Figley, 1995	Bride, Robinson, Yegidis, & Figley, 2004 as cited in Winters, 2018	Newell & MacNeil (2010)

Table 2-2: Characteristics of Vicarious Trauma and Secondary Traumatic Stress

Anyone working in traumatology should implement self-care routines and stress-reduction techniques such as the following:

- Seeking professional support through therapy or counseling

- Participating in peer support groups or supervision

- Developing healthy boundaries between work and personal life

- Engaging in continuous professional development of trauma-informed care practices

- Recognizing and addressing secondary traumatic stress is essential for the well-being of professionals in trauma-exposed fields, enabling them to continue providing support to others

Compassion Fatigue

Compassion fatigue is a form of secondary traumatic stress, a condition characterized by emotional and physical exhaustion leading to a diminished ability to empathize or feel compassion for others. It is often experienced by those who work directly with victims of trauma, such as a family member providing primary care, healthcare professionals, therapists, social workers, and first responders. Still, it can affect anyone who is exposed to complex or traumatic situations regularly.

Key characteristics and symptoms of compassion fatigue include:

- **Reduced Sympathy and Empathy**: Individuals may find it increasingly difficult to engage emotionally with others' suffering.

- **Emotional and Physical Exhaustion**: Feelings of being emotionally drained, tired, and worn out are common.

- **Increased Irritability or Anger**: There might be heightened frustration or annoyance with minor issues.

- **Detachment**: A sense of emotional numbness or distancing oneself from others, including coworkers, friends, and family.

- **Reduced Job Satisfaction**: Loss of enjoyment in work, feeling like one's efforts make no difference.

- **Sleep Problems**: Difficulty falling or staying asleep, leading to chronic fatigue.

- **Physical Symptoms**: Headaches, stomach issues, and other stress-related physical symptoms.

- **Mental Health Issues**: Increased risk of depression, anxiety, and PTSD.

Compassion fatigue can be mitigated through self-care strategies, professional support, setting emotional boundaries, seeking peer support, and, if necessary, professional counseling or therapy. Individuals in caring professions need to recognize the signs of compassion fatigue and seek help to prevent burnout and maintain their ability to care for others effectively.

Burnout

Burnout is a state of emotional, physical, and mental exhaustion caused by prolonged and excessive stress. It occurs when you feel overwhelmed, emotionally drained, and unable to meet constant demands. Initially identified in the 1970s among people in *helping* professions like healthcare and education, it is now recognized as affecting individuals across all industries and walks of life. Burnout is typically the result of prolonged exposure to stressors. A lack of supportive resources and coping mechanisms often compounds it.

Addressing burnout involves reassessing expectations, seeking support, setting boundaries, and incorporating regular physical activity, relaxation techniques, and healthy lifestyle choices. In severe cases, professional counseling or therapy can be beneficial. Some of the critical characteristics of burnout include:

- **Emotional Exhaustion:** Feelings of being drained, unable to cope, and fatigue. It is often the first sign of burnout. Chronic fatigue can produce feelings of being tired most of the time, with a sense of physical and emotional depletion.

- **Depersonalization:** This involves a sense of detachment from work and colleagues, often accompanied by a cynical or negative outlook.

- **Reduced Personal Accomplishment**: Experiencing a sense of ineffectiveness and a lack of achievement and satisfaction in one's work and personal life.

- **Insomnia**: Difficulty falling asleep or staying asleep despite feeling tired.

- **Impaired Concentration and Attention**: Inability to focus or concentrate, leading to decreased productivity.

- **Physical Symptoms**: These may include headaches, stomach or bowel problems, and other stress-related physical issues.

- **Increased Illness**: Lowered immune response leading to frequent illness.

- **Anxiety**: Symptoms include tension, worry, and edginess.

- **Depression**: In severe cases, burnout can trigger feelings of hopelessness and lead to depression. One of the antidotes for these types of workplace outcomes is to create trauma-informed communities supported by mental and physical wellness and other programs.

Transgenerational Epigenetic Inheritance

Inconvenient truths about trauma are rising to the surface, demonstrating how the evolution of our DNA during our lifetimes is then passed along to future generations. Recent research in the field of epigenetics suggests that trauma can lead to changes in gene expression, which may be passed down to offspring as distant as ten generations, thereby influencing their susceptibility to stress and trauma (Skinner, 2022).

Epigenetics is an intriguing branch of biology that delves into how behaviors and environmental factors can lead to reversible changes in gene expression without altering the DNA sequence itself. This field explores how our environment can influence the activation or deactivation of genes, effectively reading the genetic blueprint in diverse ways. Epigenetics is crucial in understanding how the environment and our choices can impact our genetic expression, offering insights into the complexity of diseases and traits. This field is especially relevant when working as an organizational effectiveness consultant, where the impact of the environment on individuals is a crucial factor.

The process of passing trauma through our DNA to future generations is often referred to as *transgenerational epigenetic inheritance*. While our genetic code (DNA) typically remains unchanged throughout our lifetime, environmental factors, including trauma, can cause chemical modifications to our DNA or associated proteins. These modifications can alter gene expression patterns without changing the underlying DNA sequence. When an individual experiences trauma, these epigenetic changes can occur in their *germ cells* (sperm or egg cells), potentially affecting the next generation. Additionally, prenatal environmental influences can also impact the developing fetus, further perpetuating the transmission of trauma-related epigenetic changes.

Epigenetic modifications suggest that individuals with different genetic makeups may respond differently to the same environmental conditions. Likewise, people with similar genetic backgrounds can follow different developmental paths based on their unique environmental experiences. These individual differences, shaped by both genetics and environment, are key principles in the behavioral sciences and in biopsychosocial and environmental models of human development.

Our personality, behavior, intelligence, and other traits are shaped by a continuous interaction between the genetic blueprint we are born with and the experiences we encounter throughout life. Some epigenetic changes are inherited, while others develop over time. For instance, research on Epigenetic Transgenerational Inheritance has shown that trauma can be passed down genetically for at least ten generations.

It's important to note that while there is evidence suggesting the possibility of transgenerational epigenetic inheritance in animals, the extent to which it occurs in humans and its specific mechanisms are still areas of active research and debate within the scientific community.

For additional information and insights, see:

- Soul Wounds Colloquium. (2018, October 22). Ancestral ghosts in your genome: Epigenetic transgenerational Inheritance by Dr. Michael Skinner https://youtu.be/b3IOUmT8YIE

- For more information see "Ancestral Ghosts in Your Genome: Epigenetic Transgenerational Inheritance" by Dr. Michael Skinner https://www.youtube.com/watch?v=b3IOUmT8YIE

- Chopra Center. (2016). Sages and Scientists Symposium 2016. For more information see https://www.choprafoundation.org/events-initiatives/sages-scientists/sas16/

Multigenerational Trauma

The biopsychosocial and environmental model also helps to explain the effects of multigenerational trauma. *Multigenerational Trauma* acknowledges how family trauma is shared and passed from one generation to another through storytelling and cultural traditions. It involves the collective emotional and psychological wounds carried across generations, often resulting from catastrophic events or oppression. It involves the transmission of the effects of trauma across generations within a family, group, or community.

With Multigenerational Trauma, the origin of trauma can be the result of various events such as war, genocide, displacement, severe abuse, or other forms of extreme stress and violence inflicted on family and community members. These events profoundly impact the individuals directly involved. Consider the Trail of Tears and other Indigenous people's stories, narratives of enslaved persons, direct experiences in recent Jim Crow, holocaust survivor stories, and Japanese internment stories as examples. Some of the critical aspects of Multigenerational Trauma include psychological impacts on those who experience trauma and who may develop psychological issues, including post-traumatic stress disorder (PTSD), anxiety, depression, or other mental health disorders that can, in turn, affect behaviors, relationships, and parenting styles.

Trauma can be transmitted to subsequent generations through a variety of mechanisms, including parenting styles and family dynamics. Traumatized parents may raise their children differently due to their trauma-influenced behaviors and coping mechanisms. For example, overprotectiveness, emotional unavailability, or aggressive behavior can impact a child's development, leading to dysfunctional relationships, communication issues, or emotional detachment that, as a result, may be passed down again to successive generations unless the cycle can be broken.

For communities that have experienced collective trauma, the effects can permeate cultural practices, beliefs, and narratives, influencing how future generations perceive their identity and history. Several communities have endured collective traumas that profoundly impacted their cultural practices, beliefs, and narratives. A few examples are discussed next.

The Holocaust, Genocide, and Enslavement

Following the Holocaust, the Jewish community perseveres by upholding its traditions and commemorating the profound loss, destruction, and displacement suffered by European Jews. This traumatic chapter has deeply influenced Jewish culture globally, shaping narratives surrounding identity, remembrance, and resilience (Bar-On, 1995). Similarly, Armenians, post-Armenian Genocide, grapple with the repercussions, leading to a widespread diaspora and a reevaluation of their history, identity, and the role of memory in their cultural narratives (Hovannisian, 1992). In the wake of the Bosnian War and the Srebrenica massacre, lasting trauma has redefined community identities and beliefs, particularly about unity, remembrance, and faith (Stover & Weinstein, 2004). For those who are of African descent, enslavement was followed by another hundred years (1865-1963) of systemic racism, Jim Crow segregation, and violence, further shaping the cultural practices and beliefs of African Americans. This collective trauma has influenced narratives surrounding identity, justice, and empowerment in the community (Alexander, 2010).

These examples highlight how communities, in response to trauma, adapt their cultural beliefs and practices while creating new narratives to process their collective experiences. These communities have in common the disparate health outcomes that most suffer when compared to the dominant culture. In terms of some of the health consequences for children and grandchildren, those who experienced trauma may be at a higher risk for various health issues, including mental health disorders, even if they did not experience the trauma directly.

Tuskegee Syphilis Experiment

Trauma produces lingering effects for those who experience it directly and, if severe enough, their progeny for generations to come. *Bad Blood: The Tuskegee Syphilis Experiment* by James H. Jones, published in 1981, is a critical historical analysis of one of the most infamous clinical medical studies. This book thoroughly examines the Tuskegee Syphilis Study conducted by the U.S. Public Health Service, which took place in Macon County, Alabama, from 1932 to 1972.

Jones (1981) details how the study involved 399 Black men who had syphilis and 201 who did not. These men were told they were being treated for "bad blood," a vague term that could have meant various ailments, including syphilis, anemia, and fatigue. In reality, they were never informed of their syphilis diagnosis and were denied treatment for their disease. Researchers observed the progression of the illness through its final stages under the guise of offering free health care to study the effects of untreated syphilis.

Jones explores the experiment's ethical, racial, and scientific dimensions, how the researchers exploited racial prejudices and economic hardships to recruit subjects, and how the study's ethical failings were ignored or rationalized by its organizers, reflecting society's broader systemic issues in medical and public health institutions. Jones also covers the aftermath of the study, including its exposure to the public in 1972, leading to significant outrage and the eventual termination of the project. This led to widespread public distrust in medical institutions among African Americans, a legacy that persists to some extent today.

Ultimately, *Bad Blood* serves as a powerful reminder of the potential for ethical lapses in scientific research, especially when it intersects with issues of race and poverty. It highlights the necessity of informed consent, and the protections needed in clinical research to prevent such abuses from occurring again. *Examining Tuskegee: The Infamous Syphilis Study and Its Legacy* by Susan M. Reverby (2009) also offers a comprehensive analysis of the Tuskegee Syphilis Study, delving deep into its historical context, ethical implications, and the lasting impact it has had on medical research and the African American community. We saw the effects during the COVID-19 pandemic when African Americans were reluctant or refused outright to get vaccinated.

Reverby provides an in-depth look at how the U.S. Public Health Service conceived and conducted the study from 1932 to 1972 in Tuskegee, Alabama. The book examines the roles of the key figures involved, the justification provided by the researchers for withholding treatment from the infected Black men participating in the study, and how these justifications mirrored broader racial and ethical issues in the United States at the time. Furthermore, Examining Tuskegee discusses the effects of the study's public exposure in 1972, leading to a national scandal and significant changes in research ethics and regulation, including the requirement for informed consent and the establishment of institutional review boards. A significant portion of the book is dedicated to the legacy of the Tuskegee Syphilis Study, emphasizing its impact on trust between the African American community and the medical establishment and its influence on the development of ethical standards in medical research.

The study affected the participants and their families significantly through untreated syphilis transmission, causing many of the men to transmit syphilis to their wives unknowingly and, in some cases, to their children through congenital syphilis. This intergenerational transmission caused health complications and contributed to the spread of the disease. Participants often suffered from severe symptoms of untreated syphilis, including blindness, heart disease, and mental illness. The consequences extended to their families, as some children suffered from congenital syphilis, which can cause developmental delays and other lifelong health issues.

The psychological aftereffects include the betrayal of trust and the lack of transparency, which led to a deep sense of mistrust in the government and healthcare systems among the survivors and their descendants. This mistrust had long-term psychological and social consequences, influencing how African American communities viewed medical institutions and research.

The Tuskegee Syphilis Experiment has had a lasting impact on the trust between African American communities and the healthcare system, influencing behaviors and attitudes toward medical interventions, including the response to the COVID-19 pandemic. Here are some key takeaways in which the legacy of the Tuskegee experiments shaped behaviors and perceptions during the COVID-19 crisis:

- **Historical Distrust:** The Tuskegee Syphilis Study is often cited as a significant reason for the distrust many African Americans feel towards the medical community. This historical skepticism contributed to hesitancy among some African Americans regarding COVID-19 vaccines, testing, and treatment. They may fear exploitation or believe that they will not receive the same quality of care as other demographic groups.

- **Vaccine Hesitancy:** Early in the COVID-19 vaccination rollout, surveys indicated that African Americans were among the most hesitant to receive the vaccine. This hesitancy was influenced by fears of being experimented on or given inferior treatment, a direct echo of the Tuskegee experiment's legacy.

- **Communication and Outreach Challenges:** The distrust engendered by Tuskegee and similar medical abuses made it crucial yet challenging for health officials to effectively communicate with and engage African American communities during the pandemic. Overcoming this barrier required tailored communication strategies that acknowledged past wrongs and engaged community leaders transparently and respectfully.

- **Health Inequities:** The Tuskegee experiment is a stark reminder of the racial inequities in healthcare access and quality, which persist today. COVID-19 disproportionately affected African American communities, underscoring these ongoing disparities. The historical context of Tuskegee helped highlight the need for targeted public health interventions and resources in these communities.

Awareness of Tuskegee's impact has led to calls for greater ethical oversight and inclusivity in medical research, which were also relevant during the COVID-19 vaccine trials. Ensuring diverse representation in these trials was crucial to building trust and ensuring efficacy across different demographic groups. The lingering effects of the Tuskegee Syphilis Experiment on the African American community contributed to significant challenges during the COVID-19 pandemic, including vaccine hesitancy and difficulties in effective community engagement. However, this awareness also spurred efforts to address these issues directly, aiming to rebuild trust and improve health outcomes in African American communities.

In 1974, a landmark $10 million settlement marked a turning point in the aftermath of the Tuskegee Syphilis Study. This class-action lawsuit paved the way for survivors, their spouses, and children to receive free medical care, acknowledging the immense harm caused by the unethical study. Additionally, it catalyzed the establishment of the National Center for Bioethics in Research and Health Care at Tuskegee University, dedicated to promoting ethical practices in medical research. President Bill Clinton's formal apology in 1997 further recognized the enduring pain inflicted by the study, solidifying its legacy as a poignant reminder of the critical importance of ethical research practices.

The repercussions of health disparities extend far beyond individual health outcomes, impacting communities and society in multifaceted ways. Disadvantaged groups face increased morbidity and mortality rates due to limited access to healthcare and preventive services, leading to a lower quality of life and heightened economic burden. These disparities perpetuate social inequities, erode trust in healthcare systems, and exacerbate public health crises, with intergenerational effects further entrenching cycles of poor health. Addressing these disparities necessitates comprehensive strategies focused on equitable access to quality healthcare and social support systems, requiring a multi-sectoral approach.

The social determinants of health (SDH) underscore the intricate interplay between social, economic, and environmental factors in shaping health outcomes. From economic stability and education to social and community context, these determinants reflect the broader forces and systems influencing individuals' health and well-being. Recognizing and addressing these determinants are pivotal for reducing longstanding health disparities and improving health outcomes across populations.

The report Unequal Treatment: Confronting Racial and Ethnic Disparities in Health Care (NIH, 2003) highlights pervasive disparities in healthcare affecting racial and ethnic minorities in the United States. Despite comparable factors, minorities receive lower-quality care, reflecting systemic biases and provider behaviors that perpetuate inequalities. Regulatory interventions and cross-cultural education are essential for mitigating these disparities and fostering equitable healthcare access and quality for all. Unfortunately, the continuing disparate healthcare outcomes and failure to have a universal healthcare system persist today because of a system of institutionalized racism. We are perpetuating a healthcare system that disproportionately disadvantages patients based on their ethnic identities, as Thom Hartmann (2021) illustrates in his book The Hidden History of American Healthcare.

Multigenerational trauma and epigenetics offer complementary perspectives on the transmission of trauma across generations. While both recognize the enduring impact of trauma on health and behavior, they differ in their mechanisms and scope. Multigenerational trauma encompasses psychological, social, and cultural dimensions, while epigenetics focuses on molecular and cellular changes. Understanding these concepts is crucial for addressing the complex interplay between trauma, health disparities, and intergenerational effects in communities.

Collective Trauma versus Individual Trauma

Collective trauma refers to the psychological impact experienced by a group of people who share a common identity or connection, resulting from catastrophic events or situations that shatter the social fabric of the community. Unlike *individual trauma*, which is personal and can result from a variety of experiences, collective trauma is shared by many and can affect entire communities, societies, or nations. Examples of events leading to collective trauma include natural disasters, wars, terrorist attacks, genocides, pandemics, and systemic violence or oppression. The effects of collective trauma can manifest in several ways:

- Shared feelings of grief, despair, and anxiety among the affected population

- Erosion of social cohesion and trust within communities

- Collective memory and identity change as communities integrate the traumatic experience into their historical narrative

- Potential for increased solidarity and social bonding as communities come together to cope with the aftermath

- Intergenerational trauma is where the effects of the trauma are passed down to subsequent generations who did not directly experience the event

Addressing collective trauma requires community-focused interventions, including public memorials, communal healing practices, supportive policies, and mental health services that acknowledge the shared nature of the experience. Healing from collective trauma is a long-term process that involves rebuilding social connections and trust, fostering resilience, and creating meaning from the traumatic event.

The long-term impacts of any type of trauma can manifest in various ways, including posttraumatic stress disorder (PTSD), depression, anxiety, dissociation, difficulty in forming relationships, and a host of other mental, emotional, behavioral, and physical symptoms. The accumulation and additive nature of traumatic events make treatments complex processes because of the interconnectedness between the pattern of aftereffects produced by each type of event, their respective trigger points, and the biopsychosocial characteristics of the individual.

In addition to creating trauma-informed communities in organizations, leaders must now also concern themselves with their employees' mental and physical wellness if they want to lower the temperature and create kinder, gentler, healthier, and more productive workplaces. Understanding and treating trauma effectively is crucial for mental health and well-being, and it is a significant area of focus in psychology and mental health care. For leaders, it is a primary component impacting employee goal behaviors.

Cultural Trauma, Colonization, and a New World Order

Cultural trauma encompasses the collective emotional and psychological wounds experienced by a community or group, often spanning generations, due to profound disruptions or destruction of their core values, identity, and way of life. Originating from significant events such as war, genocide, colonization, or natural disasters, cultural trauma alters the social and cultural fabric of a community, challenging shared beliefs and values and leading to a loss of cultural identity. Unlike individual trauma, cultural trauma is transmitted across generations, shaping collective memory and narratives that become integral to the group's identity.

Responses to cultural trauma vary, from efforts to revive cultural practices to seeking justice or fostering resilience. These experiences influence group dynamics and relationships, often fostering a sense of shared victimhood or collective grievance. Addressing cultural trauma requires a comprehensive approach acknowledging its historical and social context, with implications for social policies, reconciliation processes, and healing efforts within affected communities.

African American Communities

Communities of color in the United States have endured a legacy of destruction and displacement stemming from systemic racism and oppression. Among these communities, African Americans faced targeted efforts to hinder their prosperity and thriving. Notably, prosperous African American neighborhoods such as Tulsa's Greenwood District, often referred to as Black Wall Street, were subjected to violent attacks and destruction, as seen in the Tulsa Race Massacre of 1921. Similarly, during the era of urban renewal in the mid-20th century, many thriving African American neighborhoods across the country were demolished or disrupted by government policies, including the destruction of vibrant communities like Brooklyn's Weeksville and Chicago's Bronzeville.

Chinese Immigrant Communities

Chinese immigrant communities, for instance, faced devastating violence during the Chinese Massacre of 1871 in Los Angeles, where a mob of white residents attacked and killed Chinese residents, resulting in significant loss of life and property destruction. Additionally, Japanese American communities experienced the trauma of forced relocation and incarceration during World War II under Executive Order 9066, which uprooted over 120,000 individuals from their homes on the West Coast and placed them in internment camps.

Native American Communities

Native American communities also endured displacement and destruction throughout American history, with policies like the Indian Removal Act of 1830 leading to tragedies such as the Trail of Tears, where thousands of indigenous peoples were forcibly removed from their ancestral lands. Latino communities, too, faced displacement and destruction due to urban renewal projects, gentrification, and discriminatory policies, which led to the demolition of neighborhoods like Chavez Ravine in Los Angeles and the Mission District in San Francisco.

Systemic Racism and Marginalized Communities

These examples illustrate the pervasive impact of systemic racism and oppression on communities of color, highlighting the ongoing struggle for justice, equity, and the recognition of their contributions to the nation. Despite facing immense challenges, these communities have demonstrated resilience and determination in adversity, advocating for their rights and striving to rebuild and preserve their cultural heritage amid ongoing societal inequities.

The history of marginalized communities in the United States cannot be overlooked or dismissed despite the discomfort it may cause some in the dominant culture. To ignore this history is akin to allowing a toxic waste dump to remain unaddressed, with those responsible walking away without accountability. As a nation, our progress hinges on confronting and acknowledging our history. Failure to do so enables those in power, many of whom perpetrate harm, to evade accountability. At the same time, the consequences of their actions persist for marginalized communities. Ignoring past injustices does not erase their impact; the harm inflicted must be acknowledged and addressed for any semblance of justice to prevail.

Colonization and Induced Cultural Trauma

The impacts of colonization and cultural trauma resonate deeply across indigenous and colonized populations worldwide, leaving enduring scars that continue to shape their lives. Historically documented and still prevalent today, these impacts span various aspects of life. One significant consequence of colonization was the forced displacement and loss of indigenous lands. Indigenous communities faced the brutal seizure of their territories, stripping them of sovereignty and uprooting them from ancestral homelands crucial to their identity and survival. In the United States, each time African Americans built thriving communities such as Black Wall Street in Tulsa, OK.

Moreover, colonizers imposed their languages, religions, and cultural norms upon indigenous peoples, systematically eroding their rich cultural heritage. This suppression of indigenous languages and traditions inflicted a profound loss of identity and heritage upon these communities.

The legacy of colonization also entrenched systemic inequalities, marginalizing indigenous populations and perpetuating social and economic disparities. Limited access to essential services like education, healthcare, and employment further entrenched these inequalities, hindering opportunities for advancement and prosperity. The introduction of diseases and displacement brought devastating health consequences for indigenous peoples. Epidemics ravaged communities with no immunity to foreign illnesses. At the same time, displacement and cultural loss contributed to higher rates of mental health issues such as depression and substance abuse.

The trauma inflicted by colonization was not solely physical but also psychological, with violence and abuse leaving deep scars on Indigenous communities. This historical trauma continues to reverberate through generations, perpetuating cycles of grief, trauma, and social issues within these communities. Colonization disrupted traditional social structures and governance systems, replacing them with colonial administrations. This upheaval undermined indigenous authority and community cohesion, fracturing traditional ways of life and governance.

Furthermore, environmental degradation results from exploiting natural resources, impacting indigenous livelihoods and traditional environmental practices. Indigenous communities, closely connected to the land, saw their ways of life threatened by environmental destruction. Despite these challenges, indigenous and colonized peoples have shown remarkable resilience and resistance.

Movements to reclaim land, language, and cultural practices demonstrate a profound determination to preserve heritage and assert sovereignty. Calls for reconciliation and reparations are gaining momentum, recognizing the need to address the historical injustices inflicted upon indigenous peoples. This includes formal apologies, truth and reconciliation processes, and efforts to restore lands and rights to Indigenous communities.

The impacts of colonization and cultural trauma are profound and enduring, necessitating ongoing efforts to acknowledge, understand, and heal these deep wounds. Only through justice and reconciliation can affected communities rebuild and thrive once more.

Legacies of Colonialization and Cultural Trauma

The enduring legacies of colonization and cultural trauma are deeply woven into the social, economic, and political fabric of societies, shaping lives globally. These legacies are not just historical remnants but active forces affecting communities today, from classrooms to workplaces. For Indigenous and African American students, simple questions about family origins reveal painful histories of forced displacement and enslavement. Yet, efforts to teach critical race theory, which addresses these realities, are met with resistance, perpetuating trauma for marginalized groups while shielding others from uncomfortable truths.

The systemic inequalities, loss of cultural identity, intergenerational trauma, and environmental damage born from colonization continue to haunt communities, fueling disparities in wealth, health, and opportunity. While movements for autonomy, reparations, and justice persist, they face constant resistance from political systems that prioritize expediency over human welfare. Addressing these enduring wounds requires ethical governance, compassionate leadership, and a commitment to truth and reconciliation to break the cycle of trauma and foster healing.

Other Sources of Trauma

There are other sources of trauma worth mentioning including developmental trauma, environmental trauma, and systemic trauma.

- **Developmental Trauma** is experienced during critical developmental stages in childhood. It can result from neglect, abuse, or witnessing violence, and it often has long-term effects on emotional and psychological well-being.

- **Environmental Trauma** results from significant changes or destruction in one's living environment. It could be due to natural disasters like earthquakes and floods, or human-made issues like displacement due to development or war.

- **Systemic Trauma** is one of the most critical sources of trauma in the workplace. It should be of grave concern for leaders and supervisors because it produces advantages for some groups while disadvantaging others. *Systemic trauma* arises from policies or practices that disenfranchise certain groups. This includes ongoing racism, sexism, or other forms of discrimination embedded in societal structures.

From Oppression to Posttraumatic Wellness

Paulo Freire's seminal work, *Pedagogy of the Oppressed* (1968), stands as a foundational text in educational theory and social activism, offering profound insights into the dynamics of oppression and liberation. Freire's analysis penetrates the core of societal structures, revealing how oppression strips individuals of their humanity, leaving both the oppressed and the oppressor trapped in cycles of dehumanization. Through his exploration, Freire uncovers the insidious nature of internalized oppression, whereby the oppressed internalize narratives of inferiority perpetuated by their oppressors, perpetuating their subjugation.

Central to Freire's discourse is the notion of distorted realities fostered by oppressive systems. These distortions not only hinder those being oppressed from envisioning change but also lull the oppressor into a false sense of superiority, closing their eyes to the injustices inherent in their privilege. Both parties grapple with a fear of freedom wherein liberation threatens established power dynamics and societal norms.

In response to these challenges, Freire advocates for *praxis*, a fusion of critical reflection and action, as a pathway to liberation. He posits education as a transformative force, empowering the oppressed to critically engage with their reality and catalyze social change. Yet, the journey toward liberation is fraught with obstacles as systemic dysfunction and entrenched power structures resist transformation.

Freire's insights reverberate in contemporary discussions on trauma and healing, illuminating the pervasive nature of trauma in society. As exemplified by staggering statistics on gun violence and domestic abuse, trauma leaves indelible scars on individuals, manifesting as inner demons that haunt their psyche. However, through therapy, support networks, and cognitive reframing, individuals can confront and tame these demons, reclaiming agency over their lives.

Breaking and Being Broken

Being described as *broken* typically refers to someone profoundly affected by emotional pain, trauma, or adversity, compromising their usual coping mechanisms or psychological resilience. This state can result from personal loss, abuse, serious illness, relationship breakdowns, or other traumatic events. Emotional distress from continuous stress, abuse, or trauma can lead to conditions like depression, anxiety, and PTSD, often accompanied by a loss of self-esteem and identity crises. Overwhelming grief or sadness from significant losses or disappointments can overshadow a person's ability to find joy or contentment. Continuous stress or traumatic experiences can lead to long-term anxiety and depression, affecting daily functioning and outlook on life. Experiencing repeated failures, criticism, or trauma can erode self-worth, leading to doubt in one's value and capabilities.

The stress of being broken also has physical repercussions, including chronic fatigue, insomnia, or severe health conditions like heart disease or high blood pressure. Neglecting physical health, such as personal hygiene, nutrition, and exercise, can exacerbate health problems. Physically, the mental and emotional toll often manifests as persistent tiredness or fatigue that doesn't improve with rest. Neglected health due to harmful coping strategies compounds the issue.

Behaviorally, someone who feels broken may withdraw from social interactions, activities they once enjoyed, or even responsibilities leading to isolation. Strained relationships with friends, family, and colleagues, due to changes in behavior and withdrawal can also lead to isolation. In an attempt to escape their feelings or numb the pain, some may turn to drugs, alcohol, or other harmful behaviors. Substance abuse can become a coping mechanism, leading to substance abuse disorders. Maladaptive behaviors, such as aggression or self-harm, might also arise in an attempt to cope with circumstances. Depending on how behaviors re expressed could post threats to others.

Resilience and Recovery

For those enduring trauma and toxicity in relationships, there is a fine line between breaking and being broken. Breaking can signify a moment of growth or realization—a turning point where someone confronts their pain and seeks change. It's when they might choose to leave a harmful situation, set boundaries, or begin a journey of self-repair. In contrast, being broken describes the overwhelming weight of trauma that shatters one's sense of Self, leaving one feeling powerless, isolated, and trapped in a cycle of harm.

Navigating this space requires recognizing the difference: breaking can lead to transformation while being broken calls for urgent intervention, support, and healing. The challenge is finding the strength to regain control before the weight of toxicity causes deeper emotional and psychological damage. Recovery is possible and often requires professional support like therapy or counseling, social support from loved ones, and personal growth work, such as developing coping strategies and rebuilding self-esteem. The journey from brokenness to healing is deeply personal and challenging but achievable with the right resources.

Discussions about breaking a person must be approached with sensitivity, as the implications for the individual's well-being are severe. If you or someone you know is in an overwhelming situation, seeking professional help is critical. Self-care, setting boundaries, and building resilience through coping strategies are essential steps toward recovery. Ultimately, recognizing and addressing the factors that can break someone is key to fostering environments that support mental health, resilience, and well-being. As the Japanese principle of kintsugi reminds us, beauty can be found even in what is broken.

Impact on Life and Path to Healing

Living with multiple traumatic events can make it difficult to function normally, as the lingering harm of trauma can dominate daily life. Intrusive thoughts and ruminations— those overwhelming, unwanted thoughts—can take over, but there are ways to manage them. For me, Accelerated Resolution Therapy (ART) was crucial in breaking the cycle of trauma that affected me daily. Other effective methods include Eye Movement Desensitization Reprocessing (EMDR) and Cognitive Behavioral Therapy (CBT).

Trauma can take a toll on emotional, psychological, and physical well-being, disrupting work, relationships, and self-care. However, being broken is not a permanent state. People have an incredible capacity for resilience and healing, even after profound trauma. Recovery often involves seeking professional support through therapy or counseling, participating in support groups, and confiding in trusted friends or family. The journey from feeling broken to healing is deeply personal and may vary in length and complexity, but with compassion, support, and professional guidance, it is possible to reclaim control and begin to heal. Taking that first step toward recovery is an act of strength.

It's essential to recognize the profound impacts of trauma, the lasting and deep impacts that early and additive impacts of traumatic events can have on an individual's life, as exemplified through personal stories in this guide. The evolution of a person's story from experiencing traumatic events (in childhood or later) to dealing with their repercussions in adulthood may be highlighted with significant incidents of rage and dissociation—at least, it did for me. These personal experiences underscore the depth of the emotional scars left by early and successive traumatic events over the course of a lifetime.

It is vital to underscore that these factors all matter: the age and timing, source, context, situation, event *posturing* (the story told of the event publicly and privately), the strength of community, frequency, intensity, broader prevalence, culture, event history, as well as the individual's constitution, and capacity to withstand and recover (resiliency) from the events. Further, the narratives intertwine professional disappointments and personal challenges, illustrating how trauma can permeate all areas of life, affecting professional aspirations and personal relationships. This blend of systemic failures and personal setbacks highlights the cumulative nature of trauma and its capacity to influence broader life outcomes such as career advancement, producing generational wealth, health outcomes, and other quality-of-life issues.

Contributor Peterson Mirville emphasizes that trauma is not just a single event but often a series of repeated experiences that compound over time. He illustrates how these cumulative traumas, beginning in childhood and continuing through adulthood, profoundly shape one's self-perception and worldview. He describes how the constant barrage of insults and negative experiences, from being demeaned by a parent to being bullied in the military, led to feelings of insecurity, timidity, and a deep sense of unworthiness that affected relationships and overall life. He also discusses how the healing and empowering effects of resilience support the journey towards healing and overcoming trauma through therapy, and mindfulness. In Peterson's case, Taekwondo played a crucial role in rebuilding his confidence, strength, and worth beyond the negative perceptions instilled by his past traumas.

Societal Implications

The societal implications of trauma are its pervasive influence extending from individual experiences into workplace environments and community interactions (values, mores, ethos, policies, practices, culture, interpersonal, and intergroup relationships). When employees are hired into organizations, the organization accepts the whole person, including their personalities and belief systems, which then shape their behaviors and interactions with others. Therefore, if they hold particular beliefs about one or more groups in the workforce more generally, then those belief systems will impact how they treat the members of those groups. For example, biases about gender capabilities, or those formed that are racially based or ability-based, will likely produce subtle or overt differential treatments for those groups and result in differential outcomes for members of those groups and consequently differential long-term impacts for them as well.

Trauma in the workplace also influences home environments (values, mores, ethos alignments with company culture, and how those impact interpersonal familial relationships). We see this when workplace dynamics such as layoffs, terminations, injury, and abuse occur at work and then migrate into homes. A wrongful termination can produce lifetime consequences for the individual and their families. Contemplate the impacts of being accused of something untrue that may have been done to you to protect others or to get back at you for some reason. Consider not only the cost of defending yourself but what it does to your reputation, self-esteem, relationships, sense of quality of life, earning capacity (in a capitalist society where earnings matter), and mental health. The higher the stakes, the more significant the potential impacts. It's one thing to be fired (or jailed) for something you did and quite another when you are innocent and become the fall guy for someone else's dirty deeds.

Workplace trauma can also influence community dynamics and interactions (primarily community trauma and toxicity culture), as we can see from the decade-long Flint Michigan water crisis where the National Resources Defense Committee (NRDC) reports, "The Michigan Civil Rights Commission, a state-established body, concluded that "... the poor governmental response to the Flint crisis was a result of systemic racism" (Denchak 2024).

By examining the impact on millions of employees through workplace trauma and its subsequent effects on family dynamics, it is long past time to call attention to the necessity for systemic overhauls to include trauma-informed approaches and the establishment of trauma-informed communities. But this is a heavy lift because of the pervasive nature of trauma and the obstacles ushered in by those at the top who talk a good game, providing lip service to an existential corporate and national security threat. They do so because they, too, have been harmed by trauma in ways they may not even understand. Therefore, to protect themselves, they blame what they see in front of them as someone else creating problems that they must solve. The problem is not outside us; it is inside us. That is the point!

This is a call to action to prioritize healing and advocacy for empathy, systemic change, and the development of supportive environments that facilitate healing and resilience. It is important to recognize trauma's symptoms, support those affected, and foster environments where healing—including mental and physical wellness—is prioritized. This does two things: It provides opportunities for others to be healed. More importantly, it allows us to do the same for ourselves. Promoting trauma-informed communities changes the narrative, expectations, attitudes, and behaviors of everyone in the community.

We know this approach works from experience with how civil rights led to Affirmative Action, which launched training programs such as diversity, equity, and inclusion (DEI), which did have a positive impact (although not as much as hoped) on changing behaviors (to some extent) of those in the majority towards those in the minority. We have gone from a society that openly discriminated and harmed People of Color to a society where at least now some semblance of change has occurred to the point where Black men are no longer lynched in public ceremonies of dominance. We also know it works because if it wasn't moving us towards parity between the races, there wouldn't be so much pushback from those in a shrinking majority group.

Personal Stories: Gateways from Past to Future

Personal narratives, such as those in this guide, highlight the enduring impact of trauma, whether experienced in toxic workplaces or through internal struggles. These stories remind us of the lasting scars left by oppressive environments, yet also showcase the resilience and self-awareness individuals cultivate to reclaim control over their lives. Through this process, they empower themselves to reshape their futures and reframe their experiences, transforming adversity into personal growth.

These journeys serve as a broader commentary on the societal need to address and mitigate trauma, inspiring a shift towards more compassionate, trauma-informed practices. As readers, we are invited to reflect on how our perceptions of differences have influenced our relationships, opportunities, and the people we've included in our lives. Personal stories remind us that, while circumstances may vary, our shared human experiences reveal more commonality than division.

Being Led to Empathy

This leads me to specific thoughts about empathy, awareness, resiliency, systems issues, and advocacy. My trauma has led me to empathy. I've gone from love for humankind as I was taught in my home through a long journey of rage, and long periods of frustration, pain, and suffering. These experiences have led me to illumination, understanding, acceptance, finding capacity for empathy, and self-transcendence. My journey brought me to the point of empathy for the individual journey all people must go through to evolve into the person they can become if they are willing to find that person.

Therefore, as I read each person's story and talk to the people who cross my path, I feel a deep sense of empathy for the narrator and others mentioned in the narrative who have experienced significant trauma. Their detailed recounting of personal episodes of rage, dissociation, and the long-term impacts of such experiences makes me more aware of the complexities and challenges faced by those dealing with trauma.

Stories illustrate the broad impacts trauma has had on the person telling the story and the broad impacts on those around them. The narratives also heightened my awareness of how trauma can affect various aspects of life, from personal behavior and relationships to professional achievements and workplace dynamics. Understanding the extensive reach of trauma, including its role in workplace behaviors and systemic issues, has prompted me to reflect on similar patterns within my environments.

Stories of resilience and recovery place the focus on recovery, and the potential for overcoming trauma with the proper support and resources is inspiring. They highlight the human capacity for resilience and the importance of supportive communities and mental health resources. The narratives motivate me to continue advocating for and supporting trauma-informed approaches in various spheres, such as workplaces and their broader communities. They could also inspire a personal commitment to be more understanding and supportive of people who are dealing with trauma.

Reading about how personal trauma intersects with systemic failures in education and professional settings highlights the inadequate ways institutions often address trauma. It strengthens my belief in the need for systemic changes to better support those affected by trauma. As an organizational effectiveness consultant and educator, it drives me to be a part of that change, advocating for compassionate and informed approaches to addressing trauma within institutions.

My conclusion looks forward, envisioning a future where individuals can move beyond their contempt for differences, producing paths towards healing and hope, underlining the transformative power of supportive and informed interventions and communities.

Creating Your Own Balance

In the chapter "Creating Trauma-Informed Communities," the narrative unfolds around the critical need for society to better understand, address, and respond to the widespread impact of trauma. It begins by shedding light on the field of traumatology, which explores how trauma affects individuals, communities, and organizations. Trauma is not just a personal issue but a societal one, deeply intertwined with the environments we live and work in.

Stories of how leadership and organizations play a pivotal role in shaping whether environments become safe havens or breeding grounds for further harm are made evident in personal stories. Toxic leadership, characterized by autocratic or laissez-faire styles, can create workplaces where trauma thrives. Leaders often fail to recognize how their behaviors and management styles can aggravate existing traumas

or create new ones. The chapter recounts specific instances of workplace toxicity, where the lack of proper feedback systems and ineffective supervision led to environments where employees felt overworked, undervalued, and even traumatized by those in power. These stories serve as a reminder that leadership is not just about authority but about fostering spaces where people can feel safe, supported, and able to heal.

As the narrative progresses, the chapter delves into the complex relationship between trauma and toxicity. Trauma, as I explain, often festers within individuals until it manifests as toxic behavior that can affect others. This interplay creates a vicious cycle: toxic environments trigger trauma, and traumatized individuals can contribute to the toxicity around them. The personal reflections shared in this section illustrate how easy it is for someone who has endured trauma to feel overwhelmed, eventually reaching a breaking point where their own behavior becomes harmful to others.

But this isn't just a personal issue; it's a societal one. The chapter draws readers into the broader implications of trauma on communities, emphasizing that creating trauma-informed spaces is not just about healing individuals but about addressing systemic issues such as violence, social isolation, and mental health stigma. The constant barrage of mass shootings, workplace violence, and personal crises leaves communities feeling unsafe and disconnected. The chapter argues that, by understanding trauma and addressing its root causes, communities can foster environments of support, safety, and inclusivity.

Woven throughout are stories of resilience—individuals who, despite the weight of their trauma, found ways to heal and grow. I share personal and professional experiences, showing how trauma can become a catalyst for transformation. These stories highlight the possibility of recovery, even in the most challenging circumstances, and the power of compassionate leadership and community support.

By the chapter's end, the message is clear: trauma impacts everyone, directly or indirectly, and we all have a role in creating trauma-informed communities. Leaders, their organizations, and all individual employees must work together to break the cycle of trauma and toxicity, fostering environments where healing and resilience can flourish.

THEORY HELPS EXPLAIN BEHAVIORS

Principle 3: *Sticks and stones may break by bones, but out of control trauma and toxicity can kill us.*

CHAPTER 3

Navigating Trauma and Toxicity

Leadership, Trauma, and Group Dynamics

Leadership is intrinsically linked to group dynamics, which play a crucial role in explaining many of the events we observe globally and within organizations today. Understanding these dynamics is vital for navigating the complexities of human behavior in various social, political, and economic contexts.

When it comes to how groups function, leadership is the most consequential element because it sets the tone for everything else that follows as illustrated in Appendices 1 and 2. As part of my research in preparation for this guide, I asked AI to conduct a thought experience about what would happen to the world if countries functioned under a given leadership style for various periods of time (10 years, 25 years, 50 years, and 100 years). The findings for the 100-year timeframe are presented below as an illustration of the potential outcomes. While it is likely that not all countries would have the same leadership style at the same time, we can begin to see the impacts of various leadership styles can have on groups of all sizes including whole societies.

Autocratic Leaders

Many autocratic regimes might collapse due to unsustainable governance, potentially giving rise to new political systems. Economies could face long-term devastation, with some reverting to feudal-like systems. Societal scars from prolonged repression would be deep, possibly sparking democratic or alternative movements. Global order might be fractured, with ongoing conflicts and instability. Autocratic governance, while potentially offering short-term stability, often leads to long-term negative consequences such as economic inefficiency, social repression, and increased potential for conflict. The resilience and adaptability of human societies, however, suggest that new forms of governance and social structures would likely emerge over time, seeking to address the failures of prolonged autocracy.

Laissez-faire Leaders

The long-term consequences of Laissez-faire Leadership would be fully realized. Successful areas might still exist, driven by exceptionally self-motivated and competent individuals, but these would likely be the exception rather than the rule. Most environments would suffer from chronic issues related to lack of leadership, including deep systemic inefficiencies, widespread inequality, and potential social fragmentation. The absence of cohesive strategy and proactive problem-solving could lead to significant societal or organizational decline. There might be a shift towards more structured forms of governance as a reaction to the failures of laissez-faire leadership, with new systems emerging to address the longstanding issues created by decades of minimal oversight and direction.

Democratic Leaders

Democratic systems would show resilience and adaptability, potentially evolving to address contemporary challenges. Economies would be highly advanced, with equitable resource distribution and continuous innovation. Societal harmony would be profound, with deeply rooted principles of justice and inclusion. The international community would be cohesive, effectively collaborating to address global challenges and maintaining peace through diplomacy. Democratic leadership is likely to foster political stability, economic prosperity, and social progress. Democratic systems promote accountability, transparency, and inclusiveness, leading to sustainable development and enhanced well-being. Despite challenges like political polarization, democratic systems' resilience and adaptability can address these issues effectively, contributing to a more peaceful and stable global order.

Transformative Leaders

Transformative Leadership would be monumental. The organization or community would have evolved into a model of equity, social justice, and sustainable development. The deeply embedded practices of dialogue, reflection, and continuous improvement would have created a resilient and adaptive system capable of navigating future challenges. Overall, it would result in an environment where every individual has the opportunity to reach their full potential. The organization's sustained success in promoting social justice and equity would serve as a blueprint for others, influencing broader societal change. The transformative leadership approach would have fundamentally reshaped the culture, values, and practices, ensuring a legacy of positive impact and continuous growth.

Group Dynamics

Group dynamics help us comprehend why groups act the way they do and the outcomes of their actions, referring to the behaviors and psychological processes that occur within or between workplace or social groups. Group dynamics also explain conformity and peer pressure, as groups can significantly influence individual behavior, leading to phenomena like gangs and cults or the rapid spread of certain ideologies and trends. Individuals often align their beliefs and actions with those of their group.

Collective behavior within groups, where individuals act together in ways unique to the group, can manifest in forms such as social movements, protests, riots, insurrections, and other mass actions frequently seen in today's headlines.

Discussions within groups can lead to attitude polarization, where members develop more extreme views after discussing an issue among themselves. This contributes to the deepening of societal divides and intensifies political or social conflicts. *Groupthink*, another critical aspect of group dynamics, occurs when the desire for harmony or conformity results in irrational or dysfunctional decision-making. This phenomenon can lead to poor policy decisions, failed business strategies, or other instances where critical thinking is overshadowed by the need to maintain consensus.

Social identity theory suggests that people derive part of their identity from the groups they belong to, which can lead to intergroup conflicts, as seen in cases of racial, ethnic, or nationalistic tensions. Communication patterns within and between groups also greatly influence events. The rise of social media has changed group dynamics by enabling the rapid, widespread dissemination of information and ideas.

Events, particularly in institutional or organizational contexts, can often be explained by the degree to which individuals are willing to obey authority figures, even when performing acts, they might find questionable or unethical. The diffusion of responsibility in group settings can lead individuals to feel less personally responsible for group actions, resulting in phenomena such as bystander apathy or an increased willingness to engage in actions they wouldn't undertake alone. A leader's behaviors can impact members within various groups. Those groups can influence behaviors with nongroup members who get caught up in the moment and behave in ways that might bring them and others harm.

Understanding these aspects of group dynamics is essential for explaining and addressing the complexities of human behavior in today's interconnected world. This knowledge is crucial for leaders who aim to foster positive social change and build healthier organizations and communities.

Living with Trauma in Groups

A "neural hijack" occurs when the emotional brain (primarily the amygdala) overtakes the rational brain (prefrontal cortex), leading to impulsive or irrational behavior. This phenomenon, highlighted in Daniel Goleman's work on emotional intelligence, explains how in high-stress or emotional situations, the amygdala can trigger an intense emotional response, bypassing the logical decision-making processes of the prefrontal cortex.

In simpler terms, during a neural hijack, the emotional brain "takes over the wheel," pushing aside the thinking brain, which usually helps us make reasoned decisions. This can lead to actions driven more by emotion than logic. Once the emotional surge subsides, the prefrontal cortex regains control, allowing for more thoughtful responses.

Understanding how these brain regions interact helps us manage our reactions during emotionally charged moments. Techniques like deep breathing, pausing, or counting to ten can help calm emotional responses and prevent hijacks. Recognizing the signs of an oncoming hijack is a critical component of emotional intelligence, which can prevent toxic behaviors that often carry over into personal and professional environments.

Reflecting on personal experiences, such as reacting emotionally in stressful situations, highlights the importance of emotional management. These reactions may or may not occur in professional settings, but they still impact others, showing how trauma and emotional responses are carried into everyday life. Over time, through growth and self-awareness, one can learn to shift from reactive behaviors to more measured, thoughtful responses—transforming moments of rage into actions rooted in love and humility. With the advantage of hindsight, I'm able to see that though my path has been difficult, it has also been a journey of immense personal growth and resilience.

Trauma is a Beast

Conceptually, trauma can be thought of as a rabid beast attacking the mind and polluting it with potential aftereffects resulting from such events. Here is a case example to illustrate what I mean. Recently, I was leaving a physical therapy appointment. I approached a fellow patient who had been very nice to me because I wanted to introduce myself to them and say, "Thank you." As I approached them, what came out of my mouth was not what was intended. I was in such pain from a setback in my physical therapy treatments that I should have just left for home but instead approached the person with a behavior I didn't recognize in myself.

As I spoke to my therapist about what happened, we agreed that it was a *neural hijack*). I intended to reduce my stressors through physical therapy, which then became the stressor and overloaded my capacity to cope with my situation. In hindsight, the neural hijack was likely inevitable. I live with complex PTSD (CPTSD); I am writing a book about trauma reliving my lifetime of trauma; and I was in a car accident that completely turned my world upside down, all happening at the same time.

My physical pain was so severe that I lost my ability to cope with all the trauma at one time. Ironically, I felt the moment when the neural hijack occurred: I recognized it because I felt the light in my heart that held my joy go out. I now understand how it could happen to anyone.

When sensibilities are overwhelmed, it can lead to undesirable behaviors and outcomes, as was the case in my physical therapy, gym, and balcony examples. Also, had my guide not been there, too, chirping in my ears, my life would have been very different and likely not as productive as it has been. I speak of my *spirit guide* to say aloud, "I am truly blessed for it being in my life," and I give thanks every day for that fact.

With the ability of hindsight and now actively trying to make sense of my life, I can tell this story. I can see how my guide helps me endure my psychological battles fought daily to preserve sufficient sanity to remain functionally able to navigate a dysfunctional world. With the gift of a lengthy life, I also see the psychological war, comprising all of the little battles taking place over the length of a lifetime. Sometimes we lose a battle by doing something that brings harm to ourselves and others. But the objective is to win the war against the inner turmoil produced by trauma to become the best version of ourselves each day.

Psychological Theories Behind Trauma and Toxicity

Understanding the psychological theories behind trauma and toxicity in the workplace can provide insight into how these environments affect individuals and suggest pathways for intervention and healing. These theories explain the mechanisms through which toxic and traumatic experiences impact mental health, behavior, and well-being. Eight key psychological theories relevant to workplace trauma and toxicity are discussed next.

Attachment Theory

Attachment Theory posits that early relationships with caregivers shape our expectations and behaviors in later relationships, including those at work. In toxic workplaces, insecure attachment styles may influence how individuals perceive and react to threats, criticism, or exclusion, potentially exacerbating stress and trauma responses.

Cognitive Behavioral Theory (CBT)

CBT focuses on the relationship between thoughts, feelings, and behaviors. It suggests that negative thought patterns and beliefs about oneself or one's environment can exacerbate the impact of toxic workplace experiences, leading to increased stress, anxiety, and depression. CBT interventions can help individuals reframe negative thoughts and develop healthier coping mechanisms.

Psychodynamic Theory

Psychodynamic Theory explores how unconscious processes, including unresolved conflicts and defense mechanisms, influence behavior. In the context of workplace trauma, this theory can help one understand how past traumas and unresolved issues contribute to individuals' reactions to current toxic environments.

Social Cognitive Theory

Social Cognitive Theory emphasizes the role of observational learning, self-efficacy, and reciprocal determinism in behavior. It suggests that witnessing or experiencing toxicity can alter individuals' beliefs about themselves and their workplaces, impacting their mental health and behavior. This theory underscores the importance of role models and supportive relationships in mitigating the effects of toxicity.

Stress and Coping Theory

Developed by Lazarus and Folkman (1984), *Stress and Coping Theory* explores how individuals appraise and cope with stressful events. Workplace toxicity can be perceived as a threat, leading to coping strategies that may either alleviate or exacerbate stress. Understanding these coping mechanisms is crucial for designing interventions that help individuals manage stress more effectively.

Trauma Theory

Trauma Theory examines the psychological impact of traumatic events, including how they disrupt the individual's sense of safety, trust, and self-esteem. Workplace toxicity, especially when severe or prolonged, can be traumatic, leading to symptoms of post-traumatic stress disorder (PTSD) and other trauma-related issues.

Conservation of Resources (COR) Theory

COR Theory suggests that stress results from the loss of, a threat to, or lack of gain in valuable resources, including personal, social, and material resources. In toxic workplaces, the perceived or actual loss of resources (e.g., support, autonomy, security) can lead to significant stress and strain.

System Justification Theory

System Justification Theory suggests that individuals have a psychological motive to defend and justify existing social, economic, and political systems, even at a cost to personal and group well-being. This theory can help explain why individuals might rationalize or minimize workplace toxicity, complicating efforts to address and resolve toxic environments.

These psychological theories provide a framework for understanding the complex dynamics of workplace (group) trauma and toxicity. By applying these theories, practitioners can develop targeted interventions that address the cognitive, emotional, and behavioral aspects of trauma, promoting healing and resilience among affected individuals.

Birth, Life, and the Emergence of Difference

At birth, everyone is the same. What makes us different is the context and situation we are born into. We are all united by shared biological, psychological, and ethical traits that define *human experience*, revealing common threads of connection despite the diverse tapestry of individual lives. All humans share a set of fundamental characteristics that transcend cultural, geographical, and historical differences. Biologically, humans possess the same genetic makeup that defines the species, sharing basic physical traits and physiological functions like walking upright, possessing opposable thumbs, and relying on language for complex communication.

Psychologically, humans are inherently social beings who form relationships and communities to seek love, friendship, and belonging. They share a broad spectrum of emotions, from joy and love to fear and sadness, which shape their interactions and decision-making processes. Cognitively, humans exhibit advanced reasoning, creativity, and problem-solving abilities, enabling the development of technology, art, and societal structures.

Morally and ethically, humans possess an innate sense of right and wrong, though it varies culturally. This moral compass guides them to pursue justice, fairness, and empathy in their interactions. Moreover, all humans exhibit a desire for meaning and purpose, prompting them to explore spirituality, philosophy, or personal aspirations. Finally, humans are inherently adaptable and resilient, striving to improve their lives through learning, growth, and innovation while confronting life's challenges.

Shifting our focus toward creating cultures that truly embrace our uniqueness, would enable all of us to feel more fulfilled. This change in mindset could transform how we see and interact with each other, moving us closer to a genuinely inclusive society. Moreover, achieving this would require a deliberate effort to overcome the long-standing narratives that emphasize our differences over our shared humanity. The issue isn't that change is impossible—it's that we expend so much energy demonizing those who are different from us that we can't make meaningful progress. Instead, we remain stuck in a zero-sum mindset. But making such a shift would require toppling the idea first espoused by Aristotle to treat *equals equally* and *unequals unequally*. Such a perspective sustains the idea of differentiated classes of people to support those in power and privilege. This behavior is replicated in countries around the world that delineate in-groups and out-groups based on social category, which by definition creates an artificial construct to divide members of a society into groups based on class or some other socially defined characteristic.

Discerning Differences

Being able to discern differences is an important genetic trait that enhances the chances of survival of the individual and human species. Who we let into our groups is important because of how new individuals impact established norms necessitating reshaping the norms, practices, and behaviors of the status quo. How we come together to form groups is a naturally disruptive process that makes it possible for innovation to occur, giving the group greater capacity to produce resources for the whole of the group as the group becomes more diverse. Depending on the culture and behaviors of its members, the group organizes the rules for the distribution of their collective resources.

The cultural paradigms of our groups dictate how resources and opportunities are distributed, and decisions must be made about how these rules are applied. Should they be proportional based on specific criteria, such as family size, or should resources be shared equally to give everyone a fair chance? These rules influence the distribution of power, tools for survival, advantages, and disadvantages. Ultimately, they shape who has better or worse chances of survival over time.

Beyond our genetic differences, our focus on racial differences today stems largely from the historical creation of race and racism. The concept of race, along with the ideology of White Supremacy, was used to justify exploiting free labor, primarily from indigenous people, to generate wealth for a minority. This wealth was then used to further consolidate power, often at the expense of millions of marginalized individuals globally. Therefore, unless we can understand the impacts on various groups over the millennia, we truly cannot understand how we got to where we are today.

Pretending that the history of how we got to where we are today did not exist because it makes some people uncomfortable, does not erase the facts of what actually happened. And, what happened historically shapes everyone on the planet today. It is also true that history is made every day, which means that what we do today impacts everything that happens tomorrow. Factually then, we control our individual and collective destinies, by the decisions we make each day.

In real terms, our differences are literally killing us. Our differences reflect the trauma each group has had to endure. As a result, our path to achieving a truly color-blind society requires embracing each other's differences as to what makes us individually unique and gives us the superpower to be more effective as a species and more capable as a collective of diverse individuals. It is after all, what made the U.S. the most productive nation in the world.

Characteristics Creating Differences

Humans are distinguished by a wide range of differences that contribute to the diversity of our global population. Here are some key characteristics that create these differences:

- **Biological Differences**: Genetic variation leads to differences in physical traits like skin color, height, facial features, and susceptibility to certain health conditions. This diversity is influenced by evolutionary adaptations to various environments over thousands of years.

- **Cultural Background**: Humans belong to numerous cultural groups, each with its unique language, traditions, beliefs, values, and practices. These cultural distinctions shape worldviews, social norms, artistic expressions, and approaches to daily life.

- **Personality and Temperament**: People exhibit different personality traits, which influence behavior, thought patterns, and emotional responses. Some are extroverted and adventurous, while others may be more introverted or cautious.

- **Socioeconomic Status**: Access to resources, education, healthcare, and opportunities varies greatly due to socioeconomic factors. These disparities shape people's life experiences, perspectives, and opportunities for personal and professional growth.

- **Educational Background**: Individuals acquire different levels and types of education, leading to varied skill sets, expertise, and intellectual perspectives. This influences problem-solving abilities, career paths, and personal interests.

- **Religious and Spiritual Beliefs**: People hold diverse religious and spiritual beliefs, from atheism to organized religions, influencing moral frameworks, lifestyle choices, and community affiliations.

- **Political Ideology**: Political beliefs, ranging from conservative to liberal and everything in between, shape individuals' views on governance, social policies, and international relations.

- **Life Experiences**: Every person's life story is unique. Personal challenges, achievements, family dynamics, and the environments in which people were raised all contribute to individual perspectives and worldviews.

- **Abilities and Disabilities**: People have different physical and cognitive abilities that can impact how they navigate daily life. Some live with disabilities that require specific accommodations, influencing their interactions and opportunities.

- **Aspirations and Dreams**: People have diverse aspirations and dreams, shaped by their values, personal interests, and individual goals, which drive them toward various life paths and achievements. Differences such as these make the human population rich and varied, contributing to the broad tapestry of ideas, beliefs, and experiences that define our global society. Understanding and celebrating these differences allows for greater empathy, cooperation, and innovation across all facets of life.

On Being Human

Describing what it means to be human also encompasses a complex array of biological, psychological, social, and existential dimensions. Each perspective offers a unique lens on the human experience:

- **Biological Aspect**: At a basic level, being human means belonging to the species Homo sapiens, characterized by a set of biological and physical traits. This includes the ability to walk upright, the use of complex manual dexterity, and the possession of a highly developed brain capable of abstract reasoning, language, introspection, and problem-solving.

- **Cognitive and Emotional Capability**: Humans are distinguished by their cognitive abilities which include consciousness, self-awareness, and advanced reasoning. Emotionally, humans experience a broad spectrum of feelings, from joy and love to sadness and anger, and possess the unique ability to reflect on and be influenced by these emotions.

- **Social Interaction**: Humans are inherently social beings. The capacity to form complex social structures, communicate through language, and cooperate towards common goals is central to human life. Social interactions form the basis of cultural development and contribute significantly to personal identity.

- **Cultural and Technological Achievement**: What it means to be human is greatly shaped by cultural contexts and technological advancements. Culture encompasses beliefs, practices, arts, laws, and customs that are passed from one generation to another. Technologically, humans continually innovate, creating tools and systems that reshape their environment and condition their realities.

- **Moral and Ethical Reflection**: Humans are capable of moral thought and ethical reflection. This capacity to contemplate actions and their repercussions, to consider ethical dilemmas, and to choose actions based on some sense of moral right or wrong is a key aspect of humanity.

- **Spirituality and Existential Inquiry**: Humans have the ability to ponder existential questions such as the meaning of life, the nature of existence, and the reality of death. Many humans engage with spirituality or religion as a way to explore these questions and find community, comfort, and purpose.

- **Creativity and Expression**: Creativity is a hallmark of human experience. Through various forms of expression—art, music, literature, and more—humans convey their thoughts, feelings, experiences, and visions of the world.

- **Adaptability and Growth**: Being human involves the capacity to adapt to and influence one's environment. This adaptability is seen in responses to physical climates, social changes, and personal challenges. It includes the ability to learn from experiences and to grow personally and collectively.

- **Desire for Meaning and Purpose**: Humans have a distinct desire for meaning in their lives. This is often pursued through personal achievements, relationships, and the quest for a fulfilling life based on individual values and aspirations.

- **Awareness of Mortality**: Uniquely aware of their mortality, humans can understand the concept of death and the implications of finite existence, which can profoundly influence their actions and philosophies.

To be human then, is to navigate a rich existence of thoughts, relationships, and environments, constantly balancing between individual impulses and societal expectations, between personal desires and communal responsibilities making being human a complex interplay that shapes the uniquely human journey.

Learning About Life

This guide represents many of the most important things I've learned on my journey through a dynamic and fulfilling life. My experiences are framed within the context of never really knowing *life* without trauma. Thus, the complex nature of my trauma informs my views (perspectives) of the *real world* (my mental models of the external environment within which I exist) and how it operates. I'm certainly not alone in this space. When I compare my life to others, a normal human attempt of comparisons to others, I can say that I had at least two years of life free of any physical or cognitive abnormalities that might otherwise interfere with a healthy start to my life. We know how important a healthy start to life is for shaping our capacity to live well as we each define it over the course of our life spans.

But, despite these facts about my life, I consider myself to be the luckiest man in the world because I was born to parents who exemplified heroism, courage, and a commitment to a purpose of making life better for everyone. They shaped the lives of three sons who each rose to the top in their respective professions carrying with them a family legacy of striving towards making life better for the common good, often at great expense to themselves.

As a member of a multiethnic family, my perspectives were shaped by many traditions that were appreciated, practiced, and enjoyed at home and in the community with members representing global cultures. My experiences illustrate the very best the United States has to offer the rest of the world by teaching it that the differences between people do not matter as we can readily see when our experiences are free of the hidden hand of White Supremacy and everything it represents. The exposure to other cultures I received during this phase of my life gave me the capacity to cross cultural boundaries with ease and to seek differences with intention. Consequently, my life is so much richer as a result, giving me certain advantages in my social and work groups.

With the benefit of hindsight, I can now see how those early years were pivotal in shaping my perspectives and driving me to become who I am today. My personal stories, along with the experiences shared by others, highlight how ordinary people navigate hidden battles to overcome toxicity in their workplaces and homes. These stories serve as powerful examples of resilience and personal growth.

Understanding Human Behavior

Understanding the shared human traits and the diverse influences that shape individual and collective experiences enables us to emphasize commonalities and embrace diversity that can help foster empathy, cooperation, and innovation, contributing to a more inclusive and equitable society.

The *biopsychosocial model* is an interdisciplinary approach that understands health and illness through the complex interactions between biological, psychological, and social factors. Developed as a reaction against the reductionist *biomedical model*, which focused solely on biological aspects of disease, it represents a paradigm shift in understanding health and human behavior.

The Biopsychosocial Model

Holistic approaches in medicine, recognized since the early 20th century, emphasized the importance of psychological and social factors as determinants of health and wellness. The work of Sigmund Freud and the field of *psychosomatic medicine* highlighted the connection between mind and body. In the mid-20th century, psychosomatic medicine advanced the understanding of the interplay between psychological factors and physical health, with influential figures like Franz Alexander and Helen Flanders Dunbar leading the way.

In 1977, psychiatrist George L. Engel formally articulated the biopsychosocial model (Figure 33), criticizing the limitations of the biomedical model. Engel's seminal paper, "The Need for a New Medical Model: A Challenge for Biomedicine," published in Science, laid the foundation for this comprehensive approach. Throughout the 1980s and 1990s, the biopsychosocial model gained acceptance in medical practice and education, with medical schools incorporating it into their curricula. The model emphasized the importance of considering patients' psychological and social contexts alongside their biological conditions.

Key Components

The model's key components are biological factors (genetic predispositions, biochemical imbalances, infections, and physiological abnormalities), psychological factors (mental health conditions, personality traits, coping mechanisms, and emotional responses), and social factors (socioeconomic status, cultural influences, family relationships, social support networks, and community environments). By integrating insights from medicine, psychology, sociology, and other fields, the biopsychosocial model encourages a more holistic and patient-centered approach, fostering better communication and understanding between healthcare providers and patients.

For practitioners in human services, the biopsychosocial model (Figure 3-1) is vital in explaining human behavior. It recognizes that health is shaped by our thoughts, emotions, behaviors, and social context, making it applicable to disciplines focused on understanding and shaping human behavior. This approach helps professionals better address the complexity of human health and wellness by considering the biological, psychological, and social characteristics presented by the people with whom they work.

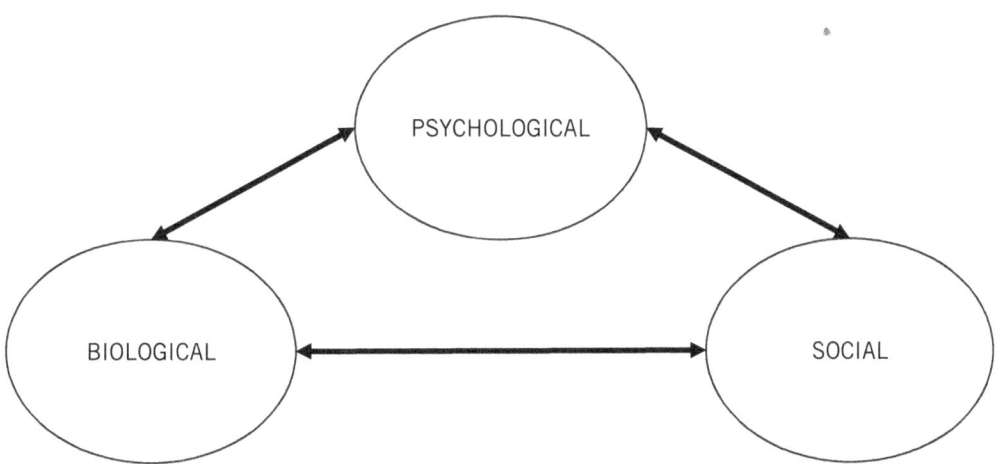

Figure 3-1: The Biopsychosocial Model of Mental Health

In the 21st century, the biopsychosocial model has continued to evolve and expand, applied to various fields including chronic disease management, mental health, pain management, and rehabilitation. Research supports its effectiveness in improving patient outcomes and satisfaction.

The biopsychosocial model provides a holistic framework for understanding individuals, allowing professionals to see the full picture of a person's health and well-being. It recognizes the uniqueness of each person, tailoring interventions to address specific factors relevant to an individual's situation. This personalized approach leads to better outcomes for employees, especially in addressing job stress, interpersonal relationships, and career advancement.

The model emphasizes prevention, allowing professionals to identify and address issues before they become severe, promoting long-term well-being, and reducing the potential for harm. It helps reduce the stigma often associated with mental health issues by acknowledging the psychological aspect alongside the biological and social context.

Moreover, the biopsychosocial model encourages comprehensive intervention and treatment strategies, fostering collaboration among healthcare providers from different disciplines. This interdisciplinary approach improves communication between professionals and those they serve, leading to better health outcomes for individuals, their families, and their social and workgroups.

In summary, the biopsychosocial model offers a complete and individualized approach to healthcare and well-being, leading to improved outcomes and a better understanding of the complex interplay between biology, psychology, and social factors in people's lives. It provides a foundation for building effective human resource support mechanisms, promoting the well-being of employees, and fostering healthier organizations and communities.

Nature versus Nurture

In the context of human behavior, the biopsychosocial model addresses the enduring question of nature versus nurture. My belief is that we are all born with a set of genetic predispositions that provide a framework for who we might become. This framework is like the chassis of a car or the foundation of a building, determining what the final object will look like and its capacity to perform as designed. The biopsychosocial model helps us understand and shape these outcomes through a comprehensive approach that integrates biological, psychological, and social dimensions.

The critical importance of comprehensive, interdisciplinary, transdisciplinary, and personalized approaches to individual and organizational well-being lies in their ability to provide a holistic and nuanced understanding of health. By considering the interplay of biological, psychological, and social factors, a comprehensive approach ensures that all relevant aspects of health and behavior are addressed, leading to more effective interventions and support. Personalized care tailor's interventions to the specific needs of individuals, recognizing their unique contexts and circumstances, which is essential for addressing root causes and promoting long-term well-being.

Enhanced collaboration and innovation are key benefits of interdisciplinary and transdisciplinary approaches. By bringing together insights from different fields such as medicine, psychology, sociology, and organizational behavior, these approaches foster better communication and collaboration among professionals. This collective expertise leads to innovative solutions and improved outcomes by leveraging diverse perspectives and skills. Transdisciplinary approaches, in particular, go beyond traditional boundaries to create new frameworks and methods, leading to a more cohesive understanding of complex issues and the development of novel, more effective strategies for enhancing well-being.

Prevention and Intervention

Effective prevention and intervention are other critical aspects. Emphasizing prevention helps identify and address potential issues before they become severe, mitigating risks and enhancing resilience and coping mechanisms among individuals and within organizations. Personalized interventions tailored to specific contexts lead to more relevant and impactful support, better engagement, and sustainable positive outcomes.

Reducing Stigma and Promoting Inclusivity

These approaches also help reduce stigma and promote inclusivity. Recognizing the multifaceted nature of well-being validates the psychological and social dimensions of health alongside the biological, fostering a more inclusive and empathetic environment. Personalized and transdisciplinary approaches ensure that cultural, socioeconomic, and individual differences are respected and integrated into care and organizational practices, promoting inclusivity and equity.

Organizational Benefits

In the long term, adopting these approaches leads to significant organizational benefits. Healthier work environments increase employee satisfaction, reduce turnover, and enhance productivity. By focusing on the holistic well-being of their members, organizations can cultivate a culture of continuous improvement, adaptability, and innovation, ensuring long-term success and resilience.

The critical importance of these approaches lies in their ability to provide a holistic, collaborative, and tailored framework for enhancing individual and organizational well-being. They lead to more effective prevention and intervention, reduce stigma, promote inclusivity, and foster long-term health and success for individuals and organizations alike.

Precursors

Precursors are factors or events that occur beforehand and contribute to the development or onset of something else, such as a condition, behavior, or situation. They act as indicators or triggers that lead to a specific outcome. Moreover, social scientists understand that to fully grasp the behaviors we observe, we must consider the context, situation, and circumstances that led to the behaviors we are studying. This requires a holistic approach that considers the complex interplay between biological, psychological, social, environmental, behavioral, and other factors such as historical, economic, spiritual, and political factors that might also influence or shape behaviors. Behavior often results from the interaction of these factors. For example, a person's genetic predisposition to anxiety might be exacerbated by a stressful work environment, leading to behaviors like avoidance or aggression.

Biological Precursors

Biological precursors include genetics, which affect traits such as temperament and susceptibility to mental health conditions, neurobiology, which involves brain chemistry and structure affecting mood and behavior, and physical health, where conditions like chronic illness or hormonal imbalances can impact behavior.

Biological precursors are foundational in behavior formation. Genetic makeup, for instance, influences temperament, susceptibility to mental health conditions, and even certain preferences. Brain chemistry and structure, involving neurotransmitters like dopamine and serotonin, significantly impact mood, cognition, and behavior. Physical health also plays a crucial role; conditions such as chronic pain or hormonal imbalances can alter an individual's interaction with their environment and responses to stimuli.

Psychological Precursors

Psychological precursors encompass cognitive processes, which involve how individuals perceive and interpret situations, emotional states, which drive behavior through feelings like anger, sadness, or joy, and personality traits such as extraversion or conscientiousness that predict certain behaviors. Additionally, past experiences, including traumas or successes, shape behavior by influencing expectations and learned responses.

Psychological precursors include cognitive processes, emotional states, and personality traits. How individuals process information and solve problems impacts their behavior, with cognitive biases shaping their perceptions and reactions. Emotions are powerful drivers of behavior, with our ability to regulate emotions influencing responses to various situations. Personality traits, such as extraversion and conscientiousness, predict consistent behavior patterns; for instance, extraverted individuals may seek more social interactions than introverts.

Social Precursors

Social precursors include family dynamics, cultural influences, and social learning, which collectively shape individual behaviors. Early family relationships and ongoing social connections influence behavior through learned responses and attachment styles, setting the foundation for how individuals perceive and interact with the world. Cultural norms and values dictate acceptable behavior within a given context, providing a framework for understanding right and wrong.

Observing and imitating others, especially role models and authority figures significantly impacts behavior formation. Media and societal trends also shape individual actions and perceptions. Understanding these social factors helps us comprehend behavior formation and modification, emphasizing the need for supportive and positive social environments to foster healthy development and growth.

Environmental Precursors

Environmental precursors, such as the physical environment, economic factors, and access to education, also shape behavior. Living conditions and workspaces influence behavior, with factors like noise and crowding contributing to stress and irritability. Economic stability impacts stress levels and decision-making processes, often leading to behaviors aimed at coping with financial strain. Access to education and information enhances behavior by fostering greater understanding and more effective problem-solving skills. Environmental stressors, such as natural disasters or political instability, cause behavioral adaptations to new circumstances, highlighting the significant role our surroundings play in shaping our actions and responses to challenges. Recognizing these environmental factors is crucial for understanding and influencing behavior, and for creating supportive environments that promote well-being and resilience.

Behavioral Precursors

In practical applications, understanding behavioral precursors is invaluable across various fields. In therapy, it helps therapists develop more effective treatment plans by addressing underlying factors. In education, it enables the creation of supportive learning environments by recognizing how different factors affect student behavior. In organizations, addressing precursors influencing employee behavior can improve workplace culture and productivity. By examining these precursors, professionals can better predict, understand, and positively influence behaviors, contributing to more effective interventions and support systems.

Simply put, behaviors are a function of the environment within which they occur. Consequently, we shouldn't really be surprised when the demonization of various groups results in attacks because of the demonization. In the same way, we should not be surprised when greater numbers of people thrive when environments are constructed to help them do so. Most importantly we should not be surprised when people who are given every advantage at birth fail and people who have what appear to be insurmountable obstacles overcome outperform members of all groups. It is a very simple formula to understand complex human behaviors. We are all slaves to our environments.

Building on Lewin's Field Theory

Lewin's Field Theory provides a comprehensive framework for analyzing human behavior by considering the totality of coexisting factors and their interdependencies, making it foundational in social psychology and organizational behavior. Understanding the multifaceted role of precursors in behavior is essential for anticipating, managing, and changing behaviors effectively across various disciplines.

Kurt Lewin (1936), the father of social psychology, emphasized this interplay in his Field Theory, encapsulated in the formula $B = f(P, E)$, where behavior (B) is a function of the person (P) and their environment (E). This theory highlights that behavior is determined by the dynamic interaction between an individual's personal characteristics and their surrounding environmental factors. Central to Lewin's Field Theory is the concept of the life space, which includes all the influences acting on an individual at a given time, both internal (needs, desires, emotions) and external (social norms, physical surroundings, interpersonal relationships). The life space is a psychological field where all these forces interact to shape behavior.

Lewin introduced the idea of force fields, representing the various factors influencing an individual's behavior. These forces can be *driving* (promoting movement towards a goal) or *restraining* (hindering movement towards a goal). Change occurs when the balance of these forces shifts, described through his three-step model of change:

- Unfreezing

- Changing

- Refreezing

Unfreezing involves creating awareness of the need for change; *changing* is the process of moving toward the new behavior; and *refreezing* establishes the new behavior as the norm.

Field Theory also highlights *topological psychology*, where behavior is mapped in a geometric space to visualize the various factors at play. This mapping helps identify the *psychological tensions* and *conflicts* within the life space, aiding in better understanding and predicting behavior.

Understanding behavior involves examining the following factors and influences:

- **Biological factors** include genetics, neurobiology, and physical health, which affect traits such as temperament, mood, and overall behavior.

- **Psychological factors** encompass cognitive processes, emotional states, and personality traits, shaping how individuals perceive, interpret, and respond to situations.

- **Social factors** include family dynamics, cultural influences, and social learning, significantly impacting behavior through learned responses and social norms.

- **Environmental factors** involve the physical environment, economic conditions, and access to education, all of which play crucial roles in shaping behavior.

An integrative approach is necessary to fully grasp these dynamics, considering the complex interplay between the factors. For instance, a genetic predisposition to anxiety might be exacerbated by a stressful work environment, leading to avoidance or aggressive behaviors. Recognizing these interactions enables a holistic understanding of behavior, facilitating more effective interventions and support mechanisms.

More than half my career was spent working for toxic and incompetent supervisors. Recently, I even fired a client last year because he waved a gun in my face thinking that was okay; and I learned afterwards that he had done that in other meetings. His behavior may have been acceptable in his environment, but it certainly wasn't in mine. It was such a shame to observe one of the most brilliant minds I've met sabotaging the thing he loved, hurting people around him who loved him, and being obsessed with proving to the world that he was the smartest most capable person in the room. However, the outgrowth of his behaviors directly led to a culture and climate survey assessment showing a high commitment to the work of the organization but a net promoter score (NPS) of 8 compared to an average NPS of 47 for nearly 100,000 companies according to Survey Monkey data during my team's analysis.

As the CEO, majority owner, and someone who was looked up to for his technical expertise and prowess in his domain, his actions carried additional weight with his frequent threats, which he dismissed as his right, at least in my case. I held privileged information about his history and could identify the probable origins of his behaviors but as an educator, I stopped short of diagnosing his mental state other than to recommend he see a licensed clinical professional.

However, in the final analysis, when discussing the precursors to behaviors, it's crucial to recognize the various factors that influence or predict an individual's actions. As I've thought about my experiences with the client as well as what I've learned through my research and experiences as a practitioner and consultant in the field over the length of my career, I was able to build the Field Theory of Goal Behavior Performance model illustrated in Figure 3-2). Lewin's Field Theory facilitates offering a new comprehensive framework for analyzing goal behavior by considering the totality of coexisting factors and their interdependencies, making it foundational in social psychology and organizational behavior. Understanding the multifaceted role of precursors in behavior is essential for anticipating, managing, and changing behaviors effectively across various disciplines.

The Field Theory of Goal Behavior Performance Model (**Figure 3-2**) functionally capitalizes on Lewin's Field Theory in how it impacts goal behavior performance by representing the relationship between an individual's precursors that filter and moderate their behaviors and that are influenced and moderated by the various environmental and social cultures with which they engage on a daily basis.

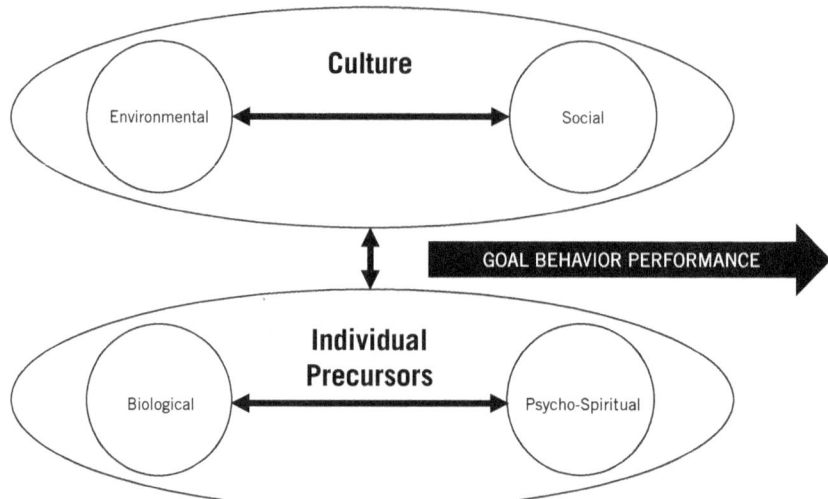

Figure 3-2: Field Theory of Goal Behavior Performance

The Field Theory of Goal Behavior Performance Model illustrates the interplay between an individual's culture (the environmental and social elements of culture) and their individual biological, psychological, and spiritual precursors which work together to induce observable behaviors. The field theory model pays homage to the biopsychosocial model but separates key elements of the culture into the environmental (group and collective experiences) and the social, more individualized components from the individual's unique personal biological, psychological, and spiritual characteristics. The bidirectional arrow indicates the reciprocal impact of culture on the individual and the interaction between the individual and their culture. That is, the environment within which they live and work, and the groups with whom they interact socially.

The outcome of these exchanges is reflected in the goal behaviors used and measured through various performance metrics. The model suggests that performance behavior depends on how individuals present themselves in their organizations and how the culture containing both the environmental (various organizational cultures) and social group cultures support or inhibit performance.

Spirituality and Behavior

What has been lacking in much of the discussion about behavior has to do with the role of spirituality and its impact on behavior. At its 52nd Assembly (1999) the World Health Organization (W.H.O.) adopted amendments to its Constitution inserting spiritual well-being into the WHO concept of health becoming "Health is a dynamic state of complete physical, mental, spiritual and social well-being and not merely the absence of disease or infirmity" (Saad, Mederios & Mosini, 2017). Montuori and Donnelly (2017) (as cited in Perry, 2025) acknowledge "... [and actively embrace] the psychological and spiritual as well as the social world and the quest for social justice ... [through which] personal and social transformation ... occurs hand-in-hand" (p.6).

Relationships and Interactions

It's undeniable that in any social system (workgroups, families, social groups, etc.) the relationships and interactions between individuals are crucial. These relationships can influence job satisfaction, communication efficiency, and organizational culture. Interpersonal and intergroup dynamics illustrate the cohesion within and between groups which is critical to organizational functioning. Organizations consist of various groups and teams, each with its own dynamics, norms, and roles, and how well members function together is critically important to not only specific teams or groups but to the organization as a whole. Therefore, being able to assess how well team members and groups are functioning is critically important to understanding how these groups function and interact, is essential to understanding the organization as a whole.

Group and Organizational Culture

Every group and organization form its own culture, which encompasses shared values, beliefs, and norms. This culture influences how members of the organization behave and interact with each other. The practices used by organizational leaders shape the culture by establishing normative behaviors. This is clearly evident through public displays of behaviors by political and other leaders who have upset long-held norms about decency and respect and established new ones that include violence, discrimination, abuse, criminalized behaviors, lack of respect, and lack of any sense of decency.

Organizational Structures

Organizations have social structures that are made up of formal and informal hierarchies, networks, and relationships. These structures play a critical role in decision-making processes, power dynamics, and the flow of information. The various systems designed to support the organization can also become sources of conflict when not designed well. Those conflicts might emerge as interpersonal conflicts when in fact system design flaws can result in interpersonal or intergroup conflicts.

Communication Patterns

We all have various patterns we use to communicate and get things done. We use phrases and ways of speaking and writing that are fairly limited. Regional and cultural nuances can result in differences that can produce communication patterns that might become misunderstood. Communication is the lifeblood of social interactions within organizations. The ways in which information is shared and the channels used for communication significantly affect organizational effectiveness.

Contributor Alan Faingold emphasizes how swearing can negatively affect the workplace environment. The behavior can lead to poor attitudes, toxic behaviors, and ultimately a decline in team morale and performance. Faingold argues that swearing is not just a minor issue but one that can undermine the integrity and professionalism of an organization, particularly when it goes unchallenged by leadership.

Transformative Leadership Matters

Transformative leaders focus on social justice (fairness) and empowerment. Over time, this leadership style can profoundly reshape organizational or community culture, fostering environments that are inclusive, innovative, and resilient. The lasting legacy of transformative leadership is characterized by sustained success, continuous improvement, and a deep commitment to social justice, influencing broader societal change, and setting standards for others to follow (Shields, 2016).

Transformative leaders are desperately needed to effect positive social change in the cultures of their organizations. After more than five decades of observation in the field, ongoing study, and research regarding an array of organizational effectiveness assessments, I can say this: There is a dearth of effective leaders and an excess of toxic leaders. This is evidenced by more than half of the U.S. workforce indicating they've been harmed in the workplace. Furthermore, in a report to a client, according to a 2023 Survey Monkey data set, the average net promoter score (NPS) for nearly 100,000 companies was 47%, which means less than half of the employees of the companies in the Survey Monkey data set would promote their workplaces as good places to work.

This sort of finding further underscores the need to place an emphasis on strengthening the human side of the enterprise by overhauling organizational cultures to align them more fully with workforce needs. By doing so, transformative leaders can focus their energies on system reforms to remove systemic obstructions, streamline processes, and increase overall efficiency. When leaders involve employees in decision-making processes, particularly those closest to where problems exist, they also increase motivation in the work being performed in addition to simultaneously cultivating the next generation of leaders, building trust, and strengthening group and organizational cohesion.

Creating Your Own Balance

The chapter "Navigating Trauma and Toxicity" explores the profound impacts of trauma and toxic environments on individuals, particularly in leadership and group dynamics. It begins by emphasizing the role of leadership in shaping group behavior, noting that leadership styles—whether autocratic, laissez-faire, democratic, or transformative—significantly influence how groups function and respond to challenges over time.

Leadership sets the tone for the entire group, impacting behaviors and decisions. Transformative leadership, in particular, stands out as a positive force, fostering equity, social justice, and continuous improvement, while autocratic or laissez-faire leadership often leads to dysfunction, inefficiency, and long-term negative consequences.

Group dynamics play a crucial role in understanding collective behaviors, such as conformity, peer pressure, and even violence, as seen in events like protests or insurrections. The chapter highlights the psychological mechanisms behind group behavior, explaining phenomena such as groupthink, attitude polarization, and the influence of authority figures on individual actions. These dynamics are pivotal in understanding toxic workplace environments and societal conflicts.

The chapter also delves into the concept of "neural hijacks," where emotional stress overwhelms rational thinking, leading to impulsive actions. This highlights the importance of emotional intelligence and the ability to manage stress in both personal and professional settings. Personal experiences of living with trauma and how this can manifest in everyday interactions, emphasize the need for self-awareness and emotional regulation to prevent toxic behaviors.

Trauma, Perry explains, is like a "beast" that can hijack the mind, leading to behaviors that may be out of character or harmful. This is particularly relevant in workplace settings, where toxic environments can exacerbate trauma, leading to a cycle of stress and negative behaviors. Understanding trauma's psychological underpinnings is essential for creating healthier, more supportive environments.

The chapter draws on several psychological theories to explain the effects of trauma and toxicity, including Attachment Theory, Cognitive Behavioral Theory, and Social Cognitive Theory. These frameworks help in understanding how early relationships, thought patterns and social influences shape behavior and reactions to toxic environments.

In conclusion, "Navigating Trauma and Toxicity" calls for a more compassionate and trauma-informed approach to leadership and organizational culture. By recognizing the deep connections between leadership, group dynamics, and individual trauma, the chapter advocates for transformative leadership that promotes healing, resilience, and a healthier workplace and societal environment.

THE HUMAN COST OF TOXIC LEADERSHIP

Principle 4: *Unless you learn to face your own shadows, you will continue to see them in others, because the world outside you is only a reflection of the world inside you.*

— Carl Jung

CHAPTER 4

Trauma and Toxicity in the Workplace and Elsewhere

Personal and Professional Selves

Unfortunately, today trauma and toxicity in our workspaces are inevitable, at least to some degree, depending on the culture of the specific organization and leadership effectiveness. Organizations in which leaders exercise *autocratic*, highly directive leadership behaviors with little input from subordinate employees tend to have low employee engagement because input is not sought and often squashed. Conversely, *laissez-faire leadership* behaviors, with little to no direct oversight by the most senior leader, are more susceptible to trauma and toxicity in unit-level workspaces. Subordinate leaders in such environments have the latitude to behave in ways that suit their individual personalities, subjecting employees to the unique behavioral tendencies of each supervisor.

In the past, it was common to view work and home as separate spheres where individuals had to present different versions of themselves. However, our understanding of human behavior has evolved, and we now recognize the interconnectedness of our actions and attitudes in various social settings. While the specific rules governing acceptable behavior may differ depending on the environment, our behavior in one setting can impact how we are perceived in another. Today, the distinction between our personal and professional selves has become less rigid, and we now acknowledge that our behavior is influenced by a range of factors, including social groups, cultural norms, and personal values. As a result, we better understand how actions in one area of life can affect others and what we must do to cultivate a more integrated sense of Self that is consistent across different environments.

What we have not yet come to grips with is how the effects of trauma and toxicity migrate back and forth between home and work, influencing the behaviors we observe in our groups. If we observe someone's behaviors change, we may try to understand or justify the changes if we like or love them. However, if we don't like them for some reason, our defense mechanisms kick in, and we find ways to isolate them or shield ourselves from their behaviors.

Linking Societal Attitudes to Workplace Behaviors

The research fully supports the idea that workplace trauma is a real and significant issue producing serious negative effects on individuals and organizations. Smith's (2016) findings reveal that 53% of working adults in the United States experienced at least one traumatic event while on the job, likely taking their trauma into their households. The U.S. Bureau of Labor Statistics (BLS) employment data for 2023 reported roughly 160 million people in the workforce. Using Smith's findings as the multiplier suggests that approximately 85 million employees experienced at least one traumatic event on the job in 2023, carrying their trauma into their homes.

These data clearly illustrate widespread abuse in the workforce. For many individuals, these traumatic events are not their first exposure to trauma, compounding the aftereffects of previous traumas. Since trauma is cumulative, increased trauma exposures makes treatment and recovery even more complex. For example, substantial detrimental behaviors occur in the workplace with millions of workers reporting being victims of workplace violence yearly. The National Safety Council (2019) found that in 2017, assaults resulted in 18,400 injuries and 458 fatalities. The National Safety Council categorized *assaults* as intentional injuries inflicted by another person, including:

- Intentional shooting by another person
- Stabbing, cutting, slashing, or piercing
- Hitting, kicking, beating, and shoving
- Strangulation
- Bombing and arson
- Rape and sexual assault
- Threats and verbal assault

Since organizations are microcosms of society, it should not be surprising that the behaviors we observe in our workplaces are being fueled, at least in part, by the attitudes exhibited in our larger society and therefore our workplaces reflect and perpetuate societal dysfunction. As a consequence, this dysfunction leads to the maltreatment of employees seen in workplaces mirroring issues in our political systems and citizenry. For example, societal attitudes towards various socially categorized groups are generally reflected in the treatment of those groups within workspaces.

Thus, mass shootings become outward expressions of people's feelings, exacerbated by the proliferation of weapons in our society making killing and suicide by guns more likely because the means are so readily available. The availability of high-capacity magazines and rapid-fire weapons ensures multiple victims whenever someone decides to kill. The increasing availability of ammunition, even in supermarkets, suggests a troubling pre-positioning strategy to make weapons more accessible.

Dr. Tracy Alloway (n.d.), a Jacksonville-based psychologist and professor at the University of North, Florida, commented: "Research suggests that [mass shooters] do have a history of aggressive behaviors, and then you have a stressful trigger, like a job loss or . . . employment concerns, where it then escalates." She further explained:

> A common misconception is that mass shooters have serious mental illness, but many times that isn't the case. Another way to look at it even for my own research in the workplace environment is looking at social connectedness, how connected does that person feel? So, if an employee does feel connected, they have that social cohesion with their colleagues, they're far less likely to have this be a trigger event for them.

Such acknowledgment illustrates the importance of healthy work relationships and the need for organizations to pay closer attention to the human side of the enterprise through regular 360-degree performance assessments, periodic culture and climate assessments, ongoing coaching and mentoring, and training programs to help employees work more effectively across cultural boundaries. These efforts enhance understanding of group dynamics, capitalize on the outcomes of healthy conflict, and serve to build social and emotional intelligence.

Healthy Conflict

From a group dynamics perspective, healthy conflict is a sign of a thriving group because differences of opinion can drive positive goal behaviors and increased productivity. Tuckman (1960), Gersick (1988), and MacGrath (1991) highlight the importance of a conflict stage in advancing a group's agenda. However, destructive conflict can become traumatizing and harmful, disrupting group cohesion and productivity.

Impact on Health and Performance

Workplace trauma is closely linked to various mental health issues. The National Institute for Occupational Safety and Health (NIOSH, 2018) found that workers who experienced traumatic events at work were more likely to report symptoms of depression and anxiety than those who had not. This connection between workplace trauma and mental health challenges underscores the need for supportive organizational measures to address and mitigate the effects of workplace trauma, promoting both individual well-being and organizational success.

Impact on Physical Health

The effects of workplace trauma extend beyond mental health, impacting physical health as well. A study by the University of Manchester found that employees who experienced bullying or harassment at work reported higher instances of physical health problems, including cardiovascular disease, gastrointestinal issues, and chronic pain, compared to those who did not experience such trauma (University of Manchester, 2016). These findings emphasize the holistic impact of workplace trauma on an individual's health.

Impact on Productivity and Performance

Trauma impacts productivity and performance, which should concern every leader. Workplace trauma also has significant implications for organizational productivity and performance. The American Psychological Association conducted a study revealing that trauma in the workplace is associated with increased absenteeism, decreased job satisfaction, and reduced organizational commitment (APA, 2019). These negative outcomes not only affect individual employees but also hinder the operational performance and efficiency of organizations.

Trauma and Violence in the Workplace

There is also a complex and multifaceted link between trauma and violence in the workplace. Trauma can be a contributing factor to workplace violence, and exposure to violence can also cause trauma in individuals. Here are some ways in which trauma and violence can be related in the workplace:

- Workplace trauma can originate from various sources, ranging from acute incidents to chronic stressors. Understanding these sources is essential for creating effective interventions and preventive measures.

- Trauma can increase the risk of violence when people who have experienced trauma, particularly if it was a violent or threatening event, may be more likely to engage in violent behavior themselves. This can be due to a number of factors such as the effects of PTSD on mental health and behavior or the development of maladaptive coping strategies as a result of trauma.

This doesn't imply that everyone with PTSD is violent. Instead, it highlights that a large portion of the world's population is significantly traumatized, which can lead some individuals to feel they must take matters into their own hands. The easy availability of weapons, combined with inflammatory slogans like *the only way to stop a bad guy with a gun is with a good guy with a gun,* can push people to dangerous actions. But who determines who the "good guys" and "bad guys" are? We see this confusion reflected in the different ways police respond to incidents involving people of color compared to those involving Whites.

Preventing Workplace Violence

It could be argued that Kyle Rittenhouse was a vigilante looking to kill someone—and so it happened. James Allen (1902), a British philosophical writer, published *As a Man Thinketh.* His core thesis encapsulates the idea that a person's thoughts directly shape their character, circumstances, and destiny. There is considerable evidence supporting that idea. Allen argues that positive, disciplined thinking leads to virtuous actions and success, while negative, uncontrolled thoughts result in detrimental behavior and failure. He emphasizes personal responsibility and the power of the mind in creating one's reality, asserting that by mastering their thoughts, individuals can achieve personal transformation and fulfillment.

Addressing trauma can help prevent workplace violence by:

- Providing support and resources to individuals who have experienced trauma

- Training supervisors to recognize distress in themselves and others

- Creating trauma-informed communities including providing access to counseling and mental health services through funded employee assistance programs (EAPs), promoting a culture of respect, empathy, and effective communication, and implementing policies and procedures that prioritize employee safety and well-being

However, as illustrated above, less than half (46%) of organizations offer support to help employees grieve, cope, or recover in the aftermath of their traumatic events (Smith, 2016).

The link between trauma and violence in the workplace is complex and multifaceted. By recognizing and addressing the ways in which trauma can contribute to workplace violence, organizations can help promote a safe and supportive workplace culture for all employees (Mathieu, 2022, pp. 131 – 132). Addressing these sources of trauma requires a multifaceted approach. Creating a safe and supportive work environment is essential to productive work environments. Implementing comprehensive policies and procedures to prevent and respond to incidents of violence and harassment is crucial. Promoting—and more importantly, supporting—a healthy work-life balance and providing access to mental health resources and support for employees are also key components of an effective strategy to mitigate workplace trauma and improve safety for all employees.

Learning from Conflicts

Teaching employees about transformative learning would go a long way in helping employees work through situations that produce cognitive dissonance and stress. Not every problem can be solved, but every problem can lead to learning.

From a leadership perspective, conflicts generally arise from three sources: interpersonal relationships, the structure and nature of the task, and the system deployed to complete the task. Regardless of the particular source of conflict, each one offers opportunities for individual and team growth. By acknowledging and addressing the diverse sources of workplace trauma—and recognizing that trauma also migrates from outside the workplace—we can foster healthier, more supportive work environments that enhance the well-being and productivity of all employees.

Sources of Workplace Trauma

Common sources of trauma in the workplace include workplace violence and safety incidents. Trauma often stems from physical violence, whether it is from coworkers, clients, or the public. Incidents like active shooter situations or bomb threats can cause significant stress and potentially trauma, even without resulting in physical harm. Accidents or safety incidents, particularly in high-risk fields like construction, law enforcement, and healthcare, can lead to severe trauma, especially when they result in injury or death.

Trauma can lead to conflicts and tensions in the workplace. People who have experienced trauma may struggle with interpersonal relationships and communication, making them more likely to experience conflicts with colleagues or supervisors. These conflicts can sometimes escalate into violent incidents, particularly if the individual is not provided with appropriate support or resources to manage their trauma.

Workplace violence itself can cause trauma. Individuals who are victims of workplace violence, such as physical assault or verbal abuse, often experience significant trauma. This trauma can negatively affect their mental and physical health, contributing to a culture of fear and mistrust in the workplace.

Organizational changes and job insecurity are additional sources of trauma. Layoffs, downsizing, or restructuring that result in job loss—or even the fear of job loss—can cause significant financial and emotional stress. Major organizational changes, like mergers or shifts in company direction, create uncertainty and anxiety. Forced retirement or demotion impacts an individual's identity and financial security, exacerbating their trauma.

Personal vulnerabilities and history also play a role. Employees with a history of trauma or mental health issues may be more vulnerable to experiencing workplace events as traumatic. A lack of personal support networks or coping mechanisms makes it harder to deal with workplace stressors.

Traumatic Events and Crises

Exposure to traumatic content, especially in professions like journalism, law enforcement, or social services, can be particularly distressing. Experiencing or witnessing critical incidents, such as serious workplace accidents or natural disasters affecting the workplace, leaves lasting emotional scars. Economic crises or industry downturns impact job security and organizational stability, adding to the stress.

Bullying and Harassment

Bullying and harassment are major sources of workplace trauma. Persistent bullying, including verbal abuse, threats, or intimidation, is a significant contributor. Sexual harassment, such as unwanted advances, comments, or gestures, creates a hostile work environment. Discrimination based on race, gender, sexuality, religion, or disability leads to feelings of exclusion and worthlessness, further contributing to trauma.

Contributor Dawn De Palma Ross shares her experiences with gender-based discrimination and harassment, highlighting the ongoing challenges women face in professional environments. From early experiences of objectification and catcalling to more overt instances of sexual harassment in the workplace, she illustrates how these issues have persisted throughout her career, affecting her professional growth and personal well-being.

Despite mandatory sexual harassment training, inappropriate behavior and gender bias continue to be significant barriers. She emphasizes the importance of resilience and assertiveness in confronting these challenges. As a transformative leader, she consistently stands up for herself and others, advocating for positive change in toxic work environments. Whether addressing harassment, confronting bullying, or fighting for the value of physical education, she demonstrates a commitment to integrity, courage, and justice. Her experiences underscore the need for perseverance and proactive efforts to create a more equitable and supportive professional environment.

Work-Life Balance

Work-life balance issues also contribute to workplace trauma. Excessive work hours or workloads lead to physical exhaustion and the neglect of personal life. A lack of flexibility in work arrangements negatively impacts personal responsibilities and family life. Poorly managed remote work environments may blur the boundaries between work and personal life, exacerbating stress.

Moreover, a toxic work culture that normalizes overwork, competition, and unrealistic performance expectations leads to chronic stress and burnout. Environments that tolerate or encourage toxic behaviors like gossip, sabotage, or exclusion create a harmful workplace atmosphere. A lack of support or recognition from management often results in feelings of undervaluation and alienation.

Toxicity in the Workplace

Workplace toxicity often sneaks up on organizations like a hidden blight, gradually eroding the well-being of employees and the organization itself. It may start with subtle signs, but over time, its harmful effects become undeniable.

Beginnings

Bullying and harassment frequently begin with persistent, demeaning behavior toward individuals or groups. When sexual harassment occurs through unwanted advances or inappropriate comments, it undermines an employee's sense of safety and respect. Verbal abuse and threats amplify the atmosphere of intimidation and fear.

Discrimination reveals itself when people are treated unfairly because of their race, gender, age, sexuality, religion, or other personal characteristics. Systemic biases in hiring, promotions, and evaluations breed exclusion and injustice, reinforcing the idea that merit matters less than personal identity.

Unethical behavior, such as dishonesty, theft, and fraud, casts a shadow over ethical standards, compromising trust in the organization. When safety standards are sacrificed for profit, employees' lives are endangered. Manipulative or exploitative behavior for personal gain further damages the organization's moral compass. In addition, customers may also suffer, as evidenced by the Boeing 737 Max disasters, which were potentially caused by cost-cutting measures aimed at increasing profits.

Results of Poor Leadership and Management Practices

Poor leadership and management practices, including authoritarian or dictatorial leadership styles, quash feedback and creativity, stifling growth and innovation. Negligent management creates chaos and confusion, while favoritism and nepotism reward relationships over merit. With 70% of the workforce not trusting HR, the rifts in the workforce become more pronounced, obstructing the path to improved behaviors (McGovern, 2022).

Making workplace dynamics more complex are toxic organizational cultures that thrive on gossip, backstabbing, and office politics. The glorification of overwork and stress often leads to widespread burnout. A lack of transparency and communication breeds mistrust and speculation. Poor work-life balance arises when employees are expected to be constantly available, even during personal time, leading to burnout. An excessive workload without adequate support adds to the pressure, and those who prioritize family or health are often penalized.

Unsafe working conditions are present in unsafe or unhealthy physical environments that threaten employees. Psychological hazards, like high-pressure deadlines or fear of job loss, compound their stress. Ignoring employees' concerns about safety only deepens the problem.

Conflict and poor communication allow interpersonal conflicts to simmer when not addressed, while poor communication leads to misunderstandings and errors. Departments working in silos, isolated and disconnected from one another, hamper collaboration.

Lack of autonomy and empowerment results from micromanagement, making employees feel like they have no control over their work. They're excluded from decision-making processes that affect them directly, and overregulation and strict adherence to procedures stifle innovation.

Lack of recognition and reward occurs when employees' efforts are ignored or under-paid, leading to frustration. Inequitable compensation practices add to this resentment, and limited opportunities for growth leave people feeling stagnant and undervalued.

Addressing Toxicity

Addressing these forms of toxicity requires a comprehensive, unified effort from leadership, HR, and employees. Clear policies should be implemented, training on respectful behaviors provided, and safe channels for reporting grievances established. Promoting practices that support work-life balance and employee well-being is essential in fostering a culture where respect, inclusivity, and transparency can flourish. Only then can organizations truly transform into positive environments where every individual feels valued and empowered.

Nine Theories of Toxicity in the Workplace

The theoretical perspectives on workplace toxicity offer frameworks for understanding the root causes, dynamics, and impacts of toxic behaviors and environments in organizational settings. These perspectives come from various disciplines, including psychology, sociology, organizational behavior, and management studies. Here are some key theoretical perspectives that can help explain and address workplace toxicity:

Psychosocial Hazard Model

This perspective focuses on how workplace stressors, such as high demands, low control, and poor support, act as psychosocial hazards that can lead to physical and psychological health problems. The model is useful for identifying work-related factors that contribute to a toxic environment.

Social Exchange Theory

Social Exchange Theory posits that relationships (including those in the workplace) are based on the exchange of resources, such as effort, support, and rewards. Toxicity arises when there is an imbalance or perceived unfairness in these exchanges, leading to negative outcomes like decreased job satisfaction and engagement.

Person-Environment (P-E) Fit Theory

According to the *P-E Fit Theory*, stress and negative outcomes occur when there is a misalignment between an individual's characteristics and the demands of their environment. Workplace toxicity can be understood as a poor fit between employees and organizational culture, values, or job demands.

Organizational Culture Theory

This perspective emphasizes the role of organizational culture in shaping behaviors and norms within the workplace. A toxic culture, characterized by negative norms and values such as competition, blame, and fear of failure, can perpetuate toxicity throughout the organization.

Systems Theory

Systems Theory views organizations as complex systems with interdependent parts. Toxicity is seen as a systemic issue that arises from dysfunctional interactions and feedback loops within the organization, requiring holistic interventions to address.

Power and Control Theory

This theory focuses on how power dynamics and the misuse of power contribute to workplace toxicity. It explores how individuals or groups with power can abuse it to dominate, harass, or marginalize others, leading to a toxic environment.

Conflict Theory

Conflict Theory, derived from sociology, examines how conflicts between different groups (e.g., management vs. employees) over resources, power, and status can lead to toxicity. It highlights the role of structural inequalities and power imbalances in creating and perpetuating toxic workplace environments.

Psychodynamic Theory

From a psychodynamic perspective, workplace toxicity can be understood through the lens of individual psychology and unconscious processes. It examines how unresolved personal issues, defense mechanisms, and projection can contribute to toxic behaviors and relationships at work.

Leadership Theories

Various leadership theories, including toxic leadership and transformational leadership, provide insights into how leadership styles and behaviors influence organizational health. Toxic leadership contributes to workplace toxicity by modeling or tolerating harmful behaviors, while transformational leadership can mitigate toxicity by fostering positive change and employee well-being. Transformative leadership can help to undercut toxicity by aggressively deploying systems to identify its occurrences and establish mechanisms to mitigate its impacts on culture to preserve social justice and fairness for all employees.

These theoretical perspectives offer valuable insights into the multifaceted nature of workplace toxicity, highlighting the importance of addressing individual behaviors, organizational structures, and cultural norms to create safer and healthier work environments. By applying these theories, researchers and practitioners can develop more effective strategies for diagnosing, understanding, and intervening in toxic workplace situations.

Sociological Aspects of Workplace Trauma

Understanding the sociological aspects of workplace trauma is essential for comprehending the broader context in which such trauma occurs and for developing effective strategies to address it. Organizational structures, cultural norms, and social interactions within the workplace all contribute to or mitigate trauma.

The culture within an organization significantly influences the incidence and impact of workplace trauma. For instance, cultures that prioritize competitiveness over collaboration may foster environments where bullying and stress are more common. Norms around communication and conflict resolution can either encourage the reporting and addressing of issues or suppress them, leading to unresolved trauma. Nonetheless, an environment that promotes open dialogue and mutual respect is crucial for preventing and addressing trauma effectively.

Power Dynamics and Hierarchies

Power dynamics and hierarchies within the workplace play a critical role in the prevalence of workplace trauma. Power imbalances between employees and management can create environments where abuse and harassment are more likely to occur and less likely to be challenged. Hierarchical structures may inhibit individuals from speaking out against injustices or seeking help due to fear of retaliation or job loss. Addressing these power dynamics is crucial for creating a safer and more equitable workplace.

Discrimination

Discrimination based on race, gender, sexuality, religion, or disability significantly contributes to workplace trauma. Marginalized groups often experience higher rates of harassment and exclusion. Societal inequalities are mirrored within workplaces, affecting individuals' experiences of trauma and their access to support and resources. Ensuring inclusivity and equity within the workplace is vital for mitigating these impacts and supporting all employees.

Policies and Practices

Workplace policies and practices play a critical role in shaping the organizational response to traumatic events. The presence or absence of clear policies regarding workplace behavior, conflict resolution, and trauma support can significantly impact how an organization handles trauma. Practices around workload management, job security, and employee welfare are crucial in either preventing or exacerbating workplace trauma. Comprehensive policies that prioritize employee well-being and offer resources are essential for creating a supportive work environment.

Economic and Industrial Factors

Economic and industrial factors further contribute to workplace trauma. Economic pressures, industry downturns, and job insecurity can create environments of high stress and anxiety, exacerbating the psychological trauma experienced by employees. Certain industries, such as healthcare, law enforcement, and social services, inherently expose employees to traumatic situations.

Understanding these industry-specific factors is important for addressing workplace trauma effectively and in a way that meets the needs of employees in that industry. For example, the needs of firefighters and police officers are very different from those of teachers and accounting workers.

Social Support

The degree of social support available from colleagues and management plays a critical role in mitigating the impacts of trauma. Supportive networks, such as employee resource groups (ERGs), can provide a buffer against stress and facilitate recovery. A strong sense of community within the workplace enhances mental health and well-being, influencing how trauma is experienced and processed. Fostering supportive relationships is key to creating a resilient workplace environment.

Societal Values

Broader societal values around work ethic, success, and mental health shape organizational attitudes and practices. Cultures that stigmatize mental health issues or valorize overwork may contribute to toxic workplace environments. Public discourse and legal frameworks around workplace safety, harassment, and mental health also influence organizational policies and employees' willingness to report issues.

Shifting societal attitudes towards a healthier work-life balance and mental health awareness is essential for creating supportive workplaces.

Comprehensive Approaches

Understanding the sociological aspects of workplace trauma underscores the importance of comprehensive approaches that address organizational culture, social dynamics, and structural inequalities. Effective interventions must go beyond individual support to include changes in policies, practices, and cultural norms to create healthier, more supportive work environments. By addressing these sociological factors, we can foster a work environment where everyone feels safe, valued, and supported.

Political Aspects of Workplace Trauma

The political aspects of workplace trauma involve the complex interplay between power dynamics, organizational policies, and the broader socio-political context in which organizations operate. These factors significantly influence how trauma is experienced, managed, and mitigated in the workplace.

Power Dynamics

Power dynamics within an organization can exacerbate trauma, particularly when those in higher positions abuse their authority. This abuse can manifest as harassment, bullying, or other forms of mistreatment. When power is concentrated in the hands of a few, it creates an environment ripe for abuse, leaving employees vulnerable and unsupported.

Moreover, employees who experience or witness trauma often feel pressured to remain silent due to fear of retaliation or negative consequences for their careers. This silencing is typically a product of power imbalances and a culture that does not protect or value whistleblowers.

Organizational Policies and Culture

Organizational policies and culture play a crucial role in how trauma is handled. The presence or absence of trauma-informed policies significantly affects organizational responses. Without these policies, organizations may inadvertently re-traumatize employees or fail to provide adequate support.

Implementing trauma-informed approaches involves recognizing the widespread impact of trauma, integrating knowledge about trauma into policies and practices, and actively seeking to avoid retraumatization. Additionally, a culture of accountability is essential. Organizations that lack this culture may allow traumatic behaviors to proliferate unchecked, particularly if these behaviors are seen as beneficial to the organization politically or economically.

Creating a culture where accountability is a cornerstone helps ensure that inappropriate behaviors are addressed promptly and effectively, which is in everyone's best interests.

Legislation and Regulation

Legislation and regulation are critical political aspects that impact workplace trauma. The degree to which existing labor laws protect mental health and address workplace trauma is a significant issue. Inadequate legal protections can leave employees vulnerable to trauma without recourse.

Strong legislation is essential for safeguarding employees' well-being and providing mechanisms for addressing workplace trauma. Advocacy and lobbying efforts by trade unions, advocacy groups, and lobbyists to influence workplace-related legislation can lead to better protections against workplace trauma. These groups play a crucial role in pushing for reforms that protect workers and promote healthier work environments.

Socio-Political Context

The socio-political context, including social justice movements like #MeToo, has raised awareness about workplace harassment and trauma, influencing organizational policies and societal expectations. These movements highlight the importance of addressing power imbalances and ensuring that workplaces are safe and equitable for all employees.

Additionally, cultural attitudes towards mental health significantly impact how workplace trauma is recognized and treated. Cultural stigma can hinder open discussions and supportive practices in the workplace, making it essential to shift societal attitudes towards greater acceptance and understanding of mental health issues.

Leadership and Management Practices

Leadership and management practices are also pivotal. Leaders who prioritize ethical practices and employee well-being can help mitigate the impact of trauma and foster supportive workplace cultures and positive organizational climates. Ethical leadership involves being transparent, fair, and empathetic, creating a culture where employees feel valued and respected.

Strategic decision-making that balances financial performance with the health and well-being of the workforce is crucial. Decisions that prioritize profits over people or neglect the well-being of employees in favor of short-term gains can contribute to an environment where trauma is more likely to occur.

Fostering Healthier Work Environments

Understanding and addressing these political aspects are essential for fostering healthier work environments that are supportive and responsive to the needs of employees who have experienced trauma. Such efforts not only benefit individual employees but also enhance the overall health and effectiveness of organizations.

By tackling these issues head-on, we can create workplaces that are not only productive but also safe and nurturing for everyone involved.

The Psychology of Fear

Fear is a complex and multifaceted emotion deeply rooted in our biology and profoundly affecting our behavior and physiology. Understanding the psychology of fear involves exploring how it is processed in the brain, its physical manifestations, and the ways it can be managed. The mind, responsible for our consciousness, perception, thinking, judgment, and memory, plays a crucial role in shaping behavior and experiences. It processes a wide range of mental activities, from reasoning and emotions to imagination and memory, enabling us to navigate our world.

Fear is a powerful emotion that exerts considerable influence on individual behavior and societal dynamics. In contemporary society, fear is strategically utilized across various contexts, often with significant impact. However, the use of fear raises ethical concerns and can have varying degrees of effectiveness. While fear can serve as a strong motivator, it can also result in negative outcomes such as anxiety, stress, and societal division. The ongoing debate centers on balancing the use of fear to inform and motivate against the risk of causing undue anxiety or manipulation.

In marketing and advertising, companies frequently choose to use fear-based tactics to create a sense of urgency or need. Advertisements might play on fears of social exclusion, aging, safety, or health to promote products like anti-aging creams, home security systems, and life insurance policies. This approach aims to drive consumer behavior by tapping into deep-seated anxieties.

Within workplace management, fear is sometimes used as a tool to drive performance. Employers might choose to threaten job loss, demotion, or other negative consequences to motivate employees. However, this strategy is generally viewed as counterproductive in modern management theories, which emphasize the importance of positive reinforcement and employee engagement.

Fear is a potent tool used across various domains in society to influence behavior and decisionmaking. While it can be an effective motivator, its ethical use requires careful consideration to avoid negative consequences and to ensure it serves the greater good without causing unnecessary harm.

Biological Basis

At the core of fear's biological basis lies the brain's specialized network for processing fear. The amygdala acts as the brain's alarm system, detecting threats and triggering the fear response. When activated, it sends signals that lead to physiological reactions such as increased heart rate and the release of adrenaline, preparing the body for immediate action.

The hippocampus is crucial for forming and retrieving fear-related memories, providing context based on past experiences to help the brain determine whether a situation is genuinely threatening. Meanwhile, the prefrontal cortex regulates the fear response by modulating emotions and promoting rational threat assessment.

When faced with a threat, the body undergoes several physiological changes to prepare for a fight-or-flight reaction. The sympathetic nervous system activation leads to the release of adrenaline, causing physical symptoms such as increased heart rate, rapid breathing, and heightened senses, all aimed at readying the body to respond to danger. The hormonal response involves the activation of the hypothalamus-pituitary-adrenal (HPA) axis, releasing cortisol to maintain a state of heightened alertness.

Impact on Emotional Experience and Behavior

Fear influences both our emotional experience and behavior. Emotionally, fear can range from mild anxiety to intense terror, evoking reactions such as panic, dread, and helplessness. Behaviorally, fear triggers primary responses such as fight, flight, or freeze.

People may also develop avoidance behaviors to prevent encountering feared situations, which can lead to phobias or other anxiety disorders over time. Cognitively, fear can distort perception, leading individuals to overestimate danger or misinterpret neutral stimuli as threatening. Fearful experiences are often vividly remembered and easily triggered by associated cues, enhancing memory consolidation due to the emotional intensity of fear.

Social and Cultural Factors

Social and cultural factors also shape fear. Different cultures have varying thresholds and interpretations of fear, influencing how fear is expressed and managed. Social learning plays a role, as fear can be learned through observation and social interactions, emphasizing the social dimension of this emotion.

Managing and Treating Fear

Managing and treating fear involves various strategies. Cognitive-behavioral therapy (CBT) is an effective treatment for fear and anxiety disorders, focusing on changing maladaptive thought patterns and behaviors. Exposure therapy involves gradual exposure to the feared object or situation in a controlled manner, helping individuals build tolerance and reduce fear over time. Medications such as anxiolytics and antidepressants can help manage the physiological and psychological symptoms of fear and anxiety.

Psychology of Fear

Understanding the psychology of fear requires recognizing its biological, psychological, and social components. By examining how fear operates within these frameworks, we can better understand its impact on human behavior and develop strategies to manage it effectively. This overview provides insight into the complexity of fear and highlights the various ways it can be addressed, emphasizing the importance of a multifaceted approach to understanding and managing this pervasive emotion within organizations.

Fear as a Weapon

In contemporary society, fear exerts a profound influence on both individual behaviors and larger social dynamics. It is crucial to acknowledge that the use of fear carries ethical implications, and its effectiveness can vary greatly. While fear can be a potent motivator in specific contexts, its misuse can lead to undesirable consequences such as anxiety, stress, and societal division.

The ongoing debate in this sphere revolves around finding a balance between utilizing fear as a tool for information and motivation, and the risk of causing unnecessary anxiety or manipulation. Its application spans a wide array of contexts, often yielding significant impacts.

In the workplace, fear can sometimes be used as a management tool, with negative consequences like job loss or demotion wielded to boost performance. However, this approach is largely viewed as counterproductive in contemporary management philosophies.

At the governmental level, in matters of national security and defense, the spotlighting of threats often serves to justify certain policies or actions, potentially rallying public support for increased defense expenditures or military interventions.

In the political arena, fear is a lever frequently pulled by politicians and political groups to sway public opinion or influence electoral outcomes. By spotlighting perceived threats stemming from specific policies, groups, or nations, they galvanize support or opposition.

Law enforcement and legal systems also choose to use fear, utilizing the threat of legal consequences, such as fines or imprisonment, and even up to lethal force, as deterrents against unlawful activities. However, today the lines of what is meant by "lawful" are being contested due to disparate treatment of various groups by law enforcement. Such disparities create safety or fear based on the color of one's skin.

In marketing and advertising, companies frequently use fear-based tactics to instill a sense of urgency or necessity among consumers. This approach can manifest through campaigns that tap into common fears such as social exclusion, aging, personal safety, or health concerns, effectively driving demand for products like anti-aging creams, home security systems, or insurance policies. Public health campaigns also harness fear as a strategic tool, aiming to encourage behaviors that mitigate health risks. This is evident in anti-smoking advertisements that lay bare the hazards of tobacco use, or in public messaging during health crises, such as pandemics, where adherence to safety protocols is crucial.

The news media, in their pursuit of capturing audience attention, may resort to emphasizing the more alarming elements of stories. This practice, often labeled as fear-mongering, not only boosts viewership or readership but can also inadvertently stoke public anxiety and foster misconceptions. On social media and online platforms, fear-based content, including conspiracy theories and alarmist narratives, frequently finds traction. Such content plays on common fears to heighten user engagement or to spread particular viewpoints. The entertainment industry, especially through genres like horror or thriller, leverages fear as a means to create suspense and captivate audiences. Unlike other contexts, here the use of fear is primarily aimed at providing entertainment.

In educational settings, fear is used to underscore the gravity of certain behaviors or situations. This is seen in driver's education programs highlighting the risks of reckless driving or in environmental education stressing the dire consequences of climate change. In educational environments, threats of academic integrity violations are used to maintain compliance among students and employees, though most employees, including the preponderance of faculty, often misapply the data provided by such AI tools as Turnitin.

Impact of Fear on Productivity

Fear in the workplace can significantly impact productivity, leading to increased absenteeism, lower job satisfaction, and impaired communication. Employees may become risk-averse, less motivated, and exhibit a narrowed focus or decreased creativity. Over time, persistent fear can result in higher turnover rates and mental health issues among staff.

Contributor Lucy J. Crowder shares her story of how the destructive impact of toxic leadership driven by ego and insecurity undermines and sabotages roles within organizations through gaslighting, bullying, and removing responsibilities. This creates a damaging work environment that not only affected her but also spread to other employees. This theme emphasizes the destructive power that a toxic leader can have on an organization's culture, morale, and overall effectiveness. The emotional toll on employees experiencing such a toxic work environment is evident in their expressions of grief over the loss of a positive organizational culture and safe leadership.

Contributor Ann M. Morgan describes the destructive effects of working under a toxic leader who undermined, manipulated, and marginalized competent employees. Her leader, the Chief Academic Officer (CAO), is characterized by favoritism, irrational decision-making, and a disregard for collaborative efforts. These behaviors not only harmed her professional integrity and well-being but also eroded the overall organizational culture, producing a toxic environment that led to a loss of morale, a decline in effective practices, and ultimately drove her to resign from a position she once valued. The internal conflicts she experienced caused her to realize that compromising her integrity was unsustainable. The pressure to conform to the CAO's harmful practices and the subsequent disillusionment with the organizational culture drove her to resign.

Mitigating Negative Effects

To mitigate these negative effects, leaders and managers must cultivate a positive, supportive, and psychologically safe work environment where employees feel empowered to pursue their goals without fear. This requires clear communication, fair and constructive feedback, recognition of achievements, and fostering a culture of trust and respect. Recognizing and understanding how fear manifests in the workplace is essential for creating healthier, more productive environments both personally and professionally.

Toxic Leaders and Fear

Research on toxic leadership reveals that a significant portion of leaders in the workforce exhibit behaviors that can harm workplace culture and employee well-being. Lipman-Bluman (2005) concluded that toxic leaders violate the basic standards of human rights, mislead their followers with untruths, subvert system structures and processes for their own purposes, and play to the basest fears and needs of their followers. We can see such behaviors played out in real-time by turning on any news channel or social media platform. These behaviors result in very real negative consequences for employees, who then become traumatized.

Other studies (Zhang & Peterson, 2019; SHRM, 2019; Sherwood & Smith, 2021; APA, n.d.) suggest that 10% to 30% of leaders may demonstrate toxic behaviors, which can include overtly abusive actions, micro-management, manipulation, and subtle forms of undermining. This toxicity often results in severe consequences, such as increased turnover rates, absenteeism, and a decline in overall organizational performance. The prevalence of toxic leadership in the workforce varies depending on the study and criteria used, but research consistently shows that 10% to 30% of leaders may exhibit toxic behaviors. These behaviors, ranging from overt abuse to subtle manipulation, can significantly harm workplace culture, leading to increased turnover, absenteeism, and decreased employee well-being.

They found that toxic leadership creates environments that suppress innovation and collaboration, ultimately damaging organizational performance. According to the Society for Human Resource Management (SHRM) (2019), toxic workplace cultures—often driven by such leadership—are costing U.S. employers nearly $223 billion over five years due to turnover and absenteeism (APA, n.d.). Sherwood and Smith (2021) found that toxic leadership substantially deteriorates workplace culture, leading to heightened stress, job dissatisfaction, and increased turnover. Similarly, Zhang and Peterson (2019) highlighted that toxic behaviors among leaders not only damage employee morale but also negatively impact productivity and organizational outcomes. Additionally, the American Psychological Association (APA) (n.d.) underlines the significant psychological damage caused by toxic workplaces, stressing that such environments, often stemming from toxic leadership, lead to widespread employee dissatisfaction and mental health issues.

These findings collectively underscore the profound and widespread effects of toxic leadership, highlighting the critical need for organizations to address these behaviors to foster healthier, more productive workplaces. As a society, we must come to grips with the prevalence of trauma rather than continuing to pretend as though the only individuals with mental health issues are those who end up in prison, commit suicide, bully, or harm others. What about the millions of people who were subject to the maltreatment foisted upon them by such individuals?

Cynthia Mathieu's (2021/2024) research and writings delve into the damaging effects toxic leaders have on organizations and their members. These leaders, often exhibiting traits linked to dark personalities such as narcissism, Machiavellianism, and psychopathy, cultivate environments dominated by fear and manipulation. This pervasive atmosphere of fear significantly impacts both employees and the organization, leading to various negative outcomes. The toxic behaviors of these leaders erode morale, stifle creativity, and increase turnover, creating a hostile and ineffective workplace.

Dark Personality Traits Across Contexts

Dark personality traits, such as narcissism, Machiavellianism, and psychopathy, can manifest differently across demographics and cultural contexts due to the influence of various sociocultural factors, including cultural norms, societal values, upbringing, and socialization practices. Below is an exploration of these influences:

Cultural Norms and Values

- **Narcissism**: In cultures that highly value individual achievement, self-promotion, and material success, narcissistic traits might be more socially acceptable or even encouraged. Western cultures, for instance, often emphasize individualism, fostering behaviors associated with narcissism, such as a strong focus on self-esteem and personal success.

- **Machiavellianism**: Cultures that place a strong emphasis on power dynamics and social hierarchy may see more expressions of Machiavellian traits. In these settings, strategic manipulation and cunning behavior might be more prevalent or considered necessary for success.

- **Psychopathy**: The manifestation of psychopathic traits can be influenced by cultural attitudes towards aggression, authority, and rule-breaking. In societies where aggression is more tolerated or where there is less stigma associated with antisocial behavior; psychopathic traits might be more visible.

Socialization Practices

- **Parenting Styles**: Overly permissive parenting might foster narcissistic tendencies, while harsh or inconsistent parenting might contribute to the development of Machiavellian or psychopathic traits.

- **Education Systems**: Environments that reward competitive, cutthroat behaviors might encourage Machiavellianism, while those promoting empathy and cooperation might mitigate the development of dark traits.

Gender Differences

- **Narcissism**: Men are more likely to exhibit traits associated with grandiosity and entitlement, while women may show more covert or vulnerable narcissism.

- **Machiavellianism and Psychopathy**: These traits are often more commonly expressed in men, possibly due to socialization that encourages risk-taking, assertiveness, and dominance. Women, on the other hand, may exhibit these traits in more socially subtle or relationally aggressive ways.

- **Socioeconomic Status**: In environments where resources are scarce or competition for status is fierce, Machiavellianism or psychopathic traits may be more prevalent as adaptive strategies for survival. Conversely, individuals from more affluent backgrounds might express narcissism through entitlement or elitism.

- **Cultural Adaptation and Migration**: Migrants may adapt their behaviors, including dark personality traits, to fit in or succeed in new environments. For example, a person from a collectivist culture might downplay narcissistic traits in an individualistic society—or vice versa.

- **Religion and Moral Frameworks**: Religious beliefs and moral frameworks can significantly influence the expression of dark personality traits. Strong religious communities might suppress overt displays of Machiavellianism or psychopathy due to ethical constraints, while some contexts might use religious beliefs to justify manipulative or authoritarian behavior.

- **Media Influence**: The portrayal of dark personality traits in media can shape how these traits are perceived and manifested. For instance, media that glorifies ruthless business practices or celebrates anti-heroes might encourage the adoption of Machiavellian or psychopathic traits.

- **Regional Differences**: Regional differences in culture, economic conditions, and social norms within a single country can affect the prevalence and expression of dark personality traits. Urban areas, for instance, may exhibit different social dynamics than rural areas, influencing how traits like Machiavellianism or narcissism are expressed.

Research Considerations

- **Cross-Cultural Research**: Studies comparing different cultures reveal variations in how dark traits are valued, expressed, or suppressed. However, such research must account for the complex interplay of variables such as economic conditions, political systems, and social norms.

- **Intersectionality**: Understanding how dark traits manifest requires considering intersectionality—how various aspects of identity (race, gender, class, etc.) interact to shape experiences and behaviors.

Addressing Toxic Leadership Behaviors Dark Personality Traits

Dark personality traits are influenced by a complex web of sociocultural factors, making their manifestation across different demographics and cultures a multifaceted phenomenon. Understanding these traits in context requires careful consideration of cultural norms, socialization practices, gender roles, and socioeconomic conditions. Cross-cultural and intersectional research is crucial for gaining a nuanced understanding of how these traits emerge and operate in various settings.

Five Aspects of Toxic Leadership

1. **Fear as a Control Tool**: Toxic leaders use fear as a primary tool to control and manipulate their subordinates. This approach significantly diminishes employee morale and motivation. Under constant stress and anxiety, employees find it difficult to remain engaged and motivated in their work, leading to decreased productivity and job satisfaction.

2. **Stifling Creativity and Innovation**: Fear stifles creativity and innovation. Employees operating under such conditions are less likely to take risks or think outside the box, hindering the organization's ability to innovate and adapt to changing conditions. This lack of innovation can put the organization at a competitive disadvantage.

3. **Increased Employee Turnover**: Stress and dissatisfaction associated with working under a toxic leader often result in higher employee turnover. Talented and capable individuals are more likely to leave the organization in search of a healthier and more supportive work environment. High turnover rates not only disrupt team dynamics but also increase recruitment and training costs for the organization.

4. **Erosion of Collaboration and Teamwork**: Toxic leadership fosters a culture of distrust and competition rather than collaboration and teamwork. Employees may focus more on self-preservation than on cooperation, leading to a breakdown in team cohesion and effectiveness. This divisive environment can further diminish organizational performance and morale.

5. **Long-Term Cultural Damage**: The long-term effects of toxic leadership extend beyond immediate employee well-being. Over time, the negative impacts on morale, innovation, and turnover can erode the organization's culture, reputation, and overall performance. This erosion makes it difficult for the organization to attract and retain top talent, ultimately compromising its long-term success and sustainability.

Insights from Research

Cynthia Mathieu (2021/2024) emphasizes that addressing toxic leadership behaviors is crucial for creating a healthier, more productive work environment. By fostering a culture of respect, support, and ethical behavior, organizations can mitigate the harmful effects of toxic leadership and cultivate a more positive and effective workplace.

Mathieu's work highlights the profound impact toxic leaders can have on organizations and their employees. These leaders, characterized by traits such as narcissism, Machiavellianism, and psychopathy, create environments dominated by fear and manipulation, which can lead to several negative outcomes. Toxic leadership fosters a culture of distrust and competition rather than collaboration and teamwork. Employees may focus more on self-preservation than on cooperation, leading to a breakdown in team cohesion and effectiveness diminishing organizational performance and morale (Mathieu, 2021/2024).

The long-term effects of toxic leadership extend beyond immediate employee well-being. Over time, the negative impacts on morale, innovation, and turnover can erode the organization's culture, reputation, and overall performance. This erosion makes it difficult for the organization to attract and retain top talent, ultimately compromising its long-term success and sustainability (Lipman-Blumen, 2004).

The Additive Nature of Trauma

Since trauma is additive, it has a compounding impact on a person. Each significant traumatic event becomes layered onto previous ones. When this occurs repeatedly or if the events are substantial enough, very complex forms of posttraumatic stress disorder (PTSD) can emerge. The more complex the entanglement, the more triggers there are to set off various aftereffects, and the more difficult it is to resolve.

Tactics of Toxic Leaders

Toxic leaders wield fear as a primary instrument to assert control and authority, often resulting in detrimental effects on both individuals and the organizational structure. They typically deploy a variety of tactics to instill and maintain this climate of fear, including intimidation and threats, using verbal aggression and the prospect of negative consequences like job loss or demotion to compel compliance. They create an environment where mistakes are met with harsh punishments, stifling creativity and risktaking. Manipulation and coercion are also commonly used by such leaders by withholding information, spreading rumors, or setting team members against each other, they foster insecurity and uncertainty.

- **Micromanagement**: Overbearing management control of every aspect of work leads to an oppressive atmosphere, leaving employees too intimidated to make independent decisions. Unrealistic goals and expectations perpetuate anxiety and feelings of inadequacy.

- **Public Humiliation**: Used to intimidate targeted individuals and serve as a warning to others. This unpredictability in reactions and decisions keeps employees in a continual state of unease, unsure of what might trigger negative feedback. Communication

- **Suppression of Dissent**: Toxic leaders also suppress dissent, creating an unpredictable and uneasy work environment. Penalizing those who voice differing opinions is compounded by a culture of favoritism and exclusion, where employees are coerced into competing for the leader's approval.

- **Emotional Abuse**: Applying pressure with belittling comments and verbal aggression will cement an environment rife with fear and disrespect.

Addressing Toxic Leadership

Such leadership styles can have far-reaching negative impacts, including diminished employee morale, high staff turnover, decreased productivity, and the propagation of a toxic work culture. Recognizing and addressing these toxic behaviors is crucial for organizations aiming to foster a work environment characterized by respect, productivity, and a positive organizational culture.

Fear in Practice

Without realizing it, early on, my fascination was with the leadership dynamic and resulting group behaviors. That fascination led me to a lifetime of studying leadership and group dynamics (organizational effectiveness), which has now become the underlying organizing principle of this guide—the nexus between trauma, leadership, group dynamics, goal behaviors, and individual and collective performance. Studying leadership in college while seeing its failings in real-time in my professional setting exacerbated my situation because I knew what should be done but saw and suffered the consequences of poor leadership practices.

Fueled by my own complex trauma, I have done my best throughout my career to create opportunities for individuals and organizations to maximize their potential regardless of the personal consequences to me. My truth includes that my pain has caused me to harm others (acts which I deeply regret), and it has given me the courage to stand against the onslaught of aftereffects that come with challenging the status quo.

Because I've lived with so much pain every day since the age of two, I've become tenacious when defending and protecting others, knowing all along that doing so has dire personal consequences. I'm not a martyr and do not have any desire to become one, but I am a humble warrior who has been trained to protect others, and I will do so whenever I feel it is called for—on the streets during protests, in my programs and classrooms, and in the boardrooms.

During my journey, I've learned that no matter how strong someone thinks they are, everyone has a breaking point when enough stress is applied. Breaking a person is a broad term encompassing various experiences that severely affect an individual's physical, emotional, or psychological state. It often involves extreme stress, pressure, abuse, or trauma overwhelming an individual's coping mechanisms, leading to significant distress or dysfunction.

Toxic environments can produce such stress, altering behaviors and compelling people to act in ways they otherwise wouldn't. In workplaces, for instance, employees might lie and cover up flaws in their work to avoid termination, which can harm themselves, their organizations, and stakeholders.

This was evident in the 2016 Wells Fargo scandal, where executives were accused of creating fraudulent bank accounts due to immense performance pressure. I was a Wells Fargo account holder at the time. My usual teller apologized to me for having to ask me whether I wanted to open other accounts—knowing full well I did not. She had to inquire because tellers were instructed to do so. Based on my training and expertise I told her the policy and practice would lead to problems downstream for the bank. Six months later, Wells Fargo was exposed for their practices, and investigations found managerial malpractice.

Years earlier, while working for the YMCA, I observed fraudulent activities driven by relentless pressure on executives to meet revenue targets. During weekly management meetings, executives were required to account for their revenues on a line-by-line basis. Any negative variances from the budget had to be explained publicly, with no discussions about expenses, the causes of revenue shortfalls, or corrective actions to balance the budget by year-end.

This environment of fear and pressure led to unethical practices as individuals sought to protect themselves and their positions. At least one executive committed fraud by manipulating revenue reporting, shifting actual revenues between line-item accounts to create the illusion that his unit's revenue streams were stable when, in fact, they were not.

Moreover, I witnessed discrepancies in financial reporting between these internal meetings—known among executives as *"machine gun sessions"*—and what was presented to the Board of Directors by the President. The President, concerned primarily with protecting his power and image, often altered the reported figures, further perpetuating the fraud.

Through these experiences, I learned early in my career about the profound impact of fear on behavior. Using the YMCA fraud example, it is abundantly clear to me that if fear were removed so the truth could be told—rather than manufacturing data as a self-protection mechanism—such behavior would not exist or be tolerated.

Unfortunately, the deception produced more significant problems for the organization that went unnoticed. Manipulated data led to profit and loss statements that appeared relatively healthy on the surface but were not. Because of poor leadership and the focus on incomplete data, no one paid attention to the annual customer sales numbers. While revenues appeared to increase year-over-year based on budget projections, actual individual sales numbers (total customer generation) were in decline, threatening the organization's sustainability.

In another example, an executive set up his budget with a $100,000 problem built into it, without any strategy to overcome such a financial hit for an already leveraged organization to absorb at the end of the year. Nonetheless, his supervisor approved the budget. The executive was promoted, and a new executive was hired, whom he then supervised.

The newly hired executive was given incomplete financial statements to analyze during the interview process. Once hired, he unknowingly walked into a financial mess and was held accountable for cleaning it up. That executive was me.

Over the length of my career, I've directly experienced or learned about the prevalence of highly toxic behaviors and the behaviors they produced through my dissertation and other research, colleagues, students and consultancies.

What is important to note here is that it does not matter how the corporate documents define the organization or which industry it operates in—people make the organization come alive. Therefore, there is a high likelihood that 70% to 90% of the workforce brings their trauma with them when hired so the strength of their emotional and social intelligence shapes their behaviors when it comes to their interpersonal and intergroup relationships. As a result, whether toxicity exists in the organization is largely the result of both leader and follower behaviors and the culture they create for the organization (Edmonds, 2021).

In one of the universities where I worked for more than a dozen years, the program director took my work, called it his own, and received good performance ratings while my performance ratings were suppressed, and I was identified as a difficult employee. This is the sort of behavior Michael LeBeouf spoke about in his 1989 book *The Greatest Management Principle in the World (GMP)*. His basic premise is that *what gets rewarded gets done.* Practically speaking, the converse is also true: *that which gets punished and causes pain can produce conditions in which someone's defense mechanisms cause them to act in illegal or illicit ways to protect themselves,* as illustrated in the previous YMCA example.

There is a lot of talk these days about the importance of authenticity in the workplace. Nevertheless, when someone, particularly a Black male such as me, comes along, outperforms expectations, and pushes against the status quo, they run the risk of being demeaned, deemed a radical, a threat, and someone to be feared rather than as someone who has talents, should be supported, and given opportunities to excel.

For example, I am personally aware of three Black executives who were targeted by one single White executive who got away with destroying their careers. I am also aware of one of those Black executives being told by his CEO, *"You always go after the dying dogs"*—in response to his penchant for choosing to work in service to low-income communities.

You would think the CEO would applaud him for his willingness to take on such difficult work in resource-poor communities, particularly in his case, where no White person would want to take such a job. Behaviors like those exhibited by the CEO harm employees by demeaning their work and their worth. CEOs control millions of dollars in resources and determine how those resources are used. They have every opportunity to steer more resources to resource-poor communities or to let those communities fend for themselves, which is generally what happened, making it possible for them to make their fundraising cases.

Equally important about this example is that the CEO's behavior is precisely what's wrong in our society and demonstrates clearly how deeply held personal beliefs impact behaviors in workplaces. The executive being referenced here was hurt deeply by what his CEO said to him, and he literally took his pain with him to his grave. *Words, like behaviors, have consequences!*

As someone who has worked in similar communities and under similar circumstances, I've observed firsthand how such attitudes impact the treatment of employees and consequently organizational performance. This kind of story is not unique, and that is the travesty and the importance of this work—to explore some of the hidden battles in organizations that undermine organizational performance and therefore organizational effectiveness.

Creating Your Own Balance

Chapter 4 *"Trauma and Toxicity in the Workplace and Elsewhere"* delves into the deep and often hidden costs of toxic leadership and how it creates environments rife with trauma, impacting both individuals and organizations. It begins by emphasizing that trauma is an inevitable part of modern workplaces, particularly in organizations where leadership styles are either too autocratic or too laissez-faire. In these settings, employees often feel powerless and undervalued, with little opportunity for input or collaboration. The lack of effective leadership oversight creates spaces where toxic behaviors, including micromanagement, manipulation, and bullying, can flourish unchecked.

The chapter highlights how workplace trauma doesn't remain confined to the office but travels with individuals into their personal lives, affecting their home environments and relationships. Referencing Carl Jung's belief that unresolved internal struggles manifest in the external world, I underscore that without confronting personal trauma, leaders and employees alike are likely to perpetuate toxic behaviors at work. This cyclical nature of trauma—moving between personal and professional lives—complicates efforts to address and mitigate its effects.

One of the most alarming aspects of workplace trauma is its prevalence. Studies show that more than half of the workforce in the United States has experienced some form of trauma on the job, affecting tens of millions of people. These experiences are rarely isolated; instead, they accumulate over time, layering on top of previous traumas and compounding their psychological impact. The chapter also connects the rise of violence in society—such as mass shootings and workplace assaults—with toxic environments, suggesting that unchecked aggression and poor leadership are part of a broader societal issue.

Workplace violence itself is a stark example of how toxic environments can escalate. Whether through physical assaults, threats, or verbal harassment, many employees face real danger in their workplaces. The chapter cites the National Safety Council's report on workplace violence, which revealed thousands of injuries and hundreds of deaths, underscoring how toxic behaviors can lead to tragic consequences. Moreover, the chapter suggests that workplace trauma, especially when compounded by societal stressors like economic insecurity or job loss, can push some individuals to violence. However, it also notes that fostering social cohesion and healthy relationships at work can act as a protective factor against such incidents.

The impact of workplace trauma isn't limited to mental health—it extends to physical well-being as well. Employees subjected to high-stress environments, bullying, or harassment often experience a range of health problems, including anxiety, depression, cardiovascular disease, and chronic pain. The chapter stresses that these issues are not just personal; they have organizational consequences as well. Companies with high levels of workplace trauma suffer from absenteeism, lower job satisfaction, and decreased productivity. This leads to significant financial losses and hinders overall performance.

Harassment and discrimination are additional sources of trauma that deeply affect workplace culture. The chapter explores how gender-based discrimination, sexual harassment, and exclusion create hostile environments that are difficult to navigate. Personal stories within the text illustrate how these experiences can leave long-lasting scars on individuals, sometimes leading them to leave jobs they once valued. The emotional toll of harassment and bullying is not easily overcome, and without proper intervention, the cycle of toxicity continues.

Toxic work cultures often develop gradually, beginning with small infractions and growing into systemic issues that erode morale and trust within an organization. Over time, environments where overwork is glorified, where competition is encouraged over collaboration, and where the well-being of employees is ignored lead to burnout, resentment, and high turnover. Toxic leadership exacerbates these issues, creating a climate where employees feel constantly pressured to meet unrealistic expectations without adequate support. The chapter argues that these behaviors are more than just personal failings—they reflect deeper organizational and societal problems.

Throughout the chapter, I reference various theoretical frameworks to explain how toxic environments emerge and persist. Theories like *Social Exchange Theory* and *Person-Environment Fit* help to illustrate how imbalances in power, misaligned values, and leadership failures create conditions where toxicity can thrive. Meanwhile, *Power and Control Theory* highlights the role of abusive leaders in perpetuating environments of fear and manipulation, reinforcing the importance of addressing these dynamics at a structural level.

The chapter concludes with a call to action for organizations to take proactive steps in preventing and addressing trauma in the workplace. It stresses the importance of:

- **Regular assessments of workplace culture:** Identifying and addressing signs of toxic patterns early.

- **Clear anti-violence and anti-harassment policies:** Establishing well-communicated expectations and zero-tolerance measures for harmful behaviors.

- **Leadership that prioritizes fairness, transparency, and employee well-being:** Promoting ethical behavior and demonstrating a commitment to supporting employees' mental and physical health.

- **Transformative leadership**, which emphasizes ethical behavior and social justice, is presented as a key solution to dismantling the toxic cultures that have taken root in so many organizations.

In sum, *"Trauma and Toxicity in the Workplace and Elsewhere"* paints a vivid picture of the pervasive nature of workplace trauma, showing how toxic leadership and harmful organizational cultures not only damage individuals but also cripple the organizations they lead. By addressing the root causes of toxicity and adopting trauma-informed practices, organizations can create healthier, more supportive environments where both people and businesses can thrive.

HEALTHY ORGANIZATIONS BY DESIGN

Principle 5: *Be the rising star rather than the shooting star. Always search for the silver lining.*

— My mother, Rose Perry

CHAPTER 5

The Human Side of the Enterprise

Leadership vs. Management

Leadership is about seeing possibilities when others see impossibilities and believing in your vision even when others doubt you. I experienced this firsthand when I became the executive leader of a branch YMCA in East Oakland, California. In my first role, I proposed consolidating two financially unhealthy inner-city organizations. When I approached my supervisor with the idea, he warned me that *if you fail, you'll be fired*. Despite the risk, I had no sense or expectation of failure. At that moment, I felt a deep connection with the communities and certainty about what needed to be done. The experience was akin to a moment of quantum alignment: I knew we would succeed.

We exceeded expectations, reversing trends in participation and revenue. Through consolidation, collaboration, and empowerment, we transformed two underperforming operations into thriving organizations doing good work in their respective service areas. This experience taught me that anything is possible with the right vision, sufficient willpower, and the right mindset.

My confidence stemmed not from arrogance but from a profound belief in our people and the solution. The previous leadership, though well-intentioned and respected, clung to outdated solutions and because two executives filled the roles for decades, no one contemplated other options. Additionally, the paradigm was that they were low-income communities and could not do any better. So, the corporate office managed two branches with two directors, doubling costs and efforts while failing to see the similarities between the communities or understand the people in them. This operational shift in mindset created two solvent branches led by a single executive director serving the largest population segment in the city with the fewest resources, and together we revitalized the organization. Mission accomplished!

Together we produced a sense of rightness about the work and the capacity to succeed against great odds. The experience is nearly *otherworldly* when perspectives and attitudes change from *can't to can*, from *hopeless* to *hopeful*, and from *impossible* to *possible*. Doing what is inherently the right thing to do against great odds is doing what is inherently kind and generative, and often very dangerous for Self and loved ones. Yet it is fulfilled with a knowing of peace that *purpose* has been achieved.

Workplace and Purpose

When discussing the workplace my perspectives as they are presented here treat the workplace as a gathering place for individuals to achieve a specific purpose as outlined in the founding documents of organizations and implemented (actualized) by the chief executive officer (CEO). They also place individuals at the center of the importance of organizations because, without them, organizations of any kind are nothing more than words contained in individual documents.

Table 5-1 illustrates a few of the defining characteristics of both leadership and management which are distinct functions that are also generally held by the same person in most organizations. All executives embody both leadership and management elements in their job descriptions. Unfortunately, in most cases, colleges do a much better job with teaching management functions than they do teaching leadership.

Leadership is so much more complex because of the complexity of human nature.

Leadership Functions *People Orientation* Quarterly/Annual Focus	Management Functions *Things Orientation* Monthly/Yearly Focus
Establishing Direction	Planning and Budgeting
Aligning People	Organizing and Staffing
Motivating and Inspiring	Controlling and Problem-solving

Table 5-1: Basic Leadership and Management Functions
(*Source: Adapted from Northouse, 2018*)

Those pursuing a master's degree in business administration (MBA) or master's in management (MSM) public or nonprofit administration (MPA or MNA) degree are generally exposed to a single leadership course if that. Therefore, when times are difficult for organizations rather than pulling employees together to problem-solve, managers tend to eliminate what is often described as soft skills training (leadership, diversity, and other programs) and then attack payroll often indiscriminately rather than through deep analysis.

No one is to blame for this because our system of education divides administration functions and leadership functions into separate disciplines. Additionally, the cost of education, shifted curricula towards shorter modules, making it easier for students to complete their degrees faster, and by offering competency-based education (CBE) which is a retooling of the correspondence courses of the nineteenth and twentieth centuries. Reducing the number of courses to speed up the degree-granting process and reducng its costs, limits how much material can be taught, learned, and how quickly.

Without intending any criticism, in my experience management functions are lower-order functions in that they are basic to the survival and ongoing sustainability of an organization through sound business systems and practices. Leadership is a higher-order function in that it is concerned with the human dynamics and behaviors of stakeholders requiring a different sort of skill set to maximize goal behaviors. While often referred to as soft skills, they are actually the more difficult to master because of the complexities of human dynamics.

The proof of this can be found in two organizations with identical management systems. All other things being equal, the differences in performance can be attributed to the effectiveness of applying leadership functions. I demonstrated these dynamics as a turnaround executive leader in resource-poor as well as resource-rich communities. There are innumerable stories in the historical record of how the leader's skills and behaviors made the difference under conditions of facing overwhelming odds against success. Success and failure of an organization lay at the feet of leaders on their hero's journey and how well they engage with their followers to maximize goal behaviors.

Today with the advent of artificial intelligence (AI) students can speed up the time to degree to weeks rather than years offering colleges and universities to remake their curricula to focus on critical thinking projects involving applied theory and computer modeling.

The difference between success and failure in two identical organizations with identical management systems is leadership. People are the most important strength for all organizations regardless of type. Ironically, calling a workforce an *asset* dehumanizes it as something disposable like all assets which we see in mergers, acquisitions, and workforce layoffs and terminations to *right-size* the entity. My perspectives as a successful executive leader have evolved from specializing in turning around and growing failing and underperforming organizations. Through practice and research, I have come to understand unequivocally that the difference between success and failure in two identical organizations with identical management systems is leadership. Furthermore, I firmly believe that people are the most important strength for all organizations, regardless of their type, including family structures organized to serve their members.

Success vs. Failure

Success comes from leaders unleashing the human potential of their employees by removing obstacles, supporting success, taking the blame for failures, and getting out of their way so they can flourish. Failure comes when management prevails and tries to solve what are inherently human performance issues such as during short-lived economic downturns or making wrong assumptions about the impossibility of successful performance by marginalized groups, poorly led teams, or the belief that organizations in economically depressed communities are doomed to failure as *dying dogs*.

Successful organizations are created through intentional design. We are where we are today, by design. We hire and elect people for office and their job is to create the structure within which everything within our borders operates and they are supposed to work on behalf of the citizenry to negotiate on behalf of our country when working with others. What we are finding though, is that more and more, the elected leaders are working on behalf of themselves. Many of them are in office to not only enrich themselves and to satisfy their own ego needs, but they are there to destroy our systems and to corrupt them for political power rather than for the benefit of the people they are supposed to serve.

Japanese and American Management Styles

William Ouchi, in his seminal work Theory Z: How American Management Can Meet the Japanese Challenge (1981), outlined the key differences between Japanese and American management styles. He explained that Japanese management often emphasizes lifetime employment, fostering a strong sense of loyalty and job security among employees. Decision-making is typically a collective process, involving input from employees at all levels, which encourages consensus and buy-in. Employee evaluations and promotions in Japan tend to be gradual, emphasizing long-term performance and loyalty rather than short-term achievements. Japanese firms often rely on implicit control mechanisms, such as shared values and norms, to guide employee behavior, rather than formal, explicit controls. Additionally, Japanese companies show a holistic concern for employees, extending their interest beyond work to encompass personal well-being and family life.

In contrast, American management often engages in short-term employment contracts, with less emphasis on long-term job security. Decision-making tends to be more individualistic, focusing on the authority and responsibility of individual managers. Employee evaluations and promotions in the U.S. are typically more rapid, focusing on individual achievements and short-term results. American companies rely more on explicit control mechanisms, such as formal rules, policies, and procedures, to manage employee behavior. They generally focus more narrowly on work performance, with less attention to employees' personal lives and holistic well-being.

Ouchi's Theory Z proposes a hybrid management approach that combines the best elements of both Japanese and American styles to create a more balanced and effective management system. This approach emphasizes long-term employment, collective decision-making, slow evaluation and promotion, implicit control mechanisms, and holistic concern for employees, aiming to foster greater loyalty, productivity, and overall organizational success.

Valuing Elders

In various cultures, the role and respect accorded to elders diverge significantly. Indigenous cultures, for example, often revere their elders, integrating them fully into the community and valuing their wisdom. In contrast, more individualistic societies might prioritize youth and self-reliance, sometimes relegating their elderly to live among peers in specialized residences. Doing so loses the value elders play in teaching the next generation of young. This division stems from deeply ingrained cultural norms and values that shape whether a society leans towards individualism or collectivism.

The Nature of Work and Organizations

The phrase *nature of the work* in this context is a nuanced term, carrying a dual meaning. It refers to the specific tasks performed by employees, as well as the broader context within which these tasks are carried out to produce goods and services.

As a species, we are confronted with catastrophe on the horizon, with a chance to alter the course of life from a destructive, hate-filled world to one that is kinder, gentler, more productive, and sustainable. The first context refers to the characteristics and attributes that define a job or occupation. It includes the tasks and responsibilities associated with a particular job, the skills and knowledge required to perform those tasks, and the context in which the work is performed. In this context, it represents the structural side of the organization, how the work is organized, and how well it is managed.

The second context embodies the organization's espoused values and norms, and the values and norms in practice representing the interests of the incumbent leader holding the most senior position. In this context, it means the expression of McGregor's (1960), idea of the human side of the enterprise where the interplay of human dynamics forms a culture with rules, norms, ethos (principles, attitudes), and mores (values, standards) that frame the behaviors and interactions of the stakeholders in the organization.

The nature of work has evolved over time, shaped by the changing needs of society, advances in technology, and shifts in the global economy. Work is purpose-specific, often aimed at providing a product or service to customers, supporting a community or organization, or fulfilling personal ambitions. The skills and knowledge required for work vary widely, from manual labor to highly specialized technical expertise. Collaboration and teamwork are central, as individuals work together to achieve common goals. Technology, a key driver of this evolution, continually changes the nature of work and how tasks are performed, making some tasks more efficient and rendering others obsolete. Flexibility is increasingly significant, allowing work to be done remotely or through other non-traditional arrangements. Career progression remains an important aspect for individuals seeking fulfillment and advancement in their work.

The nature of work is complex and multifaceted, and it continues to evolve as society and technology change. This dynamic environment underscores the importance of understanding organizations as social systems.

Organizations as Social Systems

Organizations are a vehicle to produce goods and services more efficiently and effectively than could be done alone or in smaller family units (number of employees). As a construct, the Social Systems Model developed by Getzels and Thelan (1960) depicts organizations not just as structured entities focused on economic or operational goals, but as complex social systems composed of individuals and groups often interdependently interacting with each other. This perspective emphasizes the human, relational, and cultural aspects of organizations.

Therefore, an organization is a structured group of people who come together to achieve specific goals or objectives. These goals can be varied, ranging from business profits to educational, charitable, or social aims. The key characteristics of an organization include:

- **Structure:** Organizations have a defined structure that dictates how activities are coordinated and managed. This structure usually involves a hierarchy of roles and responsibilities.

- **Purpose:** Every organization is founded with a purpose or set of objectives, whether it's to provide services, manufacture products, facilitate learning, or promote social causes.

- **People:** Organizations are made up of individuals and groups who work together. Their interactions, roles, and performance are crucial to the organization's success.

- **Processes and Systems:** To achieve their objectives, organizations establish processes and systems. These can include operational procedures, communication systems, and methodologies for decision-making.

- **Resources:** Organizations require resources to operate. These can include physical resources like buildings and equipment, financial resources, and human resources.

- **External Environment:** Organizations interact with and are influenced by their external environment. This includes market conditions, legal frameworks, competition, and socioeconomic factors.

- **Culture:** Organizations develop their own culture, which is a set of shared values, beliefs, and norms that influence how members of the organization behave.

Organizations can be of various types, including for-profit businesses, non-profit organizations, educational institutions, government agencies, and community groups. Each type has its own specific goals, structures, and ways of operating. Viewing organizations as social systems enables skilled practitioners to control and manipulate parts of the organization to maximize system productivity

Getzels and Thelan (1960) conceptualized organizations as social systems using a classroom as their example which can be extrapolated to whole organizations or smaller or larger ways of organizing. **Figure 5-1** illustrates the component parts of the social system and the relationships of the parts to the whole and to each other. The output of the system produces goal behaviors that are measurable through productivity metrics.

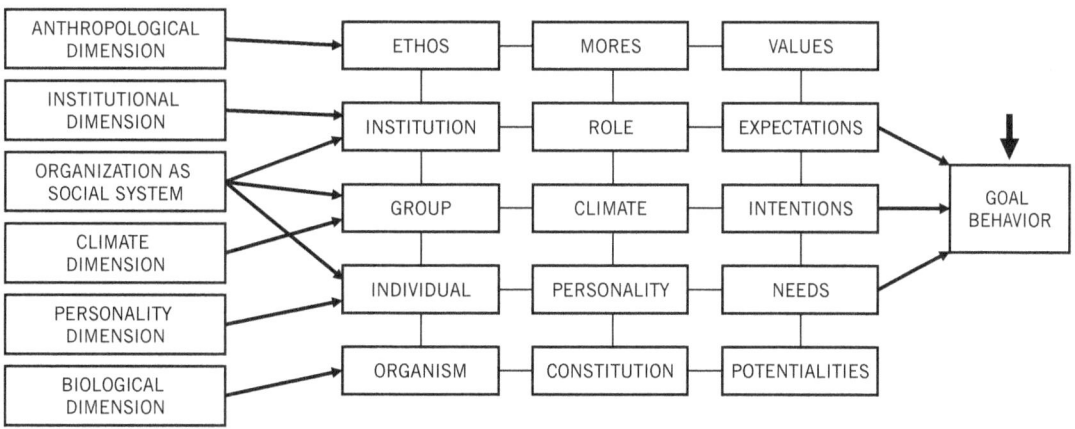

Source: The Classroom as a Unique Social System by Jacob W. Getzels & Herbert Thelan (1960)

Figure 5-1: Organizations as Social Systems

Unfortunately, most metrics and units of production fail to measure the behaviors used to produce those units. If all employees produced the same number and quality of units there wouldn't be a need to measure individual performance. However, we know that there are variations in production both at the individual and group level based on the leadership quotient that gets missed by most organizations because of the focus on output rather than the hidden human costs of production (effectiveness and efficiency). In this view, the purpose of *management* as a science is to monitor and control various aspects of operations.

The various parts (departments, teams, etc.) can be identified, defined, manipulated, observed through the goal behaviors of employees, and differentiated from other organizations through its artifacts. It also provides leaders with the ability to hone in on and adjust the interrelated parts to maximize stakeholder goal behaviors.

Goal Behaviors

In an organizational context, goal behaviors refer to specific actions or patterns of behavior that are aligned with and contribute towards achieving the organization's goals. These behaviors are often defined and encouraged by the organization to ensure that employees' actions are in sync with the organizational objectives. Understanding how to best improve performance behaviors is within the leadership domain as will be discussed further below.

Figure 5-1 illustrates the key aspects of goal behaviors including alignment with organizational objectives, performance measurement, encouragement and reinforcement, cultural fit, adaptability, and role-specific behaviors. Goal behaviors are directly related to an organization's objectives. For instance, in a sales-oriented organization, this might include proactive client engagement or effective lead generation. Organizations measure these behaviors to evaluate employee performance and understand how individual contributions aid in reaching organizational goals.

Encouraging positive goal behaviors is achieved through training, incentives, and recognition programs, with positive reinforcement used to promote and maintain these behaviors. Goal behaviors must align not only with organizational objectives but also with its culture. Behaviors congruent with the organization's values and norms are more likely to be accepted and practiced by employees.

Goal behaviors may evolve as organizational goals change in response to internal or external factors, like market dynamics or organizational restructuring. Skilled leaders monitor goal behaviors for signs of trouble, such as interpersonal and intergroup conflicts (culture assessments), system flaws (operations assessments), and employee sentiment (workplace climate assessments). Different roles within an organization have different goal behaviors. For example, goal behaviors for a manager might include effective team leadership and decision-making, while for a technician, it might involve adhering to safety protocols and efficiency standards.

Ultimately, the effectiveness of goal behaviors is judged by how well they contribute to the success and sustainability of the organization. Leaders, educators, and organizational effectiveness consultants play crucial roles in influencing goal behaviors that are key to enhancing organizational performance and effectiveness. Shaping belief systems, as Jane Elliott did in her classroom experiments and adult training protocols, demonstrates how a leader influences the goal behaviors of followers.

A Word About Leadership and Goal Behaviors

Leadership has existed since the first two people interacted and one influenced the other to act. This dynamic interplay of influence, decision-making, and adaptation is at the heart of what makes leadership both an enduring and evolving field of study.

Leadership is both a role and behavior and the behaviors shape the goal behaviors used by members in their groups. Leadership is unique to each group, defined by position titles, job descriptions, authority, and an individual's capacity to influence key organizational decisions, regardless of their title. This sphere of influence can be illustrated by the example of a mail room clerk who is the daughter of the CEO, as her connections will likely result in differential treatment compared to her peers. This is known as the *Halo Effect*.

The halo effect is a cognitive bias in which our overall impression of a person, brand, or product positively influences our perceptions of their specific traits or qualities. For example, if we perceive someone as likable or attractive, we are more likely to assume they possess other positive characteristics, such as intelligence or competence, even without concrete evidence. Who you know matters in real-world practice, as the influence of others can rub off on you through these relationships.

Leadership is not static; it evolves over time. Leaders may change their style and approach as they gain experience, as the needs of their followers' needs change, or as the external environment shifts. This dynamic nature adds to the complexity of understanding leadership. Leadership is also subjective and often in the eye of the beholder, with different people perceiving the same leadership behavior in various ways, influenced by their cultural background, personal values, and past experiences.

The study of leadership today, as it relates to human behavior in groups, can be traced back to the transformative work of Kurt Lewin in 1939. As the father of social psychology, Lewin revolutionized our understanding of how leadership behavior impacts group dynamics and outcomes. His work continues to inspire and guide our exploration of leadership today.

Kurt Lewin's 1939 study on leadership styles, conducted with colleagues Ronald Lippitt and Ralph K. White, explored the impact of different leadership styles on group behavior. The study examined three distinct leadership styles: autocratic, democratic, and laissez-faire.

They found that under autocratic leadership characteristics, the leader made all decisions unilaterally, dictated tasks and methods, and maintained strict control over the group. In response to those leadership behavioral cues) the group members exhibited high levels of productivity when the leader was present. However, this productivity dropped significantly when the leader was absent. The atmosphere in these groups was tense, and members showed a high level of dependency on the leader. Importantly, there was also more interpersonal aggression between group members and less originality in the group members' contributions.

When looking at the democratic leadership style the leader encouraged group discussion and decision-making, allowing group members to take part in the process. The leader provided guidance and offered suggestions but did not impose decisions. In response, the groups with democratic leaders were highly productive and maintained productivity even in the leader's absence. The atmosphere was more relaxed and friendly, and group members were more cooperative and engaged. Creativity and originality were higher in these groups compared to the autocratic ones. Group members showed greater satisfaction and contributed more freely.

When they examined laissez-faire leadership, the leader provided little to no guidance, allowing group members to make all decisions and work independently. In response, the groups with laissez-faire leaders had the lowest levels of productivity and organization. The lack of direction led to confusion and less cooperation among group members. The atmosphere was often chaotic, and the group's work was generally of lower quality. Members were less satisfied and more frustrated due to the lack of structure and support.

Overall, Lewin, Lippet, and White (1939) demonstrated the significant influence of leadership styles on group dynamics, productivity, and member satisfaction. Democratic leadership was found to be the most effective in promoting a positive group atmosphere, consistent productivity, and member engagement. They also demonstrated how leader behaviors influence follower behaviors, so we have known for nearly a century how one person's behaviors can influence the behavior of followers, therefore, from the leadership perspective everything that impacts human behaviors within an organization can be traced to its point of origin and to attachment points. Using systems analysis approaches to organizational effectiveness design flaws can be traced to leadership practices and behaviors.

Thanks to Lewin, Lippett, and White (1939) we know that leadership is not a static concept; it is both a role and a dynamic behavior. As a behavior, it involves constantly influencing group members' attitudes, beliefs, and actions to motivate them toward achieving common goals. This dynamic process often shifts between designated leaders and followers, especially in groups where participative leadership styles allow followers to emerge as leaders to facilitate task accomplishment. Today, as a result of their work, we can say that the study of leadership is the study of human behavior in groups.

Leadership and Group Dynamics

Leaders play a pivotal role in shaping the goal behaviors of group members as well as guiding their organizations through external changes, such as shifts in market conditions, technological advancements, or regulatory updates. This requires a deep understanding of how groups respond to and manage change, and the ability to adapt leadership styles accordingly. Effective leaders set ethical standards and norms for expected behaviors within their groups, promoting and maintaining ethical behavior, and addressing broader social responsibilities. By doing so, they not only navigate their organizations through change but also foster a culture of integrity, accountability, and goal performance.

Understanding group dynamics is critical for leaders today. Leaders who understand group dynamics can more effectively manage and motivate their teams, anticipate and resolve conflicts, and foster diversity and fairness. They can navigate change, build strong relationships, promote innovation and creativity, communicate effectively, recognize and cultivate the leadership potential in their team members, manage crises, and adapt their leadership style to meet the needs of different situations and team compositions. Understanding group dynamics equips leaders with the skills and insights necessary to manage diverse teams effectively, navigate the complexities of modern organizational life, and lead their teams to success.

Leadership plays a crucial role in shaping group dynamics, such as how individuals interact with each other, form group norms, assume roles, and achieve cohesion. Leaders navigate and manage these dynamics to ensure effective team functioning. This involves complex social interactions, including communication, conflict resolution, and relationship building. Therefore, studying leadership requires a deep understanding of the social psychology principles governing human interactions.

Effective leaders guide decision-making processes within groups, understanding how decisions are made, consensus is reached, and how to facilitate effective and inclusive decision-making. The study of leadership also examines how power, authority, and influence are exercised and perceived within groups, exploring the leader's power and how these dynamics affect group behaviors and attitudes.

Leaders play a pivotal role in shaping and changing organizational culture by initiating, managing, and sustaining change within groups. Their influence is crucial, as emotional intelligence and the management of emotions are essential for high-functioning groups. How leaders handle their own emotions and respond to group members' emotions significantly affects group morale, motivation, and performance.

Leaders are crucial in guiding groups through change. They are responsible for developing their team members, including coaching, mentoring, and creating a learning environment within the group. By understanding how groups respond to and manage change, they can guide teams in adapting to external changes, such as shifts in market conditions, technological advancements, or regulatory changes, which can significantly impact how well the group operates and achieves its mission.

Leadership Is Complex

Leadership is a multifaceted discipline involving the complex interplay of various dimensions and factors. It cannot be fully understood or explained by a single variable or factor. Here are key reasons why leadership is viewed as a multivariate construct: First, leadership is influenced by a range of factors, including personal characteristics such as personality, intelligence, and values; behaviors; the situational context; group dynamics; cultural norms; and the nature of the tasks or goals. This diversity of influencing factors highlights the complexity of leadership.

Effective leadership also varies significantly depending on the context. What works well in one setting, such as a corporate environment, might not be effective in another, such as a non-profit organization or a military unit. Factors like organizational culture, industry norms, and specific environmental challenges play a crucial role in determining effective leadership practices.

Leadership involves the interaction between individual leaders and their environments, including relationships with followers, organizational structures, and external circumstances. Effective leaders must adapt their style and approach to these varying elements, illustrating the importance of the interplay between personal and environmental factors. There are numerous leadership styles and theories, such as transactional, transformational, servant, and autocratic leadership, as well as trait theory, behavioral theory, and contingency theory, among others. Each describes different aspects of leadership, further illustrating the complexity and diversity of the construct.

Tannenbaum and Schmidt (1958) (**Figure 5-2**: *Leadership Behavior Continuum*) illustrate a continuum of leadership behavior that ranges from autocratic self-rule to democratic styles allowing participation in decision-making to varying degrees. It emphasizes the flexibility required for effective leadership, suggesting that leaders should adapt their approach based on various factors, including the situation, the leader's confidence in their team, and the team's maturity and competence.

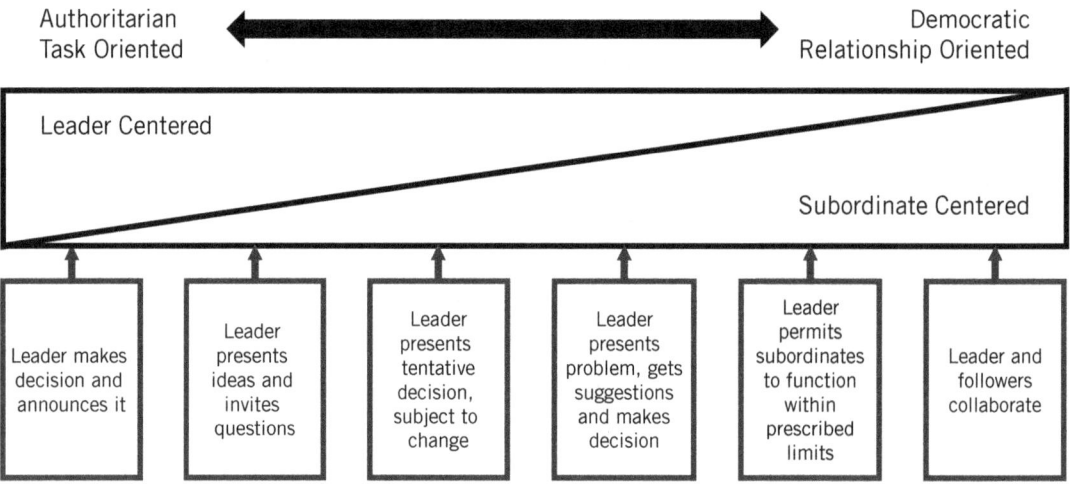

Source: Adapted From Tannenbaum & Schmidt's (1973) Leadership Behavior Continuum

Figure 5-2: *Leadership Behavior Continuum*

The model outlines how leaders can gradually shift from making decisions themselves to allowing their team more autonomy and involvement in decision-making. This transition enhances team development and performance, fostering a more participative and engaged work environment.

Thus, the Tannenbaum and Schmidt model provides a framework for leaders to balance control and delegation, ultimately promoting a dynamic and responsive leadership style to given contexts and situations. What we know from group dynamics is that once a group is formed it takes on an identity of its own as a subgroup within the limits of the larger organizational culture.

Culture Formation

Consider how quickly groups create their own identity by looking at how we organize ourselves when picking teams for a sporting event. Random people are selected from the total pool by the designated captain (leader). Once all the groups are formed, consider how quickly they establish their individual identities. Whether the contestants are shirts or skins, or given different colored jerseys, you see them get together, generally without much direction, and start forming their unique identity. Such behaviors indicate that each newly formed group becomes an in-group to which the members now create and everyone else is in one or more out-groups. Even the best of friends who end up on different teams show their allegiance to their new group rather than to their other affiliations.

Culture formation happens within seconds of forming a group, just through the process of identifying members, and becomes stronger as they create a group name, identity, and over time allegiances. An accounting department has its identity as do the subunits such as payroll, receivables, payables, and auditing. Each has its own function and if led by different supervisors or leads, its own culture based on the leader's style and behaviors.

During my most recent full-time employment, I had three different supervisors because the person who hired me (who was truly awesome) was so good that she kept being pulled to do other college projects. As such, two other supervisors led the program I was in and completely changed the culture of our unit. One was fired summarily, and the other made things so toxic that I had no other choice but to file a complaint with HR.

These examples illustrate how in general terms, followers adapt their styles and behaviors to conform to the leader's behaviors, and when they don't conflict can arise. I was the same person in the same position, working for the same organization, but what changed were the leaders. Under such conditions, my life went from bliss to toxicity, to bliss, to toxicity, to bliss to termination as part of a larger organizational layoff.

Globalization and Technology

In today's interconnected world, globalization and technology add layers of complexity to leadership. Leaders must navigate cross-cultural environments and manage virtual teams, requiring adeptness at handling diverse cultures and technological tools. Due to these factors, leadership is often studied through multiple lenses, integrating insights from psychology, sociology, management, political science, and other disciplines. This multivariate perspective allows for a more comprehensive understanding of what effective leadership entails in various settings and situations.

Studying Leadership

Studying leadership involves exploring theories that explain why certain individuals lead more effectively than others, which is what the military wanted to know at the time Lewin, Lippet, and White (1939) conducted their study. Leadership analysis ranges from trait and behavioral models to complex frameworks like transformational, transactional, and situational leadership. It focuses on the traits, characteristics, and behaviors of leaders, including charisma, intelligence, emotional intelligence, decision-making skills, and ethical standards. Additionally, it examines how leaders communicate and interact with their followers, peers, and superiors, emphasizing skills such as effective communication, conflict resolution, negotiation, and persuasion.

Understanding how leaders fit within and influence organizational structures and cultures is a significant part of leadership studies. This includes how leaders can foster positive cultures, manage change, and drive organizational effectiveness. The study of leadership also involves understanding the context in which leadership occurs, including the impact of the external environment, organizational challenges, and specific situational factors on leadership effectiveness.

Leadership studies encompass psychological and sociological aspects, including group behavior, motivation theories, power dynamics, and social influence processes. It includes learning how leadership skills and qualities can be developed and nurtured through coaching, mentoring, training programs, and self-development strategies. Ethical challenges and responsibilities of leaders, and how leadership practices vary across different cultures and global contexts, are also crucial areas of study. Historical perspectives and the impact of technology on leadership practices are examined, including virtual teams, digital communication, and social media.

In essence, studying leadership involves understanding what makes an effective leader and comprehending the broader social, organizational, and psychological contexts in which leadership occurs. It's an interdisciplinary field that draws from various areas of knowledge to build a comprehensive understanding of how to effectively guide and influence others.

Leadership is fundamentally about influencing, guiding, and organizing individuals within group contexts. It involves influencing the attitudes, beliefs, and behaviors of group members and motivating them towards achieving common goals, which is key to understanding human behavior in a group setting. Leadership plays a crucial role in shaping group dynamics, including how individuals interact, the formation of group norms, the roles individuals play, and achieving group cohesion.

Leadership involves complex social interactions, including communication, conflict resolution, and relationship building. Understanding social psychology principles that govern human interactions in a group is essential for studying leadership. Leaders guide decision-making processes within groups, understanding how groups make decisions, reach consensus, and facilitate effective and inclusive decision-making processes.

The study of leadership examines how power, authority, and influence are exercised and perceived within groups. It explores the sources of a leader's power and how these power dynamics affect group behavior and attitudes. Leaders play a key role in shaping and changing organizational culture, initiating, managing, and sustaining change within groups, which is fundamental to studying leadership and human behavior in organizations.

Emotional Intelligence

Emotional intelligence and the management of emotions are crucial in leadership. How leaders handle their own emotions and respond to the emotions of group members significantly affects group morale, motivation, and performance. Leaders are often responsible for the development and learning of their team members, including coaching, mentoring, and creating a learning environment within the group.

The Transformative Power of Leadership

The transformation of a caterpillar into a butterfly serves as a powerful metaphor for change. Similarly, we encounter numerous opportunities to evolve into better versions of ourselves throughout our lives, especially when faced with significant, unique challenges manifesting from traumatic events. It's a fascinating paradox of life that despite our individual differences, we share common experiences in overcoming adversity.

The Cocktail Party

In the work environment, what is important is that for leaders our perspectives of our workforce must evolve to account for the potential behavioral characteristics of each generation because they frame our perceptions of what motivates members in each generation to perform at optimal levels. However, what evolution looks like matters greatly for those we lead. To illustrate, T.S. Eliot expressed his concerns about the moral and spiritual decline of society in his 1949 works reflecting such concerns in his play The Cocktail Party:

> Half the harm that is done in this world is due to people who want to feel important. They don't mean to do harm—but the harm does not interest them. Or they do not see it, or they justify it because they are absorbed in the endless struggle to think well of themselves.

That is, their focus is on feeling good about themselves, which I acknowledge is an important thing for all of us to do, but it is done to serve the ego in order to feel good rather than to serve humanity which is necessary even when it doesn't make you feel good.

For those in the trenches, we do it because it has to be done rather than passing the buck to someone else. After all, it is inconvenient. For those of us who choose this line of work, we do it yes, to help offset the societal decline and moral responsibility, but more importantly, we do it to reduce suffering that could otherwise be avoided.

Eliot's views speak to the harm done by people who are self-absorbed and fail to recognize the impact of their actions on society which have dire consequences and outcomes. Egocentric leaders, who primarily focus on their own needs, desires, and interests, often lead to several negative outcomes within organizations. Some likely outcomes include:

- **Decreased Employee Morale and Engagement:** When leaders prioritize their own ego over the well-being of their team, employees may feel undervalued, leading to decreased motivation and engagement.

- **Poor Decision-Making:** Egocentric leaders may make decisions based on personal gain or recognition rather than what is best for the organization, leading to suboptimal outcomes.

- **High Turnover Rates:** Employees are more likely to leave an organization where they feel unappreciated or ignored, resulting in high turnover rates and increased recruitment and training costs.

- **Stifled Innovation:** Such leaders may be resistant to new ideas and feedback, stifling creativity and innovation within the team or organization.

- **Toxic Work Environment:** Egocentric leadership can create a culture of competition, mistrust, and conflict, leading to a toxic work environment that hinders collaboration and productivity.

- **Damaged Reputation:** Organizations led by egocentric leaders may suffer from a damaged reputation, both internally among employees and externally with customers, partners, and the public.

- **Ineffective Team Dynamics:** The focus on self-promotion can lead to poor team dynamics, as collaboration and teamwork are undermined by the leader's need to assert dominance and control.

- **Ethical and Compliance Issues:** Egocentric leaders may engage in unethical behavior to achieve personal goals, potentially leading to legal and compliance issues for the organization.

Overall, egocentric leadership tends to undermine trust, collaboration, and long-term success, creating challenges that can be difficult for organizations to overcome. However, we still tend to believe that charisma is a highly desirable trait in our leaders when there is evidence that the most highly productive leaders may very well not be viewed as charismatic; rather leaders who are selfless and humble may serve organizations more effectively, evidenced through the work by Collins (2001/2005).

Motivation: Theory X and Theory Y

To explain motivation Douglas McGregor (1960) in his book, *The Human Side of Enterprise*, introduced Theory X and Theory Y as concepts to describe two contrasting views of workforce motivation and management. McGregor (1960) described Theory X as a pessimistic view of human nature which suggests that employees inherently dislike work and will avoid it if possible. Consequently, managers who subscribe to Theory X believe they must control, coerce, and closely supervise employees to achieve organizational goals. They assume workers prefer to be directed, avoid responsibility, and lack ambition, primarily driven by financial incentives and job security. This approach often results in an authoritarian management style, where strict oversight and punitive measures are common.

In contrast, Theory Y presents an optimistic view of human nature, suggesting that employees are naturally motivated to work and can find satisfaction in their jobs. Managers who embrace Theory Y believe that work can be as natural as play or rest and that people will exercise self-direction and selfcontrol in the pursuit of objectives to which they are committed. They assume employees are capable of creativity, seek responsibility, and can be trusted to work toward the organization's goals without constant supervision. This perspective leads to a more participative and democratic management style, encouraging a supportive work environment where employees are involved in decision-making processes and have opportunities for personal growth and development.

Together, Theory X and Theory Y highlight the importance of management philosophy in shaping organizational behavior and performance, suggesting that the assumptions managers hold about their employees can significantly influence their managerial approach and the workplace environment.

Effective Leadership

Effective leadership requires active participation and engagement with stakeholder groups across the organization. Leadership is a group process. Without at least one other person it simply does not exist, making the idea of self-leadership an oxymoron. Transformational leaders strive to grow their followers and in so doing elevate the interactions between them. Servant leaders strive to serve their followers to help them meet their needs. The transformative leader strives to improve the conditions for their stakeholders by confronting obstacles brought on by the status quo that often work against various stakeholder groups and in the favor of other groups.

Lewin (1939) determined that democratic forms of leadership produce greater productivity and foster cooperation and collaboration than either autocratic or laissez-faire styles. He also found that autocratic styles tended to create a reliance on the leader for direction and produced higher levels of infighting than in either of the other styles. Laissez-faire leadership is generally associated with an absence or little leadership facilitating a culture in which independent subunits have cultures that could vary greatly because of a lack of centralized leadership.

You are only safe from a dictator if you are useful to them. Once that value is gone you become an example of how to not be for others to follow. Autocrats only want what they want. It is about satisfying their appetites for whatever may be their fancy. Kurt Lewin, a pioneer in social psychology, became famous for his leadership styles framework, distinguishing between autocratic, democratic, and laissez-faire styles.

Laissez-faire leadership, for instance, can increase autonomy and satisfaction in self-motivated and highly skilled team members. However, it may lead to a lack of direction, feelings of neglect, decreased motivation, and confusion among team members who require more guidance and feedback. Autocratic leadership provides clear direction and quick decision-making, which can be effective in crisis situations or with inexperienced teams. However, it often leads to reduced team creativity and innovation, decreased morale, higher stress levels, and feelings of resentment or lack of empowerment.

Leadership in Practice

There is an open war between those supporting autocracies and those supporting democracies the outcome of which will determine the extent of human rights globally going forward. Some segments of the population continue to promote revolution, civil war, and the denigration of democracy. As someone who studies leadership behaviors and their impacts on the organizations they lead, I can attest to the fact that there is nothing good about autocratic rule, which means self-rule.

For one eight-year period of my career serving as an executive leader and going through graduate school to obtain my master's and doctoral degrees for part of that period, I was able to witness firsthand what happened to the culture and behaviors of personnel with each change in leadership. The context was a military command. The situation was leading a nonprofit organization with a twenty-five-year history of working collaboratively with the California National Guard.

The first commander exhibited a laissez-faire leadership style. When I approached his troops for materials and facilities I needed, the general response was *whenever I can get to it, come back when I tell*. This made things difficult because my organization was on a very tight schedule for what we needed to do. As I got to know the personnel we talked about life in the Guard and at that duty station.

A couple of years later, the regular garrison command rotation brought the next commander who exhibited transformational leadership characteristics. There was an immediate change in culture. When I asked for things, it was very much *a can-do attitude* attached to *when and where do you need it*. The first time I made a request I was pleasantly surprised to see it and feel it. My relationships became friendships. In fact, one of those friendships saved me from becoming homeless years later. Our conversations shifted to how good life was under the garrison commander and that his PT scores (physical training) were the best in the Command.

My third experience was under an autocratic leader. The culture quickly became cold and distant. When I asked the same people for the things I needed, they were rigid in what needed to happen and when. Anything I needed beyond their structured job description had to have prior command approval. They were no longer able to have social relationships with contractors. The coup degras was that my organization's fees went from $25,000 twice per year to $250,000 which was an impossible threshold to meet and there were no other options of which I was aware in the state for us to move.

To make a longer story shorter, I did everything I could to resolve the issue and finally ended up having to go above his head to resolve the matter. Eventually, he was transferred up the chain to headquarters—a convenient solution I've observed throughout my career. There's an old saying that seems appropriate here, *screw up, go up!*

The observations were so timely for my personal growth and understanding. Most importantly for me, it was the application of theory in practice which is why continuous learning including studying behavioral theory is so important for practitioners to do. The point here is that there is evidence that democratic leadership styles produce greater productivity than autocratic or laissez-faire styles. The idea that autocratic leadership is beneficial is incorrect and satisfies only the autocratic leader and their acolytes for as long as they are useful. Laissez-faire leadership has become identified as the absence of leadership—particularly any sort of effective leadership.

Charismatic Leadership

Charismatic leadership can be powerful and inspiring, but it also comes with a cost. Charismatic leadership, while often inspiring and effective in the short term, carries several significant risks. One key danger is the potential for followers to become overly dependent on the charismatic leader. This dependency can reduce their own initiative and ability to act independently, stifling creativity and critical thinking within the organization. Another issue is the challenge of succession planning. Organizations led by charismatic leaders may struggle to find a suitable replacement when the leader leaves, leading to instability due to the unique influence and personality of the leader being difficult to replicate.

Charismatic leaders are known for their magnetic personalities, exceptional communication skills, and ability to inspire and motivate others. They possess a compelling vision and can articulate it in a way that resonates deeply with their followers. These leaders exude confidence and are often seen as dynamic and passionate, which helps them rally people around their ideas and goals. They are adept at building strong emotional connections, fostering loyalty, and creating a sense of excitement and commitment within their teams.

Charismatic leaders, despite their many strengths, can sometimes face significant downsides. Their strong personal appeal can lead to an over-reliance on their vision and ideas, potentially stifling input and innovation from others. This can create a dependency on the leader, making it challenging for the organization to function effectively in their absence. Additionally, the intense focus on the leader's persona can sometimes result in neglecting practical details and long-term planning, as well as fostering a culture of favoritism for allies or exclusion among those who do not align closely with the leader's vision or style.

Charismatic leaders may also suffer from ego and hubris, becoming overly confident in their abilities. This can result in arrogance and poor decision-making, with risky or unethical choices being made due to the leader's inflated sense of self.

Additionally, there is the risk of manipulation and exploitation, as charismatic leaders may manipulate their followers' emotions and loyalty for personal gain, exploiting their trust and dedication.

A culture of resistance to dissent can also develop under charismatic leadership. These leaders often expect loyalty and admiration, which can discourage dissenting opinions and stifle healthy debate, leading to groupthink. Groupthink is a psychological phenomenon where the desire for harmony and conformity within a group leads to irrational or dysfunctional decision-making. In groupthink, members suppress dissenting opinions, leading to a consensus that may not be well-considered or based on critical analysis.

Furthermore, an organization that focuses too heavily on a single charismatic leader may neglect broader systems and processes, making it less resilient and adaptable to change. This intense focus can create a cult-like atmosphere where the leader's ideas and directives are followed without question, potentially leading to unethical or harmful actions.

Another significant risk is burnout. The intense energy and commitment that charismatic leaders often demand from their followers can lead to burnout, reducing long-term productivity and well-being. While charismatic leaders can drive rapid change and achieve short-term success, they may neglect the long-term health and sustainability of the organization. Lastly, the personal magnetism of charismatic leaders can sometimes overshadow ethical considerations, leading to moral compromises and scandals.

These dangers highlight the importance of balancing charismatic leadership with strong organizational structures, ethical standards, and a culture that encourages diverse perspectives and critical thinking.

Collins: Level 5 Leadership

Jim Collins, in his influential book Good to Great: Why Some Companies Make the Leap . . . and Others Don't (2001), identified key characteristics of what he termed *Level 5 Leadership* based on his research. He introduced the concept of Level 5 Leadership, which combines personal humility with professional will. These leaders are characterized by their modesty and strong resolve to do whatever it takes to achieve greatness for their companies. They often attribute success to their teams and focus more on the organization's success than their own, displaying compelling modesty and avoiding public adulation. Despite their humility, they possess an unwavering resolve and a strong work ethic.

Level 5 leaders prioritize getting the right people on board before deciding on the company's direction, building strong teams first, and then determining strategy. They are unafraid to confront harsh realities and create a culture where the truth can be openly discussed. They help their organizations focus on what they can be the best at, what drives their economic engine, and what they are deeply passionate about, known as the Hedgehog Concept.

These leaders build a culture of discipline, ensuring that disciplined people engage in disciplined thought and action without excessive bureaucracy. They use technology to accelerate momentum rather than as the primary cause of transformation, selecting and leveraging it to support their overall strategy. They understand that great transformations do not happen overnight, and that building momentum is like turning a flywheel—persistent effort and consistent actions eventually lead to a breakthrough.

Collins (2001) utilized his research to highlight that the greatness of a company is largely dependent on the presence of Level 5 leaders who combine humility with fierce resolve, making decisions that prioritize long-term success over short-term gains. For decades, theorists posited the significance of charismatic leaders like Lee Iacocca to achieve organizational missions, when humility has proven to be the most effective style which makes logical sense when you think about it.

Humble Leaders

In contrast to charismatic leaders, humble leaders are characterized by their modesty, self-awareness, and willingness to acknowledge their limitations and mistakes. They prioritize the collective success of their team over personal recognition, often giving credit to others and celebrating their contributions. Humble leaders are excellent listeners who value diverse perspectives and are open to feedback, which fosters a collaborative and inclusive environment. They demonstrate empathy, build strong, trust-based relationships, and lead by example, showing that leadership is about serving others and facilitating their growth and development.

Humble leaders, while fostering collaboration and inclusivity, may sometimes struggle with assertiveness and decision-making. Their tendency to give credit to others and downplay their own contributions can be misinterpreted as a lack of confidence or authority. This can lead to difficulties in situations requiring decisive action or when strong, clear leadership is necessary. Furthermore, their focus on consensus and listening to diverse perspectives, while generally positive, can occasionally result in slower decision-making processes and challenges in navigating conflicts or disagreements within the team.

The Myth of Individualism

The myth of individualism, particularly prevalent in the United States, suggests that success and survival are primarily due to personal effort. I term it a myth because the reality of human existence is far more interconnected. From birth onwards, our survival hinges on the support and cooperation of others. While the ideal of self-sufficiency is appealing, it overlooks the essential fact that living within any group—be it a family or a larger society—involves a set of shared rules that ensure collective survival. Whether in peace or war, at home or work, cooperation forms the backbone of societal endurance.

Additionally, individuals are born into unique circumstances that by definition produce uneven playing fields for each person to navigate based on their genetic and demographic characteristics at birth. Various agencies in the U.S. and other countries track individuals by aggregating them into groups for study. They then track individuals and their groups during their lifetimes by following group socioeconomic and ability characteristics over time by age, gender, race/ethnicity, geographic area, education level, health, and income. These differences, while created to ensure the allocation of resources based on political policies, have become a cudgel used against various groups.

Wisdom allows individuals to apply learned principles in practical ways to navigate life's challenges effectively, anticipate the consequences of actions, and improve personal outcomes and those affecting others. It typically involves a heightened awareness of the socio-emotional dynamics of situations, empathy, and considering both short-term and long-term impacts of decisions. Wisdom is frequently seen as an attribute that mostly improves with age and experience, enriched by ongoing learning and adaptability.

When leaders prioritize their interests over those of their followers, what is often overlooked is the potential for out-group members to make significant contributions to the collective good when given the opportunity. By engaging out-group members and bringing them into decision-making processes, it increases the collective wisdom that the group can apply to any given situation. To maximize such contributions, all group members must be treated fairly by being given opportunities to achieve what interests them. Wisdom teaches us that group members are more likely to succeed when supported in collaborative environments. However, autocratic leaders often thwart this because they perceive it as a threat to their power. In contrast, environments where support can be actively provided are more effective, but this can be hit or miss in organizations led by laissez-faire leaders.

Servant Leadership

Servant leadership tends to increase team morale, cooperation, job satisfaction, and performance by prioritizing the growth and well-being of team members. However, there is a risk of overdependence on the leader for decision-making and the potential for slower decision processes due to the highly democratic nature. Transformative leadership can lead to significant societal changes, empowerment of marginalized groups, and address issues of social justice and equity. However, there is a risk of conflict or resistance as it challenges existing structures and norms and may be seen as too radical or political in certain organizational contexts.

Transformational Leadership

Transformational leadership boosts morale, motivation, and performance by inspiring team members to transcend their self-interests for the good of the group, fostering innovation and creativity. However, it can lead to burnout if demands and expectations are excessively high, and there is potential for neglect of day-to-day operations in pursuit of visionary goals.

Toxic Leadership Environments

Steven M. Walker and Daryl Watkins (2021/2023) provide a comprehensive examination of toxic leadership through their work, focusing on the dynamics within open and closed systems. Their research, presented in *Toxic Leadership: Research and Cases*, offers a nuanced understanding of how these systems impact organizational behavior and culture.

Open Systems

In open systems, toxic leadership is seen as a dynamic and interactive phenomenon influenced by internal and external factors. These systems are characterized by their permeability and responsiveness to the organizational environment, including culture, policies, and external pressures. Open systems allow for feedback from various stakeholders, which can help mitigate toxic behaviors if managed properly. Organizations operating as open systems tend to be more adaptable and capable of recognizing and addressing toxic leadership due to their transparency and effective communication channels.

Closed Systems

Conversely, closed systems are more insular and resistant to change. In these environments, toxic leaders often operate with minimal oversight, allowing their detrimental behaviors to persist unchecked. Closed systems typically lack robust mechanisms for feedback, making it difficult for followers to express concerns or for the organization to recognize toxic behaviors. The rigidity and secrecy inherent in closed systems further exacerbate the problem, hiding the true impact of toxic behaviors on the organization and its members.

Consequences of Toxic Leadership

The consequences of toxic leadership are far-reaching. Lipman-Blumen (2004) concluded that toxic leaders violate basic human rights, mislead followers, subvert systems for personal gain, and exploit the fears and needs of their followers. Such behaviors result in significant negative outcomes for employees, including disparate treatment and mental health issues. Cynthia Mathieu's (2021) research supports these findings, highlighting the damaging effects of toxic leaders who exhibit traits linked to dark personalities such as narcissism, Machiavellianism, and psychopathy. These leaders create environments dominated by fear and manipulation, leading to decreased morale, stifled creativity, and higher turnover. Over time, the negative impacts on morale, innovation, and turnover can erode the organization's culture, reputation, and overall performance, making it difficult to attract and retain top talent.

Addressing Toxic Leadership

Addressing toxic leadership behaviors is crucial for creating a healthier, more productive work environment. By fostering a culture of respect, support, and ethical behavior, organizations can mitigate the harmful effects of toxic leadership and cultivate a more positive and effective workplace. This requires significant intervention, particularly in closed systems, to break down barriers and implement changes that promote accountability and healthy leadership practices. Toxic leaders exist in part, because of toxic colleagues and followers (Edmonds, 2021). Toxic colleagues are co-workers who engage in negative behaviors like spreading rumors, undermining others, taking credit for other people's work, or refusing to cooperate with the team. When toxic colleagues are also supervisors, they can inflict harm to out-group members while treating in-group members preferentially as long as they serve their purposes. Such supervisors can also burn out and overwork by creating a work environment that demands excessive hours or places unrealistic expectations on employees, leading to physical and emotional exhaustion.

If the aim is to create healthier workplace environments, then it is important for individuals and employers alike to be aware of toxic behaviors and work towards fostering positive, healthy, and supportive work environments. If you suspect toxicity in your workplace, it is advisable to seek support from HR, management, or other relevant resources to address the issue appropriately.

Individuals with dark personalities can advance in their careers by developing higher political skills and receiving higher job performance ratings from supervisors via supervisors' assessments of their political skills. Moreover, high honesty-humility can compensate for having a reputation for low political skills, providing an additional pathway for those individuals to succeed in organizations. These dynamics shed light on the complex relationship between dark personalities, political skills, job performance, and career success in organizations. It sheds light on how individuals with dark personalities can navigate the workplace and get ahead, despite the harm they may cause to coworkers and organizations.

Reshaping Culture

Reshaping the culture of an organization is a complex and delicate process that requires thoughtful strategy, consistent action, and clear communication. When a new CEO or leader aims to transform an organization's culture, they can follow several key steps to facilitate this change effectively. The first step is to assess the current culture by understanding its strengths, weaknesses, values, norms, and underlying assumptions. This can be achieved through surveys, interviews, and observation. Identifying the gap between the current culture and the desired one helps in setting clear objectives for the change process.

Leaders have a profound impact on their organizations, and they are the primary factors that influence and shape the behaviors of the rest of the members of their groups. This does not mean they act in isolation from the other members of their groups, in fact there is a symbiotic and dynamic relationship between leaders and followers and their behaviors reflect the personalities of all members of the group. As members interact with each other the leader and their group members form independent and interdependent relationships with each other. LMX Theory explains the exchange process between the leader and each member of their group. However, as Edmonds (2021) illustrates, the followers accept or reject their leader's ways of being. Thus, toxic leaders are able to exist to varying degrees defined by the relationships with members in the group and the amount of support they receive.

Defining Culture

Next, the leader must define the desired culture, clearly articulating the vision for the new culture, including the core values, behaviors, and practices that will support the organization's strategic goals. This vision should be inspiring, realistic, and aligned with the organization's mission and objectives. Effective communication of this vision and the rationale for change to all stakeholders is crucial for gaining buy-in.

This communication should be ongoing throughout the change process, using various platforms and methods to ensure the message is received and understood by everyone in the organization.

Leaders Model Cultural Expectations

Leading by example is essential. As a leader, embodying the values and behaviors of the desired culture sets the tone for the organization and demonstrates a commitment to change. Additionally, involving key influencers within the organization who are respected and have influence over their peers can help spread the desired behaviors and attitudes throughout the organization.

Systems and Processes

Aligning systems and processes to support the new culture is also critical. This may involve reviewing and adjusting the organization's structures, systems, and processes, including hiring practices, performance evaluation criteria, reward systems, and decision-making processes to ensure they reinforce the desired values and behaviors. Providing training and development programs to help employees acquire the skills and mindsets needed to thrive in the new culture is another key step. This could involve workshops, coaching, and other learning opportunities focused on the new values and behaviors.

Cultural Transformation

Cultural transformation is a long-term endeavor that requires patience, persistence, and resilience. By following these steps, a new CEO or leader can effectively guide the organization through the complex process of reshaping its culture, leading to a more aligned, engaged, and effective workforce. Celebrating and reinforcing desired behaviors through recognition and rewards can encourage widespread adoption of the desired changes. Monitoring progress and adjusting strategies based on feedback and the evolving needs of the organization are necessary to ensure the change initiatives have the desired impact.

Communication Channels

Creating channels for open communication and encouraging feedback from all levels of the organization can provide valuable insights to help fine-tune change processes. This is where Autocratic and Laissez-faire leadership styles may undermine any such efforts and, in the end, these leaders may actively sabotage efforts for change to protect their positions.

Changes in Leadership

Changes in leadership are to be expected, and it is best to plan for it in advance. Changes in leadership bring with it changes in group culture and dynamics. The impact of new leadership behaviors on group member behaviors can vary widely, depending on several factors, including the skills of the leader, the nature of the changes being implemented, the size and type of the organization, the existing organizational culture, and how the changes are communicated and reinforced. While some immediate effects might be observed, especially in terms of employee morale and engagement, substantive and lasting change often takes longer.

New Leadership

In the short term (1-3 months), the initial impacts of new leadership behaviors may be noticeable as employees begin to react to changes in leadership style, priorities, and expectations. This period is crucial for setting the tone, where visible leadership actions can quickly influence the group's mood and immediate behaviors. Quick wins, where small but significant improvements are celebrated, can boost morale and support change.

Over the medium term (3-12 months), as new policies, practices, and behaviors are consistently applied and reinforced, more tangible changes in group member behaviors can be expected. During this period, the focus is on embedding the new behaviors into daily routines and practices. Training and development initiatives launched in the early days begin to show results as employees gain the skills and confidence to embrace new ways of working.

Lasting and Meaningful Change

Lasting and meaningful change in group behaviors often takes several years (1-3 years) to fully materialize. Cultural change, in particular, requires time as it involves altering deeply ingrained habits, values, and norms. Over the long-term, with sustained effort and reinforcement, the new leadership behaviors become integrated into the organizational culture, significantly influencing group behaviors and organizational performance.

The pace of change is influenced by several factors, including the clarity and consistency of the vision for change, effective and continuous communication, the introduction of support systems such as coaching and feedback mechanisms, the existing organizational structure, employee engagement and participation in the change process, and external pressures such as market demands and technological changes. While some effects of new leadership behaviors can be seen relatively quickly, substantial and lasting changes in group member behaviors typically unfold over a more extended period. Successful leadership change initiatives are those that are planned, executed, and sustained with patience, persistence, and a clear focus on the long-term vision.

Toxic Behaviors Impact Organizational Culture

Workplace toxicity often creeps into organizations like a hidden blight, gradually eroding the well-being of both employees and the organization itself. It may start subtly, but over time, its harmful effects become undeniable. Autocracy can take root in organizations through a gradual centralization of power, often beginning with a leader who consolidates decision-making authority and limits input from others. This shift may be subtle, arising from a desire for efficiency or control, but over time, it can lead to a culture where dissent is discouraged, and authority is unquestioned. Such environments may initially seem effective, especially in crisis situations, but they often result in decreased employee morale, innovation, and engagement. Recognizing and addressing these patterns early is crucial to maintaining a healthy, participative organizational culture.

The less input a leader allows the more authoritarian their behaviors. A review of history and what we know from modern-day experiments is that the more a leader wants to make decisions without input, the more people will let them do that until it becomes unbearable, and they revolt, particularly as things begin to fall apart, which they eventually will. The American and French Revolutions illustrate such examples. Additionally, because employees are not allowed to offer input, they are unable to contribute to solving or preventing emerging problems ahead of system failures. Further, autocrats are not experts in everything and when failure occurs, they will not take the blame for it happening.

We have plenty of historical examples to make this obvious. Autocratic leaders create a rigid scaler command structure. A *scalar chain of command* refers to the clear and unbroken line of authority that runs from the top of an organization to its lowest levels.

It represents the hierarchy within an organization where each level of employee reports directly to the level above them, and commands and instructions flow downwards through each successive level. This concept is rooted in classical management theory, particularly in the work of Henri Fayol (1916/1949), and emphasizes the importance of an organized structure where communication and decision-making follow a defined path, ensuring that responsibilities and authority are clearly delineated.

The reason the WWII Normandy invasion was so successful is that Hitler was an autocratic decision-maker, so none of his reserve units acted because they did not have Hitler's orders to make such a move. The allies, on the other hand, distributed decision-making as far down as the squad level. Consequently, when the assault became unorganized during the airborne assault, individuals knew the objectives, were able to regroup, made independent small group decisions, and therefore were able to make inroads on their objectives, and the invasion was successful.

Toxicity frequently begins with persistent, demeaning behavior toward individuals or groups. When sexual harassment occurs through unwanted advances or inappropriate comments, it undermines an employee's sense of safety and respect. Verbal abuse and threats amplify the atmosphere of intimidation and fear. Discrimination manifests when people are treated unfairly because of their race, gender, age, sexuality, religion, or other personal characteristics. Systemic biases in hiring, promotions, and evaluations breed exclusion and injustice, reinforcing the idea that merit matters less than who you are. Unethical behavior like dishonesty, theft, and fraud compromises trust in the organization. When safety standards are sacrificed for profit, employee and customer lives are endangered. Manipulative or exploitative behavior for personal gain further damages the organization's moral compass.

Poor leadership and management practices are also culprits. Authoritarian leadership styles quash feedback and creativity, stifling growth and innovation. Negligent management creates chaos and confusion, while favoritism and nepotism reward relationships over merit. A toxic culture thrives on gossip, backstabbing, and office politics. The glorification of overwork and stress leads to widespread burnout, while lack of transparency and communication breeds mistrust and speculation.

Work-life balance issues also contribute to toxicity. Employees often feel they must be constantly available, even during personal time, leading to burnout. An excessive workload without adequate support adds to the pressure, and those who prioritize family or health are penalized. When employees' efforts are ignored or underpaid, frustration builds. Inequitable compensation practices add to this resentment, and limited opportunities for growth leave people feeling stagnant and undervalued.

Unsafe working conditions, both physical and psychological, pose another significant issue. Unsafe environments threaten employees, and psychological hazards like high-pressure deadlines or fear of job loss compound their stress. Ignoring employees' concerns about safety only deepens the problem. Interpersonal conflicts simmer when not addressed, and poor communication leads to misunderstandings and errors. Departments working in silos hamper collaboration and the organization's overall effectiveness.

Lack of autonomy and empowerment is another aspect of workplace toxicity. Micromanagement makes employees feel they have no control over their work, and they are excluded from decision-making processes that affect them directly. Overregulation and strict adherence to procedures stifle innovation. Addressing these forms of toxicity requires a comprehensive, unified effort from leadership, HR, and employees. Clear policies should be implemented, training on respectful behaviors provided, and safe channels for reporting grievances established. Promoting practices that support work-life balance and employee well-being is essential in fostering a culture where respect, inclusivity, and transparency can flourish. Only then can organizations truly transform into positive environments where every individual feels valued and empowered.

My personal experience of working for toxic supervisors for nine years took a toll on me, leading to frequent cycles of trauma as the toxic relationships with my abusers worsened with each negative encounter. Despite my pleas for the behavior to stop, it only accelerated and became more vicious. After more than nine years of abuse, I finally went to HR and was encouraged to file a complaint by the HR representative assigned to my department. I never heard from her again—something that undermines the trust employees have in HR. Two years after being laid off, I still feel the aftereffects of the damage caused by my toxic supervisors.

Examining interpersonal and intergroup dynamics within the workplace reveals how trauma can impact behavior both inside and outside of work. Traumatic events can have a lasting impact, and under certain conditions, behaviors associated with trauma can manifest in the workplace. The Violence Project's research emphasizes that mass shootings are often intended as final acts of violence and can be seen as a form of suicide, whether self-inflicted or carried out by others. This means traditional measures such as increasing armed security or imposing harsher criminal sentences are unlikely to prevent such events. Instead, a more holistic approach that considers the underlying causes of such behaviors, including trauma, is needed to prevent future occurrences of mass violence.

Supervisors, who have the most frequent contact with employees and who are used by employees to gauge the organization's culture and climate, should be made aware of the aftermath of trauma. Trauma can lead to a range of emotional responses such as shock, denial, confusion, anger, sadness, and fear among others. Therefore, supervisors need to understand the role they play in creating group and team dynamics, influencing employee goal behaviors, and facilitating safe or harmful workspaces.

Understanding the nature of workplace trauma involves recognizing the complex and multifaceted ways traumatic experiences can manifest and impact individuals within their employment context. Workplace trauma can arise from specific incidents, ongoing toxic work environments, or structural and systemic issues within the organization or industry. It encompasses both direct experiences of trauma, such as witnessing or being a victim of violence or harassment, and indirect exposure, such as working in high-stress professions where employees are routinely exposed to traumatic situations.

Trauma in the workplace refers to experiences or events within a work environment that cause significant emotional distress or psychological harm. This can result from singular incidents, ongoing toxic dynamics, or exposure to traumatic content or situations as part of the job. Key aspects of workplace trauma include critical incidents, chronic stress, toxic work environments, and vicarious trauma. Critical incidents are sudden and significant events like workplace accidents, violence, or the death of a colleague, leading to acute stress and potentially PTSD. Chronic stress and toxic work environments, including harassment, bullying, or extreme pressure, can lead to cumulative psychological trauma. Vicarious trauma occurs when individuals are exposed to the traumatic experiences of others, common in professions like healthcare, social work, law enforcement, and emergency response. Teachers are now recognized as being among the first to witness or participate in the unfolding of traumatic events in their classrooms and schools.

Understanding and addressing workplace trauma involves a comprehensive approach, recognizing the various sources and manifestations of trauma, and taking proactive measures to create a supportive and healthy work environment.

Laissez-faire Leadership and Organizational Performance

As I've studied leadership over the years, I've concluded that laissez-faire leadership is harmful to organizations. My last employer was led for several years by a president who believed in laissez-faire leadership which allowed for supervisors and deans to behave in ways that they believed as best. On the surface that might be a good thing, but it opens the door for differential treatment of employees yielding some good supervisors, some mediocre supervisors, and some very toxic supervisors, and none of them were held accountable. The two toxic supervisors I worked for were in effect friends of the president when he was college dean. When I ran into an issue with my first toxic supervisor, he called me under the auspices of a student issue but did so with the intent to talk to me about my supervisor.

He brought the conversation around to my supervisor by stating, *I do not see how my two leadership experts are having so many problems.* I responded with, my supervisor is a communications person and not a leadership person. I stopped short of saying that he is not even an effective communicator. He thought for a moment and said, *that is almost insubordination!* I thought to myself, well it is not insubordination, so I did not violate any policies. He said, *well you know what I am saying right?* I said, yes, *if I can't fix the problem with my supervisor, I will not have a job.* He said *that's right, that's my guy and ended the conversation.*

As I thought about what happened, I became upset for several reasons. First, he lied about the reasons for his call. Second, my supervisor never tried to resolve whatever problems might have existed between us. He really couldn't, because he was stealing my work, causing me to do his work like writing the five-year academic program review (APR), evaluating courses, etc., and calling it his own, which in academia is a serious academic integrity violation which should have caused his termination. Third, he never asked me why there were problems which were problematic because he was in my line of authority and should have at least asked me what was going on to hear my side of the story. Fourth, he cut off my ability to seek an intervention because that was his guy, which I knew. After the supervisor was terminated for performance, the dean made me unpromotable and refused to interview me three times for a job I was well suited for and helped to create once he became president.

As noted above about laissez-faire leadership as a style, their failure to lead enables poor performers to exist at the expense of more productive employees. A hands-off leadership style where leaders provide minimal direction and allow members of the team to make decisions and solve problems on their own can produce problems when members of the team are incompetent. My supervisor was narcissistic and incompetent. He talked a good game but could not execute his job responsibilities. His work products were terribly poor as I learned writing the APR when the small work, he submitted was not usable because it was so poorly written.

Ironically, the dean who then became president was also less than competent because if it was not for his dissertation chair, who told me he had to write much of his dissertation or he would not have been able to graduate. That would have been embarrassing for not just the dean, but for the university because he was one of our students. I thought the dissertation was exaggerated until I read something the dean posted on the company's SharePoint site. It was illegible—to be kind. How embarrassing would that have been had he not passed his dissertation phase as a senior leader at the university?

Laissez-faire leadership can result in a variety of undesirable follower behaviors through lack of oversight, ambiguity, and inaction, and enabling or empowering toxic leaders to emerge. These behaviors happen because laissez-faire leaders tend to avoid taking proactive actions, which can lead to a lack of oversight and accountability. This environment can allow toxic behaviors to go unchecked, making it easier for retaliatory actions to occur (Skogstad et al., 2007). The absence of clear guidance and decisive action from leaders can create an environment of uncertainty where employees may feel less secure about reporting issues, fearing that nothing will be done to address their concerns or protect them from retaliation (Eagly, Johannesen-Schmidt, & Van Engen, 2003). Without active leadership intervention, toxic supervisors can gain undue influence and power, enabling them to target subordinates who provide negative feedback without fear of repercussions (Einarsen, Aasland, & Skogstad, 2007). As these behaviors emerge, the group and organizational cultures can shift towards toxic behaviors becoming widespread and causing disparate treatment across groups with different leaders.

In a laissez-faire leadership environment, where policies against retaliation are not strictly enforced, the risk of retaliatory actions increases. Subordinates often perceive that reporting issues will not lead to meaningful change or protection, discouraging them from providing honest feedback. This perception of a lack of support can significantly undermine the organization's efforts to maintain a fair and transparent work culture (Hinkin & Schriesheim, 2008). Retaliation can take various forms. Overt retaliation includes direct punitive actions such as blocking promotions, demotions, unfair performance reviews, or job loss. These actions can occur without proper leadership intervention, further demoralizing employees. Covert retaliation, on the other hand, involves subtle actions like social ostracism, exclusion from decision-making processes, and negative gossip. Such covert actions can thrive in a laissez-faire environment, creating a toxic work culture.

To mitigate these risks, it is crucial to strengthen feedback mechanisms. Implementing and strictly enforcing anonymous feedback processes can protect subordinates. Ensuring that all feedback is reviewed and acted upon by a neutral third party, such as HR, can also mitigate risks. Additionally, establishing and clearly communicating anti-retaliation policies, with strict consequences for violations, can help protect employees. Leadership training is another essential factor; training laissez-faire leaders to recognize the importance of proactive management and accountability can help create a more supportive environment for honest feedback (Bass, 1990).

The potential positive outcomes of these measures are significant. Enhanced employee trust is one such outcome. By implementing protective measures and demonstrating a commitment to addressing issues, organizations can enhance trust in leadership and encourage more open communication. Furthermore, improving organizational culture is another benefit. Addressing the limitations of laissez-faire leadership by promoting more active and supportive management can lead to a healthier organizational culture.

Retaliation in work environments typically arises from perceived injustices or threats to one's status, resources, or well-being. Employees may retaliate when they feel treated unfairly or discriminated against, such as through unjust performance evaluations, favoritism, or biased decision-making processes (Skarlicki & Folger, 1997). Retaliation can also occur as a defensive mechanism to protect one's job, reputation, or resources when perceived threats arise (Aquino, Tripp, & Bies, 2001). Additionally, employees may retaliate in response to aggressive behavior from colleagues or supervisors, including verbal abuse or bullying (Baron & Neuman, 1996). Sometimes, retaliation is driven by a desire for revenge against those perceived to have wronged them, often to restore a sense of balance or justice (Bies & Tripp, 1996).

Certain employees are more likely to engage in retaliation. Those with lower levels of power or status within the organization are more likely to engage in covert forms of retaliation, such as sabotage or withdrawal, due to fear of repercussions (Aquino et al., 2001). This form of retaliation can be seen in changes in employee goal behaviors (e.g., work slowdowns, decreased work quality, increased absenteeism, etc.). Employees under significant stress or experiencing high levels of job dissatisfaction are also more prone to retaliate as a coping mechanism (Fox, Spector, & Miles, 2001). Furthermore, employees who are generally more prone to experiencing negative emotions are more likely to perceive workplace situations as unjust and may retaliate more frequently (Aquino, Lewis, & Bradfield, 1999; Bradfield, 1999).

When a supervisor sponsors or supports a direct report who eventually becomes identified as a toxic supervisor and is subsequently fired for poor performance, several dynamics can interfere with judgment and lead to specific consequences. For example, bias and loyalty can interfere significantly with judgment. The sponsoring supervisor may experience confirmation bias, leading them to overlook or downplay negative feedback about the direct report due to their previous support and loyalty (Bazerman & Moore, 2012). This bias can result in the supervisor ignoring red flags and continuing to support toxic behavior. Additionally, the perceived credibility of the sponsoring supervisor can be questioned by other employees and higher management. Their judgment might be seen as flawed, affecting their reputation and authority within the organization (Tepper, Duffy, & Shaw, 2001). Furthermore, emotional attachment can cloud the supervisor's objectivity. Personal relationships may lead to favoritism, impairing their ability to make impartial decisions (Liden, Wayne, & Sparrow, 2000).

In my case, this occurred with the dean who became president of the university and two of my toxic supervisors. When my first toxic supervisor was summarily terminated for poor performance after a 360-degree performance review of all supervisors in the college, I was targeted as a prime cause and labeled a difficult employee for trying to defend myself. The dean made me unpromotable and then refused to interview me a few years later for a mission-critical initiative that then failed because he chose to allow his feelings towards me, to interfere with his judgment about the requisite leadership for the project and hired two people who failed miserably causing the initiative to fail.

My second toxic leader also retaliated against me. The only question this second toxic leader ever asked me was whether I agreed that his friend (my first toxic supervisor, my abuser, was a nice guy. All of our remaining interactions were caustic and threatening. He even went as far as trying to build a case against me based on false and inaccurate representations of the truth. Luckily, I documented everything sufficiently to finally file a complaint with HR out of survival.

The consequences of such a scenario are significant. One of the primary consequences is the erosion of trust organization wide. Subordinates who reported honestly in the 360 reviews might feel vindicated, but they could also lose trust in the supervisory chain, especially if they perceive that their concerns were initially ignored or dismissed (Dirks & Ferrin, 2002). This erosion of trust can have far-reaching implications for workplace dynamics. Morale and engagement among employees can also be affected. While the firing of the toxic supervisor might lead to a temporary improvement in morale among those who were negatively impacted, there could be lingering concerns. If subordinates believe that the sponsoring supervisor is likely to make similar errors in judgment in the future, their overall engagement and morale might suffer (Robinson, 1996). Therefore, it should be clear that when a supervisor sponsors or supports a direct report who eventually becomes a toxic supervisor and is subsequently fired for poor performance, several dynamics can interfere with judgment and lead to specific consequences for other employees and the organization as a whole.

On a broader scale, the incident can impact the organizational culture. Such an event might prompt a review of the organization's culture and policies regarding leadership development and accountability. Increased scrutiny on how leaders are selected and supported could be a consequence, with the aim of preventing similar situations (Schein, 2010). Finally, the organization might reassess its sponsorship practices. This reevaluation could emphasize the importance of objective performance assessments and the need for sponsors to remain vigilant and unbiased (Ibarra, Carter, & Silva, 2010).

Potential positive outcomes from such incidents include enhanced feedback mechanisms and improved leadership training. The incident might lead to improvements in feedback mechanisms, ensuring that honest feedback from 360-degree reviews is taken more seriously and acted upon promptly (Bracken, Rose, & Church, 2016). Additionally, there could be a push for better training for supervisors on recognizing and dealing with toxic behaviors, helping them make more informed and impartial decisions (Goleman, Boyatzis, & McKee, 2013). Supervisors must be vigilant because subordinates who provide honest feedback in a 360 review can become targets of retaliation, especially under specific circumstances. Bias, emotional attachment, and perceived credibility issues can all contribute to this dynamic, leading to significant consequences for both individuals and the organization as a whole.

In organizations where the feedback process is not truly anonymous, subordinates who provide negative feedback can be easily identified and subsequently targeted by toxic supervisors or their supporters. This lack of anonymity undermines the safety and confidentiality necessary for honest feedback (Brutus, London, & Martineau, 1999). Furthermore, in organizational cultures that tolerate or ignore retaliation, the risk for those who speak up is significantly higher. Such environments often have weak or unenforced policies against retaliation, making it easier for toxic behaviors to persist (Gundlach, Douglas, & Martinko, 2003).

A power imbalance within the organization also plays a critical role. Subordinates who have less job security or lower status are more vulnerable to being targeted, as they are perceived as less capable of defending themselves (Cortina & Magley, 2003). In addition, inadequate leadership support can exacerbate this issue. When higher-level management or HR fails to support employees who report issues, the likelihood of retaliation increases. This lack of support leaves subordinates unprotected and more susceptible to being targeted by the toxic supervisor or their allies (Edmondson, 2003).

Retaliation can take both direct and indirect forms. Direct retaliation involves overt actions such as demotion, job loss, or punitive assignments orchestrated by the toxic supervisor or their supporters.

Indirect retaliation, on the other hand, includes more subtle actions like social ostracism, negative gossip, or exclusion from important meetings and decisions (Aquino, Grover, Bradfield, & Allen, 1999). To mitigate these risks, organizations must implement strong whistleblower protections. Robust policies and a culture that supports transparency are crucial in protecting subordinates from retaliation. Ensuring true anonymity in the feedback process can also help safeguard the identities of those providing critical feedback. Furthermore, leadership accountability is essential. The active involvement of higher management in addressing and mitigating any retaliatory actions can significantly help in safeguarding subordinates (Near & Miceli, 1996).

If the prevailing leadership style in an organization is laissez-faire, specific dynamics can influence how feedback is handled and the potential for retaliation. In such environments, where policies are not strictly enforced and leadership is hands-off, the likelihood of retaliation against subordinates who provide honest feedback may be higher. The absence of proactive management and accountability allows toxic behaviors to flourish, further endangering those who speak up.

Transformative Leadership and Organizational Effectiveness

Transformational and transformative leadership are often used interchangeably, but they are not the same. Transformational leadership focuses on inspiring and developing others—coaching, mentoring, and fostering growth within individuals and teams. Transformative leadership, on the other hand, begins with deep self-reflection and a commitment to challenging systemic inequities. It is rooted in activism and social justice, aiming to create inclusive, equitable, and resilient communities.

As Shields (2010) articulates, transformative leadership starts with questions of justice and democracy, critiques inequitable practices, and addresses both individual and public good. It requires leaders to engage in critical self-reflection and to promote positive social change actively. This approach is not merely a leadership style but a way of life—a continuous process of learning, growth, and commitment to fairness in processes and systems. In essence, while transformational leadership develops individuals, transformative leadership transforms systems. Together, they offer a comprehensive approach to leadership that is both human-centered and justice-driven. This is due to its attachment to critical self-reflection and focus on self-transcendence by actively promoting positive social change and fairness by doing the following:

- Effecting deep and equitable change

- Deconstructing knowledge frameworks that perpetuate inequity and injustice and reconstructing them in equitable ways

- Addressing the inequitable distribution of power

- Emphasizing both private and public (individual and collective) good

- Focusing on fairness through democracy, emancipation, and justice

- Emphasizing interconnectedness, interdependence, and global awareness

- Balancing critique with promise

- Exhibiting moral courage

Transformative leadership is distinguished by its foundation in deep introspection and a commitment to addressing entrenched societal issues that perpetuate harm against marginalized groups. This leadership style is inherently linked to transformative learning, a process that challenges existing assumptions and promotes profound personal and organizational change. It actively critiques inequitable practices and is closely associated with activism and social justice efforts aimed at fostering equity and inclusivity within organizations and communities.

Reflecting on my own journey, I recognize that my experiences of solitude led me to engage in deep self-conversations and cultivate an insatiable appetite for understanding leadership and human behavior within group dynamics. This period of introspection, though challenging, was instrumental in preparing me for my future roles as a thought leader and transformative leader. The responsibilities I shouldered early on, which prevented me from experiencing a carefree childhood, unknowingly served as training for the path I would later embrace.

My silver lining (and superpower) is learning to live as though I've never known trauma enabling me to set the pain of my trauma aside, so I wasn't afraid of living fully. I live my life like a sponge, absorbing as much of life as possible. In so doing I recognize that my sponge will sometimes become too full and spill over the top, and that is okay. Consequently, my life has been filled with great excitement, fun, laughter, and great friends and family members.

My life's work as a transformative leader is about identifying practices that bring harm to various groups and then convincing people that we can do better than we are today if we can learn to think differently. I get this honestly from being born into an activist family heavily involved in the Civil Rights movement mobilizing people for action by teaching them about tyranny and the paths to self-determination. It was also drilled into my head by my football coaches who taught us about leveraging opponents to move them where we wanted them to go by repeating, *control the head and the ass will follow*. What they didn't tell us was that *brutalize the body sufficiently enough, and you can control the head and can do what you want with it.*

As a result, I find myself continuously tackling problems head-on when needed to cut through the fixed mindsets that often accompany deeply held beliefs. Our most deeply held beliefs are often formed throughout childhood so we grow up with an indoctrination towards various perspectives not even recognizing how much of our behaviors result from those belief systems or where they came from.

In 2023, I was traveling for six weeks to spend time with my family. During the trip, a family member had to go to the hospital. My normal response, based on family patterns well-established in childhood, was to drop everything and respond by going to support the family member. It wasn't until I discussed the situation with my therapist that it came to light that I was following a long-held family pattern originating in childhood and my role in the family dynamics that helped make the family unit work. It was a monstrous wake-up call, and I thought I knew everything there was to know about me before the light bulb went on. Such is the value of trained professionals to help us sort out what lives in our memories.

My work as a leadership and organizational effectiveness consultant and educator is to confront the most deeply held belief systems which is an uncomfortable exercise for all of us because of the facades we construct to navigate an external world. The facades make authentic discussions more difficult than they need to otherwise be. But it takes a lot to break through those facades because they evoke strong visceral responses to the emotional triggers attached to and protect the belief system.

In a case example, my consulting partner and I assessed a city recreation department to locate the source of their problems as they were explained to us. We met with the director and then the employees. We brought our findings to the director and explained what we found. We explained to the director that the fingers were pointing at his leadership style and if he did not change his, he would lose his job within a year. We agreed on an intervention strategy and began the training process.

We organized an all-staff meeting and as the meeting began the director introduced the agenda and then abruptly got up and left the meeting without any forewarning that he was not going to participate in the day's activities. Once he left the meeting space the conversations turned to *this is exactly what the problem is*. We met with the staff several times giving them as many tools as we could. When our agreement concluded I reiterated what the likely outcome would be for the director. Within twelve months he lost his job, ending a prolonged career.

If we lived in more compassionate and empathetic communities rather than ones fueled by hatred and division, thanks to the harmful rhetoric of various leaders, we would feel better about life, spend our energy on quality-of-life issues, and be healthier mentally, physically, and spiritually (whatever that means to each of us). It would fundamentally shift our interpersonal and intergroup relationships by paving the way for authentic communications and behaviors to merge. In the example of the recreation director, had he felt safe and had the willingness to show some vulnerability he might have been able to fix the issues and leave a hero with a stronger organization being left behind. Instead, he chose flight over fight. It was a choice to live with it for the rest of his life. I'm not judging the director here only offering an observation.

In contemporary terms, activism refers to efforts aimed at promoting, impeding, directing, or intervening in social, political, economic, or environmental reform with the desire to make changes in society. Activists seek to address issues through various means, including protests, advocacy, grassroots campaigns, and digital mobilization. Modern activism often utilizes social media and digital platforms to gather support, disseminate information quickly, and organize actions across global networks. Contemporary activism is characterized by its focus on inclusivity and diversity, embracing a wide range of causes such as climate change, human rights, social justice, and political accountability. The goal is to effect change and influence policies at local, national, or international levels by mobilizing public opinion and sometimes by directly engaging with decision-making processes.

Activism In An Organizational Context

My favorite professor reminded us throughout my doctoral studies to embrace conflict as a source of good. In an organizational context, activism refers to actions taken by individuals or groups within an organization to promote, advocate, or achieve reforms related to the organization's policies, practices, or culture. This form of activism is often directed towards creating a more equitable and inclusive workplace, improving environmental practices, enhancing transparency and accountability, or supporting social and ethical objectives that align with the broader goals of corporate social responsibility.

Organizational activists might employ various strategies to drive change within a company. One such strategy is advocacy, where they lobby for changes in internal policies or practices, such as promoting diversity and inclusion initiatives or pushing for environmentally sustainable operations. Another approach is campaigning, where activists organize efforts to gather support from other employees or stakeholders on specific issues. Whistleblowing is another tactic, involving the exposure of unethical or illegal activities within the organization to internal or external audiences to enforce accountability. Additionally, activists may engage in dialogue and negotiation, working directly with management or decision-makers to discuss and negotiate changes. Lastly, forming or joining groups is a common strategy, where activists establish or become part of interest groups or committees dedicated to particular causes, such as a sustainability committee or a union.

In modern organizational settings, activism is recognized as a potentially valuable force that can drive improvement, foster innovation, and help organizations align more closely with contemporary societal values and ethical standards. This activism can lead to substantive changes that not only enhance the organization's internal environment but also strengthen its reputation and relationship with external stakeholders.

As a baby boomer I have lived through segregation, experienced civil rights, have made strides in better treatment as time has gone along, and now I am experiencing open and legitimized White Supremacy and segregation again. As an organizational effectiveness practitioner with nearly six decades of experience, I agree. Our organizations are in trouble. Our society is in trouble. More than half of the workforce is being harmed while on the job and we've lost any sense of fairness when it comes to things like pay, promotions, and interpersonal relationships. Suicide rates, domestic violence rates, mass shooting rates, and trauma rates are up.

Poorly led organizations and low-income communities exist by design because leaders generally play it safe and maintain the status quo when disruption and redesign are necessary to solve the problem. Our education systems are failing to educate students. Our healthcare system serves the interests of insurance companies rather than patients. Our prison system is incentivized to retain inmates. Our judicial and policing systems are designed to protect the White population and to suppress the voices of people of color. Our entire system and way of life are largely determined by race, sometimes moderated by socioeconomic status.

Shields (2010/2016) calls out the need for leaders to be activists and to broaden their perspectives of their roles. There is so much energy in organizations lost to the fear of upsetting employees and therefore avoidance behaviors kick in. From my perspective such behaviors stem from a lack of trust and the demonization of individuals and groups. For example, I was called a radical in 2016 while being a member of a sanctioned diversity working group simply because I suggested we call our group a diversity and fairness working group rather than a DEI working group. The president was so afraid of what the working group might report after a climate survey that he delegated writing the report to someone outside of the working group. This act undermined the work of the DEI working group and became the beginning of the end of the working group because it sabotaged group cohesion.

Shields also discusses precursors to become a transformative leader and alludes to critical self-reflection as the precursor vehicle. Shields links to Freire (conscientization—critical consciousness) as does Mezirow who outlines the pathway from critical consciousness to overcoming a disorienting dilemma to adopting new ways of being. Without social justice, there is no fairness, no democracy, and no opportunity for the latest marginalized group that come under attack. We are witnessing books being banned, a refusal to discuss the history of this country, and an unwillingness to equal opportunity for all.

As organizational leaders and leadership theorists, we know the importance of fairness to promote positive goal behaviors in our organizations. Yet in organization after organization, we see leaders taking care of themselves and their *in-groups* and paying lip service to everyone else. As a consequence, those within their *in-groups* benefit and those who are not in those groups, do not benefit which can lead to *just rewards* not being given to out-group members depriving them of near-term earnings opportunities which can mean hundreds of thousands of dollars lost over the course of a career with continued negative impacts over the remaining lifetime because of lost contributions to social security and retirement programs from lower wages and earnings.

In the last several years, the flaws inherent in the U.S. way of life have been revealed, as a gift to the people. While serving the people and helping them improve their circumstances are critical actions needed from our leaders, failing to disrupt the status quo, particularly in today's environment, will be an opportunity lost. The time is now or never.

People like me are forced every day to fight for social justice in an environment that rigs its systems to produce high rates of failure. The existence of people of color cannot be separated from the degree to which social justice exists. We are seeing the same to be true for other marginalized groups. DEI would not have happened without the civil rights movement and the establishment of affirmative action. If we are going to enable employees to maximize their potential and the potential of the organizations, they serve there has to be a redefinition of fairness.

The gutting of affirmative action demonstrates that rights given are rights that can be taken away. I am fighting the same fight for survival and trying to create positive social change as my father, and my son is fighting the same fight as me to live in a world in which fairness exists—it's never-ending and it's exhausting.

Transformative Leadership and Social Justice

Shields (2010/2016) links transformative leadership and social justice and that is precisely what is missing in organizations. However, DEI is about social justice, but it has been deployed largely as lip service to meet the requirements of Affirmative Action. Without it, the progress we've made would not have happened. Now that SCOTUS gutted Affirmative Action you see the results from White backlash. As a baby boomer I have lived through segregation, experienced civil rights, have made strides in better treatment as time has gone along, and now I am experiencing open and legitimized White Supremacy and segregation again. As a person who is frequently targeted because I think differently, often perceived as uppity.

Shields offers the clearest definition of transformative leadership suggesting that when talented people emerge from those communities their paths are often made more difficult, and they are often prevented from advancing altogether. We talk about diversity and fairness, but we have yet to make it part of our DNA. Thus, teaching transformative leadership theory is important because it can help individuals become effective leaders who are committed to creating positive change. Transformative leadership theory emphasizes the importance of social justice and creating positive change in society. By teaching individuals about transformative leadership, we can help develop leaders who are committed to creating a more just and equitable world.

Transformative leadership theory encourages individuals to think critically about power dynamics and social issues. By developing critical thinking skills, individuals can become better equipped to identify and address social injustices. Transformative leadership theory emphasizes the importance of building inclusive communities and valuing diversity. By teaching individuals about transformative leadership, we can help develop leaders who are committed to creating inclusive environments where everyone feels valued and supported. It emphasizes the importance of collaboration and working together towards a common goal. By teaching individuals about transformative leadership, we can help develop leaders who are skilled in building relationships and collaborating with others. Transformative leadership theory can help individuals become more effective leaders by providing them with a framework for creating positive change. By developing a deeper understanding of transformative leadership, individuals can become better equipped to lead organizations and teams toward achieving their goals.

From a leadership perspective teaching transformative leadership theory is important for developing effective leaders who are committed to creating positive change, promoting social justice, and building inclusive communities. By providing individuals with the tools and knowledge to become transformative leaders, we can help create a more just and equitable world.

Life is a Game of Leadership and Followership

There are many definitions of leadership that are beyond the focus of this guide, so only those relevant as foundational material will be offered. When viewing leadership, we have to think about it as a multivariate construct in which many things can be true simultaneously. As an example, leadership as a position means that leaders are part of their groups and hold whatever delegated authority they've been assigned and outlined in their employment documents. The leader is then able to hold onto their power or delegate some of it and therefore empower others to act more independently.

Leadership as a behavior is defined by the words used by the leader, their attitudes, and their actions. How they present themselves matters to the members of their group. Leadership as a process recognizes the interpersonal relationships and behavioral dynamics the leader has with group members, and how the group responds to the tasks it was given.

Leadership is also both contextual and situational. When we look at the context within which the leadership occurs, we are referring to the understanding that effective leadership behaviors and strategies may vary depending on the specific situation or context in which they are applied. This approach to leadership acknowledges that there is no one-size-fits-all solution and that successful leaders adapt their actions, communication styles, and decision-making processes to fit the unique circumstances they face at any given moment.

For example, a leadership style that works well in a fast-paced, innovative startup environment may not be as effective in a more traditional, hierarchical organization. Contextual leadership emphasizes the importance of considering factors such as the organizational culture, the nature of the task or project, the needs and preferences of team members, and external environmental factors when determining the most appropriate approach to leadership.

Contextual vs. Situational Leadership

Ronald Heifetz and Marty Linsky (2002) in their book *Leadership on the Line: Staying Alive through the Dangers of Leading*, highlight the importance of contextual leadership suggesting adaptive leaders work with and within the politics of their situations rather than apart from them, and they embrace the inevitable conflicts that accompany changes as opportunities for learning and growth.

When discussing leadership as *situational* we are referring to a leadership approach that emphasizes the importance of adapting the leadership style and behaviors to fit the specific circumstances or situations at hand. Situational leadership theory, developed by Paul Hersey and Kenneth Blanchard, suggests that effective leaders are those who can assess the needs of their followers or team members and adjust their leadership style accordingly.

In situational leadership, leaders recognize that different situations may require different approaches to leadership. For instance, a directive style of leadership, where the leader provides clear instructions and closely supervises tasks, might be appropriate when team members are inexperienced or when the situation is urgent. On the other hand, a more participative or supportive style, where the leader involves team members in decision-making and provides encouragement and support, may be more effective when team members are experienced and motivated.

The key idea behind situational leadership is that there is no single *best style* of leadership, but rather that the most effective leaders are those who can flexibly adapt their approach to meet the needs of their followers and the demands of the situation. Situational leadership is expressed in families when parents recognize the different personalities, needs, and preferences of their children and modify their behaviors for those circumstances. As Blanchard, Zigarmi, and Zigarmi (1985) clarify in their book *Leadership and the One Minute Manager: Increasing Effectiveness through Situational Leadership*, situational leaders vary their leadership style according to the needs of the person they are leading and the situation at hand.

Campbell's Hero's Journey

Leadership like life is also an inside-out process. To become an effective leader requires courage to understand how personal beliefs and behaviors impact others. It also requires a moral and ethical compass if the aim is the sustainability of relationships and positive social change. The same is true if we want to become the best versions of ourselves within our social group relationships on our way to creating a personally meaningful life.

Each of us is the writer of our own life script, the actor, director, and producer of our story and as such we are both heroes and villains. Whatever fantasies we create for ourselves live in our minds as we interact with all the other actors we encounter. Like a web of overlapping stories, sometimes there are collisions that happen in which some villain brings harm to us, or we do the same to another.

Each of us is the writer, producer, and actor in our personal journeys through life and therefore we are both the heroes and villains in our life story. Joseph Campbell (1949) describes what he called the *Hero's Journey* which is a universal pattern of self-discovery that is identified in myths and stories from around the world, detailed in his book *The Hero with a Thousand Faces*. It describes the typical adventure of a hero who goes on an epic quest, faces challenges, and eventually returns home transformed. Campbell believed this journey reflects the human experience of growing, facing challenges, and transforming, which is why it resonates across cultures and time.

According to Campbell, the hero starts in the ordinary world but receives a call to enter an unknown or magical realm. Initially, the hero may hesitate or refuse the call due to fear or other reasons. The hero meets a mentor who provides advice, training, or magical equipment to help on the journey. The Greek story of Odysseus serves as an exemplar of the hero's journey. The hero leaves the familiar world behind and steps into the unknown. Along the journey the hero faces tests, meets allies, and encounters enemies, learning valuable lessons and skills.

The hero approaches the central crisis of the journey, often facing their greatest challenge in a dangerous place. As part of the ordeal the hero must traverse, the hero confronts death or their deepest fear and experiences a symbolic death or rebirth. After overcoming the ordeal, the hero claims a reward, which could be a treasure, knowledge, or reconciliation.

At some point, the hero decides to return to the ordinary world, possibly facing more challenges on the way back. On the journey home, the hero faces a final test, using everything learned on the journey to undergo a transformation. The journey ends with the hero returning home with the *elixir* or treasure to help improve the ordinary world.

When I look back on my journey, I find this path to be true for myself. I bring my treasure to share with you, so that it may help you along your hero's journey. What this frame of reference (perspective) also offers is a reminder that we are all on our hero's journeys as we come together in our social and work groups. The difficulties I've encountered completing this project, exemplify the heroes' journey in every way, and I believe my eighteen-month journey has changed me substantially and I will never be the same person I was prior to embarking on my journey to complete this project.

All groups are dynamic in that their members grow and evolve, and memberships change over time for various reasons (voluntary or forced departures). This is true in the workplace as well as in our social groups. After more than 25 years of post-doctoral research on attrition and organizational effectiveness, the evidence is clear that much if not most of what is known as avoidable attrition could be greatly reduced simply by changing from management to leadership paradigms, with a focus on improving leader and supervisor behaviors.

Leaders and Systems Thinking

Leadership is interdisciplinary as it draws from psychology, social psychology, sociology, anthropology, systems thinking, and history, to name a few. My work crosses each of these disciplines and draws on the literature from these and other areas to help organizations better align people to maximize their potential for themselves and the organization through increased productivity, maximize resource use, and to formulate strategies and tactics to maximize organizational effectiveness.

Therefore, leaders must be skilled at systems thinking because it enables them to understand and address the complexities of the organizations and environments they navigate. Systems thinking is an approach that sees complex entities as a series of interconnected parts, where each part influences and is influenced by others.

Systems thinking helps leaders develop a holistic understanding of the challenges they face by grasping the big picture, and recognizing how different elements of the organization or situation interrelate. This holistic understanding is crucial for making informed decisions that consider the potential impacts on the entire system, rather than focusing solely on isolated issues.

Strategic planning and problem-solving require understanding the interconnectedness of various components within a system, so leaders can identify leverage points where strategic interventions can lead to significant improvements. Systems thinking facilitates innovative solutions to complex problems by considering the system's dynamics, feedback loops, and potential unintended consequences.

Adaptability and change management cause organizations to operate in dynamic environments that require adaptability. Leaders skilled in systems thinking can better anticipate and respond to changes by understanding how external and internal shifts can affect the system. This ability is vital for guiding organizations through transitions, managing change effectively, and maintaining resilience.

Systems thinking encourages leaders to enhance their communications to more effectively articulate complex ideas and strategies in a way that is accessible and meaningful to various stakeholders. By framing challenges and solutions in the context of the entire system, leaders can foster a shared understanding and alignment within their teams and with external partners. Leaders who employ systems thinking are better positioned to make decisions that ensure the sustainability of their organizations. They can recognize the long-term implications of their actions, balancing short-term gains with the need for enduring success. This approach is particularly important in addressing environmental, social, and economic sustainability challenges.

Systems thinking promotes breaking down silos and encourages a more integrated and cooperative approach to achieving organizational goals. Collaboration and teamwork can encourage a culture of collaboration, as leaders recognize that cross-functional teamwork is essential to address interdependent challenges. By considering the cascading effects of decisions across the system, leaders can better predict and mitigate potential negative outcomes. This foresight helps in preventing problems that might arise from well-intentioned but poorly considered actions.

In essence, systems thinking equips leaders with the tools to navigate complexity, lead change effectively, and ensure the sustainable success of their organizations. It fosters a more nuanced and comprehensive approach to leadership that is increasingly necessary in today's interconnected and rapidly changing world.

Leadership, Culture, and Behavior

The relationship between leadership, cultures, and behavior is deeply interconnected and dynamic. Leadership sets the tone and direction for organizational cultures, which in turn shape the behaviors of individuals within that organization. This interplay is a continuous cycle, where each element influences and reinforces the others.

Effective leadership is pivotal in establishing and nurturing organizational culture. Leaders articulate a vision and set of values that serve as the foundation for the culture.

They model behaviors that align with these values, demonstrating what is acceptable and expected within the organization. For instance, a leader who prioritizes transparency and open communication fosters a culture of trust and openness. Employees observe and emulate these behaviors, creating a cohesive environment where these cultural norms are upheld.

Cultural norms, established by leadership, profoundly impact individual and group behavior. Culture acts as a social glue that binds members of the organization together, guiding their interactions and decision-making processes. In a culture that values innovation and risk-taking, employees are more likely to engage in creative problem-solving and take initiative. Conversely, in a culture that emphasizes hierarchy and conformity, behaviors may be more reserved and cautious.

Behavior, in turn, influences and perpetuates the culture. When individuals consistently exhibit behaviors that align with cultural norms, these norms become more deeply embedded within the organization. This reinforcement creates a feedback loop where culture and behavior are in constant dialogue. For example, when employees consistently collaborate and support each other, a culture of teamwork and mutual respect is strengthened. This culture then encourages new employees to adopt similar behaviors, perpetuating the cycle.

Leadership also plays a critical role in adapting and evolving culture to meet changing circumstances. Effective leaders recognize when cultural shifts are necessary to address new challenges or opportunities. They guide the organization through these transitions, fostering behaviors that support the new cultural direction. This adaptability is crucial for organizational resilience and long-term success.

The impact of leadership on group behaviors cannot be overstated. I used AI to model the behaviors of autocratic, laissez-faire, democratic, and transformative leadership styles over 10-, 25-, 50-, and 100-year framework to see what might occur if all countries were led by individuals with each style with the 100-year results presented below to look at the potential long-term impacts of each style. The fuller analysis is located in Appendices 1 & 2. The results and summaries for the impacts of each style over a 100-year timeframe are offered below as illustrations of the impacts of these four leadership styles.

Culture Defined

Culture is a broad and multifaceted concept that encompasses the values, beliefs, norms, customs, arts, history, and habits of a group of people. It is the shared characteristics that define and distinguish one group from another. Culture can manifest in various forms, from tangible elements like language, cuisine, clothing, and architecture, to intangible aspects such as traditions, social norms, ethical values, and belief systems all of which help to shape behaviors of individuals. Functionally, we are all products of culture, and we contribute to creating the culture within which we exist.

- In a sociological context, culture is the collective programming of the mind that distinguishes the members of one group or category of people from others. It is not innate, but learned and transmitted through socialization, shaping an individual's worldview, behavior, and perceptions.

- In anthropology, culture is seen as a system of knowledge, beliefs, patterns of behavior, artifacts, and institutions that are created, learned, shared, and contested by a group of people. It includes the ways people understand their environment and themselves, and how they communicate, express themselves, and solve problems.

- In organizational studies, culture refers to the shared values, beliefs, and practices within an organization that shape employee behaviors and attitudes. It influences how people interact with each other, make decisions, and perceive their roles and responsibilities within the organization. Thus, for the purposes of creating a shared understanding of culture going forward, culture is defined as a complex and dynamic system that is central to the functioning of social groups, small communities, organizations, or entire societies. It includes collective ways of thinking that make individuals in different groups different from each other and that can be observed through differences in beliefs, patterns of behavior, artifacts, and institutions that are created, learned, and shared that influence how people interact with each other, make decisions, and perceive their roles and responsibilities within the organization. It is through changing the way people think about their culture through deep inward dives to explore themselves as the focus to solving their problems rather than using superficial excuses for blaming strangers as a convenient scapegoat. How we behave is a function of our culture and our culture is something that we simultaneously experience and help create.

Schein (2010) identified four types of cultures: macro cultures, Organizational Cultures, Subcultures, and Microcultures. See **Table 5-2: Four Types of Cultures** (Adopted from Schein, 2010). Operationally speaking, from a leadership perspective each of these independent cultures act interdependently and with each other to create dynamics impacting behaviors throughout the organization. Today we have plenty of examples of how ethnic and religious groups profoundly impact our political and legal systems both increasing as well as decreasing civil rights and liberties in the United States and elsewhere.

Macrocultures	Organizational Cultures	Subcultures	Microcultures
• Nations • Ethnic Groups • Cultural Groups • Religious Groups • Occupations that exist globally	• Private • Public • For-Profit • Nonprofit/NGOs • Government Organizations	• Occupational groups within organizations • Governance • Executive Leadership • Direct Service Teams • Finance/Fund Raising • Accounting/Record Keeping • Marketing/Sales • Maintenance/IT	• Microsystems within or outside organizations • Employee Resource Groups (ERGs) / Unions • Social Interest Networks • Regulatory Bodies • Lobbyists • Donors

Table 5-2: Four Types of Cultures (*Adopted from Schein, 2010*)

Culture Matters

In 1963, after a century of legalized segregation supported by Jim Crow laws, the pendulum shifted, granting previously disenfranchised groups access to rights and opportunities. However, today, there is a reversal as efforts are made to protect the power of a particular segment of the population. The Justices of the Supreme Court must ensure impartial decision-making to prevent deeper divisions between groups. Their vision and outcome must foster understanding and collaboration between groups to benefit society.

Coexistence without meaningful interaction can lead to limited empathy, misunderstandings, and segregation, reinforcing stereotypes and biases. This prevents the full potential of diverse groups from being realized, as collaboration is necessary for innovation and progress. Historically, this lack of deeper connection has been a problem in the U.S., where racial segregation and white supremacy have shaped societal structures.

Millions of U.S. citizens who benefited from affirmative action policies think that the Supreme Court Justices who voted to overturn the affirmative action laws were influenced by personal bias. The actions of powerful people in Washington, D.C. demonstrate how personal beliefs can shape laws that affect entire populations. Leaders who serve the public must prioritize ethical decision-making over personal agendas, yet time and again, we see leaders advancing their own interests at the expense of societal progress.

Impact of Organizational Culture

We are witnessing tensions between groups with fundamentally different ways of thinking, feeling, believing, and behaving. As leaders, we must find ways to heal these rifts and unite diverse groups, despite opposition from self-interested parties who benefit from division. These self-interested groups often find division more beneficial for themselves and their allies, until, inevitably, those allies turn into adversaries. Such outcomes are typical of individualistic versus collective behaviors.

In its most rudimentary form culture shapes and influences individual behaviors. In practice, macro cultures shape organizational cultures which in turn shape subcultures, including any dynamic microcultures that emerge in response to organizational or environmental concerns such as employee resource groups (ERGs). What creates the potential for inter-cultural and cross-cultural conflicts is that we each exist within multiple cultural levels simultaneously. For example, the nation we most closely align ourselves with may be the one of our births which carries with it particular advantages and stigmas. I've spoken with dual national Canadian-US passport holders who have told me of differential treatment based on which passport they traveled under. With the national borders themselves differential treatment occurs based on other cultural artifacts such as race/ethnicity, religious preferences, etc. The legal structure of the organization itself dictates operating parameters and applicable laws that shape employee behaviors (nonprofits behave differently than for-profit organizations).

In organizations behaviors are a function of leadership (the leader's styles and behaviors). Organizational effectiveness experts such as me know that performance in most organizations can be improved through changes in culture (how people behave in organizations) and climate (how people *feel* in their organizations), both of which impact employee goal behaviors and performance. Gallup CEO Jon Clifton reported:

> . . . people's mental well-being has been worsening. In the last 10 years, the number of people expressing stress, sadness, anxiety, anger, or worry has been on the rise, reaching its highest levels since the Gallup surveys began . . . . Most employees (77%) aren't engaged, accounting for $8.9 trillion in lost productivity worldwide.

To understand the impact of organizational culture, it's essential to recognize that it primarily stems from individuals whose behaviors are shaped by and reflect both the internal dynamics of the organization and their external life dynamics and events. Each person's unique genetic predispositions, precursors, and resulting thought processes (psychodynamics) crucially influence how they react (behave) in the varying situations they encounter daily. Consequently, when they go to work, the culture of their organization becomes a unique tapestry of interactions, woven from the diverse characteristics of its individual members.

Moreover, organizational culture is not static but a dynamic, evolving entity. As the people within the organization and external circumstances change, so too does the culture, continuously reshaped by these shifting dynamics. We can see these dynamics play out most clearly through the observable dynamics we witness through our political systems as well as our favorite sports teams. Tuckman (1960) discusses how a single individual can bring about significant changes in a group and therefore suggests the group is in a dynamic process of continuous evolution for the length of its existence. Logically, therefore, if the group does not continuously evolve to meet the new conditions confronting the group it risks failure and demise. This speaks to the need for creating organizational systems and structures that can ensure sustainability including protecting the growth and development of individual employees, maximizing goal behaviors, and facilitating innovation.

Furthermore, the concept of culture within an organization is not a monolithic construct but varies significantly among individuals. That is, everyone holds their own interpretation (mental model) of what culture means, influenced by their involvement in various groups within the organization, yet not entirely synonymous with any of them. For example, employees in different departments may have very different experiences across a single organization based on their employee makeup, status in the organization, and how they perceive their supervisor if the organization is large enough where multiple supervisors exist because supervisors become the face of the organization from the employee's perspective.

This results in a complex mosaic of subcultures within the organization, sometimes conflicting, sometimes merging, but each vying to influence the organization's path. Today, as groups that have been harmed continue to retain their rights, they are clashing with groups who want to take them away. Members of each of those groups may encounter the other in the workplace. As efforts to shut down diversity programs pick up speed other mechanisms for ensuring fairness, must be developed or the pressure to revolt could become problematic. We can see that with the public threats of violence coming from individuals and groups who want what they want regardless of what others think or feel.

This dynamic mirrors the broader societal context, where organizations can be viewed as microcosms of society. It's within these organizational microcosms that people learn to live and work together productively, benefiting not only the organization (akin to society) but also each of its participating members (Schein, 1990).

Culture Shapes Workplace and Group Behaviors

Culture is a socially constructed concept that helps to explain why various groups, organizations, and societies are similar and different. It illustrates the interactions of the people within a group identifiable by their behaviors individually and collectively.

Schein (1990) suggests that first, culture comes from people who are influenced by the organization and events outside the organization. Therefore, a person's predispositions and thought processes (their precursors) coming into the organization will influence how they will react in different situations once they become an employee. The culture that is formed in an organization will be influenced by these individual variations and therefore will be unique to the organizations any given set of individuals join. While Pepsi and Coke may have similar tasting products (differentiated by discerning tastes), their real differences are in the cultures and climates and what they mean for the people producing their respective products.

Second, culture is something that is not absolute, but constantly evolves as events and people change in the organization. This is readily experienced as new CEOs and supervisors replace old ones. The CEOs' impacts are felt throughout the organization as new visions emerge while the supervisor's impacts create differential experiences for their respective employees who report to them. These differential experiences are easily identified through 360-degree performance, culture, and climate assessments and when done correctly can improve retention. It is critically important to note that an employee's perspective on the work experiences largely results from the experiences they have with their supervisors. Employees see their organizations through the experiences of their immediate supervisors. This is why two employees who love their organization's purposes but are supervised by two different supervisors can experience the organization itself differently.

Third, culture cannot be viewed as a monolithic construct because everyone in the organization has his or her own definition of culture and behaviors as a result of the culture within which they were raised and live.

This definition is similar to but not the same as the various groups of which he or she is a part. There are many subcultures in the organization that conflict, combine, and coexist. Each influences the other and tries to influence the direction of the organization. We can also see this play out in the larger context of society which illustrates organizations functioning as microcosms of societies. It is the one place where people can learn to live together in a way that is productive for the organization (society) and each of the members who are participating in the organization (Schneider, 1990, pp. 323-324).

Balancing and Organizational Values

The extent to which individuals join organizations because their personal values align with those of the organization is significant and has been a focus of research in organizational behavior and human resource management. The alignment of personal and organizational values impacts job satisfaction, engagement, and retention for the following reasons:

- **Attraction to Similar Values:** People are naturally attracted to organizations whose values resonate with their own. This is based on the principle of the attraction-selection-integration-attrition (ASIA) model, which suggests that individuals are drawn to organizations with similar values, and over time, those who fit well with the organization's culture tend to stay, while others leave.

- **Job Satisfaction and Engagement:** Employees who find that their personal values align with their organization's values often report higher job satisfaction and engagement. They are more motivated and feel a stronger connection to their work and the organization.

- **Retention and Turnover:** The congruence between personal and organizational values is a key factor in employee retention. Employees are more likely to stay with an organization when they perceive a good fit between their own values and those of the organization. Conversely, a mismatch can lead to higher turnover rates.

- **Employer Branding and Recruitment:** Organizations that clearly communicate their values attract candidates who share those values. This is an essential aspect of employer branding, which plays a significant role in attracting potential employees.

- **Performance and Productivity:** Employees whose values align with their organizations are often more productive and show higher performance levels. They are more likely to go above and beyond in their roles because they believe in what they are doing.

- **Cultural Fit and Adaptation:** While initial attraction may be due to shared values, the extent of actual alignment becomes clearer once an individual is part of the organization. Adaptation to the organizational culture and the degree of true values alignment can affect an employee's experience and decision to remain long-term.

- **Changing Dynamics:** It's important to note that both individual and organizational values can evolve over time. This dynamic aspect means that alignment may change, impacting the employee-employer relationship.

Consequently, the alignment of personal and organizational values plays a crucial role in why people choose to join and stay with an organization. It affects their job satisfaction, engagement, performance, and loyalty, which in turn impacts the success and stability of the organization.

Shaping Behaviors

Culture also profoundly shapes behaviors by setting the norms, values, and expectations that guide how individuals act and interact within a group, organization, and society. Consider how each of the cultural characteristics listed below play out in families, social groups, organizations, and societies. Here are a few key takeaways from culture influences behavior:

- **Social Norms:** Culture establishes the rules or expectations for behavior that are considered acceptable in a society. These norms influence everything from basic interactions, like greetings and manners, to more complex social behaviors, such as how people dress or conduct themselves in public.

- **Values:** Cultural values dictate what is considered important and worthy of respect within a community. These values can affect behaviors such as work ethic, priorities in life (such as family, education, or career), and how resources are used or conserved.

- **Communication Styles:** Culture determines the way people communicate with each other, including language, tone, gestures, and the degree of formality. These communication patterns can influence professional and personal interactions, potentially leading to misunderstandings if cultural differences are not understood.

- **Role Expectations:** Different cultures have different expectations for roles based on gender, age, social status, and more. These roles can dictate behaviors in family settings, workplaces, and wider social contexts.

- **Conflict Resolution:** Cultural background influences how people handle conflicts, whether through direct confrontation, mediation, or avoidance. Understanding these cultural differences is crucial in global interactions to avoid and manage potential conflicts effectively.

- **Perception of Time:** Culture also affects how time is perceived and valued. Some cultures emphasize punctuality and future planning, while others may focus more on the present or the relational aspects of time, such as spending it with family or community.

- **Adaptation and Integration:** As people move and migrate, cultures blend and adapt, influencing behaviors in diverse environments. This can lead to new cultural norms and behaviors that are a mix of various influences.

These cultural influences can provide leaders with ways to enhance communication, reduce conflict, and promote better cooperation and understanding in diverse environments.

Wrongful Terminations

The Armstrong Law Group (2017) found that 250,000 workers are wrongfully terminated annually impacting the lives of those individuals and their families—often with devastating long-lived traumatic impacts that last for decades. When cultures clash and someone is wrongfully terminated from employment, the aftermath can be profound and multifaceted, affecting the individual both personally and professionally. The most immediate concern is often financial. The sudden loss of income can make it difficult to meet everyday expenses such as mortgage or rent, utility bills, and groceries. This financial strain can extend to long-term financial stability, especially if the individual has to dip into savings or retirement funds. The stress of losing health insurance and other benefits can also add to the financial burden, making it harder to cope with unforeseen medical expenses or emergencies.

The emotional and psychological effects of wrongful termination can be significant. The sense of injustice and betrayal can lead to intense stress, anxiety, and depression. The emotional impact can include a decreased sense of self-worth and confidence, leading to a loss of identity, especially if the job was closely tied to the person's self-concept. The stigma associated with being terminated, even wrongfully, can further exacerbate these feelings.

Professionally, a wrongful termination can disrupt career trajectories. It creates a gap in the resume that needs to be explained to future employers, which can be awkward and challenging. The circumstances surrounding the dismissal might also lead to questions and skepticism from potential employers. In some cases, the individual may feel compelled to accept positions below their qualification level to re-enter the workforce, which can stall career progress.

Many individuals choose to pursue legal action against wrongful termination. This can be a complex, stressful, and costly process that involves hiring attorneys, gathering evidence, and enduring lengthy legal proceedings. Successful legal action can result in compensation for lost wages, benefits, and possibly punitive damages. However, the process itself can be emotionally draining and time-consuming.

Being wrongfully terminated can tarnish a person's professional reputation. News of the termination can spread within the industry, creating a negative perception that can impact future job prospects. This reputational damage can be particularly harmful in close-knit industries where word-of-mouth and personal references play significant roles in hiring decisions.

The stress and uncertainty of wrongful termination can strain personal relationships. Financial difficulties and emotional turmoil can lead to tension within families and among friends. The support network may also feel the strain as they try to provide emotional and possibly financial support.

The prolonged stress from wrongful termination can lead to various health issues, including cardiovascular problems, hypertension, and a weakened immune system. Mental health can also suffer, with increased risks of anxiety disorders, depression, and even substance abuse as individuals may turn to unhealthy coping mechanisms.

Being removed from a job often means losing access to professional networks, which are crucial for finding new opportunities. Networking events, professional associations, and informal connections within the industry can become less accessible, making the job search more isolating and challenging.

The experience of wrongful termination can affect future job searches, both in terms of the individual's confidence and how potential employers perceive the termination. The individual may feel less confident in interviews and networking situations, and potential employers might have reservations about hiring someone who has been terminated, even if wrongfully.

Sometimes, wrongful termination forces individuals to reconsider their career paths. This can lead to pursuing different opportunities, further education, or even a complete career change. While this can be a positive outcome in the long term, the transition period can be fraught with uncertainty and additional stress. Wrongful terminations can have a devastating impact on an individual's financial stability, emotional well-being, professional reputation, and personal relationships. The process of recovery often involves significant legal, financial, and personal challenges. Understanding these potential consequences can help organizations develop fairer policies and provide better support for employees who find themselves in such difficult situations.

Tribalism, In-groups, and Out-groups

Tribalism is the behavior and attitudes that stem from strong loyalty to one's own tribe or social group. It often involves a sense of identity and belonging derived from being part of a group, leading to strong in-group cohesion and sometimes to the exclusion or hostility towards those not in the group.

When speaking of tribalism, we are technically speaking about in-groups and out-groups. In-groups are a group with which an individual identifies as a member. This could be based on various characteristics like social groups, families, race, nationality, gender, religion, hobbies, professions, or any other defining trait. People tend to have a psychological attachment to their in-group, and they often view members of their in-group in a more positive light. This favorable bias toward the in-group can manifest in greater trust, cooperation, and empathy toward fellow in-group members.

The concepts of in-groups and out-groups are central to understanding various social phenomena such as group dynamics, prejudice, discrimination, and intergroup conflict. These biases are not necessarily fixed and can change depending on context and individual experiences. This can be observed in the behaviors of members who break away from gangs, White Supremacy groups, cults, changing religious affiliations, etc. Understanding and being aware of our own in-group biases is crucial for promoting more inclusive and harmonious interpersonal and intergroup relationships. It is through cohesion that strength exists rather than through division which only weakens whatever is being divided.

Conversely, out-groups are any group that an individual does not identify as belonging to. People often perceive out-group members as being more different from themselves than they actually are. This can lead to out-group homogeneity bias, where individuals see out-group members as being more similar to each other than they are to members in their in-group. Accompanying such perspectives can be negative biases against out-groups, which might manifest as distrust, discrimination, or even hostility.

Using race as an example, the vitriol existing between races may be momentarily set aside simply by donning a piece of clothing or secret handshake or code words that illustrate a political or other affiliation between two people. As a result, a person belonging to a group normally vilified by one group might be accepted by that same group when that same person shows allegiance to the group by wearing symbols of affiliation such as a hat or other paraphernalia or behaves in a manner that shows allegiance to the group. Ironically, when the paraphernalia is removed that individual may again be targeted.

It is my contention that here is where the work must be done because culture clashes are the source of much of the observable conflict. It is the intergroup relationship between one culture and other cultures in any type of group that must be the focus if we are ever going to see peace. This means doing everything possible to foster open discussions about differences between groups rather than shutting such discussions down. Anyone working to shut such conversations down is trying to assert their position as dominant at the exclusion of other ways of being that are equally legitimate. This is unacceptable because in the long term, it leads to violent conflict as we see in the 110 shooting conflicts globally and as the backdrop for many of the mass shootings in the United States and elsewhere observed today.

In our exploration of workplace environments, we encounter several significant challenges: trauma, toxicity, and tribalism and how they interact to create cultures of inclusion or exclusion in our workplaces and social groups. These elements create barriers to a healthy, thriving organizational culture and can severely hinder both individual well-being and collective productivity.

What would happen to your perspective of a senior leader introducing themselves as the department head for your part of the organization and when they do so, they identify themselves as a Redneck and then mock the way a member of the department spoke because he was foreign-born? What if that person treated selected groups differently from others? A person identifying themselves in this way identifies their primary tribal group affiliation and puts everyone in their out-groups on notice that they are not respected for their uniqueness. It also demonstrates a substantial lack of awareness or sensitivity to life in the 21st century.

Our tribalism in the United States is and has always been openly visible. We cannot go around saying that the United States is not a racist country when the behaviors of large swaths of the population, maybe as much as 40% of the population, are actively working to undermine progress towards a multicultural society; and almost all of the White population benefits from the institutionalized racist structures built into the fabric of this country through its laws and practices going back to its founding.

Today, there are continued calls for the United States to be identified as a White Christian nation so how can anyone pretend that it's not a country steeped in its past? My parents fought to resolve the race-based question of whether Whites are superior to all groups, a long-held belief system by many in that segment of the population. They also fought to undermine the socioeconomic class warfare waged against the poor and marginalized segments of the population in the United States. Ample evidence illustrates that in the wealthiest country on earth, the wealth gap has been increasing with disparate negative health and other outcomes for the rest of the population. Today, sixty years after my father's death, I am left to wage the same struggles as my father.

If it looks like a duck, acts like a duck, and quacks like a duck, then it is a duck. Like the addict, if we can admit that we have a problem then we can begin to resolve and fix it. But it begins with the admission of a problem and understanding how our propensity for tribalism interferes with our ability to move towards a multicultural society in which all members of the society have equal opportunities to maximize their individual potential.

The person or group that is doing the harm does not get to determine when harm has been done. That right is in the purview of those being harmed. A person who owns a weapon cannot waive it in the face of someone else and then say that person wasn't being harmed. What if that incident triggered the target because the person had personal experiences with friends and loved ones being murdered by that same sort of weapon? Where do one person's rights end and another's begin in a civil society? I suggest in a civil society the rights of the person facing the weapon outweigh the rights of the person wielding it. In a society where incivility and privilege exist, individuals will wield the weapon out of a sense of privilege.

When tribalism exists in the leadership ranks the benefits inure to the members of the in-groups at the expense of out-group members. Capozzoli (2003) (as cited in Mathieu (2021) discussing leadership and culture argues: [certain] . . . organizational factors may be conducive to violence in the workplace: autocratic management, disciplinary actions by a supervisor, a negative appraisal, lack of support from an employee's superior or workgroup, change in the workplace if not managed well, and downsizing. (p. 135).

Psychopathy and Tribalism

Robert D. Hare (1993/2006), a leading expert on psychopathy, has extensively studied and described the impact of psychopathic individuals in the workplace. His work, particularly in developing the Psychopathy Checklist-Revised (PCL-R), provides insight into how individuals with psychopathic traits might operate within professional settings.

Psychopathy is a personality disorder that manifests through a blend of affective, interpersonal, and behavioral traits. Individuals with psychopathy typically exhibit a profound lack of empathy, shallow emotions, and an absence of guilt or remorse. Interpersonally, they tend to be manipulative, superficially charming, grandiose, and deceitful. Behaviorally, they are often impulsive, irresponsible, and prone to engaging in antisocial activities, including criminal behavior. These characteristics make it difficult for them to form genuine emotional attachments, leading them to exploit others for personal gain without regard for the consequences. The disorder is commonly assessed using the Psychopathy Checklist-Revised (PCL-R), a tool developed by Robert D. Hare to evaluate psychopathic traits (Hare, 1993).

The connection between psychopathy and tribalism lies in how individuals with psychopathic traits might exploit tribalistic tendencies within groups for personal gain. For example, psychopathic individuals, characterized by their manipulative and deceitful nature, can leverage the strong loyalty and cohesion present in tribalistic groups. They may use their superficial charm and manipulative skills to influence group members and attain power or resources. Psychopaths might exacerbate tribalistic tendencies by promoting division and conflict between groups. Their lack of empathy and remorse allows them to create and exploit rifts, often for personal or strategic advantage.

In highly tribalistic environments, the characteristics of psychopathy, such as grandiosity and assertiveness, may be mistaken for strong leadership qualities. This can result in individuals with psychopathic traits rising to positions of influence, where they can further manipulate group dynamics to their benefit. Psychopathy coupled with extreme forms of tribalism can involve a degree of moral disengagement. Psychopathic individuals naturally lack moral concern, while tribalism can sometimes lead to dehumanizing those outside the group. This overlap can result in actions that are harmful to others being rationalized or overlooked.

Understanding these connections helps in recognizing how psychopathic individuals might navigate and exploit tribalistic settings, highlighting the importance of fostering ethical leadership and inclusive group dynamics to mitigate such risks.

Hare (1993) describes psychopathic individuals as exhibiting a range of traits that can be particularly disruptive and damaging in the workplace. These individuals often present themselves with superficial charm, making them appear engaging, charismatic, and articulate, which can initially be appealing in professional settings. A fundamental characteristic of psychopathy is a profound lack of empathy, affecting their interactions with colleagues and leading to unethical decisions and behaviors. They are highly manipulative, using deceit and coercion to achieve their ends without concern for the harm caused to others.

Psychopaths frequently have an inflated sense of their own importance and abilities, leading to overconfidence and reckless behavior in business decisions. Habitual lying is common, and they find it easy to lie to cover up misdeeds or manipulate others. A key trait is the lack of remorse or guilt for their actions, even when those actions harm others or the organization. Additionally, emotional depth is lacking in psychopathic individuals, resulting in shallow effect where their emotional responses can be faked or superficial, making them appear cold or unemotional. In the context of the workplace, Hare has pointed out that these traits can lead psychopathic individuals to seek positions of power and to thrive in environments where cut-throat and aggressive behaviors are rewarded. They might be drawn to roles that offer high rewards and have low supervision, allowing them more freedom to exploit situations and individuals. This also suggests that autocratic or laissez-faire leadership styles may suit their personalities.

Hare's (1993/2006) insights are particularly valuable for organizational leadership and HR professionals, as they highlight the importance of rigorous screening and oversight in hiring and promotion processes, especially for positions that offer significant power and influence. Understanding the potential impact of psychopathic traits can help in developing better management strategies to mitigate the risks associated with such individuals in the workplace. Mathieu (2021) also suggests that change can create chaos, and chaotic environments are the perfect hiding place for individuals with dark traits and intentions.

The Culture-Behavior Paradox

Paradoxically, behaviors shape culture through a dynamic and reciprocal process where individual actions and interactions contribute to the development, reinforcement, and transformation of cultural norms, values, and traditions. This relationship between behavior and culture is foundational to understanding social evolution and cultural diversity.

Behaviors that are consistently repeated by individuals within a group form an observable pattern, especially noticeable to younger generations. These patterns, transmitted across generations through mechanisms like imitation, teaching, and storytelling, become embedded as cultural norms or traditions. Individual behaviors can also lead to cultural innovation when new ways of doing things are adopted by the wider community. Innovations that solve problems or improve the quality of life are often integrated into cultural practices, aiding a culture's survival, especially in response to environmental changes or contact with other cultures.

Behaviors significantly contribute to the formation of social identity and group cohesion by distinguishing in-group from out-group members. Rituals, customs, and shared practices reinforce a sense of belonging and identity among members of a culture. Through participating in these shared behaviors, individuals affirm their membership and contribute to the continuity and unity of their culture.

Behaviors also play a crucial role in maintaining social order through the establishment of norms and laws that dictate acceptable conduct within a society. Deviant behaviors challenge these norms, potentially leading to social change by prompting a reevaluation of existing rules and values. This dynamic process illustrates how behavioral shifts can influence the evolution of cultural standards and legal systems.

Additionally, behaviors often carry symbolic meanings that reflect and reinforce cultural values. Rituals, ceremonies, and everyday practices can embody a culture's beliefs, priorities, and ethics. By engaging in these behaviors, individuals communicate and perpetuate the underlying values of their society.

The interaction between individuals and their environment through behaviors such as farming, hunting, and urban development reflects and shapes cultural attitudes toward nature and resource use. These behaviors lead to cultural adaptations that are specific to the geographical and ecological context of a group. As such, behaviors shape culture through their role in transmitting values, fostering innovation, defining social identities, regulating social life, communicating symbolic meanings, and interacting with the environment. This interplay between behavior and culture is central to the development of diverse cultural landscapes and the ongoing process of cultural change.

Culture is a hidden force ever-present in the background of every person's behavior. It profoundly influences behavior by shaping social norms, communication styles, perception, decision-making, workplace dynamics, responses to change and conflict, mental health attitudes, and consumer behavior. It dictates what is deemed acceptable or unacceptable in a society, affects how people communicate and interact, and influences their values and thought processes.

Cultural background plays a crucial role in individual and collective actions, from personal decisions to workplace practices and responses to societal changes. Therefore, since culture significantly influences human behavior, shaping how individuals think, feel, and act within their social environments understanding cultural impacts is essential for effective communication and cooperation in our increasingly globalized world.

The impact of culture on behavior can be seen in various aspects such as through social norms and values that guide behavior. These norms dictate acceptable and unacceptable behaviors in a society. For example, culture influences how people greet each other, how they dress, and their attitudes toward work, other groups, and leisure. It affects how people perceive the world and process information including attitudes towards different concepts like time, space, and individualism vs. collectivism. For instance, in individualistic cultures, emphasis is often placed on personal achievements and independence, whereas collectivist cultures emphasize group harmony and interdependence. It also influences communication styles including language, non-verbal communication, and the interpretation of gestures and expressions. In some cultures, direct communication is valued, while in others, more indirect or contextual forms of communication are preferred.

Cultural values and beliefs influence decision-making processes. In some cultures, decisions may be more community-oriented and consensus-driven, while in others, decisions might be made by individuals or based on hierarchical structures as can be observed in the application of various leadership styles, how employees approach teamwork, and employer-employee relationships.

Different cultures have different expectations regarding formality, power distance, and work-life balance. Cultures influence how individuals respond to change and manage conflict. Some cultures might be more resistant to change and prefer traditional ways, while others are more open to innovation and change. It can influence how mental health issues are perceived, treated, and supported. In some cultures, there may be a stigma attached to mental health issues, affecting the willingness of individuals to seek help.

Significantly for all organizations, culture impacts purchasing decisions and consumer behavior. This includes preferences for certain products, brand loyalty, and attitudes towards domestic vs. foreign goods. Consequently, understanding the impact of culture on behavior is crucial in a globalized world, as it fosters better communication, reduces cultural misunderstandings, and enhances cooperation among people from diverse backgrounds.

Culture, Goal Behaviors, and Attrition

Attrition is a process rather than an event and therefore the significance of supervisory leadership cannot be overstated. Employees formulate many of their perceptions about an organization through the treatment they receive when interacting with their supervisors. That is, two people in the same organization with different supervisors may very well have significantly different views about the quality of the organization because of how they perceive their respective supervisors. **Figure 5-3** illustrates the process employees go through during the hiring, acculturation, and attrition process suggesting that attrition is a process and not an event.

Acculturation & Values Matching

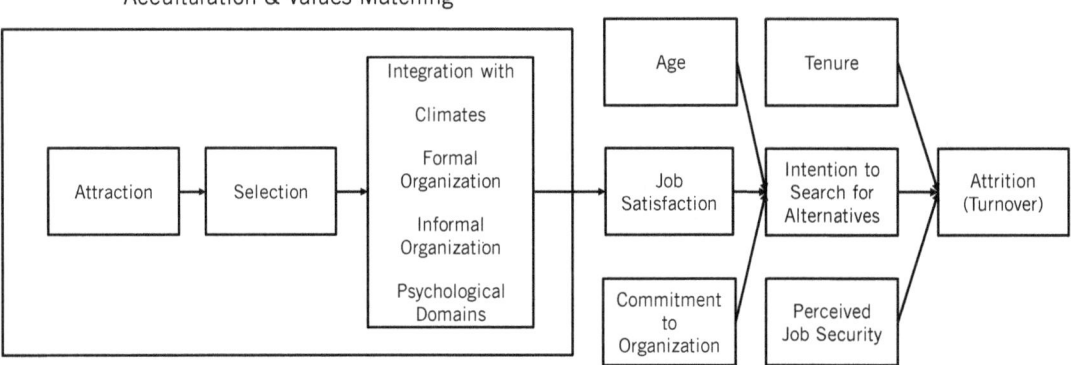

Figure 5-3: Attraction, Selection, Integration, Attrition (ASIA)
(*Perry, 1995*)

The Attraction, Selection, Integration, and Attrition diagram illustrates how job candidates become employees. The employment process begins with prospective candidates applying for a position with a company. The hiring processes used by organizations reflect elements of the organization's culture. For example, the position announcement lists various aspects of the organization including its mission statement, vision statement, values important, amenities, and a description of the position requirements.

Since the COVID-19 pandemic, most organizations have used a virtual screening process to begin narrowing the range of candidates for interviewing and potential site visits. Some organizations are using static video captures requiring prospects to answer questions with video captured for further processing or screening. Whatever the application and selection requirements might be, the candidate begins to make decisions about their experiences with the process, which reflects characteristics of the culture. As they move farther along in the process, they begin to feel what it's like to work in the organization basing their feelings on their perceptions of the selection processes they are being led through to become the successful candidate.

Once hired, the new employee experiences more and more about the organization's culture as they proceed through orientation programs, training, and observing the behaviors of their colleagues as part of an entire acculturation process of adapting to new surroundings and patterns of behaviors. The longer the employee works for the organization, the more they adapt to patterns of behaviors reflecting the status quo.

Since attrition is a process and not an event, much of what happens with avoidable leavers is resolvable with the right interventions, and therefore leaders and supervisors can do something to lower it. The findings from my 1995 dissertation on attrition found that common reasons for attrition fell into two categories of *Leavers*: *Avoidable Leavers* (those within the control of the organization and *Unavoidable Leavers* (those who leave for reasons outside any control of the organization.) **Table 5-3** outlines the characteristics of Avoidable and Unavoidable Leavers in a nationwide study of a large nonprofit organization.

Avoidable Leavers	Unavoidable Leavers
• Values didn't match the organization's values • Burnout • Poor working conditions • Poor leadership / supervision • Conflicts with supervisor • Low pay • Harassment • Career advancement	• Retirement • Imposed relocation • Stay home to care for spouse / child • Reduction in workforce • Career change

Table 5-3: Avoidable and Unavoidable Leavers

In a more recent study, the characteristics of what a good organization looks like are outlined in a study by Indeed (2022). They include:

- Competitive compensation

- Company Culture

- Sense of Community

- Trust

- Fairness

- Open Communication

- Innovation

- Professional Development

- Engagement

- Caring

- Desirable Employer

- Transparency

- Honorable Mission

- Effective Leadership

- Diversity

My fascination with the reasons why people leave organizations they love led me to my dissertation on the topic of attrition. There are several reasons why people leave organizations but for those who are Avoidable Leavers, it is largely due to culture, particularly the values in practice as demonstrated through the behaviors of their supervisors and other leaders. Some of the primary reasons include:

- **Company culture and values:** Employees want to work for an organization that aligns with their values and beliefs. If they feel that the company culture is toxic or does not align with their values, they may choose to leave.

- **Lack of opportunities for career growth and development:** Employees want to feel like they are progressing in their careers and gaining new skills. If they feel that their organization does not provide adequate opportunities for career growth and development, they may start looking for other job opportunities.

- **Poor Supervision, Management, and Leadership**: Managers and leaders play a crucial role in the workplace. If employees feel that their managers are not supportive or are micromanaging, they may become disengaged and lose motivation, leading them to leave the organization.

- **Poor work-life balance:** Many employees value their personal lives outside of work and want to achieve a good work-life balance. If an organization demands too much of their time or does not provide flexibility, they may choose to leave in search of a better work-life balance.

- **Low job satisfaction:** Employees want to enjoy their work and feel fulfilled by it. If they feel that their job is unfulfilling or not aligned with their interests and passions, they may become disengaged and seek other opportunities.

- **Compensation and benefits:** Fair and competitive compensation is important for attracting and retaining talent. If employees feel that their compensation and benefits are not adequate, they may look for better-paying opportunities elsewhere.

Employees leave organizations for a variety of reasons, but addressing these primary factors can help organizations reduce turnover and retain top talent. The point illustrated here is that over time the reasons for attrition are largely stable and they have everything to do with organizational culture which is in the leader's authority to establish. My 1995 dissertation findings as well as the 2022 Indeed study clearly illustrate that what employees want from their organizations is effective leadership, a healthy culture, good interpersonal relationships, and an organizational mission that is personally meaningful. Some slight variations might exist between organizations, but these data points are stable and consistent over time, demonstrating the significance of the degree to which effective or poor leadership and supervision exist and make a difference in organizational productivity.

The disconnect for organizations is that most leaders, as will be shown, pay lip service to the importance and value of employees as critical assets but treat them as interchangeable cogs in wheels. The fact that leaders consider their employees as assets (a thing) rather than as beings with lots of upside potential that will manifest themselves under the right conditions, frames their belief systems and establishes a self-fulfilling prophecy of people as assets, something that can be bought, sold, and dispensed as needed. While it makes us uncomfortable to think about it this way, those attitudes prevalent in today's organizations are the same attitudes held by masters of enslaved persons through the nineteenth century. Leaders have the power to create the cultural conditions that determine how their employees are treated.

Strategies to Reduce Attrition

After obtaining my doctorate I began contemplating several questions.

- What strategies will reduce attrition?

- What strategies will increase productivity through improved goal behaviors?

- What strategies will increase positive sustainable change?

- What strategies will reduce workplace trauma?

Studying the dynamics related to poor performance and attrition for nearly three decades has given me a unique perspective regarding what organizational effectiveness truly means. There are substantial costs related to turnover and high attrition rates including the subsequent and very real destructive ripple effects negatively impacting goal behaviors in which employees are not working at the levels of their potential, and leaders who are less than fully effective in getting the most from their direct reports are allowed to sustain mediocrity.

Poor supervision undermines organizational performance and increases attrition. In some cases, three-year turnover rates may be as high as 50% or more with five-year rates as high as 70%. When you factor in that the replacement costs per employee can range from 17% to 200% (lowest to highest-paid employee) and consider that payrolls can be as much as 70% or more of an organization's budget, it is not unreasonable to suggest that organizations are literally bleeding green to the tune of hundreds of millions, if not, billions of dollars when avoidable attrition is high (SHRM, 2020).

What is truly most remarkable is that the bulk of the turnover we see in organizations is preventable. My dissertation study of attrition demonstrated that eight of thirteen reasons for attrition (the reasons given by people who left their organization) were completely controllable by the organization. In other words, excessively high turn-over rates don't have to happen in organizations! While pay is often cited as the reason someone leaves an organization, my research suggests otherwise. I contend that people understand the pay when they join the organization and that other reasons (toxic cultures) contribute more fully to attrition such as conflicts between espoused organizational values and values actually in practice, and poor leadership/supervision. Today, we see people saying I've had enough, and I am not going to take it anymore!

Smith (2016) found that more than half (53%) of working Americans experienced a traumatic event while on the job. Their trauma is then carried back into their households. If you look at the U.S. Bureau of Labor Statistics (BLS) employment data for 2023 there were roughly 160,000,000 people in the workforce. If we use Smith's findings, we can extrapolate that approximately eighty-five million (84.8 million) employees experienced at least one traumatic event on the job in 2023 and took their trauma into their homes.

What has become abundantly clear from the data is that greater than half (53%) of the U.S. workforce identify some type of abuse in the workplace annually and there are more than a quarter million wrongful termination lawsuits filed annually. Depending on their previous life experiences, those traumatic events may very well not be their first traumatic event and therefore may add to the impacts of previous traumatic events. In other words trauma is additive with each subsequent event.

The conditions we find ourselves in today offer tremendous possibilities for our collective futures if we can stop the wars being fought in our organizations, our communities, and our societies. Therefore, I am left to do my best to convince people that we can do much better as a society if we can reconcile our differences (diversity) but to do so we must be willing, individually, and collectively to transform ourselves into better versions of who we are today. To do so, we must confront our internal discomfort produced by what psychologists call cognitive dissonance which occurs when events and circumstances challenge our most deeply held beliefs and the systems that support them. Conscientization is the gateway to transformation.

Courage to Face Fear

It takes courage to stand up to a bully, and meeting trauma can certainly be like confronting a bully staring us in the face at the most inopportune times. Courage is a complex human virtue that involves the willingness to face and overcome fear, difficulty, danger, uncertainty, or pain. It requires a level of bravery to confront such challenges, whether they are physical, moral, emotional, or psychological—the scariest of all. Key aspects of courage include:

Facing fear requires courage that involves acknowledging fear and choosing to act in spite of it. This doesn't mean the absence of fear, but rather the assessment and management of fear. Emotional courage involves being open and vulnerable, particularly in expressing one's feelings or in facing emotional pain.

Moral integrity is the courage to stand up for one's beliefs or principles, even if this goes against the majority opinion or might result in personal loss or hardship. It requires perseverance which requires the resilience to keep going in the face of obstacles, setbacks, or failures.

Courage can also manifest as taking action to protect or defend others who are vulnerable or in danger. In doing so, being courageous often involves a willingness to take risks that others might avoid and requires putting one's own interests or safety at risk for the sake of others or for a higher cause. Courage comes in many forms and can be seen in a wide range of contexts, from extraordinary acts of bravery to the everyday courage of facing life's many challenges.

There is a desperate need for courageous leadership. Courageous leadership refers to a style of leadership characterized by boldness, integrity, and the willingness to take risks in the face of adversity or uncertainty. It involves making decisions that are guided by ethical principles and a clear vision, even when these decisions are unpopular or come with personal or professional risks. Here are some key aspects of courageous leadership:

- Courageous leaders make choices based on what is right and just, rather than what is easy or advantageous. They do not shy away from difficult situations or decisions, understanding that growth often comes from addressing challenges directly. They are transparent, communicate openly with their team, share both successes and failures and encourage an environment where honest feedback is valued.

- Courageous leaders inspire and empower their team members to take initiative and make decisions, fostering a sense of ownership and accountability. They demonstrate resilience in the face of setbacks and adapt to changing circumstances, maintaining a focus on long-term goals. They are not afraid to challenge the status quo and encourage innovative thinking to achieve their vision. They lead by example, showing consistency between their words and actions, and hold themselves accountable to the same standards as their team.

In an organizational context, embracing courageous leadership can be vital for fostering a culture of trust, innovation, and ethical practice. It's about leading in a way that respects and advances the values and goals of the organization while also being mindful of the broader impact on stakeholders, society, and the environment.

The Courage to Be Disliked by Ichiro Kishimi and Fumitake Koga (2019) is a thought-provoking book that delves into the psychology of Alfred Adler, a contemporary of Freud and Jung. The book is structured as a dialogue between a philosopher and a young man, exploring various aspects of Adlerian psychology. They emphasize that happiness is a personal choice, not something dictated by past traumas or experiences. It asserts that everyone has the freedom to change their life at any moment, regardless of what they've been through. This idea is central to the book's message that we are not prisoners of our past but can choose our path forward.

A significant aspect of Adlerian psychology presented in the book is the focus on teleology rather than causality. This means that our behavior is shaped more by our goals for the future than by the events of our past. Instead of dwelling on what has happened, Kishimi and Fumitake encourage readers to consider what they want to achieve and how they can direct their actions toward those goals. The importance of social connectedness is another key theme. The book argues that feeling connected to others and contributing to the well-being of the community is essential for personal happiness. It suggests that true fulfillment comes not from seeking superiority over others but from striving to be the best version of oneself and making meaningful contributions to society.

Overcoming feelings of inferiority is also central to their philosophy. Rather than striving for superiority or defining success as an end goal, the book encourages readers to aim for their personal best and to focus on contributing to others. This shift in perspective can lead to a more satisfying and purposeful life. The title, *Courage to Change*, reflects the idea that real courage lies in being honest with oneself and being willing to change, even when it's uncomfortable. The book challenges the victim mentality, advocating instead for taking responsibility for one's life and choices. It encourages readers to reject the notion that they are victims of their circumstances and to embrace their power to shape their own destinies. The concept of the separation of tasks is another important lesson. Kishimi and Fumitake (2019), teach the value of understanding what is within our control and what is not, and of focusing on our own tasks rather than trying to take on the tasks of others. This approach can lead to greater clarity and peace of mind.

Effect of Positive Leadership

Positive leadership practices have a significant impact on improving productivity in the workplace. Studies and research in this area demonstrate the various ways in which positive leadership behaviors contribute to better organizational outcomes. A study by Arakawa and Greenberg (2007) investigated the effect of positive leadership practices on project performance and employee engagement. They found that positive managers, who use a strengths-based approach, maintain a positive perspective during challenges, and provide frequent recognition and encouragement, lead teams with higher performance and engagement. This research aligns with earlier Greenberd and Arakawa (n.d.) findings that show a strong connection between employee engagement and key business outcomes like retention, productivity, profitability, and safety.

Research conducted by Kim Cameron (2012), a prominent positive organizational scholar, over 15 years shows that positive leadership and practices can significantly improve various organizational aspects. These include profitability, productivity, staff well-being, motivation, quality of work, innovation, customer satisfaction, and staff retention. Positive leadership is characterized by several key behaviors such as intellectual stimulation, individual consideration, inspirational motivation, and idealized influence, which prioritize employee well-being over self-interests.

Likewise, the concept of psychological safety in the workplace, an essential element fostered by positive leadership, is linked to high performance in teams. This includes being open-minded, resilient, motivated, and solution-oriented. Positive leaders create environments where employees feel safe to express concerns, challenge the status quo, and take calculated risks.

Investing in employees' development is another critical aspect of positive leadership. Practices like offering strength assessments and training programs have been shown to enhance well-being, job performance, satisfaction, and social relationships within teams. Additionally, leaders demonstrating positive behaviors set the tone for the entire organization, influencing the emotional climate and encouraging similar positive behaviors among employees. Thus, positive leadership practices are demonstrated to not only improve the immediate workplace environment but also have far-reaching effects on the productivity and success of an organization.

Dana Arakawa and Margaret Greenberg (2007) investigated the effect of positive leadership practices on project performance and employee engagement, specifically among information technology professionals at The Hanover Insurance Group. Their study aligns with previous Gallup (2007) research indicating the crucial role of supervisors in employee engagement and its linkage to key business outcomes like retention, productivity, profitability, customer engagement, and safety.

The University of Sussex (2023) highlights how positive leadership and practices improve profitability, productivity, staff well-being, motivation, quality of work, innovation, customer satisfaction, and staff retention. Additionally, it discusses the importance of fostering a culture of psychological safety and investing in employees' development to enhance workplace productivity and well-being.

Toxic Leaders and Toxic Cultures

The Dark Triad personalities: narcissism, Machiavellianism, and psychopathy are discussed by Mathieu (2021). *Narcissism* in the workplace often manifests as a sense of entitlement, a constant need for admiration, and a notable lack of empathy for others. She also discusses *sadism* which involves deriving pleasure from inflicting pain, suffering, or humiliation on others. When sadism is included, the construct is sometimes referred to as the *Dark Tetrad*. Individuals with this trait can create environments where they dominate conversations, take undue credit for successes, and dismiss the contributions of others, fostering a toxic atmosphere.

Machiavellianism involves manipulation and exploitation of others, a cynical disregard for morality, and a focus on self-interest and deception. In a professional setting, Machiavellians might engage in backstabbing, spreading misinformation, or manipulating situations to their advantage, often at the expense of their colleagues' well-being and the organization's overall health. Psychopathy in the workplace includes traits such as insensitivity, lack of empathy, and often impulsive or antisocial behaviors. These individuals may engage in reckless decision-making, exhibit a blatant disregard for rules and norms, and create a threatening or hostile work environment.

Mathieu delves into how these dark personality traits influence workplace dynamics, leadership styles, team interactions, and organizational culture. Mathieu challenges these personalities and suggests they foster toxic work environments, promote unethical behaviors, and negatively impact employee well-being and productivity. She also offers strategies for managing and mitigating the impact of these traits, including leadership approaches, organizational policies, and individual coping mechanisms.

Mathieu (2021) explores how these dark traits infiltrate organizations, secure management positions, and create harmful dynamics. She discusses the Dark Triad Model, the influence of organizational culture on these traits, and best practices in employee selection to reduce the risk of hiring individuals with such characteristics. Additionally, she covers impression management tactics used by individuals with dark personalities, their connection to leadership styles, and the role of organizational culture in mitigating their negative effects. Mathieu's work (2014/2021) provides valuable insights and practical tools for managing these challenges and emphasizes the importance of fostering a positive and healthy organizational culture.

Identifying Toxic Leaders

Identifying a toxic leader is crucial for maintaining a healthy work environment. When I use the term toxic leader, I am talking about toxic people who also have a positional power differential from another person, and they use it to get whatever it is that they want. Toxic leaders often show a lack of empathy, demonstrating little concern for the emotions and well-being of their employees. They might focus solely on performance and results, disregarding personal circumstances. Manipulative behaviors are also common, with such leaders using deceitful or indirect tactics to achieve their goals, often at the expense of others. This can include playing team members against each other or using information for personal gain.

Poor communication is another hallmark of toxic leadership, with communication often being vague, overly aggressive, or one-way. Employees might feel that their voices are not heard and that the leader does not effectively communicate expectations or feedback. A blame culture is prevalent, with toxic leaders avoiding responsibility and blaming others for failures or mistakes, fostering a culture of fear and discouraging risk-taking or admitting errors. They may react negatively to criticism or feedback, perceiving it as a personal attack rather than an opportunity for growth.

Toxic leaders often overemphasize hierarchical power, constantly reinforcing their authority and status, which discourages open dialogue and collaboration. This creates a gap between the leader and the team. There is often a lack of transparency about decisions and organizational changes, leading to mistrust and speculation among employees. Unrealistic expectations are set to perpetually keep employees feeling inadequate or unsuccessful.

These leaders foster a hostile work environment through intimidation, bullying, or creating unnecessary competition among employees. They also fail to invest in the growth and development of their team members, leading to stagnation and low morale.

Recognizing these signs is the first step toward addressing toxic leadership. In academic or consultancy settings, being aware of these behaviors can help advise organizations on leadership development and organizational health. Resources like the Harvard Business Review and Forbes offer extensive research and articles on this topic, providing deeper insights and strategies for dealing with toxic leadership.

The presence of toxic leaders in an organization can have far-reaching and detrimental implications. Toxic leadership often results in a demoralized workforce, with employees feeling undervalued, overworked, or mistreated, leading to a lack of engagement and commitment. High levels of stress and dissatisfaction can lead to higher turnover rates, which incur significant costs in recruiting and training new employees, impacting the organization's bottom line.

Toxic leaders can foster an environment of mistrust and competition, hindering effective teamwork and leading to silos within the organization, reducing efficiency and productivity. The word of a toxic work environment can spread beyond the organization, damaging its reputation. This can make it harder to attract top talent and harm relationships with clients, investors, and stakeholders. In such an environment, employees may be less likely to take risks or propose innovative solutions due to fear of repercussions, stifling growth and adaptation in a rapidly changing business landscape.

Long-term exposure to a toxic leader can lead to physical and mental health issues among employees, including stress, burnout, anxiety, and depression. Toxic leadership behaviors can sometimes cross the line into harassment or discrimination, leading to legal challenges and compliance issues. These leaders may make decisions based on their own interests rather than the organization's best interests, leading to poor strategic choices. Over time, a toxic leader can significantly alter the culture of an organization, making it more cynical, aggressive, or unethical. All these factors can culminate in reduced productivity and the performance of the organization.

Understanding these implications is crucial when advising organizations on leadership and organizational effectiveness. Developing strategies to identify and mitigate the effects of toxic leadership can significantly enhance the health and performance of an organization. Resources like the Academy of Management Journal and McKinsey Quarterly offer valuable perspectives and case studies on this topic.

Negative Outcomes of Toxic Leadership

Lipman-Bluman (2005) found that toxic leaders create trauma and often leave their followers worse off than when they found them. Toxic leadership can have a number of negative outcomes for both individuals and organizations, including:

- Violating basic standards of human rights

- Feeding followers illusions enhances the leader's power and impairs their capacity for independent action

- Exploiting the basest fears and needs of their followers

- Stifling constructive criticism by focusing on compliance rather than encouraging questions about the leader's actions

- Misleading followers with untruths

- Subverting systems and processes for personal gain

- Building totalitarian or narrowly dynastic regimes and undermining the law

- Failing to nurture other leaders and creating divisions among constituents

- Treating close associates well while persuading them to dislike others

- Ignoring or promoting incompetence, cronyism, and corruption

Such leadership deliberately undermines, incapacitates, demeans, disenfranchises, seduces, imprisons, marginalizes, tortures, intimidates, terrorizes, demoralizes, and even kills. Such leadership results in:

- **Reduced morale and job satisfaction among employees:** Toxic leaders often create a toxic work environment characterized by fear, intimidation, and harassment. This can lead to decreased morale and job satisfaction among employees, which can in turn lead to decreased productivity and increased turnover.

- **Decreased productivity:** Toxic leaders may focus on their own personal goals at the expense of the organization's goals. They may also engage in micromanagement or other behavior that hinders productivity and efficiency.

- **Increased absenteeism and turnover:** Employees may choose to leave the organization rather than continue working in a toxic environment. This can lead to increased absenteeism and turnover, which can be costly for the organization.

- **Decreased creativity and innovation:** Toxic leaders often discourage creative thinking and innovation. This can stifle new ideas and limit the organization's ability to adapt to changing circumstances.

- **Legal and financial consequences:** Toxic leaders may engage in unethical or illegal behavior that can result in legal or financial consequences for the organization.

- **Damage to the organization's reputation:** Toxic leadership can damage the organization's reputation both internally and externally. This can lead to decreased trust and respect among employees, customers, and other stakeholders.

Reasons for Following Toxic Leaders

Toxic leadership can have a wide range of negative outcomes for individuals and organizations. It is important for organizations to take steps to identify and address toxic leadership in order to minimize these negative consequences. When talking about toxic leaders we have to ask ourselves, what sort of people want to follow a dictator? People who follow dictators often do so for various reasons, each influenced by their personal circumstances, beliefs, and the societal context that triggers them to do so such as:

- **Desire for Stability and Order**: In times of chaos or economic hardship, people may support dictators who promise stability and safety.

- **Nationalism and Pride**: Dictators often appeal to national pride, offering a vision of restoring or improving the nation's standing.

- **Fear and Coercion**: Many follow dictators out of fear, as opposing a dictatorship can lead to severe consequences.

- **Propaganda and Control of Information**: Dictators often control media and information, influencing public opinion and suppressing dissent.

- **Ideological Alignment**: Some individuals may genuinely believe in the dictator's ideology or political goals.

- **Disillusionment with Previous Systems**: People frustrated with previous democratic or corrupt systems might support a dictator promising change.

- **Personal Gain**: Some support dictators for personal or professional gain, such as career opportunities or financial benefits.

- **Social and Peer Pressure**: In some contexts, there's social or community pressure to conform and support the ruling regime.

These factors can combine in complex ways, and the decision to support a dictator is often a result of multiple influences rather than a single cause.

Quiet Quitting

Quiet quitting is a term that gained popularity in the workplace context. It describes a situation where employees are not outright quitting their jobs, but they are disengaging

from extra efforts and doing only the minimum required tasks. Essentially, these employees are quitting the idea of going above and beyond at work.

This concept is not about leaving the job but rather about setting boundaries.
Employees who are *quitting* typically fulfill their job responsibilities but avoid extra
work, such as working overtime without pay, taking on tasks outside their job description, or consistently putting in effort beyond what the role requires. This behavior might
stem from a variety of reasons, including:

- **Work-life balance**: Employees might want to ensure they have time and
  energy for their personal lives.

- **Burnout**: After extended periods of high stress or overwork, employees
  may reduce their engagement to cope.

- **Lack of recognition or advancement**: Employees might feel their extra
  efforts are not being acknowledged or rewarded.

Quiet quitting reflects a shift in the employee's mindset regarding their relationship
with work, emphasizing personal well-being and work-life balance over the traditional
norms of workplace commitment and extra unpaid effort. Quiet quitting illustrates the
impact of corporate culture on goal behaviors. The less cultures meet the individual
needs of their members the more psychological, sociopsychological, and behavioral
separation begins to occur.

In my case, I was experiencing so much trauma and toxicity in the workplace that
I not only began missing social events in national meetings by disappearing into the
crowds and exiting when it was convenient, I began eating in my hotel room or going
to restaurants on my own dime just to find peace. At one point, after spending years
collecting company merch, I donated it all to Goodwill because it triggered me. I also
found it almost impossible to go to social events for more than a few minutes because of
the sensory overload I experienced in crowds. I am still not recovered and tend to avoid
crowds now altogether, because of additional complications brought on by my motor
vehicle accident.

I did not let what was happening to me because of toxic supervision and organizational leadership stop my efforts to produce exemplary work, which often happened as
evidenced by the number of times my work was identified as exemplary and often show-
cased as examples. This construct has been discussed in various business and human
resource articles, reflecting changing attitudes towards work and employment. For a
deeper understanding, it might be valuable to look into recent discussions on employee
engagement and workplace culture in business publications.

Moonlighting

Moonlighting refers to the practice of holding a second job or additional jobs outside
of one's primary employment. This term is often used to describe situations where an

individual works these additional jobs during their off-hours, such as in the evenings or on weekends, hence the term "moonlighting," which implies working by the light of the moon. The reasons for moonlighting vary. They can include:

- **Financial Necessity**: Many individuals take on additional work to supplement their income from their primary job, often due to financial needs or to achieve specific financial goals.

- **Career Development or Diversification**: Some people moonlight to gain experience in a different field, develop new skills, or pursue interests that they cannot in their primary job.

- **Passion Projects**: Moonlighting can also be a way to work on personal projects or hobbies that may also provide additional income, such as freelance writing, arts, or crafts.

Moonlighting can have implications for a primary job. Some employers have policies restricting or regulating secondary employment, especially if it poses a conflict of interest or affects job performance. Therefore, it's generally advisable for employees to be aware of and comply with their primary employer's policies regarding secondary work.

Complacency

Complacency can lead to a range of negative effects, both on an individual and organizational level. When people become complacent, they often experience stagnation in their personal growth. This lack of motivation to improve or learn new skills results in personal or professional stagnation. In a work or business environment, complacency can significantly reduce competitiveness. Organizations that become complacent may fall behind more proactive and innovative competitors, struggling to keep up with industry advancements.

Being content with the status quo can also result in missed opportunities for advancement or improvement. Complacency decreases adaptability, making it harder to adjust to changes or new challenges because there is less incentive to seek out or prepare for them. This can be particularly detrimental in a crisis situation. Complacent individuals or organizations might be ill-prepared for emergencies, leading to inadequate or slow responses that could exacerbate the situation.

The quality of work and overall performance can decline as well. Complacency often leads to a lack of attention to detail and a diminished commitment to maintaining high standards. In the workplace, this attitude can cause employees to become disengaged, feeling unchallenged and unmotivated. This disengagement further contributes to a decline in productivity and morale.

Moreover, complacency might result in ignoring constructive criticism or feedback, which is essential for improvement and growth. Without this crucial feedback, individuals and organizations miss out on opportunities to identify and address areas that need development.

While being content with one's achievements can be positive, complacency implies a level of self-satisfaction that overlooks potential risks, opportunities, and the need for continuous growth and change. This can create a significant barrier to achieving long-term success and resilience in an ever-evolving environment.

The Failure of HR To Protect Employees

Whether or not an employee goes to human resources (HR) may largely be due to their feelings of trust in HR (assuming an HR department exists). If the employee feels that HR is trustworthy, they may be more likely to go to HR. However, anyone who has worked for any length of time knows that HR's role is to first and foremost protect the organization. It should not be surprising that under such conditions, productivity may drop as disaffected employees find ways to sabotage performance by going on strike, producing less through work slowdowns, increasing absenteeism, or terminating their employment. In extreme cases, irate employees may even resort to violence in the workplace.

Based on my research, generally speaking, employees use Human Resources to handle administrative items like updating direct deposit forms, making leave requests, and enrolling in benefits. However, many employees do not use Human Resources for larger issues that are related to company culture, policies, and procedures. Employees are reluctant to speak to Human Resources because they believe that HR has the best interest of their company in mind more so than that of their employees. Further, employees tend not to use Human Resources because they feel like HR does not have enough power to effect change, and it may be a wasted effort to make a complaint.

Writing for *Forbes*, Segal (2021) found that "When employees face troubles, they'd rather reach out to their manager, a trusted colleague or another leader in the company. What's really scary: Some would do nothing at all rather than turn to HR." He goes on to identify that:

- 75% of employees don't trust that their HR leader cares about their needs.

- 71% of HR employees in the survey stated that less than 30% of complaints they received in the last 2 years resulted in any disciplinary action. Having less than a third of cases result in disciplinary action led employees to wonder—if they bring complaints forward, will anything even result?"

- 47% don't feel safe confiding in or getting assistance from the HR leader.

- 38% of employee respondents feel HR does not equally enforce company policies for all employees, with 18% of that group believing managers get special treatment.

- 37% felt HR was more concerned about advocating for the organization.

- 9% felt their HR leader would advocate for them.

However, when it comes to problems with their direct supervisors' employees may not be able to confide in HR because of a lack of trust, particularly in toxic workplace environments. They also may not have the ability to contact their supervisor's supervisor for advice when that supervisor is close with their toxic direct supervisor. The bottom line is that there is a deep lack of trust in toxic organizations preventing open conversations and thwarting positive interpersonal interactions. This leaves employees with having to make decisions about whether to stay or leave the organization. Those who have the resources or financial capacity might leave when things in the workplace environment become too toxic. However, large percentages of middle- and lower-income employees may find themselves stuck without the ability to leave their employment because of the substantial disruption to their quality of life increasing the impact of whatever workplace trauma they may be experiencing.

Creating Your Own Balance

The chapter titled "The Human Side of the Enterprise" delves into the intricate relationship between leadership, management, and organizational success. It explores the differences between leadership and management, emphasizing that while both roles are often held by the same individual, leadership is more complex due to the human dynamics it entails. Leadership is described as a higherorder function that focuses on aligning people, inspiring and motivating them, and establishing direction. In contrast, management deals with organizing resources, planning, budgeting, and controlling operations.

The chapter recounts a personal experience of leadership transformation in the context of the YMCA, where consolidating two financially struggling branches into a single, thriving organization illustrated the power of vision, collaboration, and empowerment. This success story highlights the importance of seeing possibilities where others see impossibilities, a key characteristic of effective leadership.

The discussion extends to the role of education in developing leaders, noting that most business programs focus heavily on management functions, leaving leadership skills underdeveloped. This gap often leads to short-sighted decisions, particularly in challenging times, when soft skills like leadership and diversity training are often eliminated.

Additionally, the chapter contrasts American and Japanese management styles, explaining that while Japanese firms emphasize long-term employment and collective decision-making, American companies prioritize short-term results and individual achievements. I advocate for a balanced approach, combining the best aspects of both management styles to foster loyalty, productivity, and long-term success.

The chapter also touches on cultural differences in valuing elders and the evolving nature of work, shaped by technological advancements and changing societal needs. It argues that organizations should be viewed as social systems where leadership plays a vital role in shaping culture, behaviors, and interactions.

Finally, the chapter emphasizes that successful organizations are created through intentional design, where leadership unleashes human potential and fosters environments that allow employees to thrive. It warns against autocratic and laissez-faire leadership styles, which can lead to inefficiency and long-term damage, and instead advocates for transformative leadership that promotes equity, social justice, and continuous improvement.

THE POINT

Principle 6: *If you don't put time into something, don't expect to derive its benefits.*

CHAPTER 6

From Wounds to Wisdom

The Alchemy of Adversity

Life is a journey of perpetual transformation, a narrative woven from the threads of aspirations, experiences, efforts at overcoming adversity, and the constant pursuit of self-realization. From the moment we draw our first breath to the instant we exhale our last, we are in a state of perpetual evolution, forever becoming the architects of our destinies.

Life is a process of always becoming, yet it is also a solitary journey even though, as a species, we are social creatures. Every day we live creates opportunities for us to become a better version of ourselves. However, we define it. In childhood, we are innocent voyagers, wide-eyed and eager, exploring the vast terrain of possibility with boundless curiosity. Every discovery fuels our imagination, propelling us to understand and discover the Self, defined by and moderated by the situation and context within which we live.

As we traverse the landscape of adolescence, we grapple with the complexities of self-discovery and, knowingly or not, start charting a course through the turbulent waters of identity formation and personal growth. Amidst the storms of change, we forge our identities, carving out a space for ourselves. In adulthood, we shoulder the burdens of responsibility, navigating the demands of work and relationships, and pursuing our dreams. Each day, we refine our purpose, honing our skills and talents as we strive to leave our mark on the world.

The trick, then, is to survive and live long enough to learn how to effectively navigate what is inherently dangerous and unpredictable. Successfully navigating the storms in a tumultuous world in which anything can happen at any time is a substantial feat in and of itself. Still, it strengthens our constitution and is the gateway to wisdom.

This is a story about proactively drawing on various aspects of experiences and using a form of alchemy to transform adversity and trauma into wisdom. By teaching individuals how to reframe adversity into opportunities for growth, we can create learning organizations through which employees can embrace transformative learning as a lifelong learning practice.

Alchemy

Alchemy of adversity uses the metaphor of *alchemy*—the medieval practice believed to turn base metals into precious gold—to describe transforming difficult or negative experiences into something valuable or enriching. This concept suggests that adversity, while challenging and often painful, can be transformed and lead to personal growth, wisdom, and positive change. In this context, the alchemy involves:

- Learning from hardships and using them as lessons that fuel personal improvement

- Increasing personal capacity by developing resilience and strength through overcoming obstacles

- Gaining insight into personal values and priorities due to facing challenges

When confronting tough situations, the alchemy of adversity is about finding the silver lining surrounding our darkest moments and mining those experiences to foster a deeper understanding of life and oneself. It reflects that personal and collective growth often arises from the most challenging periods.

Challenges

For as long as we breathe, life happens, and it routinely presents challenges that shape our behaviors and future actions. Outside forces can impact us without warning, forcing us in an instant to contend with something that was never conceived in our worst nightmares. For example, being in psychological turmoil and encountering unexpected events can disrupt the peace at any time. There is evidence to suggest that this is what may occur in violent outbursts on airplanes and in other public spaces, domestic violence, or mass shooting cases. We can encounter toxic supervisors or family members that our circumstances do not allow us to escape, creating the type of dynamics that can lead to harmful health outcomes and sub-optimal goal behaviors, negatively impacting productivity.

Today, more than any time in our history, we are all under threat of domestic terrorism and violence that could break out anywhere individuals gather. As a result, in an instant, we can find ourselves in myriad life-threatening circumstances that could not have been anticipated.

Events such as these remind us that the only person, we truly have control over is ourselves and our responses to the daily challenges we face, regardless of our circumstances. They should also serve as a reminder to be mindful that our feelings and capacity to control them impact others around us. As it becomes clearer, we too can have our destiny turned on a dime by an event that is completely out of our control.

The Playing Field of Life

The playing field of life is seldom fair and rarely level. This reality necessitates the development of critical thinking about our capacities, situational awareness, and understanding of the contextual circumstances surrounding us. Taking personal responsibility means acknowledging ownership of our existence and the events that unfold in our lives. We have the power to choose whether to approach difficulties with a positive or negative mindset and that choice not only shapes the outcomes but how we live and our perceptions about the resulting outcomes themselves.

Interpreting Experiences

Paradoxically, while life exists only in our minds, we attribute profound meaning to our experiences. How we interpret our experiences shapes how we perceive others, sometimes as friends or enemies, depending on the mental constructs we've developed. Each significant experience is stored in our memory banks, with emotionally charged memories residing closer to the surface. These memories can resurface unexpectedly, impacting our present state.

Our capacity to extract lessons from our experiences significantly influences our future paths. By examining our past decisions, we can better understand the psychological crossroads we've encountered. This hindsight enables us to connect the dots of our journey to present moments, aiding us in navigating our future with informed intentionality. Although we may carefully consider our course, unforeseen events may still disrupt our plans. Therefore, resilience and our capacity to rebound after negative events become crucial in adapting to life's unpredictability. Through resilience, we can weather the storms that come our way and continue to navigate toward our goals with determination and perseverance.

Training, Growth, and Personal Development

There are ways we can partially inoculate ourselves to help lessen the effects of seismic events by going through training for specific situations, which is the purpose of CPR, First Aid training, active shooter drills, disaster drills, and other forms of training, including life coaching to live more fully. Training facilitates skills development and enables better responses when those responses are necessary. These are proactive responses to specific potential concerns of something catastrophic occurring in the future that may or may not happen.

In the case of trauma, there is an absolute certainty that everyone at some point in their lifetime will suffer trauma, and therefore, to maximize the quality of life over the life span, we should teach people how to overcome inevitable difficulties through embracing transformative learning as a lifelong practice. Embracing transformative learning offers a gateway to overcoming disorienting dilemmas that throw us off balance forcing us to change our ways or continue down a path of potential ongoing distress, further harm, or even death.

Shifting our perspectives from an external to an internal focus helps us to take ownership of our existence. If we want to take control of our lives, then we have to find a way to ask ourselves, at what point do I change my behaviors from *they* are the problem to *I* am the problem? For example, we often blame homeless people for being homeless rather than admitting that home insecurity and homelessness result from poverty, poorly constructed mental and other health maintenance systems, antiquated K-16 and trade school education systems, poorly constructed socio-economic development programs to support citizens striving to achieve the American Dream, wrongful terminations, toxic leadership, and sometimes just bad luck during layoffs.

Instead, we adopt negative paradigms and belief systems about various demographically assigned groups that shape misguided policies and practices. The perceptions (mental models) held by policymakers are often based on deficit learning models, and marginalized groups' perceived lack of capacity to improve their socioeconomic condition is one such example.

Life is an inside-out process, a solitary journey that each of us must navigate. It is akin to being both the game developer and the player, navigating the challenges we mentally construct and observe in our personal movie theaters locked inside our brains. Imagine life as a game where we set the rules and objectives. Our minds generate the scenarios— whether a love story, an adventure, or a horror story—and we navigate them, striving to achieve the goals we envision for each game. Our game is unique to each of us, living solely in our minds, guiding our actions, and influencing our interactions with others.

At first glance, this concept might seem abstract, even implausible. However, our perceptions fundamentally shape our sense of reality. As we play this game of life, we collaborate with others, weaving shared experiences and collective narratives. The game expands and contracts, and the storyline evolves as players come and go.

Recognizing this internal journey empowers us to address external challenges with clarity and purpose. It encourages us to own our existence, by looking beyond surface-level conflicts and focusing on the deeper, shared human experiences that unite us. In doing so, we can harness our collective capacity to create meaningful change and build a more cohesive, harmonious world.

Understanding that our internal world defines our external experiences can revolutionize our approach to problem-solving and collaboration. As Gandhi purportedly said, be the change you wish to see. By focusing on inner growth and self-awareness, we begin to cast aside those things that no longer serve us well and adopt new ways of being.

As we shift our way of seeing and interpreting our existence, we alter how everything in our personal universe responds to the newly emerging person. This transformation allows us to celebrate the changes we've made along our journey or appreciate our journey once it's over at the end of our time. Therefore, changing our perspective about the game changes the game itself, along with the potential outcomes for every player.

For example, shifting from a zero-sum game perspective to one of collective abundance means capitalizing on the unique contributions of individual team members for the benefit of the whole. Consider the current state of global affairs, where we often fight over perceived differences that only matter in a game of accumulating the most at others' expense. This rule pits everyone against each other in a survivalof-the-fittest contest. We can be better than that!

In the wake of the pandemic, our lives have been profoundly altered, intensifying mental health issues in already traumatized societies. Yet, this crisis has also opened up new opportunities to deploy existing technologies and revolutionize how work is conducted as we've experienced with virtual conferencing. We stand on the verge of long-term space exploration but continue to clash over ancient belief systems and paradigms.

Instead of engaging in these conflicts, we have the potential to come together and use our collective resources to employ and feed every person on the planet. By focusing on collaboration and mutual goals, we can harness our combined potential to create a more equitable and sustainable future for all. We could even harness our collective efforts to explore and inhabit other worlds, unlocking new technologies and opportunities along the way.

By shifting our focus from external to internal challenges, we change how we address the issues facing us. Refocusing our negative energy into positive outcomes through a shift in perspective allows us to evolve positively, regardless of what happens. A simple shift from scarcity to abundance has huge impacts on how we feel about ourselves and our condition, producing a shift in how the world responds to us.

Here's an example of what I mean: I attended a presentation in Seattle, WA which is about eighty miles from home. The presenter was a friend, and the content of her presentation was done well. After her presentation ended, we hung around and talked for a bit. I shared that I thought she did a great job presenting, and she said thanks, but explained she was disappointed there wasn't much engagement. I said candidly, with her permission, you never smiled. I explained that it's the weirdest thing, that by making changes in yourself everything around you shifts and responds to you differently. I suggested that the next time she went out in public, she should try it.

The next day she called me excited and exclaimed, why didn't you tell me that when I did it, people would just start talking to me! We laughed. She went on to explain her experience on the bus, and how other people just started to talk to her, which was a new experience for her. I knew her life would change because it happened to me when I paid my undergraduate fees, a story I tell later about fear.

Life is a journey of learning how to survive and make meaning of our experiences. Our journey to find that meaning is a journey to discover the Self and help it evolve over whatever time we have. The problem is, most of us do not understand or even know about that fundamental truth. Life as a human is to explore what it means to live fully, experience, understand, cope with, shape, be shaped by, learn from, and knowingly advance to create that which is experienced. This may sound complicated but it's not.

Simply put, we define our life by how we capture it to define our Self—the essence of how we define our being; and whatever we make of it, however we see it, resides in our minds. We define the meaning of our experiences—which will be made clearer as we go along. Defining the Self captures who we are at any given moment—a snapshot in time on our continuous path of becoming, lasting until our final breath. This inward focus enhances personal growth, changes the way we see our world, and drives our individual, and when done together, our collective potential to new heights.

When I close my eyes for the final time in preparation for taking my final breath, my hope is that I die with a smile on my face, thinking about all the wonderful moments I experienced. The wisdom I gained from knowing how far I traveled from the beginning to my highest points will be my final solace. One thing will be for sure, I will have accomplished one of my goals of always being the rising star rather than the shooting star, in honor of my mom who gave me that advice.

Life, the game designed by the player and whose outcomes are determined by the player, exists solely in the mind of the player. Yet, each player joins a universe with other players intent on playing their game by their own rules, creating infinite possibilities of outcomes for all participants. The point is, we must prepare ourselves to respond to a chaotic universe where anything can happen beyond our control.

Those of us who have faced life's uncertainties and engaged in end-of-life reflections understand the importance of deliberate self-assessment. When we evaluate our lives, our interpretation of events informs how well we feel we played the game of life. When others assess our contributions to the community, they will measure our accomplishments against our capacity to overcome adversity. For Christians, the stories of Moses, Job, and Jesus serve as such examples, but every culture has stories of such role models.

Finding Self

The ultimate formation of the Self is a deeply personal journey, influenced by individual choices and interpretations of experiences. This evolution is shaped by the dynamic interplay between a person's constitution and their willpower. Constitution refers to the physical and mental health and robustness of an individual, while willpower is the internal drive and determination that propels one to make decisions and persist in the face of challenges.

A strong constitution provides the necessary stamina and resilience to pursue goals, enhancing mental fortitude and fueling the willpower required to stay motivated and focused on long-term objectives. Physical health significantly impacts mental well-being; a healthy constitution promotes a positive mental state, which in turn fosters a strong source of willpower capable of managing stress and overcoming adversity.

Interestingly, individuals grappling with chronic health issues may find their circumstances foster even stronger willpower as they make choices to manage and potentially improve their health, illustrating how determined willpower can reciprocally fortify one's constitution.

Resilience, stemming from a robust constitution, enables individuals to adapt to changes and recover from setbacks. This resilience is closely linked to willpower; the determination to conquer difficulties can encourage lifestyle choices that promote health and proactive wellness. Furthermore, the environment significantly shapes both constitution and willpower.

Living conditions, social support, and access to healthcare and nutritious foods can either bolster or challenge these aspects of a person. A supportive environment enhances willpower, empowering individuals to take actions that improve their constitution, while less favorable conditions necessitate stronger willpower to navigate and surmount additional challenges. This dynamic may propel many athletes and others growing up in poverty to excel professionally, regardless of the industry or discipline. But it can also be the source of negative pressure that can overcome the ability to successfully resist system failure likely producing catastrophic consequences if safety nets are unavailable or nonexistent. In such cases lower order basic human needs such as food, clothing, shelter, and basic safety and security are all threatened.

The relationship between constitution and willpower is dynamic, with each influencing and reinforcing the other. Understanding this relationship highlights the holistic nature of health and well-being, showcasing how intertwined physical and mental strengths are in shaping human experience and achieving personal growth.

The evolution of the Self is intricately woven through the interplay of constitution and willpower, each profoundly shaping an individual's identity and experiences. At the heart of this developmental journey is the constitution, which serves as the foundational physical and mental framework. A robust constitution often equates to better physical health and mental clarity, allowing individuals to engage more deeply with the world around them. This strength enables them to explore a wide array of interests and challenges, thereby enriching their life experiences and shaping a more complex Self. On the other hand, a weaker constitution may restrict these experiences but can also foster a unique kind of growth where resilience and adaptability become key themes in an individual's evolution.

Willpower acts as the dynamic force driving change and without it, nothing happens. Over the duration of my career, I've initiated or otherwise been part of various change initiatives. Two of the change initiatives were a northern California high school and a statewide nonprofit organization that sustained continuous change for eight years because of the stability of the senior leaders in both cases. Organizations tend to not have the willpower to effectuate and sustain long-term systemic change because of CEO (senior most leader) turnover, but these were two success stories.

The solution to the CEO turnover problem that produces the next cycle of change is to carefully construct the desirable culture and train it upwards and top to bottom.

Building the desirable culture enables the construction of systems to support that culture. For example, building innovation centers, labs, or mechanisms to encourage continuous improvements. Embrace conflict rather than attack and squash it. Embrace new ideas and ideas that challenge the status quo. Build workforce support mechanisms such as coaching, mentorship, wellness, and learning programs to continuously develop and maintain a robust, dynamic workforce and coveted culture. Provide opportunities for employees to collaborate with each other in safe spaces.

It is the inner strength that motivates an individual to pursue goals, face challenges, and remain steadfast in their long-term aspirations. The potency of one's willpower determines how effectively they can utilize their constitutional strengths and weaknesses in pursuing personal growth. Strong willpower enables individuals to transcend physical or psychological barriers, molding their Self in alignment with their deepest values and visions—even in the face of great adversity.

As life unfolds with its array of challenges and opportunities, the interaction between constitution and willpower significantly colors how individuals perceive and respond to their circumstances. For example, someone endowed with a strong constitution and who is resolute in their determination may embrace challenging roles that cultivate leadership and resilience, sculpting a self-identity centered on success. Conversely, an individual with a less formidable constitution but a vigorous level of willpower might carve out a niche that values creativity and strategic thinking, leveraging their mental sharpness to overcome physical constraints.

Furthermore, the twin forces of constitution and willpower are essential for navigating the unpredictability of life. They equip an individual with the adaptability and resilience necessary to adjust and recover from life's inevitable setbacks. This resilience not only facilitates personal growth but also deepens self-understanding.

The process of reflection and self-awareness, fueled by an individual's will, is integral to this journey. Continuous self-evaluation helps one recognize their strengths and limitations, refine their goals, and gain a clearer understanding of their place in the world. This introspective practice is crucial for weaving one's varied experiences into a cohesive and meaningful self-identity.

In essence, constitution and willpower are the critical drivers in the ongoing evolution of the Self, determining not only the breadth and depth of experiences one encounters but also shaping how one engages with their experiences to forge a distinct identity and deeper self-understanding.

The Evolution of Self—Always Becoming

The gift of life brings with it an existence that is evolutionary, lasting until we take our last breath. That means life as a process is itself a process of always *becoming*. But what is it that is *becoming*? As I've thought about this question, I've come to conclude that *becoming* is a process of evolving the *Self* to maximize what we learn from our experiences over the course of the lifetime, for whatever length our lifetime might become.

That is, life is an ongoing dynamic process of developing the Self, or Self-development. In many ways life sculpts us using experiences as much as water erodes surfaces to bring new shapes and forms to the otherwise bland landscape.

The concept of the Self is a fundamental yet complex aspect of human psychology and philosophy, encompassing the essence of an individual's identity and consciousness. It refers to the coherent, integrated set of perceptions and values that an individual holds regarding who they are as a distinct, unique entity. The Self includes components such as an awareness of the *Self*. Self-awareness is the ability to reflect upon oneself, recognize one's own existence, and consider one's own actions, thoughts, and feelings. It involves consciousness of one's individuality and separateness from others.

The Self as a concept represents all the beliefs and understandings an individual has about their own attributes, roles, and capabilities. It includes self-esteem (how much value people place on themselves), self-image (how they see themselves), and the ideal Self (how they would like to be).

The Self is also shaped by social interactions and the broader societal context. It includes the roles one plays in society and how societal norms and relationships define aspects of who a person is. The Self provides physical and psychological continuity. The Self is perceived as persisting over time, maintaining a continuous identity despite changes in circumstances, experiences, or physical alterations. The Self is considered the source of actions and decisions, possessing agency (the capacity to act independently) and autonomy (self-governance).

Lewin's Force Field Theory can also be applied to explaining the evolution of the Self. Using Lewins Force Field Theory explained in Chapter 3, illustrates how the forces as the Self evolves influences an individual's behavior. The forces promoting movement towards a goal are represented by the + sign. The restraining forces hindering movement towards a goal are represented by the – sign in Figure 7: Change occurs when the balance of these forces shifts, described through his three-step model of change: unfreezing, changing, and refreezing. Unfreezing involves creating awareness of the need for change, changing is the process of moving towards the new behavior, and refreezing establishes the new behavior as the norm.

Field Theory also highlights topological psychology, where behavior is mapped in a geometric space to visualize the various factors at play. This mapping helps identify the *psychological tensions* and *conflicts* within the life space, aiding in better understanding and predicting behavior.

Understanding the Self involves exploring how these elements are formed, how they change over time, and how they influence behavior and interactions with others. Different disciplines, such as psychology, philosophy, sociology, and neuroscience, offer diverse perspectives and insights into the nature of the Self. **Figure 6-1:** *The Field theory of the Evolution of Self* illustrates various aspects of life that shape us as we grow over the lifespan. In essence, self-transcendence is about transcending the ego or the individual Self to embrace a more inclusive and expansive view of life, fostering a sense of unity with all beings and a commitment to contributing to something greater than oneself.

If the outcomes of navigating the various environments are negative, they can produce a drag on our progress and ability to move forward. If they are positive, they can help to propel us forward towards achieving whatever goals we set for ourselves. The complexities of life create plenty of opportunities for collisions to occur where things may be going very well in one environment and not so well in another. When this occurs issues, arising, in one environment can impact what is happening in others and alter our feelings and behaviors in another. For example, losing a job can disrupt what occurs in the home and social group environments. Likewise, a severe illness or illness of a family member can have profound impacts on job performance and career trajectories.

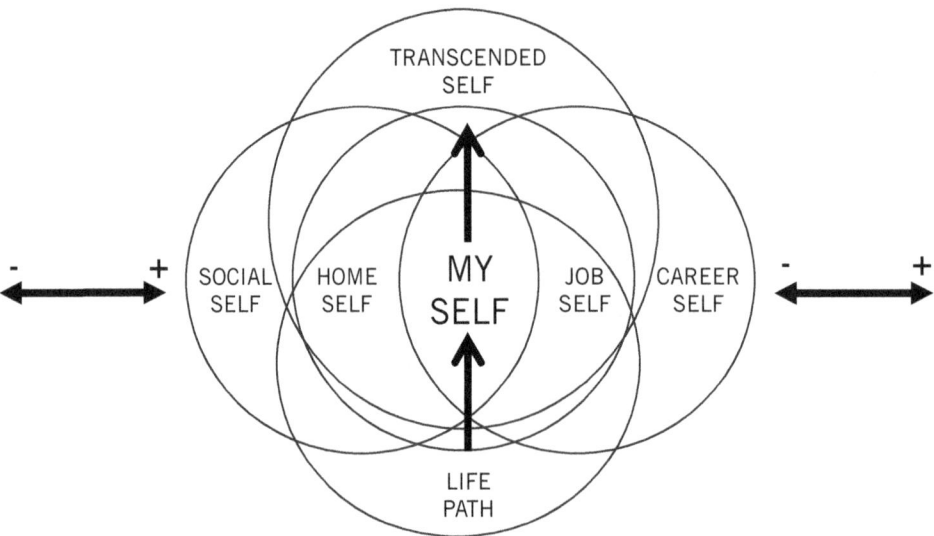

Figure 6-1: *The Field Theory of the Evolution of Self*

The formation of the Self is a complex, multidimensional process influenced by a combination of biological, psychological, and social factors shaping how the Self is typically formed. Biological factors provide the initial ingredients to form the container that houses what becomes the Self. The Self begins with the innate aspects of an individual, including genetic predispositions and the basic temperamental traits present from birth. Neurological development also plays a critical role, as brain structures and functions related to memory, perception, and cognitive processing contribute to self-awareness and selfregulation.

Childhood

Early interactions and attachment during infancy and childhood, interactions with primary caregivers are crucial for the initial formation of the Self. Attachment theory suggests that the quality of the early emotional bond formed with caregivers can significantly influence an individual's sense of security and self-worth. Secure attachments promote a healthy self-concept, while insecure attachments can lead to challenges in self-esteem and identity.

As children grow, they are increasingly influenced by broader social contexts, including family, peers, schools, and media which provides the early socialization situations and contexts. Socialization involves learning the values, norms, and behaviors of one's culture, which integrate into one's selfconcept. This includes gender roles, cultural identity, and moral beliefs. The development of cognitive abilities enables children to think about themselves in abstract ways, consider different perspectives, and construct narratives about their own lives. Theories such as Jean Piaget's stages of cognitive development show how the capacity to understand complex ideas about the Self evolves through childhood.

Individual Experiences

Individual experiences, including education, relationships, successes, failures, and traumas, continually shape the Self. The environment a person grows up in—whether it's nurturing or abusive, stable, or chaotic—plays a significant role in developing self-esteem and self-efficacy. Reflection and self-perception during adolescence is a critical period for self-discovery and identity formation. During this part of the life cycle, teenagers and young adults, experiment with different roles and ideologies to find a personal identity that fits them as self-perception becomes more detailed and differentiated.

Agency and Autonomy

It is also critical to forming a sense of agency and autonomy through recognizing one's ability to make choices and influence one's own life. This sense of personal power is integral to shaping their identity and life path through lifelong development. The Self is not static but continues to evolve throughout a person's life. Adulthood brings new roles, challenges, and changes, including career choices, parenthood, and aging, all of which can reshape the self-concept.

Ongoing Process

The formation of the Self is an ongoing process of development that starts from birth and continues throughout life, shaped by an interplay of genetic factors, personal experiences, and social influences. It is this interplay of circumstances that produces the uniqueness that makes each of us one-of-a-kind individuals. How far we go as individuals is a matter of luck, capacity, skill, situations, and circumstances. The rest is up to each of us to find the willpower to derive the most we can from our existence to become the best versions of Self we can. We can choose to develop the Self with intention and live on purpose or we can let our circumstances define us and let them take us where they may. The choice is ours to make, and we are the only ones who can make it.

Life as a Process of Self-Transcendence

We do not live in isolation from others and therefore we must also think about our individual actions and their impacts on others. Societies consist of individuals, making everyone's well-being relevant because we're all in the same boat. The same is true of our workplaces. While each person's journey to this moment is unique, there are commonalities beneath the surface, masked by the facade we wear in the theater of life. It's a lesson that everyone will face or has faced trauma, often multiple times, so when interacting with others, we must be mindful that behind smiles may lie hidden pain.

Interconnected Communities

Living in interconnected communities means our actions impact others and therefore we must concern ourselves with life beyond ourselves. Poor performing employees impact other employees and the organization as a whole. Noisy neighbors impact their neighbors as well as the neighborhood. Threatening behaviors impact those being threatened and can intimidate entire communities. Recognizing our collective existence on this planet is crucial. Together, we possess immense potential to tackle any challenge. Unfortunately, we often waste efforts on conflicts rooted in perceived differences. The solution begins internally since our personal journeys affect the world around us.

Modern Civilization

Looking at modern civilization, we see a web of challenges that are diverse, interconnected, and complex, highlighting the precariousness of our era. At the forefront, we are confronted with an environmental crisis that looms large, characterized by climate change, loss of biodiversity, and pollution. The planet warms, ice caps melt, and sea levels rise, threatening coastal communities and island nations. Forests, vital lungs of the earth, are cut down at alarming rates, leading to loss of species and habitats. Air and water pollution continue to plague large swaths of humanity, affecting health and quality of life.

Environmental Degradation

Environmental degradation and climate change is leading to displacement, as people are forced to migrate from areas affected by severe weather, rising sea levels, or unsustainable conditions. This displacement strains resources leading to competition and conflict among communities. Individuals may also experience anxiety and distress over environmental changes, impacting mental health. The impacts of environmental degradation, such as natural disasters caused by climate change, can lead to direct trauma. Experiencing or even anticipating events like hurricanes, wildfires, and floods can cause acute stress and long-term post-traumatic stress disorder (PTSD). Furthermore, the loss of one's home or community can lead to feelings of grief and dislocation.

Technological Advancements

Technological advancements create ethical dilemmas that must be managed effectively, or they can destroy civilization in very real terms. Alongside environmental issues, rapid technological advancements present both opportunities and challenges. Artificial intelligence and automation promise efficiency and innovation but also pose risks to jobs and privacy. The digital divide separates those who have access to technology and those who do not, exacerbating existing inequalities. Ethical dilemmas abound, from data privacy breaches to the potential for surveillance states.

Rapid advancements in technology can lead to job displacement due to automation, increasing economic anxiety. The digital divide might isolate individuals who lack access to technology, limiting their educational and professional opportunities. On a social level, while technology connects people digitally, it can also lead to isolation and a decrease in face-to-face interactions. Rapid technological changes and digital overexposure can lead to psychological stress and anxiety. Issues such as cyberbullying, privacy violations, and the constant pressure from social media can induce emotional distress. The pace of change can also cause a phenomenon known as *technostress*, where an individual feels overwhelmed by keeping up with new technologies.

Economic Trauma

In my experience, the only time trickledown economics works is through the disparate outcomes that economic inequality produces. Economic disparities both within and between countries are growing. The rich get richer, and the poor struggle to meet basic needs. This inequality fuels social discontent and can lead to unrest and violence. Resource scarcity, particularly of water and arable land, heightens tensions and competition, that often leads to conflicts. Growing economic disparities can lead to a sense of injustice and social exclusion for those on the lower end of the spectrum. This can breed resentment and hostility between different economic classes and reduce social cohesion. Individuals may feel powerless or disenfranchised, which can decrease civic participation.

Economic trauma occurs through economic instability, such as job loss, financial insecurity, and poverty which can lead to chronic stress and anxiety. The uncertainty and struggle associated with economic hardship can severely impact mental health, contributing to depression and a reduced sense of personal efficacy making self-transcendence more difficult as the focus must become survival and meeting basic needs. Economic trauma also produces disparate health outcomes between those who do and don't have adequate economic resources to live well. Accordingly, public health challenges, especially highlighted by the COVID-19 pandemic, demonstrate the vulnerabilities of global health systems. The disparity in healthcare access and quality between developed and developing nations is stark. Pandemics illustrate not only the biological threats from viruses but also the societal and economic shocks that can result from a global health crisis.

Health Crises

Health crises like pandemics disproportionately affect those with less access to health-care, leading to higher morbidity and mortality rates in these groups. The fear and uncertainty associated with health crises can lead to social stigmatization and discrimination against those perceived to be at higher risk of spreading diseases. Disparities in health access and outcomes, as well as experiencing or witnessing severe illness during pandemics, can be deeply traumatic. The fear of disease, death, and the stress of caregiving can lead to long-term psychological distress.

Political Instability and Fragmentation

Political instability and fragmentation within societies in the global political landscape is increasingly fractured. Nationalism and populism have risen, challenging global cooperation and multilateralism. Democracies face internal pressures from misinformation and polarization, while authoritarian regimes use technology to tighten their grip on power. Political instability and cultural fragmentation divide segments of the population fostering environments of mistrust and hostility. Misinformation and polarized media can influence individual beliefs and exacerbate divisions, making cooperative dialogue and consensus-building more challenging.

Cultural and Social Fragmentation

Cultural and social fragmentation is evident as societies grapple with identity politics, migration, and the integration of diverse populations. Social media platforms, while connecting people, also facilitate the spread of misinformation and create echo chambers that polarize public opinion. Political unrest, social upheaval, and cultural conflicts can lead to a collective sense of insecurity and fear. Experiencing violence, discrimination, or severe societal division can lead to emotional trauma. This kind of environment can also exacerbate existing mental health conditions or lead to new issues such as anxiety disorders or depression.

Multifaceted Challenges

The confluence of these challenges—environmental, technological, economic, health-related, political, and social—demands a coordinated and comprehensive response. Our ability to address these issues holistically, to foster resilience and adaptability, will likely define the future trajectory of human civilization. As we navigate these turbulent times, the interconnectedness of our global society means that solutions must be collaborative, inclusive, and forward-thinking, keeping in mind not just the immediate impacts but also the long-term well-being of our planet and its inhabitants.

The multifaceted challenges facing civilization today significantly influence individuals on a personal level and affect how they interact with one another. Collectively, these issues can lead to increased stress, anxiety, and a sense of insecurity among individuals. They can also challenge traditional social structures and norms, necessitating new forms of adaptation and resilience as people navigate these global challenges in their daily lives.

The challenges facing civilization today can indeed produce trauma in various ways that spill over into our workplaces and social groups and ability to move forward towards self-transcendence. These sorts of traumatic experiences can affect individuals' ability to function and interact with others, influencing their behavior, emotional responses, and social relationships. The ongoing stress from these societal challenges can also lead to complex trauma, which occurs due to repeated exposure to stressful events over time, profoundly affecting an individual's well-being.

Triggering

Societies are composed of individuals and therefore everyone's well-being should matter to each of us because we all share the same proverbial boat. So, the stories of how we each got to this very moment in time while unique, have more commonality than what is evident on the surface and that's why we call it a façade, the mask we wear to the costume ball we call life. The lesson here as we'll discuss is that we are all living with, or will experience trauma during our lifetimes, with the statistical norm being multiple events. Therefore, when interacting with others, we never know how much pain might lie behind their smiles, so be mindful and kind.

If we assume that Abraham Maslow is right and the objective of life is to transcend the Self in order to live more fully and holistically in community with others, then we have to be able to successfully navigate the various environments that shape our lives including our home and family, social groups, the dynamics surrounding the jobs we take, as well as the careers we pursue. Interestingly, the effects from the environments that impact our lives can negatively thwart or positively aid in our capacity to achieve what Abraham Maslow labeled as *Self-transcendence*.

Catalysts

Catalysts are essential for self-transcendence to occur. These catalysts can be external events, experiences, or internal shifts in perspective that prompt individuals to move beyond their egoic selves and connect with something greater. Without these catalysts, individuals may remain entrenched in their current state of consciousness (status quo) and may not embark on the transformative journey toward self-transcendence. Catalysts for self-transcendence can vary widely and may include profound life events, moments of awe and wonder, spiritual practices, acts of compassion and service, creative expression, and encounters with wisdom and insight. Each of these catalysts has the potential to ignite a spark within individuals, propelling them toward a deeper understanding of themselves and their place in the world.

Moreover, while catalysts are essential for initiating the process of self-transcendence, the journey itself requires active engagement and willingness on the part of individuals. It involves introspection, selfawareness, and a willingness to explore new perspectives and experiences. Without this active participation, the transformative process may stall, and individuals may struggle to progress toward self-transcendence.

While catalysts are crucial for initiating the journey toward self-transcendence, individuals must also actively engage in the process to fully realize its potential. Through a combination of external catalysts and internal exploration, individuals can embark on a transformative journey that leads to profound shifts in consciousness and a deeper sense of connection and meaning in life.

Self-transcendence is a profound concept often depicted as the journey of an individual reaching beyond their immediate self-interests, personal desires, and life's mundane aspects to connect with something larger and more universal. Imagine a person standing on a beach, staring out at the vast ocean. As they gaze into the horizon, they experience a moment of clarity where their everyday concerns seem to shrink in significance compared to the immensity of the sea and sky. In this moment, the individual feels a deep connection with nature, a sense of being part of a larger whole. Such a state helps to explain my experiences during the Lummi Nation Salmon Ceremony.

Self-transcendence involves expanding one's boundaries to include the wider universe, embracing a broader perspective of life that emphasizes connectivity and purpose beyond the self. For many, this can come through spirituality, deep relationships, commitment to a cause, or profound experiences in nature that evoke a sense of awe and wonder. Through self-transcendence, individuals often find a deeper meaning in life, seeing themselves as integral parts of the bigger picture. It shifts focus from personal gain to the welfare of others and to broader existential questions. This journey might inspire acts of charity, create a deeper understanding of life's interconnectedness, or lead to significant changes in how we live and interact with the world.

Self-transcendence is often sparked by experiences and practices that invite individuals to move beyond their limited sense of Self and connect with something greater, whether it be the universe, humanity, or the divine. These catalysts can lead to profound shifts in consciousness and a deeper sense of meaning, purpose, and interconnectedness in life. The journey to self-transcendence is deeply personal and can vary greatly from person to person. What works for one individual may not resonate with another, so it's essential for each person to explore and discover their own path toward self-transcendence.

Achieving self-transcendence often involves personal growth, spiritual development, and a shift in perspective. Like most things about being human, there are several pathways we can take to reach self-transcendence. Intentionally seeking meaning and purpose by engaging in activities or pursuits that align with our values and contribute to the greater good can foster a sense of purpose beyond self-interest. This might involve volunteering, pursuing a meaningful career, or engaging in creative endeavors that contribute positively to society. Developing self-awareness through practices such as meditation, mindfulness, or therapy can help individuals gain insight into their thoughts, emotions, and behaviors. This heightened awareness can lead to a deeper understanding of oneself and one's place in the world, fostering a sense of interconnectedness with others.

Certain experiences, such as awe-inspiring natural landscapes, profound moments of connection with others, or transcendent spiritual experiences, can evoke feelings of self-transcendence. These experiences often challenge our sense of separateness and expand our awareness of the interconnectedness of all life. Cultivating compassion and empathy towards others can shift the focus away from the individual self and towards the well-being of others. By empathizing with the experiences of others and taking compassionate action to alleviate suffering, individuals may experience a deep sense of connection and purpose beyond themselves. For many individuals, spiritual practices such as prayer, meditation, or contemplation can be a pathway to self-transcendence. These practices often involve transcending the ego and connecting it with a higher power, universal consciousness, or the divine.

Challenges, Setbacks, and Personal Growth

Embracing challenges, setbacks, and periods of personal growth can lead to profound transformations in consciousness. By facing and overcoming obstacles, individuals may develop resilience, wisdom, and a deeper understanding of themselves and the world around them, ultimately leading to self-transcendence. Self-transcendence can be sparked by a variety of experiences, perspectives, and practices that prompt individuals to shift their focus from the individual Self to something greater.

Significant Life Events

Significant life events such as childbirth, near-death experiences, loss of a loved one, or major life transitions can prompt individuals to reevaluate their priorities, values, and sense of self. These experiences can lead to a deeper understanding of the interconnectedness of all life and foster a sense of self-transcendence. Experiencing moments of awe and wonder, such as witnessing a breathtaking sunset, exploring the vastness of nature, or contemplating the mysteries of the universe, can evoke feelings of humility and insignificance in the face of something greater than oneself. These experiences can open individuals to a sense of awe and interconnectedness, sparking self-transcendence.

Creative Endeavors

Engaging in creative endeavors such as art, music, writing, or dance can provide a pathway to self-transcendence. These activities often involve tapping into a deeper source of inspiration or creativity beyond the individual self, leading to experiences of flow, connection, and transcendence. Reading inspiring literature, listening to wisdom teachings, or engaging in meaningful conversations with mentors or spiritual guides can provide insights and perspectives that expand one's understanding of oneself and the world. These encounters can spark moments of insight and self-transcendence.

Spirituality and Religion

Spirituality plays a significant role in the concept of self-transcendence. According to a report by the Pew Research Center, about 84% of the global population is affiliated with a religious group. This includes major world religions like Christianity, Islam, Hinduism, and Buddhism, as well as other traditional, indigenous, and folk religions. Additionally, there are people who may not identify with a specific religion but consider themselves spiritual in some way, often expressing belief in higher powers, spiritual forces, or a universal spirit without aligning with the tenets of organized religions. Thus, it is reasonable to estimate that a significant portion of the world's population has some sort of religious or spiritual belief system, reflecting a widespread human inclination towards belief in something greater than oneself.

Religious spirituality refers to the personal practices and beliefs that connect individuals to a divine or higher power within the framework of a specific religious tradition. It encompasses a range of practices, beliefs, and emotions that relate to the sacred or the transcendent. Key characteristics of religious spirituality include a connection to a higher power, engagement with sacred texts and doctrines, participation in rituals and worship, adherence to moral and ethical guidelines, a sense of community and fellowship, and a focus on personal transformation and growth.

Many religious and spiritual traditions also include beliefs about the afterlife and eschatology, providing a framework for understanding human existence in a broader cosmic context and often motivating adherents to live their lives in certain ways. Religious spirituality is about seeking meaningful connections with something greater than oneself, often expressed and experienced through the specific teachings and practices of established religious traditions.

Indigenous spirituality encompasses a diverse range of beliefs and practices that are deeply rooted in the cultural traditions and histories of indigenous peoples around the world. These spiritual practices are inherently connected to the land, the natural world, and the community, reflecting a profound relationship with the environment and the cosmos. Indigenous spirituality often involves a deep, sacred connection to the land, viewing the Earth as a living entity. This connection informs practices that respect and honor the natural world, including animals, plants, and geographical features. It relies heavily on oral traditions to pass down knowledge, stories, rituals, and wisdom from generation to generation, with ancestors holding a significant place as guides and protectors.

Spiritual practices are generally communal rather than individualistic, involving community rituals, ceremonies, and festivals that reinforce social bonds and cultural identity. Rituals and ceremonies may include music, dance, storytelling, the use of sacred objects, and rites of passage, which serve to maintain the balance between the physical and spiritual worlds. Leaders such as shamans, elders, or other respected figures play crucial roles in guiding spiritual practices, healing, and maintaining the health of the community. Indigenous spirituality typically embodies a holistic approach, integrating aspects of the physical, spiritual, social, and cultural lives of the community, emphasizing balance and harmony. It is not monolithic but varies widely among different indigenous groups, each with its own unique beliefs, practices, and connections to their environment.

While indigenous spiritual practices and organized religious practices both encompass beliefs about the sacred, rituals, and community involvement, they differ significantly in their origins, structure, and the way they are practiced. Indigenous practices are typically deeply rooted in the traditions and histories of specific tribes or cultural groups, with a strong connection to the land and the natural world, passed down orally through generations. In contrast, organized religions often have more documented histories with formal scriptures and a well-defined founder or group of founders. Indigenous practices generally lack a formal hierarchical structure seen in many religions, with leadership roles such as shamans or elders focusing on serving the community's spiritual needs rather than governing.

Organized religions typically feature a defined hierarchical structure, including roles such as priests, bishops, and popes, with specific doctrines and rules. Indigenous practices often focus on the interconnectedness of all living things, ancestral spirits, and a deep connection to specific landscapes, while organized religions generally center around a defined deity or deities, with practices often including regular worship services, prayer, and the observance of holy days related to specific religious histories.

Despite these differences, there are notable similarities between indigenous spiritualities and organized religions. Both use rituals and ceremonies to mark important life events, seasonal cycles, and other significant occasions. Both provide ethical guidelines intended to shape moral behavior, foster community cohesion, and outline the responsibilities of individuals to their communities and the natural world. Both play significant roles in forming and maintaining community identity and cohesion, offering a sense of belonging and an integral part of cultural or community identity. Both have figures who are considered to have special spiritual authority, whether shamans, elders, priests, or rabbis, who provide spiritual guidance and maintain the traditions of the community. Both seek to connect individuals to a transcendent reality beyond everyday existence, offering explanations for life's mysteries and the nature of the universe. Understanding these distinctions and connections can enrich our appreciation of how people across different cultures and histories make sense of the world and their place in it.

In essence, self-transcendence is about transcending the ego or the individual self to embrace a more inclusive and expansive view of life, fostering a sense of unity with all beings and a commitment to contributing to something greater than oneself. This journey can manifest through spirituality, deep relationships, commitment to a cause, or profound experiences in nature that evoke a sense of awe and wonder. It is a universal aspect of human experience that bridges individual and collective existence, offering pathways to greater fulfillment and a deeper sense of purpose.

Self in a Sea of Others

Complicating matters for all of us is that we live in an era marked by significant upheaval and transitions generating extreme external pressures, casting a shadow of uncertainty over our future as a species. In these critical times, decisive leadership is essential to mitigate the anxiety that, if sustained, can lead to trauma. Unfortunately, what we often encounter instead is leadership that could at best be described as mediocre, driven by the self-interests of leaders focused on their own power and personal gains.

What exacerbates the situation is that many influential figures actively and intentionally use divisive rhetoric that stokes fear. This kind of speech has tangible effects not only on their supporters and opponents but also on innocent bystanders, as we often observe in public political discussions that lead to violent outbreaks. The influence of such rhetoric extends into our personal spaces like homes, social circles, and workplaces, as individuals carry these influenced attitudes and behaviors across different environments.

In the United States, we see considerable energy wasted in conflicts over our differences, rather than embracing our differences as a source of strength, that has propelled us to the status of a superpower. Politicians and other leaders often exacerbate this division, to a point where many analysts draw parallels between today's polarized climate and the tense pre-Civil War era of the 1850s and more recently to Nazi Germany with the rise of fascist sentiments here at home.

Some people have expressed harmful rhetoric and undue skepticism about Black pilots' qualifications, which not only underscores this division but actively inflicts trauma on those targeted (PatriotTimes, 2024). Such remarks, which are made publicly and without any factual basis, reflect profound ignorance and malice. These attitudes are not only harbored within certain workplaces but are also broadcast with the ease of a click-through social media to large audiences, who may then carry these harmful stereotypes into their own professional environments.

Life is imperfect in the sense that we all might want it to be, imagined to be filled with romance, happiness, great health, easy living, and the ability to do whatever we want, whenever we want, for as long as we want, and with whomever we want. In fact, many of us want to be so carefree that if whatever we want interferes with whatever someone else wants, we behave as though our wants should supersede all others because it is our wants.

Such perspectives produce the basis for future conflicts because of the disregard some individuals have for others and for the collective good of the whole. Moreover, we often champion the ideal of rugged individualism, yet this principle is frequently applied selectively, to satisfy personal desires and beliefs. When others express their individuality in ways that differ from our own, there's a tendency to intrude into their lives, dictating how they should live.

In scenarios where there is a power imbalance, the more dominant party usually prevails until those less powerful begin to unite and advocate for their rights. In the workplace, these conflicts often boil down to class and status struggles embedded in the belief systems of those in power. This distinction is crucial for understanding the dynamics inherent in social categorization and as my favorite professor taught during my doctoral studies, is what must be embraced to effect meaningful change. That is, we must learn to embrace conflict as a source of potential positive change rather than run from it.

Mental Models and Belief Systems

Mental models are the frameworks or representations that individuals create in their minds to understand, interpret, and interact with the world around them. These models are cognitive constructs that help people process information, make decisions, solve problems, and navigate their environment. Mental models are shaped by personal experiences, education, culture, and environment, and they influence how individuals perceive and respond to situations. Mental models:

- Simplify the complexity of the real world by focusing on certain aspects while ignoring others. This helps in managing and making sense of vast amounts of information quickly.

- Form the basis for prediction and allow individuals to predict outcomes and explain events based on their understanding of how things work. They are used to anticipate consequences and plan actions.

- Play a crucial role in decision-making processes. They influence how options are evaluated, and which course of action is chosen.

In short, mental models are the lenses through which we view and interpret the world around us. They are the internal representations of external reality that our minds create to understand how things work and guide our decisions and actions. Think of them as mental shortcuts or simplified maps of complex landscapes, helping us navigate through life's challenges and opportunities without having to start from scratch every time.

Mental Models are important because they frame how we see others, our circumstances, and our lives. Mental models are just that, the images we create in our minds when we think about life events or plans. A supervisor with a Theory X mental model will treat their employees very differently than if they hold a Theory Y mental model. (Theory X and Theory Y are explained more fully below.) Senge's *Ladder of Inference* is a visual concept developed by Chris Argyris and used by Peter Senge in his (1990) book *The Fifth Discipline*. It describes the mental process of moving from observable data and experiences to a conclusion or action, often without being aware of the intermediate steps and assumptions involved. This model is particularly relevant in understanding how people form beliefs and make decisions, and it can be used to enhance personal and organizational learning.

Senge's Ladder of Inference

Senge (1990) outlines the steps on the *Ladder of Inference* as follows:

- **Reality and Facts:** Starting at the bottom of the ladder, we have facts and our sense of reality. Facts are the observable data that is the same for everyone. For example, if the temperature is factually measured as 70 degrees (F), then it is 70 degrees (F) for everyone even when each person experiences the temperature differently. However, each person's sense of reality in terms of their experience with the event will likely vary. The difference is in how each person's body regulates its respective temperature as well as how each individual *experiences* the temperature neurologically. The point is, even though two people can experience the same thing at the same time, how they process the experience will be unique to them.

- **Selected Reality:** We select specific data and facts from what we observe. We can't notice everything, so we subconsciously select data that seems relevant to us.

- **Interpretation:** We interpret the data, giving it personal meaning based on our existing assumptions and prior experiences.

- **Assumptions:** Our interpretation is based on the assumptions we are making, often unconsciously.

- **Conclusions:** Based on our interpreted data and our assumptions, we draw conclusions.

- **Beliefs:** We develop beliefs about the world or the situation, influenced by the conclusions we have drawn.

- **Actions:** We take actions that seem appropriate based on our beliefs.

- **Reality Check:** We confirm our beliefs by interacting with our surroundings and either reinforce or continue to challenge our belief systems through a reflexive loop that continues the process. It's at this point we have to be careful about confirmation bias reinforcing our beliefs to the exclusion of considering space for reconsideration.

In the case of the 70-degree temperature how we experience the temperature may influence how we dress, what we choose to do, and set our frame of mind for the day. The *Ladder of Inference* also suggests how easily we can jump to conclusions without considering all the facts and perspectives when confirmation bias sets in.

Practically, we make assumptions about the weather based on temperature rather than the overall weather pattern for the day. I recently traveled to Las Vegas for my grandson's first birthday. Because I've been to the area, I made some assumptions about how to dress on my outbound flight to Las Vegas as well as assumptions about how to dress on my return flight to the Pacific Northwest, where I reside. It shows how our beliefs and actions are often based on interpreted reality, not objective reality, and these interpretations are influenced by our past experiences and cultural norms.

Awareness of this process can help us in questioning our own thinking and making more informed, less biased decisions. It can also improve communication and understanding in groups by revealing how different people can interpret the same data in very different ways, leading to different conclusions and actions. For example, *policing* has very different connotations in different communities.

Mental models are indispensable tools for understanding the world, but their effectiveness is greatly enhanced by the breadth and depth of our knowledge and the willingness to update them in light of new information. The more varied and accurate our mental models are, the more effectively we can navigate the complexities of life. Challenging our mental models can create internal discomfort through what is known as cognitive dissonance which challenges our thinking and deeply held belief systems. As an example, growing up in segregated communities may make it difficult for a family to accept a child marrying someone whose culture is unlike the culture of the dominant group.

Mental models are built from our experiences, education, cultural upbringing, and the information we absorb from our environment. They include beliefs, assumptions, and generalizations about how the world operates. For example, the concept of supply and demand in economics is a mental model that helps us understand how prices are determined in the market. Similarly, the mental model of cause and effect aids us in understanding the relationships between actions and outcomes.

The power of mental models lies in their ability to help us predict outcomes, solve problems, and make decisions more efficiently. However, they also have limitations. Because mental models are simplifications, they might not always accurately represent the full complexity of reality. They can lead to cognitive biases and errors in judgment if we rely too heavily on oversimplified or incorrect models. This is why it's beneficial to cultivate a diverse set of mental models—drawing from different disciplines and perspectives allows us to view situations from multiple angles and increases the likelihood of making better-informed decisions.

Mental models and belief systems are both frameworks that guide how we perceive and interact with the world, but they serve different functions and are structured differently. Mental Models are cognitive constructs that represent how things work in the external world. They are practical and often based on observable phenomena, allowing us to predict outcomes, solve problems, and make decisions. Mental models are more about understanding and applying principles from various domains (e.g., physics, economics) to navigate specific situations.

Belief Systems

Belief Systems, on the other hand, are comprehensive collections of beliefs and values that provide a broader worldview and a sense of meaning and purpose. These systems encompass moral, ethical, religious, or philosophical beliefs and are deeply personal. They shape our attitudes, and how we judge right from wrong and influence our motivations and aspirations.

In essence, while mental models are tools for practical reasoning and decision-making about how things work, belief systems offer a foundational framework for understanding why things matter, guiding our principles and values in life. Mental models can be easily updated or changed with new information, whereas belief systems are more deeply ingrained and evolve more slowly over time.

Mental models influence perception and behavior by shaping not only how individuals perceive the world but also how they behave in it. Mental models can determine a person's reaction to various situations and challenges, and they are not static, so they evolve over time as individuals gain new experiences, learn new information, and encounter different perspectives. Interestingly, different individuals can have vastly different mental models for the same concept or situation, leading to variability and different interpretations and responses to the same stimuli. Since mental models affect understanding, they play a significant role in communication making it possible for misunderstandings to occur when people have different mental models of the same subject.

There are numerous types of mental models across various fields, such as economic models, scientific theories, social and psychological theories, and personal belief systems. A number of mental models are presented here to illustrate various concepts through visual images or pictures to support what the text explains for the same concept. Understanding and occasionally revising mental models is important for personal growth, effective decision-making, and better communication. Being aware of our mental models and recognizing that others may have different models is key to empathy and effective interpersonal interactions.

Throughout life, mental models are dynamic; they are constantly being tested, adjusted, and sometimes completely overhauled as we gain new information and experiences. The flexibility and adaptability of these models are crucial for learning and effective decision-making and being aware of them is also important for personal growth, enhancing empathy, and improved communication with others. Mental models begin to form very early in human development and continue to evolve throughout a person's life. The formation and refinement of these models are influenced by a combination of cognitive development, personal experiences, social interactions, and cultural context.

Belief systems play a critical role in shaping our self-concept, which is our understanding and perception of ourselves based on our beliefs, attributes, and personal identity. These belief systems include our views on the world, our values, and our perceptions of our place within it. They significantly influence how we see ourselves and, consequently, our self-esteem, or how much value we place on ourselves.

Belief systems impact our Self-concept in the following ways:

- The values and norms we adopt from our culture, family, and social groups provide a framework for evaluating our behaviors, achievements, and characteristics. If we believe we are living up to these values, our self-concept will likely be positive, enhancing our self-esteem.

- Our interactions and experiences with others contribute to our belief systems. Positive feedback and successful experiences can reinforce beliefs that we are competent and valuable, bolstering our selfconcept and self-esteem. Conversely, negative feedback can lead to beliefs that undermine our selfconcept and diminish our self-esteem.

- Our belief systems often include ideas about where we stand in comparison to others. These comparisons can significantly affect our self-concept. If we believe we are doing well compared to our peers, our self-esteem may increase. However, unfavorable comparisons can lead to a poorer self-concept. These comparisons also shape our perspectives of fairness in our organizations.

Subsequently, belief systems play a crucial role in shaping individual behavior, societal norms, and world events. They influence how people make sense of their experiences, how they interact with others, and how they respond to challenges and opportunities in life. Understanding different belief systems is key to appreciating the diversity of perspectives and motivations in the world.

If we engage in transformative learning as a way of being in our organizations, then any cognitive dissonance that arises from the way we see the world and experience it becomes fuel for continued growth and personal development. Transformative learning brings with it a way of understanding ourselves more fully and it supports resiliency when it is needed. It aids in perspective shaping, tolerance for ambiguity, empathy, and compassion and supports positive mental health. It is also foundational to effective transformative leadership, effective coaching, and overall mental and physical wellness.

My father, self-taught, along with my mother who was an avid reader, created a home library containing about three thousand books according to my mother. It was such an extensive Black history book collection that it is now in a museum in Chicago. It was the beginning of my understanding why I was having so many conflicts with my teachers and why my feelings were so strong about the harm teachers and others were creating for people of color.

Belief systems are comprehensive frameworks of ideas and values that individuals or groups use to understand and interpret the world around them. Belief systems provide a lens through which individuals and groups view the world. They offer a sense of understanding, purpose, and identity, and can strongly influence behavior, relationships, and societal structures. Despite their diversity, all belief systems fulfill a fundamental human need to make sense of the world and one's place in it.

Mental Models, Belief Systems, and Behavior Converge

Belief systems and mental models are not just abstract psychological concepts; they are practical tools that, when understood and managed effectively by leaders, can significantly enhance an organization's ability to navigate challenges, capitalize on opportunities, and maintain a competitive edge in the dynamic business landscape. In a professional business context, understanding how belief systems and mental models construct our sense of reality is crucial for effective leadership, decision-making, and organizational dynamics. Both belief systems and mental models are integral cognitive frameworks that shape our perceptions, interpretations, and interactions within the organizational environments.

There is a nexus between belief systems and trauma. Belief systems can both shape the experience and response to trauma and be transformed by it. Understanding this nexus can help in developing therapeutic approaches and support structures that align with an individual's core beliefs. Belief systems and trauma are interconnected in several ways, often influencing each other deeply. Coping mechanisms may develop beliefs to cope with trauma, such as seeing the world as inherently dangerous or unpredictable, or adopting spiritual/religious views to make sense of their experiences. Trauma can lead to negative self-images like unworthiness, guilt, or shame, which influence behavior and future interactions.

Pre-existing belief systems shape how individuals perceive and interpret traumatic events, and they can become precursors for future behaviors. For example, a person with a strong belief in justice may find it particularly challenging to cope with trauma caused by an injustice. Positive beliefs, such as optimism or faith, can offer resilience and help individuals navigate through their trauma. Conversely, rigid or negative beliefs can increase vulnerability, making it harder to recover.

The shared narratives and beliefs within a community also play a significant role in how trauma survivor's cope. Communities that emphasize healing and resilience can provide a supportive environment that aids recovery. However, communities that stigmatize those affected by trauma can lead to further isolation and exacerbate the survivor's distress.

Cultural or religious practices, which are deeply rooted in these belief systems, can offer structured ways to process trauma. Rituals and healing practices provide a framework for recovery, helping individuals find meaning and solace in the aftermath of traumatic events. These practices can be crucial in fostering a sense of community and shared experience, which are vital components of the healing process.

Cognitive Distortions and Maladaptive Beliefs

Trauma can lead to cognitive distortions and maladaptive beliefs, such as thinking *the world is a bad place* or *I can't trust anyone,* which reinforces negative behaviors and interactions. These distorted thinking patterns can significantly impact a survivor's perceptions of safety, influencing their ability to form relationships and engage in everyday activities.

Belief Systems as Triggers

Belief systems can serve as powerful triggers, particularly when trauma reminders are tied to certain situations, symbols, or concepts related to the original traumatic experience. For instance, the idiom *cutting off your nose to spite your face* describes self-destructive retaliation or revenge, where the person ends up harming themselves more than anyone else. This idiom likely originates from stories of nuns in the Middle Ages who would mutilate their faces to avoid being attractive to invading soldiers, demonstrating how deeply held beliefs can lead to significant self-harm.

We see beliefs play out in real-life scenarios, such as people marching and protesting for or against issues they feel strongly about, even risking arrest to support their cause. Unfortunately, the rise of violence overtaking discourse, fueled by fiery political speeches promoting aggression as a primary solution, exemplifies the dangerous outcomes of rigid belief systems. I had a former client who thought it was acceptable to wave a gun in my face. After terminating my contract with this client, I discovered that I was not the only one to experience such behavior. Despite discussing the inappropriateness of their actions, the client insisted on continuing this practice, reinforcing my decision to end our professional relationship.

Reflecting on my childhood, I realize how cruel the world can be due to socially constructed views of differences. These perspectives define who belongs and who does not, creating in-groups and out-groups. Membership decisions, whether conscious or subconscious, determine who receives benefits and rewards and who is demonized without reason beyond that they are excluded members of a group.

Our perspectives shape how we view the world and establish our belief systems and mental models. These systems influence our interpretations and responses to experiences, either confirming or challenging our previous views. For example, as a child, I disliked avocados, but as an adult, I enjoy them as a creamy addition to sandwiches and in guacamole. As we grow, our upbringing, education, and training influence how we confirm or reject beliefs. Family dynamics, social groups, and childhood experiences produce biases and prejudices that affect our treatment of others. These biases, formed over a lifetime, become deeply ingrained and challenging to change.

Trauma can exacerbate cognitive distortions and maladaptive beliefs, such as *the world is a bad place* or *I can't trust anyone*, reinforcing negative behaviors and interactions. These distorted thinking patterns impact perceptions of safety, influencing the ability to form relationships and engage in everyday activities. Pre-existing belief systems and shared community narratives can either provide resilience or increase vulnerability to trauma, highlighting the complex interplay between individual experiences and broader social contexts.

Triggering Responses

Adding another layer of complexity to reshaping perspectives is the potential for triggering responses. These responses can become problematic as individuals confront either previously hidden or newly revealed traumas. I witnessed this dynamic often in an undergraduate course I taught, which was designed to encourage students to think about crafting meaningful lives. As they delved into their past and their aspirations for change, several students found themselves emotionally overwhelmed highlighting the sensitive nature of addressing deep-seated personal issues and the importance of navigating these discussions with care. Ensuring that psychological support is available is also important when doing this work because trauma is pervasive, and it often alters behaviors including the ability to cope with new stressors.

Culture profoundly shapes how individuals and groups behave and interact, playing a crucial role in defining the values, norms, and communication styles within any group. It serves as a lens through which individuals interpret their experiences, influencing behaviors in diverse group settings. For instance, in collectivist cultures, group harmony and collective decision-making are highly valued. This contrasts with individualist cultures, where personal autonomy and individual achievement are prioritized. These cultural values significantly impact on how groups operate and make decisions and how individuals behave.

Ala story Communication styles also vary across cultures. High-context cultures rely heavily on non-verbal cues and the surrounding context of communication, while low-context cultures prefer direct and explicit communication. These differences can affect how effectively group members interact and understand each other. Leadership styles are similarly influenced by cultural backgrounds. Hierarchical cultures may favor autocratic leadership, where decisions are made by leaders without much input from others. In contrast, egalitarian cultures often prefer democratic leadership, encouraging participation and shared decision-making. Conflict resolution methods are also deeply rooted in cultural norms. Some cultures emphasize face-saving and indirect approaches to resolve conflicts, avoiding direct confrontation. Others might encourage open discussion and direct confrontation to address issues head-on.

However, culture can also be a significant source of conflict, particularly when groups with different cultural backgrounds interact. Several factors contribute to such conflicts such as ethnocentrism and the belief that one's own culture is superior can lead to misunderstandings and conflicts. This attitude can cause individuals to misinterpret or devalue the behaviors and customs of others. Differences in communication styles and norms can lead to misunderstandings. For example, a gesture or phrase acceptable in one culture might be offensive in another, leading to conflicts.

Conflicts often arise when groups with different cultural values interact. For instance, a culture that values individual achievement might clash with one that prioritizes community well-being. Longstanding historical conflicts rooted in cultural differences can perpetuate ongoing tensions and disputes. These grievances can be challenging to resolve and may flare up in various contexts.

The Power of Belief Systems in Organizations

Belief systems form the foundation of an organization's culture, encompassing shared values, norms, and practices that guide employee behavior and decision-making. For example, a company that values innovation will encourage risk-taking and creative problem-solving. Employees' belief systems significantly influence their commitment to the organization's vision and strategy; when personal and organizational beliefs align, motivation and engagement are enhanced. Additionally, a company's ethical belief system dictates its approach to moral dilemmas and corporate social responsibility, impacting its reputation, stakeholder trust, and long-term sustainability.

Leaders' belief systems shape their management approach, communication style, and how they motivate and inspire their teams. These mental models influence how leaders and employees perceive problems and opportunities, affecting their decision-making processes. Effective leaders are aware of their mental models and actively seek diverse perspectives to avoid biases. Complex problem-solving in business often requires challenging existing mental models and developing new ones, particularly in rapidly changing industries. Mental models can either foster or hinder innovation; recognizing and adjusting them can open up new possibilities and drive innovative thinking.

In business, effective communication and negotiation hinge on understanding the mental models of colleagues, clients, and stakeholders to ensure messages are interpreted as intended. There is a critical interplay between belief systems and mental models in a business environment, determining how individuals and groups interpret internal and external business events, trends, and information.

Leaders who are cognizant of this interplay are better equipped to foster a culture that aligns with the organization's goals, navigate complex business landscapes with informed and nuanced perspectives, drive change and innovation by encouraging diverse thinking and challenging status quo mental models, enhance collaboration, and reduce conflict by understanding and respecting differing belief systems and mental models within their teams.

Elliott's Blue Eye-Brown Eye Experiments

Dr. Jane Elliott demonstrated how teachers set student intentions through the instructions they provided students in her Blue Eye-Brown Eye experiments beginning in 1968. She demonstrated how belief systems are the frameworks of principles and values through which individuals interpret, understand, and engage with the world around them. They consist of a set of convictions or practices that guide actions, attitudes, and a sense of meaning or purpose.

Jane Elliott's *Blue Eyes/Brown Eyes* experiment revealed several key findings about prejudice and discrimination. The experiment demonstrated how easily prejudice could be instilled. Within a very short period, children quickly accepted the assigned superiority or inferiority based on their eye color.

Behavioral changes were immediately noticeable. The children designated as superior, initially the blue-eyed group, quickly adopted discriminatory behaviors. They exhibited dominance, arrogance, and mistreatment toward the inferior group, the brown-eyed children. Conversely, the children labeled as inferior displayed signs of low self-esteem, frustration, and resentment.

The experiment also showed a significant impact on performance and confidence. The superior group performed better in tasks and felt more confident, while the inferior group performed worse and exhibited signs of stress and helplessness. This highlighted how discrimination can directly affect individuals' abilities and self-perception. When the roles were reversed, the previously superior group experienced discrimination firsthand. This reversal led to increased empathy and a deeper understanding of the effects of prejudice among the children who were initially in the superior position.

The long-term impact of the experiment was profound. Many participants reported a heightened awareness of discrimination and a stronger commitment to social justice in their later lives. The exercise left a lasting impression, emphasizing the arbitrary and destructive nature of racism. Overall, Jane Elliott's experiment underscored the powerful influence of social constructs on behavior and self-perception. It highlighted how quickly and easily prejudice can be created and its far-reaching effects on individuals and groups.

Self-Fulfilling Prophecies

The greatest threat from self-fulfilling prophecies is the rapidity with which behaviors change because of them. The Stanford Prison Experiment, conducted in 1971 by psychologist Philip Zimbardo, became infamous for its extreme and violent behavioral changes in participants, leading to its abrupt termination after only six days. The experiment aimed to explore how individuals conform to roles of authority and subordination in a prison-like environment. The basement of Stanford University's psychology building was transformed into a mock prison, and 24 psychologically stable male college students were randomly assigned the roles of guards or prisoners.

The guards, equipped with uniforms, clubs, and mirrored sunglasses, quickly began to exhibit authoritarian and abusive behaviors. They enforced arbitrary rules and punishments, some reveling in their newfound power. Conversely, the prisoners, subjected to a simulated arrest and detention, were overwhelmed by stress and helplessness, rapidly losing their individuality. The line between reality and role-playing blurred as the guards' tyranny and the prisoners' subjugation intensified.

The rapid onset of these behaviors highlighted the profound impact of situational forces and assigned roles on human behavior. Normal, psychologically healthy individuals quickly engage in atypical behavior when placed in this particular setting. The experiment, initially planned for two weeks, was terminated after only six days due to the escalating emotional turmoil and abuse.

In the aftermath, the Stanford Prison Experiment was heavily scrutinized and criticized for ethical transgressions. The lack of fully informed consent, the psychological scars borne by participants, and the passive observance of the research team sparked ethical debates. This experiment not only reshaped ethics in psychological research but also left a lasting impact on our understanding of the human psyche.

Years later, further scrutiny raised questions about the experiment's validity. Critics questioned whether the guards' behavior was spontaneous or influenced by expectations of their role. Zimbardo's involvement and his influence on the outcomes were also called into question.

The Stanford Prison Experiment

My experiences as a night group supervisor at a juvenile detention center while pursuing graduate studies mirrored the results of the Stanford Experiment. Responsible for a group of young, serious offenders, I gained profound insight into the mutual effects of oppression, reinforcing the notion that harm inflicted on others also impacts the one who inflicts it. These experiences, combined with the lessons from the Elliott Blue Eye/Brown Eye experiments and the Stanford Prison Experiment, illustrate how situational forces and defined social roles can dramatically influence human behavior, often leading to unintended and harmful consequences. They also illustrate how quickly individual belief systems can impact behaviors or be impacted by them depending on the circumstances.

Despite its controversies and ethical quandaries, the Stanford Prison Experiment remains a pivotal reference in social psychology. It serves as a stark reminder of the potent influence of situational forces and authority on human behavior, continuing to provoke introspection and debate in the realms of psychology and beyond.

Over the decades since that experience, as I've thought about my time at the Juvenile Detention Center, I can see that Paulo Freire was correct that the oppressor cannot escape the oppression he is perpetrating on others. Today, with what I now understand about trauma and human behavior, I am acutely aware of how our own trauma shapes our behaviors when interacting with others.

The Stanford Prison Experiment is a profound example of the dynamics that can unfold when ordinary people are given authority and the responsibility to create rules and the power to enforce them over a second group. This experiment vividly demonstrates how quickly negative traits of human nature can surface. When individuals are categorized into *in-groups* (groups one identifies with) and *out-groups* (groups one does not identify with), and power is allocated to the in-group to dictate rules for both groups, it often leads to detrimental outcomes. In the case of the Stanford experiment, it only took six days for the situation to deteriorate to the point where intervention was essential to prevent further trauma from being inflicted on students (both guards and prisoners).

Looking at this experiment through a contemporary lens, it may offer insights into the phenomenon of White grievance in the United States. The institutionalized oppression that was woven into the fabric of American democracy by its founders might provide a backdrop for understanding these grievances. The claims that the United States is fundamentally a White Christian Nation and the continuous efforts to undermine hard-fought human rights reflect the anxieties of those who seek to oppress others to bolster their own self-esteem. This is driven by a baseless fear of losing a perceived genetic superiority and a birthright to rule over others. Such fears are so deeply ingrained in certain parts of the population that they are willing to compromise the principles of democracy just to maintain their hold on power.

Perceptions and Experiences

In navigating life's complexities, I've learned that we adjust our perceptions based on our experiences, using mental models (our internal representations of how the world operates) and belief systems (shaped by education, experiences, and philosophies) to navigate life. The challenge with this approach is the risk of becoming ensnared in a cycle of confirmation bias if we don't periodically challenge our perceptions. A vivid example of this was my neighbor, who harbored deep-seated hatred towards people like me, a prejudice ingrained from childhood by his family's teachings. It shows how easily we can base our understanding of the world on false assumptions, especially if they are all we have known since childhood. This pattern of self-deception is noticeable in many areas of our lives. For instance, some people, due to misinformation or lack of information, believe that fossil fuels do not contribute to the current climate crisis. However, this belief is in stark contrast to the substantial scientific evidence linking fossil fuel use to the degradation of Earth's atmosphere and the stainability of life on the planet. The global pandemic offered concrete proof of this, as seen in the environmental changes during the period of reduced travel and economic activity. Yet, climate denialism persists in certain sections of society. This phenomenon prompts important questions: Why does this continue to happen? How do these misconceptions persist despite clear evidence to the contrary?

The messages we receive and internalize from our environment, including media, peers, and authority figures, become part of our belief system. Positive messages can enhance our self-concept, while negative, critical messages can harm it. However, our belief systems are subject to cognitive biases, which can distort our perception of self or others. For example, a confirmation bias might lead us to focus on information that confirms our existing beliefs about ourselves or others, either positive or negative, reinforcing our current self-concept. Performance review systems such as 360-degree reviews, culture, and climate surveys provide comparative metrics that can help offset some biases by increasing sources of feedback.

Belief systems that include a growth mindset—the belief that we can grow and change through effort—can positively influence our self-concept. This adaptability and resilience can lead to a more positive self-view and higher self-esteem, especially in the face of challenges. In essence, belief systems form the foundation of how we interpret our experiences and view ourselves. They shape our self-concept by influencing how we perceive our abilities, worth, and place in the world. Consequently, a positive selfconcept, nurtured by empowering beliefs, contributes to higher self-esteem, while a negative self-concept, influenced by limiting beliefs, can lower self-esteem.

From Trauma's Darkness to Wisdom's Light

In addition to the twenty-four-hour clock, we each get to define what's valuable for ourselves. Interestingly, issues generally only arise when we start measuring ourselves against others. This dynamic is part of a social justice construct in which individuals tend to compare themselves.

In exploring the concept of social justice, one crucial aspect is how individuals measure their value relative to others. This process, known as social comparison, was first introduced by psychologist Leon Festinger in 1954. Festinger proposed that people determine their own social and personal worth based on comparisons with others. There are two primary forms of social comparison: upward and downward. Upward social comparison involves comparing oneself to those who are perceived to be better off, which can inspire self-improvement but also lead to feelings of inadequacy. Conversely, downward social comparison involves comparing oneself to those who are perceived to be worse off, often boosting self-esteem.

In the realm of social justice, these comparisons play a significant role. When individuals become aware of economic, racial, and gender disparities through social comparison, it can drive movements for equity and systemic change. For example, noticing income inequalities among peers can lead to awareness and activism for social mobility and economic justice, as highlighted in Wilkinson and Pickett's work, *The Spirit Level* (2009). Similarly, recognizing racial and gender disparities fuels initiatives like Black Lives Matter and gender equality movements, as discussed by Kimberlé Crenshaw in *Mapping the Margins* (1991).

Furthermore, social media has amplified the impact of social comparisons, often highlighting societal standards and inequalities. This phenomenon can exacerbate feelings of inadequacy while also bringing attention to widespread issues, prompting collective action for social justice.

Notably, the process of social comparison is a powerful tool in understanding and addressing social justice issues, helping individuals recognize disparities and motivating efforts toward a more equitable society.

I recall a friend sharing stories of being in Africa to offer her professional services. She expressed her sorrow about the poverty she witnessed, showing me pictures from her time in the country. The photos depicted children playing, smiling, and having fun, just like children everywhere. However, their surroundings showed what we might consider extreme poverty by Western standards. The children reminded me of those I worked with in ghettos and some impoverished rural U.S. communities. Yet, she seemed to pity them because of their living conditions. I wondered how many U.S. ghettos she worked in and in some ways, I pitied her for using her own privileged standards as a benchmark for measuring others' lives—a rather colonial mindset. This tendency to measure others against ourselves to gauge our own well-being is prevalent in the U.S.

The length of life is unique to each of us, so no one knows how much of it they will have for their purposes. This unknown quantity raises the stakes for how much we invest of ourselves (our time, talent, and treasure) in future activities when that future is unknowable. The best we can do is to invest in the future and at the same time live in the present.

Time provides the opportunity for personal growth, learning, and self-improvement, and opportunities to change circumstances. It allows individuals to gain new experiences, acquire knowledge, and develop skills. Each moment is a chance to become a better version of oneself. Spending time with loved ones is fundamental to building and maintaining strong relationships. Time invested in family and friends creates memories, strengthens bonds, and fosters emotional connections that are essential for mental and emotional well-being (Harvard Study of Adult Development).

Time management is crucial for achieving goals and fulfilling ambitions. How individuals allocate their time directly impacts their productivity and success. Effective use of time can lead to significant accomplishments and a sense of fulfillment (Covey, 1989 "The 7 Habits of Highly Effective People"). Time is essential for maintaining physical and mental health. Allocating time for exercise, rest, and hobbies contributes to general well-being. Studies show that taking time for relaxation and leisure can reduce stress and improve quality of life (American Psychological Association). Time allows for reflection and mindfulness, helping individuals to understand themselves and their place in the world better. This introspection can lead to greater self-awareness and a deeper appreciation of life (Kabat-Zinn, 1994).

Therefore, how we choose to spend our time shapes our legacy and the impact we leave on others. Time dedicated to meaningful causes and contributions can create lasting positive effects on society and future generations. Time's irreplaceable nature and its critical role in various aspects of life underscore *why* it is regarded as a precious gift.

Simon Sinek (2009) is a renowned author, motivational speaker, and organizational consultant, best known for his work on leadership and inspiring change in organizations. His most famous concept is the *Golden Circle*, introduced in his book *Start with Why: How Great Leaders Inspire Everyone to Take Action* (2009). This model emphasizes the importance of starting with *why*—the purpose or belief that drives individuals or organizations—rather than focusing first on *how* (process) or *what* (product).

Sinek argues that great leaders and organizations inspire others by clearly communicating their purpose, which fosters loyalty, trust, and long-term success. His work extends beyond this concept, addressing themes of leadership, trust, collaboration, and the impact of the modern work environment on well-being and innovation.

Nurturing the Existence of a Healthy Self

Family structures and their equivalents act as incubators nurturing the development of the Self from birth through the transition into adulthood, a process often marked by cultural rites of passage. These rites, whether they are formal ceremonies or simply reaching a certain age like eighteen, are intended to signal a person's entry into adulthood within their culture. However, these markers don't always align with the individual's personal development. For example, a fourteen-year-old who has run away from home might exhibit a maturity level that exceeds their years, shaped by the harsh realities they may have faced. This level of maturity might surpass that of a twenty-year-old who remains living comfortably at home with parents or other family members.

My incubator for making sense of my world included a family devoted to improving the quality of life for all people. We lived a middle-class lifestyle but over the length of my life I've experienced poverty and know what it's like waking up to an empty refrigerator and cupboards as though I had yet to move into my apartment. My parents were activists who played a crucial role in the transition from segregation to integration, producing a life that many have only read about in textbooks or novels. My parents, who led by example would say, no matter what happens, any job worth doing is a job worth doing well!

Largely, because of my parents, my life mission is to improve individual and organizational effectiveness by promoting positive social change, social justice, and peace in all that I do. My vision for getting to such a state is by fostering kinder, gentler, healthier, and more productive organizations and communities.

Despite this unique background, I've experienced deep frustration from consistently outperforming my peers while watching them be the ones who receive rewards. I've been targeted and defamed in the workplace, accused of crimes that could have led to imprisonment if true, and seen reports sanitized and false documents placed in my personnel file. I know what it's like to be stuck under awful supervisors for long stretches, with little ability to defend myself or escape.

What I've learned through my own experience is that achieving what others deem impossible often invites painful treatment for proving them wrong. People are adept at promoting themselves through bravado, but when they've declared something impossible or failed due to flawed strategies, they may turn against those who succeed, feeling threatened by the contrast. For committing such offenses, I've been knocked down and kicked in the teeth, but never stayed down. My parents taught me to light the way in both the best and worst of times, standing tall amidst the storm so others might find safe harbors to flourish.

Rejection and the Evolution of Self

Rejection is an experience familiar to everyone, manifested in personal relationships, professional environments, and social interactions. It's the act of being dismissed or spurned, of having our ideas, desires, or presence not accepted. This can trigger feelings of anger, sadness, frustration, or inadequacy, making it a common yet deeply impactful human experience.

Learning to cope with rejection is essential for building resilience to the adversity we are likely to face periodically through the processing that comes with being alive. Handling rejection positively builds emotional resilience, enabling us to recover from setbacks and adapt to challenging circumstances. This resilience is crucial for both personal and professional growth. It allows us to bounce back stronger and more determined, turning setbacks into setups for future success.

Rejection often provides an opportunity for self-reflection and improvement. It serves as a motivator to address areas of weakness, refine skills, or adjust behaviors. By embracing rejection, we can transform it into a powerful tool for personal development. Experiencing and coping with rejection helps set more realistic expectations for future endeavors. It teaches us that not all efforts will be successful, which is a normal part of life's challenges thereby fostering patience and perseverance, qualities essential for long-term achievement.

Learning to handle rejection enhances our emotional intelligence by teaching us to manage our emotions, develop empathy by understanding how rejection affects others, and navigate social interactions more effectively. Emotional intelligence is key to building and maintaining healthy relationships. In many cases, rejection can redirect us towards opportunities, relationships, or careers better aligned with our strengths and values. It acts as a guide, steering us away from paths that aren't right for us and towards those where we can truly thrive.

Effective coping mechanisms prevent the negative emotional spirals that can arise from rejection, such as chronic stress, depression, or anxiety. By developing healthy strategies to manage rejection, we can protect our mental health and well-being. Developing strategies to cope with rejection—like maintaining a strong support network, practicing self-compassion, and staying committed to personal goals—significantly influences our mental health and well-being.

For those who never learn to handle rejection effectively, several negative outcomes can arise, impacting various aspects of their lives in lowering self-esteem. Persistent struggles with rejection may lead to a diminished sense of self-worth. Individuals might internalize rejection as a reflection of their personal failings, perpetuating feelings of inadequacy. It can produce avoidance behaviors to prevent the pain of rejection by trying to avoid situations where there is a risk of being rejected. This can result in missed opportunities in relationships, careers, and personal growth.

It can produce relationship challenges with difficulty in managing rejection that can further strain relationships. It may cause over-sensitivity to criticism, defensive behaviors, or withdrawal from social interactions, hindering the development of healthy relationships. It can lead to long-term mental health issues with a chronic inability to cope with rejection contributing to mental health issues such as anxiety, depression, and chronic stress. These conditions can further exacerbate feelings of isolation and unhappiness.

Rejection can result in stunted professional growth for those who can't handle rejection and who then might avoid risks or new responsibilities, limiting their career development. They may also struggle with feedback, which is essential for professional improvement. In some cases, individuals may turn to unhealthy coping mechanisms, such as substance abuse or aggressive behavior, to manage the distress caused by rejection. Rejection can also produce a resilience deficit in which a lack of resilience can emerge, leaving individuals less equipped to deal with life's challenges. This can result in a fragile approach to obstacles, where even minor setbacks lead to disproportionate distress.

Therefore, learning to cope with rejection is crucial for maintaining a healthy, balanced, and progressive life. Support from friends, family, or professionals, along with personal development efforts, can help build the necessary skills to manage rejection effectively. Sometimes, we must accept that others may not want what we offer. Those with sponsors inside organizations or coveted groups often have an advantage, gaining access that others must work for. Such relationships can offer distinct benefits and sometimes protect those with preferential treatment. In the end, rejection, like many challenges in life, is an opportunity for growth. Embracing it with resilience, self-reflection, and a willingness to adapt can lead to personal and professional success, paving the way for a richer, more fulfilling life.

During one particularly challenging episode, a senior leader in my chain of command explicitly showed his loyalty to my supervisor, disregarding the harm being inflicted on me. He never inquired about the dynamics between my supervisor and me. Instead, he made it clear that it was my responsibility to mend the relationship, or I would risk losing my job. The issue was that my supervisor was stealing my work, assigning his tasks to me, and treating me horribly. I wasn't the only one suffering under his management, but I was his primary target. Despite the abuse we endured, all of us were too afraid to report it to Human Resources, which we did not trust.

As a result, I was labeled as a difficult employee and deemed unpromotable. This became evident as I was never promoted despite applying for more than a dozen positions, including three instances for a role I had significantly contributed to creating. Many colleagues expressed their belief that I deserved the job when they learned others had been hired. Nonetheless becoming targeted is the reality for those standing up against abuse in the workplace.

My career has been marked by numerous instances of rejection, but I remain steadfast in my commitment to improving the human condition wherever I go. I see myself as a leader dedicated to positive social change, inclusion, and transformative, transformational, and servant leadership. My life's work focuses on enhancing individual and organizational effectiveness by advocating for diversity, fairness, and peace. My vision is to foster healthier, more compassionate communities and organizations.

Life in a Complex World

Each of us must choose our path and my path has brought me to this moment of capturing some of my experiences and things I've learned that I am now sharing with you. While we share the same world, how we experience and interpret that world can differ marginally or greatly. Marginal differences are usually negotiable but when they vary greatly, they can lead to war. Why does this happen? Applying the principles of Ocham's Razor by finding the simplest explanation it is contained within the differences in perspectives, which I will illustrate more fully as we continue.

Johnson on Polarized Thinking

Barry Johnson's (1992) methodology for managing polarized thinking offers a path to transform perspectives when differences exist between individuals or groups. For those interested in working specifically in the political and policy domains William Benet's work on the polarities of democracy is supported by doctoral research of his own and more than 30 dissertations using his research written on various aspects of democracy. Benet applied Johnson's work to produce his dissertation findings, and he is now expanding his work in countries like Belgium and by teaching doctoral students.

Barry Johnson is known for his work on polarity management, a concept that addresses how to handle situations involving interdependent but opposite perspectives—polarities that are often viewed as problems to be solved or conflicts to be resolved. Unlike problems that can be permanently solved, polarities are ongoing, chronic issues that require ongoing management rather than resolution.

Johnson's framework highlights that many of the challenges we face are not so much either/or scenarios but rather both/and situations where both sides of a polarity have positive and negative aspects. For example, in organizational settings, common polarities might include centralization vs. decentralization or stability vs. change. Each pole has benefits and drawbacks, and the goal is not to choose one at the expense of the other but to find a way to leverage the upsides of both while minimizing the downsides. To manage polarities effectively, Johnson proposes a process that includes:

1. Identifying polarities by recognizing when a situation is a polarity perspective rather than a problem to solve.

2. Mapping the polarity by using a polarity map (essentially a 4X4 grid) to lay out the positive and negative aspects of each pole.

3. Assessing and learning by evaluating the current state and gather feedback on the impacts of overemphasizing one pole at the expense of the other.

4. Leveraging the polarity by developing strategies to maximize the benefits of both poles, aiming for a dynamic balance that respects the strengths of each side.

Johnson's methodology promotes the acceptance of modern life's complexity, particularly in addressing ongoing strategic challenges that cannot be solved with straightforward, permanent solutions. His insights into polarity management enhance the effectiveness of individuals and organizations by acknowledging and adeptly navigating the inherent tensions that arise from polarized perspectives. By appreciating the nuances of differing viewpoints, we can forge a path toward mutual understanding, provided that finding common ground is the objective.

Achieving a profound understanding of life necessitates that individuals shift their perspectives, recognize the motives behind different viewpoints, and work toward consensus. This journey requires the courage to endure the discomfort of cognitive dissonance that arises when our core beliefs are questioned. However, by educating individuals through transformative learning processes, we can create avenues that enable them to find hope amid conflicts, adversities, and disruptive events. These experiences, while challenging, provide valuable opportunities for growth, development, and gaining wisdom—which is the essence and purpose of living.

Embracing Conflict

One of the many things my favorite professor Dr. Robert Lamp drilled into our heads was the importance of embracing conflict as a source of potential good. However, getting leaders to consider perspectives they do not agree with is a very important capacity to help them develop. Leaders who smother conflict do a disservice to their group members because conflicts arise out of differences, and if those differences never have a chance to work themselves out, then they sit, fester, and can erupt at a time that puts everyone at risk. I believe the same is true for parents who try to stop sibling rivalry which prevents the siblings from learning how to problem-solve with others they do not agree with later in life. How we resolve our differences matters and conflicts can illuminate issues that have not yet fully surfaced that might threaten the group or organization.

Group conflicts often emerge from a variety of deep-seated and complex issues. Divergent interests and goals are a primary source of tension, as individual objectives may clash with those of the group or with other members. For instance, some members may face restrictions on workdays due to religious practices, while others might push for modern technological solutions that less tech-savvy members find daunting.

Resource Scarcity

Resource scarcity is another trigger, where limited access to time, money, or materials pits members against each other as they vie for these essential resources. Outdated technological tools can exacerbate this struggle, leading to frustration and inefficiency. Role ambiguity within the organization often causes conflict too. Unclear or overlapping responsibilities, coupled with inadequate training, can lead to confusion over who is supposed to perform certain tasks, undermining the group's efficiency. Clearly defined roles and comprehensive training can help alleviate these issues.

Even when roles are clearly defined, personality clashes can occur which can also contribute significantly to group conflicts. The diverse personalities within a team can lead to misunderstandings and disagreements if not effectively managed. Tools like the Myers-Briggs Type Indicator, Decision Style Inventory, Herrmann Brain Dominance Instrument, and Leadership Practices Inventory can provide valuable insights into individual behavioral styles, helping to shift the focus from personal differences to how team members process information and make decisions.

Communication Barriers

Communication barriers further complicate group dynamics, where poor communication can result in misunderstandings and misinterpretations. Enhancing communication through training and strategic development activities can help bridge these gaps, allowing team members to better understand each other's perspectives and intentions. Addressing these factors requires a combination of leader role modeling, effective communication, clear systems and organizational structures, and strategic leadership to prevent and resolve conflicts, thereby enhancing group cohesion and productivity.

Working Through Differences

Working through differences is an absolutely necessary skill in the 21st century, particularly in highly diverse societies like that of the United States. Meaningful progress towards a unified solution is feasible only when all parties approach the discussion with openness and receptivity. Johnson and Benet demonstrate how the polarity management approach can be applied in various organizational settings, where some decisions, like redesign strategies, are relatively straightforward, while others, such as politics, can be emotionally volatile and complex, especially in the current climate.

Their applications of the polarity management model offer a potentially flexible framework that can adapt to an array of applications illustrating how processing polarized thinking might be resolved across diverse fields. I used the polarity model in a leadership course with eight graduate students working in different domains (entrepreneurship, nonprofit community resource building, and the arts) to get them to think about the opposition they face currently in their change management work or could face in a project of their own design. The Polarities Model Activity enabled them to consider strategies for getting to both/and decisions. I believe the Polarities Model can be easily taught across the social sciences in courses such as leadership, education, human development, counseling, administration, mediation, social work, criminal justice, and social psychology offering a useful tool for navigating difficult interpersonal and inter-group challenges.

Cultural Influences and Conflicts

Cultural influences and conflicts can result from workplace diversity. In multicultural workplaces, cultural diversity can enhance creativity and innovation but also lead to conflicts if not managed well. Differences in work ethics, communication styles, and leadership expectations can cause friction among employees. The significance of our workplaces as a place where difference (diversity) is largely set aside to produce something of common value goes beyond what an individual could produce alone is the point and illustrates the reliance we have on each other to work collectively for the good of the whole.

Cultural differences play a significant role in international relations and other forms of in-group and out-group diplomacy. Misunderstandings between nations due to differing cultural norms and values can lead to conflicts and complicated diplomatic efforts. The integration of immigrants into a new culture can be challenging. Host cultures may have expectations that clash with the cultural practices of immigrant communities, leading to social tensions and conflicts.

Culture profoundly influences group behaviors and can be a source of both harmony and conflict. Therefore, understanding and appreciating cultural differences is crucial for fostering positive interactions and resolving conflicts in various settings, from workplaces to international arenas. Recognizing the role of culture can help individuals navigate complex group dynamics and contribute to more effective and harmonious group interactions.

The Role of Difference in Relationships

Our nation's history is a tapestry woven from diverse cultures, each contributing its unique flavors, traditions, and customs to our shared societal fabric. This rich diversity fosters a vibrant community life but also sets the stage for conflicts rooted in the complex psychodynamics of our collective past. Recognizing the limits of individualism at the juncture where cooperation becomes essential is not just a lesson but a necessity for harmonious coexistence.

Recently, I had the privilege of attending the Lummi Nation Salmon Celebration at the community's K-12 school. The event marked the sharing of the season's first salmon with hundreds of attendees. I was graciously guided to a section reserved for elders, where I took my seat. Having previously been a part of several other indigenous cere-monies, I felt deeply honored to sit in the area designated for elders, recognizing their lifelong contributions as custodians of wisdom, traditional ways of being, and guard-ians of the stories handed down through oral traditions to future generations. In this moment, apart from birthdays, I cannot recall any other ceremony I've experienced where elders are revered with such profound respect.

The Lummi are known as the Salmon People, with narratives deeply rooted in their struggle to preserve their sovereignty and way of life, which centers on protecting salmon and preserving other wildlife crucial to their ecosystem for future generations. The Salmon Ceremony was an incredibly moving experience that filled me with a pro-found sense of pride for their community and their enduring traditions. I learned that the event was primarily organized and led by students, with enthusiastic support from faculty, staff, administrators, and the larger community surrounding the school.

Traditional songs, dances, and blessings enriched the ceremony, and as I took part in these celebrations, I felt deeply connected to something far greater than myself, swept up in the collective spirit and heritage of the Lummi Nation. My connection to this nation of people was heightened further as I heard stories of how young people from a nearby public high school called these students Lummi dummies. Listening to their stories caused me to reflect on the many putdowns I heard in school about the failure I would become because of my differences compared to others in the communities where I lived.

The experience tapped into the portions of me that are of Choctaw and Creek descent making it deeply personal for me. They remind me of the oneness I feel when hearing ancestral songs, drums, and dance of the indigenous peoples of the Americas. But that is only part of who I am. I'm also of African descent but mostly Sicilian ethni-cally speaking.

Something I find interesting about myself is that when I experience indigenous drums from the Americas my body responds differently with what feels like a higher level of energy resonance than when I experience the indigenous drums from Africa. On the other hand, when I hear the languages of the indigenous Americas and Africa, I am most resonant with the spoken language of Africa. Culturally, I consider myself most influenced by Sicilian and the Black culture of the United States. Trust me when I tell you that my most difficult struggles are the internal ones, I have with myself when making genetic makeup of my blood goes to war with itself.

However, in the Black and White world within which I grew up caused me to align myself most fully with people of the African diaspora, even though I never felt accepted anywhere outside of the circle of friends my parents created, because of political-cul-tural like-mindedness I mostly felt. When in the circle, my father's celebrity status also gave me cover and a sense of extra protection I did not feel anywhere else. In fact, a few years ago I realized that I never felt a sense of safety anywhere, even to this day.

This initial description of myself is offered because living in the United States, how I describe myself in the morass of humanity is important for my Self-identity and for you to fully understand and appreciate the perspectives shared here. One important perspective to acknowledge is that in the United States, factors such as race, religion, and socio-economic status significantly influence people's lives. Similarly, in other countries, ethnicity, religion, and other characteristics play crucial roles in shaping the behaviors of their people in unique ways.

While we often pretend these differences do not matter, their impact is clearly visible in the behaviors we observe and the disproportionate outcomes they produce for members of various groups. These factors define us in various ways—through the circumstances of our birth, the identity of our parents, our birth location, and the historical period we are born into. These sorts of factors combine with all the decisions we make to frame how we experience life.

Because of my Sicilian heritage, circumstances have given me a deep appreciation for the perspectives and privileges generally afforded White people. I also have a very deep understanding of the pain suffered by Black, Indigenous, and People of Color (BIPOC) to use a contemporary term; and based on my observations over the course of my lifetime I know that if my complexion was like that of a Sicilian, my life would have been very different professionally, and yes, my Self as well.

Here is a brief story to illustrate what I mean. One of the most traumatic events in my life occurred as the result of a wrongful termination lawsuit I filed for maltreatment by my employer. When I followed my attorneys into the office of the Federal Magistrate who was to hear my case, as I crossed the threshold into his office, he said, well, my estimation of you has gone up a hundred percent! One of my attorney's asked, why is that your honor? The magistrate responded with, you could have made this a race-based case and didn't! My attorney retorted with, we tried to get him to do that your honor, but we think we can win the case on its merits! If race does not matter, then why did it come up when it was not part of the case being presented? And why did it matter enough for the magistrate to comment on it?

In my case, that single difference (race) and its impacts is a point upon which a life can hang in the balance to be filled with opportunities and safety nets or obstacles and harm. Race is but one of many characteristics we've come to use as a point of differentiation that impacts how we relate to each other as individuals and groups. The mechanism used for socially differentiated groups is based in socially categorizing individuals into groups: Some groups we belong to (called in-groups) and some groups we don't belong to (called out-groups).

Moreover, our focus on difference rather than similarities keeps us from our collective humanity through a process of differentiation inflamed by rhetoric to pit us against each other. Ironically, the characteristics we use such as race do not exist in nature; they were manufactured as a way of dividing people into classes and treating each group differently based on socially defined characteristics. Such perspectives go back to at least Aristotle who proffered class distinctions through treating equals equally and those unequal unequally. Such perspectives permeate everything we do and how we behave in our homes, social groups, and workplaces.

Making Sense of the World

Montuori and Donnelly (2017) (as cited in Perry, 2025) suggest that in the times of transition "... *there is a need for new ways of making sense of the world. This process requires a new approach to inquiry, and to the relationship between theory, action, reflection, and practice.*" This formula is utilized here for telling a story of new ways to make sense of our world in the face of deliberate violence used to produce political ends for individuals, at the expense of a majority of the world's population who are the victims of their violence.

Bridging the gap between the theoretical and the practical, Montuori and Donnelly's insights invite us to reimagine our approach to leadership in these transitional times. As we pivot from understanding new ways of inquiry and sense-making, it becomes clear that leadership too, must evolve to become truly transformative.

Leadership is inherently a forward-looking endeavor. Unlike management, which typically focuses on short-term decision-making (usually within a twelve-month timeframe), leadership involves actions and decisions that extend well beyond the immediate horizon. Leaders must use current conditions as a foundation for understanding and anticipating future events that may unfold over a year or more. This means that each decision a leader makes can and will set behaviors in motion, and these behaviors will have long-term consequences. Therefore, it is vital for leaders to base their decisions on the best available information at the time. Yet, during my nearly six decades in the field, I've witnessed leaders time and again, instead base their decisions on their personal preferences filtered by their own biases producing negative outcomes for their organizations.

Critical to effective decision-making is understanding the precursors that influence both leaders and their followers. Specifically, it is essential to examine how the perspectives of both leaders and their followers are formed, as these perspectives significantly shape the culture of the organization or group they lead, regardless of its size.

In today's rapidly evolving world, the challenges faced by civilization are not just external crises but also profound sources of trauma that affect individuals at a deep psychological level. Environmental degradation, for example, manifests through natural disasters exacerbated by climate change—like hurricanes, wildfires, and floods—leading directly to acute stress and long-term post-traumatic stress disorder (PTSD) for many who find their lives impacted by nature's devastation. The loss of homes and communities can trigger profound grief and dislocation, unsettling the very foundation on which individuals build their lives.

Technological advancements, while beneficial in many ways, also bring about technology stressors (*technostress*) through the necessity to constantly adapt to new systems and the omnipresent glare of social media. This digital overexposure can lead to psychological strains such as cyberbullying and privacy concerns, fostering an environment ripe for emotional distress.

Economic instability further compounds the trauma landscape. Job insecurity, financial strain, and poverty create a chronic backdrop of stress, fueling anxiety and depression. Such economic pressures erode personal efficacy, making everyday survival a source of anxiety.

Health disparities and global health crises like pandemics intensify these experiences. The fear and reality of disease and death, alongside the strain of caregiving, contribute to psychological trauma. Individuals facing these health challenges often experience a sense of helplessness and persistent sorrow, impacting their mental health over the long term.

Sewing sociopolitical unrest—from political conflicts to cultural clashes—creates a pervasive sense of insecurity. Experiences of violence, discrimination, and deep societal divisions can lead to individual and collective trauma, exacerbating mental health issues and affecting people's ability to form and maintain healthy relationships.

These various sources of trauma, stemming from the macro challenges of our times, profoundly influence how individuals interact and relate to one another in their families, social groups, and workspaces. Trauma shapes behaviors, emotional responses, and social dynamics, often leading to a cycle of stress and trauma that impacts communities and the very fabric of society. Contributor Janine Crifasi emphasizes how early-life trauma, developmental challenges, and neurological factors shaped her personal and professional life. She discusses the lasting effects of trauma on neurological development and the importance of addressing these issues through therapeutic approaches, self-awareness, and personal growth. She also illustrates the ongoing struggle to overcome these challenges and the determination to not let past traumas define one's future.

Bidirectional Trauma

The migration of trauma between our homes and workplaces is a dynamic process, reflecting the interconnectedness of our personal and professional lives. In an increasingly integrated world, the boundaries that once separated these spheres are now permeable, allowing stressors from one area of life to influence the another in profound ways. Telecommuting has made it possible for employees working in highly toxic environments to at least partially separate themselves from the physical toxic energy within the walls of a physical workspace.

When individuals experience stress, trauma, or instability in their home lives—whether from financial worries, family conflicts, or personal health issues—these emotional burdens do not simply vanish during work hours. Instead, they accompany them into the workplace, often manifesting decreased productivity, heightened irritability, or withdrawal from collaborative engagements. This personal distress can affect team dynamics and a sense of workplace morale, potentially leading to a broader environment of stress and anxiety among colleagues.

Conversely, trauma originating in the workplace—due to factors like job insecurity, workplace bullying, or ethical conflicts—does not remain confined to the professional domain. Employees often carry these stresses home, which can disrupt their personal life and relationships. The strain of a toxic work environment can lead to increased domestic tension, diminished parenting capacity, or withdrawal from family activities, thereby spreading the psychological impact of workplace trauma into the familial setting.

This bidirectional flow of trauma between home and work underscores the critical need for supportive structures in both domains. Creating trauma-informed workplaces that recognize and respond to the emotional and psychological needs of employees, alongside nurturing home environments where individuals can recuperate and reconnect, is essential. By addressing the holistic mental and physical well-being of individuals across all aspects of life, we can work towards mitigating the migration of trauma and at the same time foster healthier, more resilient communities.

Culture and Difference in the U.S.

The culture in the U.S. is one of individualism, competition, and success often derived through subterfuge and violence. We see how such values become precursors to behaviors by driving organizational leaders to act in ways that mostly serve their own interests and the interests of their few *in-group* members rather than the broader community of stakeholders. Ironically, many such leaders take as much as they can for themselves and simultaneously suppress the opportunities and wages of their employees who then find it difficult to own the very things their companies produce. We also see how external forces shape employee belief systems that frame and impact the behavioral forces within our workplaces and social groups.

For those of us living in the United States, we are tethered to our history of colonization, White privilege, racism and the effects of slavery, and subsequent rules of law, all of which shape the behaviors that define our culture. But like any founding document or set of policies and procedures, they are only as good as the people who make them living documents.

To illustrate this point, all employees bring their biases and prejudices into their workplaces where their belief systems emerge through their observed behaviors. In one case example, a senior leader identified himself as a *Redneck* during his self-introduction to the unit he would supervise on his path to becoming company president several years later. The leader felt so emboldened that he then mocked a staff member who was originally from India by imitating his speech pattern. The most despicable part was that the Indian employee was also present in the room, and he was responsible for the leader getting through his doctoral process.

His leadership proved to have deleterious effects for many employees over the duration of his tenure. The leader was never held accountable for his actions, but the harm done that day lived on until his termination many years later. Since there were never any repercussions for the leader, he eventually became president of the company to the dismay of many of the employees, me included. That case, is an example of White privilege when compared to what often happens to non-White executive leaders, as was the case with Dr. Gay, an African American president at Harvard who made comments that were less than sensitive, and as a result of her remarks, was attacked and forced to resign.

From Difference to Sameness in Management Curricula

However, when you look at the structure of MBA and management curricula it is *thing* based rather than *people* based. That is one of the reasons leadership development programs emerged. But what if I told you that such perspectives have a more sinister legacy that shapes how the workforce is treated today? Caitlin Rosenthal (2018) offers a history of how the mechanisms of *the business practices used for the accounting of enslaved human assets* were so solid that they carried over from the plantations through business practices during industrialization and remain foundational in today's business language and practices.

Considering this perspective, there isn't any irony that today we commonly refer to the organizations workforce as an *asset* thereby dehumanizing it as something disposable like all assets which we see in mergers, acquisitions, and workforce layoffs to *right-size* the entity; and under the conditions where poor supervision and working conditions create other types of attrition because of the negative views many supervisors have of their workforce. Such perspectives shape the behaviors leaders use in their decision-making practices, impact their interpersonal relationships with various individuals and groups, and produce self-fulfilling prophecies that support their belief systems.

Violation of Trust

In another case example, I had dinner with my Board chair and his wife at the Napa Valley Wine Train Mystery Dinner. It was an enjoyable evening where passengers participated in solving a mystery. During dinner, my Board chair asked about my personal goals. I very innocently mentioned that I would like to experience earning a hundred thousand dollars. At the time, I was making seventy thousand dollars annually and I knew other executives in the organization with less complex operations earned more than my goal.

A few weeks later, the Board chair called me for a meeting. We met in another Board member's office, where a regional director was also present. To my surprise, I was harshly criticized as if I had demanded to be paid a hundred thousand dollars a year. When I departed the meeting, I heard the three of them laughing, with one of them saying, *I bet he'll never do that again!* I was livid.

My Board chair violated my trust with a personal conversation of dreams turned into a nightmare. My words had been twisted and taken out of context. The Board chair had previously told me that he needed safeguards to protect those around him because he was an autocrat and unconcerned with people's feelings. I understood what he meant at that moment. Our relationship never recovered from his breach of trust.

Blaming the Victim

When I talk about blaming the victim I'm referring to a behavior in which in-group members blame out-group members for who they are as a vehicle for justifying their maltreatment. It's an age-old practice of one group justifying their behaviors towards another. William Ryan (1970) illustrates how this works in his book titled *Blaming the Victim*.

The book was given to me by a consulting partner while working on a community economic development project in Berkeley and Oakland in the San Francisco, Bay Area. It became one of my bibles for understanding the dynamics of how trauma is perpetrated, cultivated, and sustained in low-income communities where I choose to do the majority of my work. Blaming people for their existence and condition is the ultimate act of oppression that, as Freire reminds us of the harms to both those oppressed as well as those who oppress. Again, we can identify the nexus between the workplace trauma of the customer (those being served) and the employees who provide the service.

Ryan challenges the pervasive mindset of attributing the causes of poverty and social issues to the individuals who suffer from them rather than to systemic inequalities. Ryan identifies and critiques a set of myths that perpetuate this victim-blaming mentality. For example, he disputes the idea that minority children perform poorly in school due to cultural deprivation or that poor health among impoverished populations is due to ignorance and disinterest in healthcare. He particularly targets the culture of poverty thesis, exemplified by the Moynihan Report, which argued that the instability of African American family structures caused socioeconomic disadvantages.

Ryan counters this by demonstrating that these views overlook the broader socio-economic and political factors that contribute to poverty and inequality. He argues that blaming victims serves to divert attention from the need for societal change and reinforces the status quo by suggesting that the poor and marginalized are responsible for their own circumstances. These perspectives are then used to frame a narrative of fear against these very same populations justifying police brutality and armed vigilantism.

But, what about the targets of such perspectives on how societal attitudes towards race and class contribute to ongoing social injustices supported by establishing oppressive systems as a response? What happens to them? Victim-blaming can significantly impact the self-concept and the psychological outcomes of victims. When individuals are blamed for their own misfortunes, several adverse consequences can occur including negatively impacting the evolution of the self-concept. Those who are targeted may start to internalize the blame, believing that their circumstances are a result of their own failings. This internalization can lead to feelings of shame, guilt, and unworthiness, which can severely damage their self-esteem and self-concept.

Repeated experiences of being blamed for situations beyond their control can lead to learned helplessness, where victims feel powerless to change their circumstances. This can diminish their motivation to seek help or improve their situation, perpetuating a cycle of victimization and dependence. They may struggle with their identity and social roles. For example, if they are consistently told that they are responsible for their misfortune, they may adopt a victim identity, which can limit their potential and aspirations.

Being targeted may have psychological and emotional outcomes associated with various mental health problems, including depression, anxiety, and post-traumatic stress disorder (PTSD). The stress and emotional turmoil caused by being blamed can exacerbate these conditions. They may withdraw from social interactions due to fear of further blame or judgment which can lead to a lack of support and increased feelings of loneliness and despair.

When individuals are blamed, particularly by institutions meant to protect them (e.g., law enforcement, and social services), they may lose trust in these systems which can deter them from seeking help in the future and foster a sense of alienation and disenfranchisement.

There can be long-term consequences as well, such as chronic health issues, hypertension, cardiovascular disease, and other stress-related conditions. It can impact economic and social mobility, often creating feelings of being trapped in their socioeconomic status due to reduced opportunities for advancement. This can perpetuate cycles of poverty and limit access to education, employment, and other resources necessary for upward mobility.

Causes of Poverty

Blaming others for their circumstances not only undermines their self-concept but also has far-reaching psychological, emotional, and social consequences. Addressing these issues requires a shift from blame to support, focusing on systemic changes and providing resources that empower victims rather than stigmatize them. Poverty is a complex phenomenon created by a variety of interconnected factors.

Understanding the causes of poverty involves examining its economic, social, political, and environmental dimensions. These factors collectively contribute to the creation and perpetuation of poverty, forming a complex web of influences that affect individuals and communities.

Economic factors play a critical role in poverty. The lack of job opportunities or the prevalence of underemployment can prevent individuals from meeting their basic needs. Economic downturns, technological advancements, and globalization can exacerbate these issues, leading to widespread unemployment and insufficient wages. Economic inequality, where wealth is concentrated in the hands of a few, further deepens poverty by limiting access to essential resources such as education, healthcare, and job opportunities. Policies that favor the wealthy, such as tax breaks for the rich and austerity measures, can widen the gap between the rich and the poor, making it harder for low-income individuals to escape poverty.

Social factors also significantly contribute to poverty. Limited access to quality education can trap individuals in low-paying jobs, perpetuating the cycle of poverty. Education is a key driver of economic mobility, and without it, opportunities are severely limited. Health is another critical factor, as poor health and lack of access to health-care can prevent individuals from working or force them to spend a significant portion of their income on medical expenses, thus contributing to poverty. Family dynamics, such as single-parent households or families with many dependents, can strain financial resources and contribute to economic hardship. Political factors are crucial in under-standing poverty. Poor governance and corruption can hinder economic development and the fair distribution of resources. Ineffective policies can lead to a lack of infrastruc-ture, social services, and economic opportunities. Political instability, wars, and con-flicts can destroy infrastructure, disrupt economies, and displace populations, creating conditions that lead to widespread poverty.

Environmental factors also play a role in perpetuating poverty. Climate change and natural disasters can destroy homes, reduce agricultural productivity, and deplete nat-ural resources, leading to loss of livelihoods and increased poverty. Resource scarcity, such as lack of access to clean water, arable land, and energy, can limit economic activi-ties and further contribute to poverty.

Structural factors, such as discrimination based on race, gender, ethnicity, or dis-ability, can limit individuals' access to education, employment, and other resources, perpetuating poverty among marginalized groups. Globalization, while creating eco-nomic opportunities, can also lead to job losses in certain sectors, wage suppression, and increased competition, affecting vulnerable communities the most. Poverty is often transmitted from one generation to the next, creating a cyclical nature of pov-erty. Children born into poverty are more likely to experience poor health, limited educational opportunities, and reduced economic prospects, continuing the cycle of poverty. Addressing poverty requires a multifaceted approach that includes improv-ing access to education, healthcare, and employment opportunities; implementing fair economic policies; combating discrimination; and ensuring political stability and good governance. Reducing poverty also involves addressing environmental chal-lenges and supporting vulnerable communities through targeted interventions.

Scapegoating and Blaming

Scapegoating and blaming individuals or specific groups detracts from addressing broader systemic factors such as economic inequality, lack of access to quality edu-cation and well-paying jobs, inadequate healthcare, discrimination, and ineffective policies and governance. Addressing poverty effectively requires a shift from blaming the victims to tackling the structural and systemic issues that perpetuate it. Blaming individuals and specific groups for poverty shifts the focus away from broader societal and structural causes. Individuals are often blamed for their situation due to perceived personal failings such as lack of effort, poor financial management, or inadequate skills. This perspective suggests that poverty results from individual choices and behaviors rather than external factors. Marginalized groups, such as racial and ethnic minorities, single parents, and immigrants, are frequently blamed for their economic hardships. These groups face stereotypes and prejudices that suggest their culture or community practices contribute to their poverty.

When marginalized individuals are blamed for their circumstances, the psychological impact can be profound and multifaceted. For example, the narrative below explores the psychological effects on individuals who face such blame, highlighting the need for a more comprehensive and compassionate approach to understanding and addressing poverty.

Maria, a single mother working two jobs, constantly hears that people like her are poor because they lack ambition or make poor life choices. These messages come from the media, community leaders, and sometimes even from those close to her. Over time, Maria begins to internalize these negative perceptions.

Initially, Maria's self-esteem takes a significant hit. She starts believing that her financial struggles are entirely her fault, leading to feelings of shame and guilt. This self-blame creates a vicious cycle of self-doubt and decreases motivation, making it even harder for her to seek better opportunities or advocate for herself. According to research, this internalized stigma can lead to chronic stress and mental health issues such as depression and anxiety.

As Maria navigates daily life, she becomes increasingly isolated. The fear of judgment and the stigma attached to her circumstances make her withdraw from social interactions. She avoids community events and hesitates to seek help from social services, fearing further stigmatization. This social withdrawal exacerbates her sense of loneliness and helplessness.

Moreover, Maria's trust in societal institutions erodes. When schools, healthcare providers, and government agencies perpetuate the narrative that her poverty is her own fault, she feels abandoned and unsupported. This mistrust further discourages her from accessing the resources she desperately needs, trapping her in a cycle of poverty and isolation.

Despite her best efforts to provide for her children, Maria worries about the long-term impact on them. They too are exposed to the stigma and blame directed at their family, which can affect their self-concept and aspirations. They might internalize these negative stereotypes, affecting their academic performance and future prospects, perpetuating the cycle of poverty across generations.

Blaming marginalized individuals like Maria for their circumstances leads to internalized stigma, decreased self-esteem, chronic stress, social isolation, and eroded trust in institutions. This narrative highlights the profound psychological toll of such blame, emphasizing the need for a shift in societal attitudes and systemic support to break the cycle of poverty and marginalization.

This focus on blaming individuals or specific groups detracts from addressing broader systemic factors such as economic inequality, lack of access to quality education and well-paying jobs, inadequate healthcare, discrimination, and ineffective policies and governance. Addressing poverty effectively requires a shift from blaming the victims to tackling the structural and systemic issues that perpetuate it.

From Victimhood to "Robin Hood"

Trauma is an unavoidable part of life. Although we can't prevent it, we have the power to decide how we respond. The world can be harsh, making it easy to feel victimized. However, I have never seen myself as a victim. Embracing a victim's mentality gives power to those who cause harm, and I refuse to do that. It took me a long time to come to grips with the fact that while I can't control everything that happens to me, I can control my reactions. This doesn't diminish the pain inflicted by those who treated me as a scapegoat instead of confronting their own issues.

When it comes to my career, I see myself as a canary in a coal mine, signaling deeper problems than whatever issues were being mined at the time. Because of my upbringing I was never afraid to take up issues I felt harmed me or those around me. My loyalty to others, including my employers, has been steadfast and I often give more than I receive, frequently offering everything I have. Despite my commitment to my employers, several of my employers brought substantial direct and intentional harm to me for whatever personal reasons they might have. It has taken a long time for me to grasp that they could not see me in any other way than they were capable of seeing me based on how they developed as a human being.

For example, a department chair at a university tried to sabotage my career because I had become friends with the previous department chair. When the previous chair was promoted, the most senior faculty member took over and immediately started undermining me. She changed my job responsibilities without any prior discussion, and I only discovered this during a student open house where printed materials outlined my new duties.

When I approached the Union Steward to explain what had happened, he was taken aback, unable to understand her actions. It turned out that the previous department chair had treated her similarly, and because I had formed a close friendship with him, she directed her anger and frustration towards me.

Lessons from Robin Hood

Paradoxically, the lesson of the Robin Hood story revolves around the themes of justice, rebellion against tyranny, and the defense of the powerless. At its core, the legend underscores the importance of standing up against oppression and fighting for social equity. The enduring appeal of Robin Hood lies in his representation of the universal fight for justice and the hope that even in dark times, there are heroes who will rise to challenge injustice and defend the powerless.

Achievement and Flux

Like anything we do that's of real value to us, achieving it takes lots of hard work. While outliers might be born with extra genetic superpowers in a given area (savants come to mind), no one could seriously argue that sustained effort isn't required to master something. Whether we can capture the benefits of that which we master is a complex story told here. Like characters in a story, we navigate the plot twists and turns of existence, encountering challenges, triumphs, and unexpected detours. Each chapter unfolds with its lessons, shaping our beliefs, values, and identities as we journey toward a horizon ever on the move.

Yet, even as we journey through the seasons of life, we remain in a perpetual state of flux, forever in the process of becoming. Each moment is an opportunity for growth, a chance to redefine ourselves and rewrite the narrative of our lives. In the end, life is not a destination to be reached but a journey to be embraced—a journey of self-discovery, growth, and transformation. And as we surrender to the rhythm of existence, we discover that the true beauty of life lies not in the destination but in the journey itself.

Interpreting Experiences

Paradoxically, while life exists only in our minds, we attribute profound meaning to our experiences. How we interpret our experiences shapes how we perceive others, sometimes as friends or enemies, depending on the mental constructs we've developed. Each significant experience is stored in our memory banks, with emotionally charged memories residing closer to the surface. These memories can resurface unexpectedly, impacting our present state.

Our capacity to extract lessons from our experiences significantly influences our future paths. By examining our past decisions, we can better understand the psychological crossroads we've encountered. This hindsight enables us to connect the dots of our journey to present moments, aiding us in navigating our future with informed intentionality. Although we may carefully consider our course, unforeseen events may still disrupt our plans. Therefore, resilience and our capacity to rebound after negative events become crucial in adapting to life's unpredictability. Through resilience, we can weather the storms that come our way and continue to navigate toward our goals with determination and perseverance.

Creating Your Own Balance

The chapter "From Wounds to Wisdom" is a reflective narrative on life's journey, emphasizing personal growth through adversity. It uses the metaphor of alchemy to describe how life's challenges, whether emotional, psychological, or external, can be transformed into wisdom and strength. The chapter explores various life stages, from childhood innocence to the complexities of adulthood, and highlights the importance of resilience in navigating life's unpredictability. It suggests that adversity can serve as a powerful catalyst for personal transformation, urging individuals to take ownership of their responses to challenges and use them as opportunities for growth and self-discovery. Through training, reflection, and a shift in perspective, individuals can evolve, becoming more aware of their impact on the world and those around them. Ultimately, the chapter advocates for embracing adversity as a tool for wisdom, shaping both personal and collective growth.

HIDDEN POSSIBILITIES

Principle 7: *What might initially appear as a limitation or obstacle can be transformed into a powerful opportunity for growth and innovation with the right mindset, creativity, and sufficient willpower.*

CHAPTER 7

The Art of Becoming

On Becoming

Life is a process of always *becoming*, so owning the *becoming process* is the first thing we need to do if we want to create a meaningful life for ourselves. No one can define for us what a meaningful life means. The people around us, as loving as they might be, can only tell us what is meaningful to *them*, by giving us their perspectives about life. What we choose to believe is up to each of us, which means that we have to own the beliefs we choose to adopt and whatever behaviors and actions resulting from our belief systems. Factually then, the outcome of who we are at any given moment is the result of every belief we've adopted, decision made, behavior exhibited, and action taken.

Life is a solitary journey whether we live in isolation in a forest, alongside others in communities, or in a stadium of one hundred thousand other sojourners, we each have to figure out what life means for ourselves when it comes to living life itself. Therefore, whatever our circumstances, if we want to change them, we have to learn how to change our condition so that we can flourish. From my lived experience, how this might be done will begin to emerge once the decision to act has been made and energy is put into figuring out in what ways to change.

My own healing process is ongoing and will continue for the rest of my life. I had to first learn to be kind to myself and to forgive myself for the things I've done that may have harmed others. I've learned that when I harm others, I can't escape harming myself in the process—a fact I've already explored with you. Life has a way of humbling us, reminding us that despite our best efforts to improve our circumstances, unforeseen obstacles can still emerge. During the time I spent writing this book, I experienced the loss of a cherished possession, the loss of someone dear to me, significant financial setbacks, and I'm still on the mend from an accident. That's life—just as Odysseus learned in his epic journey. I recall a moment when I was lamenting my hardships, asking aloud, "Why me?" My younger brother responded, "What makes you think you're so special?" It was a poignant reminder that navigating life's challenges is a universal experience.

Looking at the course of my life, the one constant, has always been trying to convince people that they should consider thinking about things differently, just as I am trying to do with you now. I challenged my parents' thinking because my beliefs about how to solve problems were different than theirs. I challenged my teachers because what I was being taught at home was very different than what I was being taught at school. Professionally, I tackled the problems I saw out of the belief that there was always a better way of doing things. By being a transformative leader, I demonstrated that what my supervisors thought impossible was doable by shifting perspectives about the capacity of employees and other stakeholders to achieve great things when they are committed to purpose and supported by leaders. Admittedly, because of the maltreatment I've endured over the full length of my lifetime, I've always challenged the maltreatment of others more fiercely than anything else.

Thanks to some tough love from my mom and the problem-solving skills I honed while in school, I've come to a pivotal understanding: whatever happens to me on my journey to *becoming* is mine to own fully because those things occurred as the direct result of my own decisions. That is, my decisions set in motion the events I will experience as I navigate my existence. For me, embracing full ownership of my life and everything in it translates to absolute freedom—the freedom to evolve into the best version of myself. My takeaway has been when there's no one else to blame, there's nothing holding me back except myself.

Writing today and being forced to think about how I've become *me* at this moment, I recall professional development exercises in which the participants were guided to write their epitaph. Early in my career (1970s) my supervisor who was a really nice guy, asked me what I would write for myself on my tombstone, and I responded, "Here lies a Man." When I finally saw my father's headstone in my mid-twenties I had them create a larger headstone inscribed with, "For the people." Today, if I was to inscribe my tombstone it would be very simple, "A teacher of possibilities."

We are all shaped by our environment and the people in our lives. Reflecting on my journey, I recognize three pivotal influences that have shaped who I am today. Firstly, my father's unwavering dedication to serving humanity inspired me to commit to a similar path of service. Secondly during the tumultuous 1970s—a period marked by the nation's struggles with civil rights and the Vietnam War—I was deeply engaged in my personal quest for equality and identity. Lastly, in hindsight, it's clear that my life's trajectory has always been aligned with teaching others the lessons I've learned about overcoming adversity to achieve profound personal fulfillment.

With these things in mind, while this story is about providing tools to better understand the nature of trauma and what to do about it, it is also about the possibilities that can emerge from the harm inflicted by traumatic events and toxic people. Unfortunately, trauma is inevitable, and no one leaves this world without experiencing it. Accordingly, the question becomes how can traumatic events be overcome to ensure life is lived in the most meaningful way despite whatever happens?

My mother would say, be the rising star rather than the shooting star; and no matter what happens always search for the silver lining even when the clouds are darkest. What I've learned is that living long is quite a matter of luck no matter how careful we might be, but living well is a matter of choice. We get to choose how we live and respond to the adversity that is likely to befall us at some point during our lifetimes. Since life is always about *becoming*, then for as long as we are alive, we have the capacity to become better versions of ourselves each day. We just have to take the first step in that direction which is to develop the right perspective.

Lessons From Experiences

Life in many ways is a figment of our imagination. It only exists in the mind and yet we attribute all sorts of meaning to our experiences. Because life is in the mind's eye, we can manipulate the meaning of any experience we choose. We can choose to see someone as an enemy or friend. The difference reflects clips of the memories we hold and the meaning we ascribed to those experiences.

Each experience is subconsciously labeled, categorized, and filed away in our memory banks. The experiences involving the greatest emotions become starred, so they live closer to the front of the filing system in our minds making them easier to access when needed. But every experience has been recorded in our memory banks, so they are always there making it possible for painful or good memories hidden deep in the recesses of our minds to find their way to the surface when triggered by some event. This happened to me in 2023 when long-forgotten family-pattern memories resurfaced after being triggered, causing great discomfort, substantial stress, upending my wonderful plans, and leading to an automobile accident.

Our capacity to maximize the lessons from our experiences substantially determines our destiny. We can actually trace our path at any given time by tracking our decisions like breadcrumbs. We can track them to each crossroads we encountered and the decisions we made. The advantage of hindsight enables us to connect the dots which helps us make sense of why we are who we are at that moment. It's like plotting the course we've traveled. If we can plot the course we've traveled, then we can plot the one in front of us assuming we know what compass point we want to travel.

Traveling anywhere requires the decision to take the first step. Metaphorically, when talking about life, taking the first step requires a commitment to a different way of being, having the courage to confront whatever obstacles emerge, the willingness to face uncertainty, all while quieting the mind from creating intrusive thoughts about imagined what-ifs. It requires the motivation and courage to create a different future than the one appearing as inevitable based on the information available at the time.

Insights often arrive unexpectedly, triggered by a visceral response that connects our present circumstances to childhood experiences. These moments of clarity prompt deep reflection. Recently, while facing a challenging decision, I realized that my struggle was deeply rooted in familial patterns from my childhood, charged with negative thoughts, emotions, and energy. Recognizing such influences not only clarifies the nature of our personal and professional dilemmas but also gives us a chance to alter our approach to resolving them.

This type of transformative learning underscores the critical importance of self-reflection in personal growth efforts, leadership styles, and relationship management, offering substantial opportunities to foster healthier, more effective ways of being that can positively influence interpersonal dynamics, most importantly when times are tough.

Perspective Shaping

In the context of leadership and organizational effectiveness, perspective shaping is an important tool. Leaders can shape the perspectives of their teams or organizations by promoting certain values, setting examples through their behavior, and framing challenges and solutions in specific ways to strengthen the goal behaviors of group members. This helps in cultivating a shared vision and aligning the group's efforts towards common goals. When done effectively trust is built and group cohesion is fostered. These dynamics occur in social groups as well as those including our families, sports and recreation teams, personal interest groups, etc.

Effective perspective shaping can lead to enhanced teamwork, improved communication, and increased effectiveness in achieving organizational objectives. It also plays a crucial role in areas such as change management, where shifting the collective perspective is often necessary to overcome resistance and gain buy-in for new initiatives.

Let us acknowledge that individuals often face uneven starting points in life. Not everyone is afforded the same opportunities, and many encounters significant hurdles from the outset. However, our perspective plays a critical role in how we perceive these challenges—whether as insurmountable barriers or as opportunities for growth. The way we view these obstacles can transform them from daunting trials into valuable steps toward success, enriching our experience through the lessons learned in overcoming them. Adversity can either forge character or cause setbacks. Yet, even in moments of setback, the process of recovery and rebuilding can lead to profound transformation and renewal. Ultimately, it is our perspective that shapes the outcome, turning potential breaks into breakthroughs.

What becomes clear is that life is a continuous process of becoming, and individuals must take responsibility for defining and creating their own meaningful lives, independent of others' definitions. Therefore, the sum of our beliefs, decisions, behaviors, and actions determines who we are at any moment, highlighting the importance of conscious choice in shaping our lives. Life is also a personal journey where each individual must determine their own meaning and purpose, regardless of their surroundings or the people around them. Thus, to change our life circumstances, we must commit to changing our conditions and invest energy into finding solutions, emphasizing the importance of action and perseverance. Such attitudes are likely what Freire (1970) was seeking to understand when contemplating the idea of conscientization and whether an individual decides to stay or live in their existing conditions when those conditions might be harmful to them actualizing their true potential.

Being kind to oneself and forgiving past mistakes is crucial for personal healing and growth. Trauma and adversity are inevitable, but they can lead to meaningful growth and the development of resilience, provided individuals adopt the right perspective and approach. We each have the power to shape perspectives by promoting desirable values, finding and setting positive examples, and by framing challenges positively to foster shared vision and trust within groups.

Self-transcendence, as described by Maslow and influenced by the Blackfoot perspective, extends beyond personal fulfillment to include a broader, more inclusive focus on community and spiritual well-being. Therefore, reflecting on past decisions and experiences can help individuals navigate future challenges and create a more meaningful life. Viewing challenges as opportunities for growth rather than insurmountable barriers can transform adversity into steps toward success and personal enrichment.

The Hawthorne Effect

The Hawthorne Effect, or Hawthorne Theory, originates from a series of studies conducted at the Hawthorne Works plant of the Western Electric Company in Cicero, Illinois, during the late 1920s and early 1930s. These studies, which initially aimed to investigate how various physical conditions (such as lighting, rest breaks, and work hours) affected workers' productivity, unexpectedly highlighted the impact of psychological and social factors on work performance and employee behavior.

There are key findings and implications of the Hawthorne studies for all groups. For example, studies revealed that worker productivity increased not just in response to changes in physical conditions but also when researchers paid attention to them. This suggested that social and emotional factors, such as feeling valued and being part of a group, significantly influence worker performance. The research underscored the importance of human relations in the workplace, including the way managers interact with workers and the social interactions among workers themselves. It highlighted the role of employee attitudes, morale, and group dynamics in productivity.

The Hawthorne Effect is a term coined to describe the phenomenon in which individuals modify an aspect of their behavior in response to their awareness of being observed. In the context of the studies, the mere fact that workers knew they were being studied and given attention by researchers led to a temporary increase in productivity. The findings from the Hawthorne studies led to a shift in management practices, encouraging a more employee-centric approach that considers workers' needs for recognition, social interaction, and a sense of belonging. It marked a move away from the traditional views of scientific management, which focused primarily on optimizing work processes and efficiency without considering workers' psychological needs.

The insights from the Hawthorne studies contributed to the development of the human relations movement, which emphasizes the importance of people in organizational success, advocating for management approaches that foster a positive work environment, enhance worker satisfaction, and promote team spirit. The Hawthorne Effect and the broader conclusions drawn from the Hawthorne studies have had a lasting impact on the field of organizational behavior, highlighting the complexity of human dynamics in the workplace and the importance of considering psychological and social factors in managing and motivating employees.

Psychodynamics

The psychodynamic approach to understanding leadership recognizes that leadership as a behavior occurs in groups and influences follower behaviors based on the leader-follower relationship with each member (Northouse, 2018). The impact of group member behaviors on psychodynamics refers to a psychological approach and theory that emphasizes the systematic study of the psychological forces underlying human behavior, feelings, and emotions, and how they might relate to early experience. It's rooted in the theories of Sigmund Freud and further developed by several other psychologists like Carl Jung.

Psychodynamics stresses that much of our mental life is unconscious, meaning we are not fully aware of the motivations behind our behaviors and feelings. It suggests that human behavior and emotions are the result of dynamic interactions and conflicts between different parts of the mind, particularly the conscious and unconscious.

Early life experiences, especially those in childhood, are believed to play a significant role in shaping an individual's personality and psychological state. According to psychodynamic theory, people use defense mechanisms, such as repression, denial, and projection, to manage conflicts and feelings that arise from interactions within the mind.

Freud's theory of psychosexual development is a cornerstone of psychodynamics, suggesting that early experiences in life are centered around pleasure and play a critical role in the development of the adult personality. Psychodynamics looks at how people develop their sense of Self and their relationships with others based on early experiences with primary caregivers. In therapy, transference refers to the phenomenon where patients project feelings about important figures in their lives onto the therapist. Psychodynamic therapy involves exploring these unconscious patterns, bringing them to awareness, and understanding their impact on a person's current behavior and emotions.

Jung and Freud

Carl Jung, a Swiss psychiatrist, was initially a close collaborator of Sigmund Freud, the founder of psychoanalysis. However, Jung eventually developed his own theoretical framework, which both complemented and diverged from Freud's views. Carl Jung's perspective on psychodynamics, which developed into analytical psychology, both builds upon and diverges from Sigmund Freud's theories in several significant ways.

Freud's theory of psychosexual development focused on stages in early childhood while Jung proposed that development continued throughout life, with a critical phase in midlife, where individuals confront and integrate elements of the unconscious into their conscious awareness. Freud often interpreted symbols, especially in dreams, as disguised fulfillments of repressed desires.

Jung saw symbols and archetypes as manifestations of the collective unconscious, conveying universal human experiences. He believed symbols in dreams and myths were not merely disguises but messages to the conscious mind about important life issues. Freud's model of the psyche consisted of the id, ego, and superego while Jung's model included the ego (conscious self), the personal unconscious, and the collective unconscious. He also introduced concepts like the persona (the social face presented to the world), the shadow (unconscious aspects of the personality), the anima/animus (the gender-opposite qualities inherent in each person), and the Self (the unification of consciousness and unconsciousness in an individual).

While both Freud and Jung recognized the complexity of the unconscious mind and its influence on behavior, Jung extended these ideas to include a collective dimension and placed greater emphasis on ongoing psychological development and self-realization throughout the lifespan. Together Freud and Jung help us explain the individual and collective behaviors that can be observed in organizations and other groups. They also reinforce the idea that we must concern ourselves with both the evolution of individual and group behaviors and the interplay between them.

We can see evidence of the impact of the collective unconscious come to life through cultural traditions brought into the workplace by employees through their natural behaviors as well as through the cultural traditions adopted by the organization. IBM's identity as *Big Blue* is a case in point where the unwritten cultural code became identifiable by the blue suits worn by employees.

In a professional context, let's consider an individual seeking to undergo a process of transformative learning by understanding their own psychodynamics for personal development and fostering better workplace interactions and relationships. Consider the role of an executive coach or mentor, paralleling the therapist in psychodynamics. This professional helps you to excavate and examine these deeply rooted experiences and patterns. Through this exploration, you gain insight into how these past experiences influence your current professional behavior and decision-making

Psychological Archive and Professional Unconscious

Reflecting upon early career experiences, analogous to childhood in psychodynamic terms and how they relate to *a way of being* today, these formative professional experiences, stored in your *psychological archive*, significantly shape current leadership styles, problem-solving approaches, and reaction to workplace challenges. For instance, a past failure in a high-stake project might unconsciously influence your current risk assessment, similar to how early life events shape our adult behaviors and attitudes. In this scenario, confronting unexpected emotional reactions or biases in decision-making is akin to recognizing the influence of the unconscious mind. These reactions are not arbitrary but stem from the amassed experiences and learned behaviors deeply embedded in our *professional unconscious*.

In this professional narrative, psychodynamics is about understanding how an individual's past experiences and internalized beliefs (the 'professional unconscious') shape their current approach to leadership, decision-making, and workplace relationships. The objective is to bring these underlying influences to the forefront of conscious awareness, facilitate perspective shaping for personal growth, more effective leadership, and healthier workplace interactions.

Biases and Prejudices Shape Behaviors

Bias is an inclination to favor or disfavor certain perspectives, people, or groups, often leading to partiality or unfairness in judgment. It can arise consciously or unconsciously and may result in either favoritism or discrimination. In this guide, bias refers to this tendency, whether positive or negative, that influences judgment.

Prejudice is a preconceived opinion or attitude, typically negative, rooted in stereotypes and not based on actual experience or reason. It involves making assumptions or judgments about individuals or groups based on characteristics such as race, gender, religion, or socioeconomic status, often leading to discrimination or exclusion.

Biases and prejudices are shaped by various factors that influence our perceptions and attitudes over time. Socialization and family traditions play a significant role in forming early beliefs and attitudes, which affect how individuals perceive others. Cultural and social norms can reinforce stereotypes and biased attitudes toward certain groups. Media exposure, especially to stereotypical representations, can further entrench these biases. Selective information from biased reporting can also contribute to confirmation biases.

Personal encounters, whether positive or negative, can strengthen existing beliefs or create new biases. Observing how others interact with certain groups can shape one's perceptions. Being part of a particular social group often leads to in-group favoritism, where individuals favor their group and discriminate against others. Mental shortcuts, such as stereotypes, help people make quick decisions but often result in oversimplified judgments.

Confirmation bias further reinforces these tendencies by favoring information that aligns with pre-existing beliefs. As we discussed above, confirmation bias can also exacerbate these dynamics by reinforcing existing beliefs about both in-groups and out-groups. Individuals tend to notice information that supports their preconceived notions, further entrenching stereotypes and limiting opportunities for out-group understanding or perspective-taking.

Systemic Biases

Systemic biases in institutional practices can perpetuate prejudice and discrimination. In learning environments, curricula and teaching methods can shape perceptions of different groups, and historical events can create lasting prejudices and power imbalances. Recognizing these factors is crucial for individuals and organizations to mitigate bias and prejudice.

Shared Similarities

Bias and prejudice share similarities, often overlapping in how they manifest and influence behavior. Both involve personal judgments that cloud objective thinking, leading to decisions based on preconceived notions rather than facts. They rely on stereotypes, resulting in incorrect assumptions about individuals within a group. These attitudes influence how people treat others, affecting interactions and opportunities, and potentially leading to discrimination or exclusion. Often operating unconsciously, biases and prejudices are shaped by societal, cultural, and familial influences, reflecting the prevailing norms and assumptions of a particular group or segment of society.

Despite these similarities, they differ in that prejudice is more often associated with a negative attitude or belief about a group, while bias can be either positive or negative and refers more broadly to a tendency or inclination in perception or judgment. Therefore, what makes bias and prejudice so important to understand is that they can serve as hidden hands that significantly shape behaviors toward in-groups (groups we identify with) and away from out-groups (groups we don't identify with).

Favoritism and Discrimination

In-group favoritism can lead to preferential treatment, as people tend to show more empathy, support, and cooperation toward members of their own group. This often results in better access to opportunities for in-group members. Shared identity characteristics within the group reinforce beliefs and values, promoting solidarity while excluding differing perspectives.

Out-group discrimination often involves stereotyping and dehumanization, reducing out-groups to negative characteristics and thereby fostering distrust. This exclusion can manifest in unfair treatment, such as workplace hiring biases, educational access disparities, health disparities based on membership in marginalized groups, or social exclusion, leading to unequal opportunities based on group membership.

"Us" versus "Them" Mentalities

Bias and prejudice distort perceptions of group members, leading to "us" versus "them" mentalities that lay the foundation for conflict and hostility. These attitudes can escalate intergroup conflict, fostering competition, rivalry, and even violence against out-group members. The influence of these biases can be seen in various aspects of life, from toxic workplace behaviors to political decisions regarding promoting individuals who challenge the status quo.

Reducing Discriminatory Behaviors

Understanding how bias and prejudice affect group dynamics is crucial for reducing discriminatory behavior and promoting inclusion. Organizations and individuals can implement strategies to foster fairness and increase understanding across groups. Taking responsibility for defining and creating a meaningful life in the context of working with others is crucial because each individual has to determine for themselves what is meaningful to them. Our beliefs, decisions, behaviors, and actions shape our identity, how we interact with others, and our life outcomes, underscoring the importance of making conscious, intentional choices about how we spend our time and with whom. Personal growth in the workplace requires an intentional commitment to change by applying proactive effort, highlighting the necessity for intentionality, perseverance, and action to reduce barriers to productive goal behaviors.

Creating a fulfilling and meaningful life amidst its many challenges demands resilience, compassion, and forgiveness—both for ourselves and others—as we navigate the complexities of being human. Embracing self-compassion allows us to treat ourselves with kindness during times of suffering or failure, fostering emotional resilience and well-being. By acknowledging our shared human experience, we recognize that adversity is a universal aspect of life, which can lead to personal growth and transformation when approached with a compassionate mindset. Forgiving ourselves and others for our imperfections enables us to move forward unburdened by past mistakes, opening the door to healing and a deeper understanding of our common humanity.

Different cultural perspectives, such as the Blackfoot's focus on communal well-being, offer valuable insights into achieving both personal and collective fulfillment. These perspectives provide a broader understanding of human potential and growth. Opening ourselves to differing viewpoints increases the number of perspectives that can be brought to bear when problem-solving. Viewing challenges as opportunities rather than barriers can also transform adversity into steps toward success, illustrating the power of perspective-shaping in producing a desirable life. Playing countless games of dominoes with my mentor gave me vivid examples of how perspectives shape experiences. Each time he scored, he'd smile and say, "Ain't no hill for a stepper, obstacles ain't nothing but stepping stones," turning every challenge into a lesson in hope, perseverance, and resilience for achieving a better outcome than what might otherwise appear to be the case. He was training me to overcome difficulties through a simple game we both enjoyed.

Learner-Centered Psychological Principles

McCombs and Miller (2006/2007) present a comprehensive framework for educational reform based on learner-centered psychological principles. They emphasize the importance of understanding the cognitive, emotional, and social aspects of learning to create more effective and engaging educational environments. Key principles include fostering intrinsic motivation, the role of self-regulation and metacognition, and the need for personalized and adaptive teaching strategies. They argue that aligning educational (training) practices with these principles can better meet the diverse needs of students and promote deeper, more meaningful learning experiences. These principles also apply to other organization types interested in employee development.

Human Behavior and Decision-Making

Milton Rokeach (1973) *The Nature of Human Values* explores the fundamental values that guide human behavior and decision-making. Rokeach identifies a set of core values that are universally held across different cultures and societies, categorizing them into terminal values (end goals of existence, such as happiness and security) and instrumental values (modes of behavior, such as honesty and ambition). He examines how these values influence individual attitudes, perceptions, and actions (behaviors), as well as their role in shaping social norms and cultural practices. Rokeach provides insights into the psychological underpinnings of values and their impact on personal and societal levels, offering a foundational perspective for understanding human motivation and behavior. He discusses how values are fundamental beliefs that guide attitudes and behaviors, deeply rooted in our psychological makeup. They play a crucial role in shaping human motivation and behavior, forming part of our cognitive structure and functioning as standards or criteria that influence perceptions, evaluations, and actions. Values help individuals make sense of the world by providing a framework for interpreting experiences and making decisions.

Shaping Perspectives

Perspectives are subjective lenses through which individuals interpret the world, influenced by personal experiences, cultural background, education, and social interactions. These perspectives are flexible and can evolve over time as people encounter new experiences and information. In contrast, belief systems are structured sets of principles that form the foundation of an individual's or group's worldview. Unlike perspectives, belief systems are more rigid and comprehensive, encompassing various aspects of life such as religion, philosophy, or ideology.

While perspectives are contextual and situational, adapting to different circumstances, belief systems are more stable and resistant to change. Perspectives reflect individual viewpoints, often shifting with new insights, whereas belief systems provide a consistent framework for understanding and interacting with the world.

Educational background plays a significant role in shaping perspectives. For example, someone with an education in environmental science might view climate change differently from someone whose perspective is influenced by economic concerns. This underscores the importance of education in shaping how individuals interpret and respond to complex issues.

Psychological and Sociological Underpinnings of Values

Schwartz (1992) suggests an emotional association indicating values are often associated with strong emotional responses and are not just intellectual concepts but instead are tied to feelings of right and wrong, which can motivate action. Moreover, according to Schwartz, when individuals act in accordance with their values, they experience positive emotions, whereas acting against their values can lead to guilt or discomfort or what Mezirow (1991) called a disorienting dilemma.

Bandura (1977) found that there is a social influence on values that are shaped and reinforced by social interactions and cultural norms. It's through socialization that individuals learn what is valued in their community, which influences their own value system. For example, peer pressure, family upbringing, and cultural traditions all play a role in the formation and reinforcement of values. Hitlin (2003) observed that values are closely linked to an individual's identity and self-concept. They are a reflection of what is important to a person and help define who they are. In practice, people strive for consistency between their values and their actions to maintain a coherent self-identity.

Impact on Human Motivation and Behavior

The psychological underpinnings of values significantly impact human motivation and behavior in several ways including goal setting practices, decision-making processes, and behavioral outcomes like persistence, resilience, and interpersonal relationships. Locke and Latham (2002) discuss goal setting and prioritization and how values influence the goals individuals set for themselves and the priorities they assign to different aspects of their lives. For instance, someone who values achievement highly will be motivated to pursue career success and set ambitious professional goals.

Rokeach (1973) observed that values serve as a guiding framework for decision making. When faced with choices, individuals evaluate options based on their values, leading to decisions that are consistent with their core beliefs. This process helps reduce cognitive dissonance and aligns actions with personal values. Schwartz (1992) also examined how values regulate behavior by setting standards for acceptable and unacceptable actions thereby acting as internalized rules that individuals use to judge their own behavior and that of others. This individualized regulation is crucial for giving members in a democratic society a locus of control for maintaining social order through personal integrity. Such personalized regulations are vital in a democratic society because they empower individuals to take responsibility for maintaining the rules and values governing society.

Deci and Ryan (2000) found that strongly held values can enhance persistence and resilience in the face of challenges. When individuals are committed to their values, they are more likely to persevere through difficulties and remain motivated to achieve their goals. Fiske (2004) demonstrated how values play a key role in forming and maintaining interpersonal relationships. Shared values can strengthen bonds between individuals, while conflicting values can lead to misunderstandings and conflicts. Understanding and respecting others' values is essential for effective interpersonal and intergroup communication and cooperation.

Values and a person's constitution are deeply intertwined, shaping an individual's identity, behavior, and overall life direction. A person's constitution, which encompasses their fundamental beliefs, principles, and character, is significantly influenced by their core values. These values act as internal guides that dictate how individuals perceive the world, make decisions, and interact with others.

At the heart of this connection is the idea that values provide a framework for understanding what is important and meaningful in life. They serve as benchmarks for evaluating experiences and making choices that align with one's inner beliefs. For instance, a person who values honesty will integrate this principle into their constitution, striving to be truthful in their interactions and expecting the same from others. This value shapes their character, guiding their actions and reinforcing their sense of integrity.

Furthermore, values play a crucial role in forming and maintaining an individual's identity and self-concept. As Hitlin (2003) notes, values are closely linked to who we are and help define our personal identity. They reflect what matters to us and influence how we see ourselves in relation to the world. This connection means that when individuals act in ways that align with their values, they experience a sense of coherence and authenticity, reinforcing their self-identity.

Values also contribute to resilience and persistence, essential components of a person's constitution. Deci and Ryan (2000) suggest that strongly held values can enhance an individual's ability to persevere through challenges and stay motivated to achieve their goals. When individuals face obstacles, their commitment to their values can provide the inner strength needed to overcome difficulties and remain steadfast in their pursuits.

Interpersonal relationships further illustrate the connection between values and constitution. Shared values can strengthen bonds between individuals, fostering trust and cooperation, while conflicting values can lead to misunderstandings and conflicts (Fiske, 2004). This dynamic shows how values influence not only personal identity but also social interactions and relationships. Further, matching values between individual members and those espoused by their groups and organizations is critically important to retaining group and organizational cohesion, as well as low levels of attrition (Perry, 1995).

In conclusion, values are fundamental to a person's constitution, shaping their identity, guiding their behavior, and influencing their resilience and interpersonal relationships. They provide a stable foundation upon which individuals build their character and navigate the complexities of life, ensuring that their actions remain true to their core beliefs and principles. This intricate relationship highlights the profound impact of values on the essence of who we are and how we live our lives.

On Being Human

In many ways, our attitude determines our altitude, and it can be the difference in the perspective of whether life is viewed as meaningful or not. As they say, perspective is everything and therefore the game of life requires us to shape the perspective with which we want to live. Perspective frames the quality of life we have, and therefore *life itself and what we make of it is an inside out process*. It seems to me that at its most fundamental level, *life* is *simply* a process of always becoming the best version of *Self* possible, no matter how difficult the obstacles before us. To use any variation of the term *simple* when discussing life which is highly complex, appears on the surface to be an oxymoron, but it really isn't.

Meaningful Pursuits

Creating something meaningful in our lives is essential for fostering a sense of purpose and direction. When we engage in activities that resonate with our core values and passions, we experience a deeper sense of fulfillment. This intrinsic motivation drives us to continue pursuing our goals, providing a sense of satisfaction that external rewards cannot match (Ryan & Deci, 2000).

From a psychological standpoint, meaningful pursuits are linked to better mental health outcomes. Engaging in these activities can significantly reduce symptoms of depression and anxiety, as they provide a sense of accomplishment and personal fulfillment. This connection between meaningful work and psychological well-being highlights the importance of aligning our actions with our personal values (Steger, 2012). Moreover, the process of creating something meaningful helps build resilience. When we face challenges in pursuit of our meaningful goals, we develop perseverance and adaptability. These experiences teach us to cope with adversity more effectively, strengthening our ability to overcome future obstacles (Frankl, 1963).

Meaningful activities also play a crucial role in building and maintaining strong social connections. By engaging in collaborative efforts and sharing our passions with others, we form supportive relationships that enhance our well-being. These social bonds provide a sense of community and belonging, which is fundamental to our happiness

(Baumeister & Leary, 1995). Furthermore, creating something meaningful allows us to leave a lasting impact on the world. This sense of contributing to something greater than ourselves can be deeply satisfying and inspiring. It gives our lives a greater sense of significance and purpose, knowing that our efforts can make a difference (Erikson, 1968).

Finally, the journey of creating meaningful work encourages self-reflection and personal growth. It challenges us to expand our skills, knowledge, and understanding, leading to continuous development and improvement. This ongoing process of growth and self-discovery is vital for achieving our full potential (Maslow, 1943). In essence, the importance of creating something meaningful in our lives cannot be overstated. It enriches our personal experiences, enhances our mental and emotional well-being, builds resilience, fosters strong social connections, and leaves a lasting impact on the world around us.

From Pain to Purpose

To transform anything requires effort and energy but to transform the Self requires a willingness to work through the things that make us most uncomfortable and often lead to painful events we've encountered. Herein lays a transformative learning opportunity we can go through as a structured process aimed towards personal growth through deliberate intention. Moreover, the best version of *Self* can only be known through some sort of lessons to be learned by undergoing and overcoming one or more challenges. *The Hero's Journey* described by Joseph Cambell (1949) more fully below illustrates the path heroes take and since we are the actors in our own life scripts, it describes our individual journey which is unique to each of us.

Rites of Passage

Rites of passage are ceremonies or rituals marking significant transitions or milestones in a person's life and signifying a change in social status or role. These rituals are common in many cultures and often serve to formally introduce individuals to new stages in their life cycle. The concept was first extensively studied and named by the anthropologist Arnold van Gennep (1909) in his work *Les Rites de Passage*.

Rites of passage typically consist of three main stages:

- Separation in which the individual is separated from their previous status or role. This phase often involves physical separation from the community or a symbolic breaking away from the former identity.

- Transition (Liminal Stage) in which the individual is between statuses or identities, experiencing a liminal or "in-between" state where they learn, undergo challenges, or are prepared for their new role.

- Incorporation in which the individual is reintegrated into the community in their new role or status. This stage often includes celebrations or ceremonies that recognize and honor the new identity.

Some of the common examples of rites of passage include birth and baptism which are rituals that mark the birth of a child and their introduction into a religious or cultural community. Puberty and coming of age ceremonies signify the transition from childhood to adulthood, such as bar/bat mitzvahs, quinceañeras, or various indigenous puberty rites. Completing courses of study such as secret society ceremonies, Boot Camps, college or technical degree programs, training programs, etc. Marriage is the ritualistic joining of two individuals into a new social status as a couple. Death and funerals represent rituals that mark the passage from life to death, often emphasizing the transition of the deceased to another realm or existence. Rites of passage provide individuals and their communities with a structured way to understand and celebrate life's major changes, reinforcing social cohesion and the continuity of cultural norms.

Overcoming significant trauma and traversing the Dark Nights of the Soul is a rite of passage that can yield substantial post trauma growth, long term wellness, and wisdom. As we go through the healing process, we have opportunities to learn in ways that are truly transformative contributing to personal growth and long-term well-being.

Kintsugi: Beauty Can Be Found in What is Broken

My mother was one of the most intuitive people I know. She almost always knew exactly what to say at a given moment. She was also very good at predicting things that most around her could not envision. One of her many gifts to me was to teach me how to always seek the silver lining no matter have foreboding or dark the moment might appear. In doing so, she taught me to always search for the hope in what appears hopeless and the possible in the impossible. Boy, was she right! It works and when you experience it, it changes the frame of reference and by altering the frame of reference it changes how we perceive what we are looking at, revealing new solutions to what was previously thought hopeless and impossible.

Recently, a friend named Tom Hodge introduced me to the Japanese concept of Kintsugi, which translates to *golden joinery* in Japanese. It is the art of repairing broken pottery using lacquer mixed with powdered gold, silver, or platinum. This unique technique not only restores the functionality of the broken item but also adds to its aesthetic appeal. Shifting from *something that is broken* to *something that is broken still has value and can be made beautiful* shifts the perspective from casting the broken thing in the garbage to going about a deliberate process of finding beauty in all things when we look for it, and in many ways, the kintsugi process can create something with even greater beauty than when it was in its original state.

This shift in perspective is essential for experiencing posttraumatic growth, a profound state of being that emerges once the consequences of trauma are managed, and new approaches are developed to navigate a reality reshaped by the traumatic experience. Reaching a stage where the trauma no longer defines you is a vital part of the healing journey, opening doors to transform adversity into new possibilities.

Kintsugi is a philosophy of embracing flaws because kintsugi is rooted in the philosophy of wabisabi, which sees beauty in the flawed or imperfect. The repair method highlights, rather than hides, the cracks, and breaks. It is a way of celebrating the object's history in a way of honoring and celebrating the life and history of the object, rather than discarding it because of imperfection or damage. Kintsugi is considered an art form, as the repair process often results in something more beautiful than the original. It turns the object into a unique piece of art, with each crack and repair telling a story. It contains a metaphorical significance often seen as a metaphor for healing and recovery, symbolizing resilience, and the ability to become stronger and more beautiful in the face of adversity.

For those of us wishing to reframe what brokenness means, we have a wonderful metaphor for taking what is broken in us a recreating it into something that is even more beautiful than what we had before. It is the manifestation of posttraumatic growth when we navigate our way through the pain to a higher state of beauty that comes from transformation, very much in the same way that the caterpillar transforms itself into the butterfly. Without such a process of transformation, the butterfly would not exist.

One of the most important lessons is that *beauty can be found in What is broken*. Always looking for hope in hopeless situations and possibilities in the impossible, as a way of changing our frame of reference can reveal new solutions. The Japanese art of repairing broken pottery with gold, silver, or platinum, transforms broken items into more beautiful and valuable objects, emphasizing that brokenness can be a source of beauty and value. Embracing flaws as a way of celebrating imperfections and seeing beauty in the flawed or imperfect, highlighting an object's history rather than discarding it for its imperfections. Kintsugi serves as a powerful metaphor for healing and recovery, symbolizing resilience and the potential to become stronger and more beautiful in the face of adversity. The shift in perspective is crucial for experiencing posttraumatic growth, a state of being that emerges when trauma is managed, and new approaches are developed to navigate a reality reshaped by the traumatic experience. Embracing and transforming brokenness within ourselves can lead to a state of greater beauty and resilience, similar to a caterpillar transforming into a butterfly.

Kintsugi teaches us to honor and celebrate the history and life of objects and ourselves, understanding that imperfections and damage add to our unique story and value. The process of kintsugi not only restores functionality but also enhances aesthetic appeal, turning repaired objects into unique pieces of art, illustrating that healing can create something more beautiful than the original. The ability to embrace flaws and see beauty in brokenness strengthens our resilience, helping us navigate through pain and emerge transformed and empowered. Transforming personal brokenness into a state of beauty and strength exemplifies the manifestation of posttraumatic growth, demonstrating the potential for profound personal growth and transformation.

The Person Before and The Person After

When trauma upsets our life, we can never go backwards in time to undo it so our only option is to keep going forward, otherwise we could succumb to the obstacles in front of us that serve to prevent us from achieving our goals. While we cannot go backwards, we certainly can go forward in search of a better version of the person we were prior to the seismic traumatic event upsetting our equilibrium and knocking us off our feet. It's in these times that we must remind ourselves that out of the most significant events in our lives will come opportunities for substantial growth and wisdom from periods of bliss, pain, or ongoing suffering. How we handle ourselves during such moments of ecstasy or adversity reflects our constitution as a biological organism.

Kintsugi reflects a sustainable approach to living, encouraging repair and reuse, rather than a culture of disposability. Kintsugi also offers a thoughtful perspective on damage and repair, suggesting that breakage and repair are natural parts of an object's history and can be embraced without shame or concealment—an exceptionally important metaphor for healing and moving beyond the aftereffects of trauma (events) as well as toxicity that produces trauma over time. For me, learning about kintsugi has changed my perspective about my own brokenness, thereby enabling me to reframe my own story as I continue my journey into my future.

From Los Angeles to Altadena

To better illustrate how I have become the person I am today, my life took a dramatic turn when I was eleven years old and we moved from Los Angeles to Altadena, California. We lived in Altadena by necessity because it was the only home my mom could find with external (detached) living quarters for my father who contracted TB and was not allowed to come home without such conditions being met. Since she was Sicilian, she was able to find a family willing to sell to her during a time of rampant redlining. So, when we showed up as a multiracial family the signs went up and my parents received bomb threats to blow up our home with us in it.

At the time we moved to Altadena in 1961, both race and complexion (degree of lightness or darkness) mattered more than it seems today because of the times but also, I believe because the numbers of us (multiracial children) have increased sufficiently to be counted as a discrete group in the census and other surveys. It's also true that enough time has elapsed since anti-miscegenation laws were finally struck down by the 1967 Supreme Court decision Loving v. Virginia, that interracial relationships are now at least tolerated in most of the country.

However, most Black men I know who enter into a relationship with a White woman still have a conversation with them about places that could be dangerous for them to be seen together. I see the same sorts of conversations happening with other cross-cultural relationships, but in the United States the most tabooed of all relationships viewed through the lens of White Supremacists is for a Black man to be with a White woman—AKA *the forbidden fruit.*

It also matters enough that a discussion of "I've never been with a Black man or White woman" might very well occur as though the two are different species. While I understand why it happens, the fact of the matter is, it does happen. As I explained to one person not too long ago, there aren't any differences between Black people and White people, they both want the same things. What is different, is that while Black people and White people live in the same community, their experiences within that community are very different solely because of race. Race is such a top-of-mind experience that a couple of months ago after attending a chrch service, a White parishioner approached me, looked me in the eye, and then apologized profusely for the harm his perceived privilege did to me. That is the impact of race on our society in 2025 and that is the impact and experience of race on me throughout my life making it very personal and real.

My parents married in 1949, during the height of Jim Crow segregation in many parts of the United States. Their union—and the family they built—stood on the frontlines of the long, slow march toward desegregation. Looking back now, it's clear that race has shaped much of my journey. Whether in the workplace or the neighborhoods I've lived in, it has too often been the undercurrent of the trauma I've endured.

Telling this story in 2025 isn't just about reflecting on the past—it's about naming what's still true today because it has real impacts on real people. We see it in the uneven treatment with the excessive force often used by police in communities of color, and in the vilification of those seeking a better life by moving across our borders. This ongoing maltreatment doesn't just harm immigrants or non-Christians, non-White citizens—it harms everyone. Those being targeted experience fear and anxiety to the point it changes behaviors which are classic markers of trauma. Even those who inflict the harm may be impacted with anger, aggression, and frustration, and experience these feelings as markers of trauma.

This collective unease around race has always been part of our national culture and it produces a climate of fear, mistrust, hate, and poorer outcomes for the majority of people, and we can't begin to heal without naming it. Ironically, science tells us that race doesn't exist in nature so there isn't any scientific basis for the idea of any group being superior to another based on race. However, we can readily see the impact that the idea of race-based superiority has on behaviors.

In other words, we want choice when it is convenient for us individually but want to eliminate it for others when it isn't because it is something *they want,* and we do not. As such, we behave as though life is a zero-sum gain rather than life exists in a universe of abundance rather than scarcity. For example, when we try to work through the Second Amendment issues there is a segment of the population that believes they have the absolute right to own, carry, and even brandish their weapons whenever and wherever they want. But at what point do those rights infringe upon the rights of all those who do not want to be in the presence of weapons when they are out in public? I witnessed my neighbor get murdered about twenty feet from me. After killing my neighbor, the gunman looked at me as though he was going to shoot me, but didn't, and then got into the waiting vehicle and drove off. I have a family member who was murdered. I've had a weapon pointed at my stomach at point blank range, and I have had someone waive a pistol in my face and then say it was what he wanted to be able to do.

Fear is an outgrowth of uncertainty about the outcome of some future event. In its extremes it produces the sensation of fighting or taking flight. But it is not always a logical response to the events we encounter. Here is a case in point: I went to the cashier's office to pay my undergraduate fees. As I approached the counter, the cashier looked panicked and quickly moved backwards to distance herself from me as much as possible and literally ran into her desk. I said, *excuse me, I am here to pay my graduation fees*. The cashier calmed down, approached the counter, took my money, and never said anything. So, why did this happen?

It is impossible for me to know why the cashier responded the way she did because we did not have much conversation other than about my purpose for approaching the counter. For my part, I pitied the cashier. But let me add some additional context. It was the mid-1970s. At the time I had a large Afro and was most closely identified as Black and likely a member of the Black Panther Party, which I was not. I was also at San Francisco State University where the first Black Studies Department was formed in 1968. There are a couple of points being made here with this example and that will be further illustrated later: First, context and situation always matter, and second belief systems also always matter.

Ekhart Tolle teaches that if something is not a problem in the moment then it is not a problem because the moment has not arrived for the problem to matter. It's hard to wrap the mind around such a concept, but I've learned his wisdom is correct. We live anticipating things that may never occur and in so doing we continuously live in fear which has its mental and physical consequences when in the extremes.

My story and the stories of those who volunteered to share their stories are meant to bring to life how theory when applied well in practice can lead to transformative learning, new ways of being, and greater wisdom. For myself, borrowing from William Ernest Henly (Invictus, 1875) *my head is bloody, but unbowed*. Now in my seventh decade of life, I can see how I got to where I am today. The gift of time brings with it the gift of a broader perspective. How we exercise that perspective makes the difference in how we and others experience the world because, as we will discuss throughout this story, our behaviors are inextricably linked to our shared experiences with others.

Life's Curriculum for Finding Meaning

We have to stop to ask ourselves why do we go through all the trouble to learn this stuff? The response is simple, it is life's curriculum. The sooner you learn and the sooner you sharpen your skills the more effectively you can work towards creating a meaningful life. For me, the simplest definition I can offer for a meaningful life is one filled with smiles and in the end, smiling on your way out. I'm reminded of a story I heard when my son and I traveled to Santa Rosa, California for one of his hockey games.

After his game, we went to the Charles M. Schulz Museum and Research Center to check it out. Charles Shulz was the creator of Charlie Brown, Snoopy, and the rest of the Peanuts Gang. During the visit, I was told that Schulz died in his sleep with a smile on his face. It seems to me that when it is all said and done that would be the legacy to leave our family members and friends.

But while that might become the final objective, it is also true that smiles are fickle little things that hold hidden secrets, so you simply never know the pain that exists behind a smile. Smiles are wonderful and powerful enough to change a person's mood. I've learned that I cannot stay in a bad mood when I smile, so when I am upset, I try to remember that when *enough is enough* and I've acknowledged what's bothering me sufficiently to move on, is to turn the frown upside down and smile.

Benefits of Smiling

In summary, smiling initiates a complex interplay of muscle activation, neural communication, and neurotransmitter dynamics that not only lift your mood but can also have a positive impact on your health. When you smile, a series of physiological processes occur in addition to activating facial muscles, involving the nervous system, and even the brain. Here's a breakdown of what happens:

- **Neural Messaging**: When you smile, your brain sends signals through nerves to the facial muscles, instructing them to contract. This signal is mediated by the cranial nerves, particularly the facial nerve (seventh cranial nerve), which carries impulses to the muscles of facial expression.

- **Release of Neurotransmitters**: Smiling activates the release of certain neurotransmitters, including dopamine, endorphins, and serotonin. These chemicals are associated with feelings of pleasure and pain relief. Serotonin acts as an antidepressant, while endorphins act as a mild pain reliever and give a sense of well-being.

- **Reduction of Stress-Related Hormones**: Smiling can lead to a decrease in stress-induced hormones such as cortisol, adrenaline, and dopamine, thereby reducing stress levels. This physiological change can help your body relax and lower your heart rate and blood pressure.

- **Brain's Reward Mechanism**: Smiling stimulates our brain's reward mechanisms in a way that even chocolate, a well-regarded pleasure-inducer, cannot match. The act of smiling can increase the level of dopamine in the brain, helping to elevate moods.

- **Immune System Boost**: There is some evidence suggesting that smiling may boost the immune system. The relaxation that comes with smiling and laughing is thought to contribute to improved immune function, as stress can suppress the immune response.

There are health benefits derived from smiling. Beyond the immediate physiological effects, smiling has been associated with a better mood, increased positivity, and potentially even longer life. People who smile more often are generally perceived as more likable, which can impact social interactions and personal relationships positively.

A smile is often a façade to cover our pain, and it helps us feel better at the same time. The people who know us best can detect slight changes in our moods and behaviors when we are not fully ourselves, but the public sees the façade. Being vulnerable enough to work through our own deception is critical to healing and moving beyond our traumatic events to posttraumatic growth and long-term wellness. The term *events* is used here because most of us will experience multiple traumatic event exposures over the course of our lifetimes so learning to cope with trauma is something we should learn about, teach to others, and confront more openly in well-conceived trauma-informed communities. By understanding and integrating these lessons, individuals can navigate their personal journeys with greater resilience, purpose, and fulfillment.

Lessons About Life

My professional and academic training causes me to see the world as a collection of individuals, groups, organizations, societies, and the totality of humanity. My areas of research and focus are interpersonal, intergroup, and intragroup behaviors and the dynamics caused by the various levels of interactions.

The process of growing older offers greater insights when looking through our rearview mirrors to connect the dots. We learn that we cannot understand the path we've taken until it has been walked. Looking forward offers speculation, anticipation, and hope but until we step into the next moment, we cannot know it until we are in it. We learn that living (the gift of life itself) is a process of navigating the circumstances we encounter on a moment-to-moment basis as we *find our way* through life. Some of us learn to live with a greater sense of purpose than others but all of us are shaped by the context and situation we find ourselves in at any given moment.

For each of us, our country of origin, time of birth on the historical timeline, our life choices, how we experience life, and our genetics conspire to shape us but do not define us unless we allow them to do so. Therefore, while we cannot control the future, we can control our response to it when it is encountered. We just need to learn that what we encounter is of our own making. That in truth, life is a continuous process of creation and responding to what was created. From the moment we are born we begin our process of always becoming until the moment we cease to breathe and the energy that brought us life is converted back to the energy of the collective universe to serve another purpose.

By this I mean our experiences growing up shape who we become as adults. Consciously or not, life is a survival game in which we dodge the traps and overcome the obstacles we encounter while navigating the hills and valleys found along our route from start to finish. The goal of the game is for each of us to decide what we want to accomplish with the time we have, who we will become, and by the end of the game, to have accomplished our purpose.

The Game of Life and How to Play It, written by Florence Scovel Shinn and first published in 1925, is a metaphysical book that delves into the power of thought and the importance of having faith in oneself. Shinn, drawing on her understanding of *New Thought* principles offers readers a guide to living a fulfilling and prosperous life. The central thesis of the book is that our thoughts and beliefs shape our realities, and by changing these, we can alter our lives for the better.

Shinn uses biblical stories and metaphors to illustrate her points, emphasizing the law of attraction, the importance of positive thinking, affirmations, and visualization as tools for manifesting one's desires. She discusses several key themes, such as the power of the spoken word, the law of prosperity, the law of nonresistance, and the law of karma, presenting them in a way that readers can apply to everyday situations to overcome obstacles and achieve their goals. These concepts were again popularized in *The Secret* by Rhonda Byrne (2006).

The idea that life can be viewed as a game with rules, and by understanding and applying these rules, we can navigate life more effectively. Shinn encourages readers to recognize and claim their divine right to life's riches, advocating for a spiritual approach to problem-solving and goal achievement. I was fortunate enough to come across Shinn's work during my days as an undergraduate student and it helped me reframe the way I wanted to approach my own life.

From that moment on, I gave my *inner child* permission to always come out and play—which it does even during my most desperate times. Life is a real-world version of some *survivors show* and each of us is a contestant. In a warped way, the object of the game of life is to see who can outlive whom so the stories can continue, handed down from generation to generation.

Since my introduction to Shinn later reinforced by Byrne and lived experiences I've come to fully understand how much of our experience we control. My life has been greatly enriched by learning five simple lessons which I offer here to you:

What experience has taught me is that we create much of our own pain and our own happiness by the choices we make individually and collectively. After all, don't we all choose our attitudes about what happens on any given day and how we feel about it afterwards. However, to live this way, in a manner that is on purpose, requires *owning the life we live* and everything in it. That doesn't mean we control everything that occurs, but *we do have to own the things that we do as well as their outcomes* if we're taking full responsibility (ownership) for our lives.

Here is a personal example to illustrate what I mean. When I was fourteen, my mom was cooking dinner, and I decided I did not want what she was cooking. So, she gave me some money to go to the market which was two blocks from our home. I got on my bike and was waiting for a car to pass. I thought the car was coming toward me, so I tried to maneuver around it. The driver hit me broadside launching me into the air for about seventy-five feet causing me to land with my head a few inches from the curb. I recall flying in the air, landing, and then coming back to conscious awareness after blacking out from the shock of landing on the ground.

Luckily, I landed on my butt in such a way that somehow my head also did not hit the pavement or the curb. When I came to, I looked at my bike and it was stuck at a forty-five-degree angle under the car's bumper, and I was screaming for my mom. I also remember that prior to getting hit, kicking my left leg above the crossbar which after seeing my bike and its angle to the vehicle probably saved my life. I remember thinking (and it has haunted me since) that had I been pinned between the car and the angle of my bike to the bumper I do not see how I would have lived or at minimum not suffered much more extensive bodily damage if I survived at all.

Years later, my mom and I were talking, and the accident came up in our discussion. My mom quipped, *well, if you had eaten what I was cooking for dinner, you would never have gotten hit by the car.* I realized at that moment that she was so right! That day and her comment changed me forever, because my mother taught me to *own my life* and everything in it.

Taking responsibility for my behavior was a strong theme throughout my upbringing. It was continuously reinforced through the stories told around our dinner table in much the same way other families do when they eat together. It is through family stories, stories told about courageous freedom fighters who are seen as heroes, being taught to take a stand against injustice, and taking responsibility for our actions were thoroughly reinforced by my parents.

This way of being was indicative of how we learned in our family, and it has carried over as a family cultural artifact to all our children and grandchildren in one way or another. We'll discuss this more fully later, but this is an example of how culture is transmitted in families and societies and why, how we act in our families is important to long term attitudes and behaviors as we work with and interact with others in our social and work groups.

When we can look through our pain to see the lesson in it, we have opportunities every day to learn from each other. If we stopped fighting each other long enough to truly listen with respect and intention to *hear* what we each have to say we could completely change our individual and collective circumstances for the better. This would, however, require challenging the cognitive dissonance (mental conflicts that bring with them discomfort) that will arise with active listening when long held beliefs are challenged, but it would fundamentally change everything about how we see the world operating if we had the courage to try. The likelihood of this ever happening for everyone is small yet it illustrates a different kind of possibility available to those who are willing to make the effort.

We all want the same basic things in life. If we subscribe to Abraham Maslow's view of the world, we all have identifiable needs such as food, clothing, shelter, safety, a sense of belonging, positive selfesteem, the ability to become who we wish to become through a process of self-actualization, and ultimately to transcend ourselves spiritually in support of the collective good.

Destiny

My appetite for information is insatiable so I absolutely love the *Age of* Information and the advances we've made with our various technologies. Unfortunately, the gifts we are given with such advances bring with them opportunities for misuse and abuse. But that is true with everything we learn. What is being learned is largely neutral, it is how we use it that makes it good or bad. In my line of work which largely is to convince people that they can do things they never thought possible, I utilize what I know about learning and teaching as tools for shaping the thoughts of students. Their thoughts about what I am trying to teach them, if adopted, then shape their future behaviors.

Being an educator provides an environment that fosters learning for both teacher and student. The teacher has to organize the learning context in such a way as to stimulate the student to learn it. The teacher's frame of reference and belief systems inform everything that goes on in the classroom. When done well, students outperform their own expectations, and they go on to take what they've learned and use it in their lives in ways they never expected. In that didactic process the teacher also has to understand the information sufficiently well, so that they can deliver it in a way that is digestible and makes sense.

One of my favorite authors is Kevin Cashman who wrote Leadership from the Inside Out (2000). Cashman talks about how it is not so much about learning new things but rather learning to see the world with new eyes. That is, seeing the same things differently which is a simple yet profound thought.

William Jennings Bryan (1826-1925) offered, "Destiny is not a matter of chance; it is a matter of choice; it is not a thing to be waited for, it is a thing to be achieved." Such a sentiment resonates deeply with my belief, now well supported by experience, that without taking charge of our destiny, life is left completely to others to control (Perry, 2020).

Destiny generally refers to the events that will necessarily happen to a particular person or thing in the future. It's often seen as a predetermined course of events that may be beyond a person's control but shaped by a combination of fate and one's own choices and actions. The concept of destiny is commonly associated with a philosophical or spiritual belief that there is a purpose, or a specific path set out for each individual's life. My perspective on destiny is that it is the sum total of decisions made over the course of the lifespan that produced experiences whose outcomes were defined by the behaviors of the individual. The question of whether destiny is predetermined is a complex one and varies greatly depending on cultural, philosophical, and individual beliefs:

Philosophical and Religious Views of Determinism: In philosophy, determinism argues that all events, including human actions, are ultimately determined by causes external to the will. Some philosophers assert that because of the laws of nature, everything that happens can only happen in one particular way.

Theological Fatalism: Many religious viewpoints suggest that a higher power or divine force has a plan for the universe, and that each person's life unfolds according to this plan. This is often seen in monotheistic religions where God's will is considered as shaping individual destinies.

Free Will: Contrary to determinism, the concept of free will holds that individuals can make choices that are not determined by past events. According to this view, while some aspects of life might be influenced by circumstances or predispositions, humans are capable of making decisions that can change their paths in significant ways.

Combination of Factors: Many people believe in a combination of destiny and free will, where certain events might be preordained, but how individuals respond to these events involves personal choice. This perspective allows for a destiny that is flexible and can be shaped by one's decisions and actions.

Modern Psychology: From a psychological standpoint, destiny is often seen more as a construct of human perspective, focusing on how individuals attribute meaning to events and how they respond to the perceived challenges and opportunities of life. Psychological theories, such as those pertaining to human motivation and goal setting, suggest that while external factors may set certain parameters or influences, individuals can shape their own paths through choices and actions.

Ultimately, whether destiny is viewed as predetermined or not largely depends on one's worldview and the philosophical or religious frameworks one adheres to. What I believe about destiny is that it is our purpose as we define it consciously or not. I believe that we are each born with particular genetic traits that define the body metaphorically speaking as a machine, if you will. As the body matures over time it is exposed to various experiences that imprint on the brain and collectively work to guide the actions of the body, or person we experience in our encounters in our shared physical plane. With its own unique characteristics. That machine is energized through its own life source I will call Spirit.

When discussing concepts like the spiritual plane, physical plane, or dimensions, the term physical plane refers to the tangible, material world that we can see, touch, and interact with using our physical senses. It's the dimension of reality that is governed by physical laws, such as gravity, and encompasses all things made of matter and energy. Here's how it contrasts and relates to other planes or dimensions like the spiritual plane:

The physical plane is the realm of concrete reality that includes everything from our daily environment to the observable universe. It's where biological, chemical, and physical processes occur. The physical plane is often considered the most immediate and real aspect of our experience because it involves direct sensory and empirical interaction. The spiritual plane is often described as a non-physical realm that exists beyond ordinary sensory experiences and material existence. This plane is associated with the soul, spirit, or consciousness, and is thought to be a realm where abstract concepts such as thoughts, feelings, values, and beliefs reside. It's considered less tangible and is often associated with religious or spiritual experiences, mysticism, and metaphysics. The spiritual plane is believed by many to be a higher, more subtle level of reality that is not bound by the physical laws governing the physical plane. It's where experiences like enlightenment, spiritual encounters, or connections with a higher power are said to occur.

Many philosophical, religious, and spiritual traditions discuss interactions between these planes, suggesting that events on the spiritual plane can influence or correlate with events on the physical plane and vice versa. For example, a person's spiritual growth and intentions might manifest as changes in their physical reality or behavior. In more esoteric or metaphysical contexts, additional dimensions or planes might be discussed, each representing different aspects of existence and consciousness. These are often seen as layers of reality that coexist but operate under different sets of rules or vibrations. Understanding these concepts typically involves an exploration of both empirical science and metaphysical beliefs, bridging the gap between what is physically observable and what is spiritually or philosophically theorized.

Discomfort as the Gateway to a Meaningful Life

What happens when we work through the things in life that bring us discomfort? Working through things in life that bring discomfort can lead to a range of positive outcomes, both personally and professionally. This process, often referred to as facing or embracing discomfort, is a critical component of personal growth, resilience building, and emotional intelligence. Here are some key benefits and results of engaging with uncomfortable situations or feelings:

Confronting discomfort often leads to personal development. It forces individuals to adapt, learn new skills, and rethink their beliefs or strategies. This growth can manifest in improved problem-solving skills, greater adaptability, and a deeper understanding of oneself. Regularly facing uncomfortable situations can build resilience. Over time, individuals learn to handle stress and adversity more effectively, developing a stronger capacity to bounce back from challenges.

Working through discomfort can enhance emotional intelligence by improving one's ability to manage emotions, relate to others, and communicate effectively. Understanding and navigating one's own discomfort can lead to better empathy and interpersonal skills. Discomfort often arises from challenges or problems that need to be addressed. By engaging these issues rather than avoiding them, individuals can sharpen their problem-solving abilities, finding innovative solutions that they might not have considered otherwise.

Successfully working through uncomfortable experiences can boost selfconfidence and self-efficacy. Each success reinforces an individual's belief in their ability to handle future challenges. Openly addressing issues that cause discomfort in relationships—whether personal or professional—can lead to healthier and more honest relationships. It encourages transparency and trust, as parties learn to communicate their needs and boundaries more clearly.

Breakthroughs in Professional Life: In a professional context, pushing through discomfort can lead to significant breakthroughs. Whether it's tackling a difficult project, dealing with conflict, or adapting to changes, navigating these challenges can lead to career advancement and recognition. Regularly stepping out of one's comfort zone expands it. What was once daunting becomes less intimidating over time, allowing individuals to take on even greater challenges.

Working through discomfort often requires a level of mindfulness, which can improve one's mental health. Being present with uncomfortable emotions reduces anxiety and depression and increases well-being. While discomfort is not pleasant at the moment, addressing the underlying causes of discomfort can lead to greater happiness and fulfillment in the long term. Avoidance often leads to unresolved issues simmering below the surface, affecting long-term happiness and well-being.

In summary, while discomfort is naturally something most people seek to avoid, actively engaging with it is a crucial step towards achieving a more fulfilling, successful, and balanced life. By integrating these lessons, individuals can transform discomfort into a powerful catalyst for personal and professional growth, leading to a more meaningful and fulfilling life.

Limiting Access to Knowledge Because of Discomfort

Collectively, teaching and learning are foundational to the growth and health of all societies. We have to ask ourselves what happens to societies that limit information? Societies that limit access to information typically experience a range of effects, both internally and in their interactions with the wider world. The control of information can be achieved through censorship, media control, restricting internet access, and other forms of suppression.

Limiting information often goes hand in hand with suppressing freedom of speech and expression. People in such societies may be unable to express their opinions freely or share information without fear of repercussions, leading to a climate of fear and self-censorship. Access to diverse and comprehensive information is crucial for effective personal and collective decision-making. When information is limited, both citizens and leaders may make poor decisions based on incomplete or biased data, potentially leading to adverse social, economic, and political outcomes.

Innovation often thrives in environments where ideas can be freely exchanged and critiqued. Information limitations can stifle creativity and slow down technological and scientific advancement, leaving societies less competitive on the global stage. When information flow is controlled or restricted, it becomes easier for corruption and abuses of power to go unchecked. Transparency and accountability typically suffer, as watchdog functions of media and the public are undermined. Limited access to information can contribute to misunderstandings and misconceptions among different groups within a society. This can exacerbate divisions and lead to social conflict, as people are not exposed to diverse perspectives that could foster empathy and understanding.

Economically, information limitations can deter foreign investment and hinder business development. Investors and businesses often seek environments where information flows freely, ensuring better market analysis and risk assessment. On the international stage, countries that severely limit information may find themselves isolated. They might face sanctions, reduced diplomatic relations, or exclusion from global forums, as they are perceived as repressive or untrustworthy partners.

Culturally, when the flow of ideas and cultural expressions is restricted, it can lead to stagnation. Exposure to new and different cultural ideas is a key driver of cultural evolution and dynamism. Interestingly, in many cases, efforts to suppress information can lead to increased resilience and resistance among the populace. Underground networks, alternative media, and cyber activism can flourish as people seek ways to bypass restrictions and access or disseminate information.

The extent and specific impacts of limiting information vary depending on how such controls are implemented and the societal context. However, the general trend suggests significant negative repercussions for societal progress and global integration.

Going through the discomfort of learning about differences and how we ascribe those differences to ourselves and other individuals as we associate them with groups, is a mental process of social categorization to make things easier for us to comprehend. It is how we discern friends from enemies. However, the more we limit what is available for people to learn, the more we have shifted from education to indoctrination to a particular way of thinking.

So, it becomes a matter of perspective and intention. And, as one of my classmates, reminded me during our doctoral studies, is that you have intention, and you have impact. Consequently, even something done with the best of intentions can have dire impacts with long-term implications.

For example, a parent can say something to a child with the intention of helping them grow into a more capable adult, but the impact on the child is negative (maybe even devastating) to the child because of how it is received. Much of this difference comes from all the previous parent-child interactions and how those became interpreted by the child. My son played hockey, and one of his teammates had so much abuse at home, that if a coach yelled at him his eyes glazed over; you could actually see the change as his brain processed what was happening.

There is so much for us to learn from youth sports, which I believe in wholeheartedly, that would be good for parents to learn so they could become better parents. Too many parents do not fully understand that how they treat their child during the most developmentally significant period in their lives, will shape their behaviors for the rest of their lives. Too many parents are stressed to the point of having little capacity for carrying the burden of parenthood on top of everything else. We see this when parents say, oh pick up your big boy/girl pants life is tough so you've got to learn to deal with it.

By understanding these lessons, societies and individuals can work towards creating environments that promote free access to information, critical thinking, and empathy, leading to healthier, more innovative, and inclusive communities.

Dimensions of Human Capacity

In the context of what it means to be human, capacity can refer to several interrelated aspects of human potential and abilities. Here are some key dimensions of human capacity:

Physical Capacity
This includes the body's ability to perform tasks, endure physical challenges, and respond to the demands of the physical environment. It encompasses strength, endurance, flexibility, and health and wellness.

Intellectual Capacity
Intellectual capacity refers to cognitive abilities such as reasoning, problemsolving, learning, and understanding. It encompasses the capability to think abstractly, apply knowledge, analyze, synthesize information, and adapt to new situations through learning.

Emotional Capacity
This is the ability to manage and express emotions effectively. Emotional capacity includes recognizing one's own feelings and those of others, managing emotional reactions, and navigating interpersonal relationships through empathy, compassion, and social skills.

Creative Capacity
Human creativity involves the ability to generate new ideas, innovations, and expressions that are original and valuable. This capacity is evident in all forms of artistic expression, technological innovation, and in the ability to think and act 'outside the box.'

Moral and Ethical Capacity
This involves the ability to discern right from wrong, make ethical decisions, and behave in a manner that is considered morally correct. It includes a sense of justice, integrity, responsibility, and respect for others.

Spiritual Capacity
For many, this includes the ability to understand and connect to something greater than oneself, which can involve religious faith, spiritual beliefs, or a deeper sense of purpose and connection to the universe.

Social Capacity
This entails the ability to interact effectively with others, build relationships, and function within social institutions. Social capacity includes skills in communication, cooperation, negotiation, and conflict resolution.

Developing an adaptive capacity gives us the ability to adjust and thrive in new or changing environments, overcoming adversity, and utilizing flexibility to cope with external pressures and stressors. Related to adaptive capacity, resilience refers to the ability to bounce back from hardship, trauma, or failure, learning from experiences and continuing to pursue goals and growth. There is a range of abilities and potentials humans possess to function, adapt, and thrive in various dimensions of life. These capacities define the scope of what humans can achieve and experience, influencing personal development, social structures, and cultural evolution.

When it comes to creating a meaningful life, perspective shaping frames our mental models about how the world works and how we fit into that world. Perspective shaping is often considered one of the most important capacities to have because it fundamentally influences how individuals interpret their experiences, relate to others, and make decisions. This ability to shape and reshape one's perspective can determine the impact of life's events and life's trajectory. Perspective shaping is so pivotal because people perceive and interpret their experiences directly. Therefore, it affects their emotional responses and the lessons they derive from those experiences. A positive and constructive perspective can turn challenges into opportunities for growth, whereas a negative perspective might lead to feelings of despair, stagnation, and potential for retaliation. Moreover, perspective shaping is critical in building resilience. By reframing setbacks and difficulties as part of a larger, often beneficial process of personal development, individuals can maintain motivation and continue striving towards their goals despite adversity. The ability to adopt multiple perspectives enhances empathy. Understanding where others are coming from can lead to stronger, more meaningful relationships, which are key components of a fulfilling life. This capacity allows for deeper connections and a better understanding of diverse viewpoints.

The perspectives people adopt can heavily influence their decision-making processes. A broader, well-considered perspective can lead to more thoughtful and effective decisions, impacting virtually all aspects of life, from career choices to personal relationships. Perspective shaping helps in setting realistic and meaningful goals. By evaluating what truly matters from a well-rounded viewpoint, individuals can pursue aspirations that align more closely with their values and long-term life vision.

The ability to alter one's perspective on stressful situations can significantly affect stress levels and mental health. Viewing stressors as manageable and temporary can reduce their negative impact and promote a healthier, more balanced life. In a globalized world, the ability to understand and appreciate different cultures and social norms is crucial. Perspective shaping enhances one's ability to function effectively and respectfully in diverse settings, enriching life experiences and broadening one's worldview. Continuously shaping one's perspective promotes lifelong learning and personal growth. It encourages curiosity, openness to new ideas, and the willingness to change outdated or unhelpful views.

Perspective shaping can also lead to an increased capacity for joy and gratitude. By focusing on positive aspects and maintaining a grateful stance, individuals can enhance their life satisfaction and well-being. Ultimately, the ability to shape one's perspective can directly influence one's sense of meaning and purpose. Perspectives that align with personal values and goals contribute to a sense of living a purposedriven life. In essence, perspective shaping is a dynamic capacity that affects almost every aspect of human experience. It allows individuals to navigate life's complexities with more wisdom, balance, and effectiveness, directly contributing to a richer, more meaningful life.

Whether someone maximizes their capacity or not is influenced by a combination of internal and external factors. These factors can either enhance or hinder a person's ability to develop and utilize their full potential across various domains of life.

Genetic factors play a significant role in determining physical abilities, cognitive potential, and even predispositions to certain behaviors or traits. These inherent qualities set the foundation for one's capacities. The environment in which a person grows and lives, including family, education, socioeconomic status, and cultural background, profoundly impacts the development and maximization of their capacities. A supportive, resource-rich environment enhances opportunities for growth, while a restrictive or impoverished one can limit them.

Access to education and continuous learning opportunities is crucial for intellectual and skill development. Quality education can unlock potential and foster critical thinking, creativity, and knowledge acquisition. Physical and mental health are foundational to maximizing human capacity. Good health allows individuals to fully engage with life's opportunities, while health challenges can significantly restrict one's ability to reach their full potential.

Personal drive and goals influence the extent to which individuals strive to develop and use their capacities. Motivation can be intrinsic (driven by personal satisfaction) or extrinsic (driven by external rewards), and both types can propel individuals toward maximizing their potential. Relationships and social networks provide emotional support, advice, and access to opportunities that are crucial for personal and professional development. Supportive relationships can encourage risk-taking and resilience, key factors in realizing one's potential.

Traits such as resilience, self-esteem, and openness to experience are critical psychological factors that affect capacity maximization. These traits influence how individuals face challenges, adapt to changes, and seize opportunities. Availability of financial resources, technology, information, and professional guidance can significantly affect the ability to maximize capacity. Resources provide the necessary tools and opportunities needed to develop skills and knowledge.

The cultural and societal context can either constrain or enable capacity development. Norms and values that emphasize learning, innovation, and self-expression can promote capacity maximization, whereas those that impose strict roles or limit access to opportunities based on gender, race, or class can hinder it. Life experiences, including challenges and successes, shape personal growth and capacity development. Experiences teach valuable lessons, build character, and influence perspectives, impacting how one approaches personal potential.

By understanding and addressing these factors, individuals and societies can better support the realization of human potential and capacity across diverse contexts.

Creating Your Own Balance

The chapter "The Art of Becoming" revolves around the theme that life is a continuous process of personal growth, shaped by our choices, experiences, and the perspectives we adopt. It highlights the idea that what may seem like limitations or obstacles can be transformed into opportunities for growth and innovation through creativity and willpower. Life, as the chapter explains, is an ongoing journey of becoming, and the key to living a meaningful life is owning that process.

The chapter stresses the importance of adopting a mindset that takes responsibility for one's beliefs, decisions, and actions. Every individual must define what a meaningful life looks like for themselves, independent of others' opinions. It underscores the solitary nature of life, suggesting that regardless of our circumstances, each person must figure out how to change and flourish. I share a personal realization about the power of shifting one's perspective, recounting moments where painful memories surfaced unexpectedly and how these moments provided insight into personal growth.

The chapter further explores how life is, in many ways, a product of our imagination, with experiences shaped by the meanings we ascribe to them. The ability to reflect on past decisions and behaviors allows individuals to understand their current state and navigate future challenges more effectively. It encourages taking the first step toward change by cultivating a mindset that faces uncertainty with courage and quiets negative, intrusive thoughts.

In leadership and organizational contexts, the chapter introduces the concept of "perspective shaping"—the ability of leaders to influence the views of their teams by promoting shared values and aligning group efforts toward common goals. Effective perspective shaping leads to better teamwork, communication, and group cohesion.

The chapter concludes with the idea that challenges in life can either be seen as barriers or as steppingstones to success. The way we perceive and approach these challenges determines whether we succumb to setbacks or use them to foster transformation and renewal. Ultimately, life is about becoming better versions of ourselves every day, and this is achieved by maintaining a perspective that sees the potential for growth in every experience.

LIVE IN FULL EXPRESSION

Principle 8: *Our perception of the world deeply influences our response to life events, and by intentionally shifting our mindset and embracing new perspectives, we can foster personal growth, resilience, and a more meaningful life.*

CHAPTER 8

Life is What We Choose to Make It
Seeing the World with New Eyes

To live life well means to live life in full expression of who we truly are. The research tells us that 60% of people who experience trauma report posttraumatic growth (Calhoun and Tedeschi 2006). This provides hope for us all that we can find posttraumatic growth and wellness if we try hard enough. That is not to say it is easy and when we are hurting it's even harder to find hope, so sometimes just knowing others have found a way to do it gives us the silver lining we need to simply put our heads down in the darkness taking one step at a time until we find the light at the end of the tunnel.

What I have learned through my own journey is that a significant portion of how I respond to a given event has a lot to do with how I see the world in the moment. This was made abundantly clear when I experienced a neural hijack in my physical therapist's office. The way I saw the world changed in an instant with the thought I had at the moment of the hijack, that my physical therapy setback reverted me to the beginning of my treatments. That thought changed how I was seeing the world with the speed of thought—and I am still recovering from that brief moment nearly four months later illustrating in clear detail what can happen simply by the perspective we hold.

Kevin Cashman (2008), a well-regarded leadership coach and author, explores the transformative power of seeing the world with new eyes in his book *Leadership from the Inside Out*. Cashman emphasizes that authentic leadership requires a deep personal transformation that goes beyond traditional skills and competencies. It involves a shift in perception and consciousness, allowing leaders to see themselves, others, and their environments in fundamentally new ways.

Seeing the world with new eyes, according to Cashman, begins with self-awareness and self-discovery. Leaders must embark on an inward journey to understand their core values, strengths, and weaknesses. This process of introspection helps leaders align their actions with their true selves, fostering authenticity and integrity. By understanding their inner landscape, leaders can approach challenges and opportunities with a fresh perspective, unburdened by preconceived notions and biases.

Cashman also highlights the importance of embracing diversity and different viewpoints. Seeing the world with new eyes involves actively seeking out and valuing diverse perspectives, which can lead to more innovative solutions and more inclusive environments. Leaders who are open to learning from others and who encourage a culture of curiosity and respect are better equipped to navigate the complexities of today's interconnected world.

Moreover, Cashman underscores the role of purpose in leadership. By connecting to a higher purpose, leaders can transcend their personal ambitions and focus on creating positive impact for others. This purpose-driven approach enables leaders to see beyond the immediate challenges and to envision a broader, more meaningful future.

In essence, Kevin Cashman's concept of seeing the world with new eyes calls for a holistic and transformative approach to leadership (and life). It requires leaders to cultivate self-awareness, embrace diversity, and connect to a higher purpose. By doing so, leaders can unlock their full potential and lead with greater empathy, creativity, and effectiveness. This approach not only enhances personal growth but also contributes to the development of more resilient and adaptive organizations.

The power of life is in our hands and all around us. The friends we've chosen, the people we've met, the decisions we've made when choices presented themselves, our behaviors in response to problems and challenges, the teachers we've adopted to teach us, the sacrifices we've made, the opportunities missed and taken converge to create what we used to call in the day, the school of hard knocks.

LIFE: Live in Full Expression

My friend Jill Cody shared something she'd learned from one of her mentors which is that LIFE as an acronym means Live in Full Expression, which I am now adding to my lexicon, thank you very much. Jill was the Host of the Be Bold America talk show on KSQD 90.7FM serving Santa Cruz and the California Central Coast. In the spirit of full disclosure, Jill was a colleague who transitioned from city government recreation to become department head for recreation and leisure studies at San Jose State University. She was kind enough to invite me to be a guest on her show several times and then invited me to co-host with her, which we did for a couple of years until my life took a significant turn. When we adopt a growth mindset, all things become possible. Whether they are probable or not is another thing; resolved by among other things determination, constitution, skills, and pure luck.

My point for sharing this part of my story is that here is another example of how you just never know when one experience or contact will blossom into a beautiful friendship or relationship that is beneficial to advancing your life (the same is true for circumstances that lead to negative outcomes). Again proof that life is always a process of becoming.

Nonetheless people determine to a large extent how far they go and what they accomplish as I illustrated throughout this guide. Things may not turn about precisely as you have in mind (although sometimes they do) but they very well might give you much of what you dreamt of for yourself. I worked my fingers to the bone, to move an organization towards celebrating its 50th Anniversary, I got to the gala event, and the meanness of people who were unscrupulous created the circumstances upon which everything I worked so hard for, I never got to witness. It was every bit the story of Moses who never got to see the thing he lived and worked so hard to create for his people.

It happened again, in another organization in which my work gave the organization a chance to become a model of diversity and inclusion work and yet, egos got in the way. Two others were hired into a position that I was best suited for, and the five-year long initiative died because of egocentric leaders who got in the way.

The point with these two examples is that we can do our best and be the best at what we do, and others may very well likely expend energy to undermine everything we are attempting to do. At that point the question becomes how we respond. I chose to continue producing exemplary work, because of how I was raised that a job worth doing is a job worth doing well. I never took the job for any other reason than to do my best. Everything else was out of my control because I was an employee and not the CEO.

My mantra as an employee has always been that I can only do as much as the people above me allow me to do. What they did not count on is just how much I could accomplish by pushing the envelope to achieve things that were thought impossible and in many cases they didn't even understand. I refuse to allow other people to determine how much I am going to get out of my life. Because I live my life like a sponge, I look for every positive moment to file in my memory banks and use my skills to mitigate the harm because I challenge the status quo to maximize employee and organizational potential. I do so to the best of my ability as an experienced executive leader with a penchant for identifying and resolving blockages to performance. That is my craft.

We can pout about the cards we were dealt at birth; we can blame our parents, we can blame the external world for everything that has gone wrong, and we can perceive life as cruel. But if you've gotten this far, you know that you have the power within you to change your perspective, as you know by now, which is something only you can do and in so doing, the same world appears differently.

Cultivating New Skills and Ways of Being

Look at the world with new lenses developed by cultivating new skills and ways of being. Look for what is around you rather than what is missing or lacking. Use whatever pain that comes into your life as your fuel to create the life you desire for yourself and loved ones. If you wonder how to take the next step just begin asking that question: How do I take it? It is through the question process that we learn, and we reshape our lives.

It's not where we start but where we finish that matters. As long as you have breath in your body you can make of life what you will. So, choose to be the rising star and not the shooting star. Be observant and learn from what you see and experience. Cultivate an inquisitive mind. When others tell you how screwed up you are, believe in yourself and your ability to find ways to create the life you want for yourself. Search for people who can teach you how to become better at what you want to do. Choose peace over conflict. Choose benefiting the entire collective over just benefiting yourself.

Once the foundation is created, everything else is shaped due to personal preferences established over time and the amount of energy placed into creating the final version of the thing being created. From this perspective, nurturing (personal treatment, family dynamics, socioeconomic dynamics, life experiences, etc.) shapes who and what we become more than our genetic predispositions. We are who we are at the moment of our birth. But our birth does not define who we will become over the length of our existence.

In general, what defines us is how we respond to whatever experiences we encounter, and those responses shape and alter who we become when it is all said and done. To that end, one of the themes conveyed throughout this guide is that out of adversity, suffering, and pain come opportunities for significant personal and professional growth.

Willpower

The development of willpower is a dynamic process involving the interaction of both genetic predispositions and environmental influences. For example, a person with a genetic predisposition for strong impulse control may still struggle with willpower if they are raised in a chaotic environment lacking structure and support. Conversely, an individual with genetic tendencies towards impulsivity can improve their self-control through positive environmental influences and deliberate practice.

When exploring the impact of nature as the basis of willpower we have to look at both the genetic influences as well as the brain structure and its function. Research suggests that genetic factors contribute to differences in willpower among individuals. Certain genes may influence neurotransmitter systems, such as dopamine and serotonin, which are involved in self-control and reward processing. For instance, according to Casey et al. (2011) variations in the DRD4 gene, which affects dopamine receptors, have been linked to differences in impulsivity and self-regulation. Neuroimaging studies have shown that certain brain regions, particularly the prefrontal cortex, play a crucial role in willpower. The prefrontal cortex is responsible for executive functions such as decision-making, planning, and impulse control. Further, genetic factors can affect the development and functionality of these brain areas, thereby influencing an individual's capacity for self-control.

Moffitt et al. (2011) found that the environment in which a person is raised significantly impacts their development of willpower. Early childhood experiences, including parenting styles, education, and social interactions, shape an individual's ability to exert self-control. For example, children who grow up in structured environments with clear expectations and supportive relationships tend to develop stronger self-regulatory skills. Cultural norms and societal expectations can also influence willpower. Societies that value and reinforce self-discipline and delayed gratification can encourage individuals to develop stronger willpower. Additionally, social support networks, such as family, friends, and community, provide encouragement and accountability, which can bolster an individual's ability to maintain self-control.

Life experiences and learning can also shape willpower. Willpower can be cultivated and strengthened through experiences and practice. Educational programs, cognitive-behavioral therapies, and mindfulness training have been shown to enhance self-control by teaching individuals to formulate strategies that manage their impulses and make conscious, deliberate choices. Positive reinforcement and habit formation also play a role in nurturing willpower over time. (Duckworth & Seligman, 2005).

Therefore, both nature and nurture significantly contribute to the development and expression of willpower. Genetic factors provide a foundational basis for self-control, influencing brain structure and neurotransmitter systems. Environmental factors, including early childhood experiences, social and cultural contexts, and life experiences, shape and reinforce an individual's capacity for willpower. Understanding this interplay can help individuals and organizations develop strategies to enhance self-control and achieve personal and collective goals. From a leadership and organizational effectiveness perspective goal behaviors are intimately intertwined with the willpower an individual brings to their group. More importantly their willpower largely determines the outcomes they will achieve as they navigate their workplace environments. In my case, during the most difficult periods in my life, my willpower to achieve despite the roadblocks facilitated my ability to do what was perceived as impossible. Willpower gives you staying power!

Purpose of Life

The question of the purpose of life is profound and varies significantly across philosophical, spiritual, and individual perspectives. Many philosophers suggest that the purpose of life is to find happiness and fulfillment. Aristotle coined the term eudaimonia, which is often translated as flourishing or the good life. This concept is about living in a way that is consistent with one's virtues. In many religions, the purpose of life is to fulfill the dictates of a divine being or beings, achieve spiritual enlightenment, or live according to certain moral and ethical principles. For example, in Christianity, the purpose of life is often seen as serving God and loving other people. Indigenous spiritual practices are inherently connected to the land, the natural world, and the community, reflecting a profound relationship with the environment and the cosmos.

From a biological standpoint, the purpose of life can be viewed as survival and reproduction, ensuring the continuation of one's genetic material. Many people find their life's purpose in personal goals and values, such as pursuing passions, achieving career ambitions, nurturing relationships, or contributing positively to society. Existential thinkers often claim that life inherently lacks purpose, but they also argue that individuals can create their own meaning through their choices and actions.

Ultimately, the purpose of life is a personal discovery that reflects our beliefs, values, and experiences. In essence, in sum it reflects every decision we made while alive. No matter who we are, to live most effectively requires generally good health and wellness. The concept of wellness can be explored through various dimensions that contribute to an individual's health and well-being. The original six dimensions of wellness were developed in 1976 by William Hettler co-founder of the National Wellness Institute as a holistic strategy for understanding wellness. Since then, other researchers added two more dimensions to create today's eight dimensions of wellness.

Wellness and Effective Living

To live most effectively requires generally good health and wellness. The concept of wellness can be explored through various dimensions that contribute to an individual's health and well-being. Originally, six dimensions of wellness were developed by William Hettler in 1976, and since then, researchers have added two more to create the eight dimensions of wellness recognized today. These dimensions are:

- *Physical wellness* involves maintaining a healthy body through regular exercise, proper nutrition, adequate sleep, and avoiding harmful habits. It emphasizes the importance of listening to the body's signs and responding appropriately through healthcare and personal hygiene.

- *Occupational wellness* relates to deriving personal satisfaction and enrichment from one's work. It is about enjoying your occupational endeavors and appreciating your contributions, fostering a sense of purpose and fulfillment.

- *Financial wellness* involves learning how to successfully manage financial expenses. Money plays a critical role in our lives, and not having enough of it impacts health as well as academic and professional performance. Financial stress is repeatedly found to be a common source of stress, anxiety, and fear.

- *Environmental wellness* inspires us to live a lifestyle that is respectful of our surroundings. This realm encourages us to live in harmony with the Earth by taking action to protect it, promoting interaction with nature and personal environments.

- *Intellectual wellness* encourages creative and stimulating mental activities. It involves expanding knowledge and skills while discovering the potential for sharing these gifts with others. Engaging in lifelong learning and activities that foster critical thinking and mental challenges is essential.

- *Social wellness* involves developing a sense of connection, belonging, and a well-developed support system. It emphasizes participating in and contributing to the community, country, and world, fostering relationships and social networks that are supportive and enriching.

- *Emotional wellness* relates to understanding and respecting our feelings, values, and attitudes. This dimension emphasizes the ability to manage our feelings and behaviors, cope with stress, and seek support and guidance when needed, promoting emotional resilience and balance.

- *Spiritual wellness* involves seeking meaning and purpose in human existence. It includes the development of a deep appreciation for the depth and expanse of life and the natural forces that exist in the universe, fostering a sense of inner peace and connectedness.

Fostering and integrating each of these dimensions can contribute to an individual's overall sense of well-being and health, supporting their ability to lead a balanced and fulfilling life. Reflecting on these wellness dimensions, we can see how the spiritual, emotional, social, and intellectual dimensions shape our physical, occupational, financial, and environmental dimensions, influencing how we function in the world.

However, striving to foster each of these wellness areas may produce considerable stress depending on the individual's current situation and context. For example, a person in an abusive situation may not feel physically or emotionally safe in their environment, which may also have consequences for financial and occupational security. Addressing challenges in wellness involves understanding and mitigating factors that hinder well-being. For instance, Paulo Freire's work on education and social justice highlights the importance of addressing systemic issues that impact wellness. Ensuring equitable access to resources, supportive environments, and opportunities for personal growth are crucial for fostering wellness.

No matter who we are, achieving and maintaining good health and wellness is fundamental to living effectively. Each dimension of wellness contributes to our overall ability to function, thrive, and find fulfillment. By integrating and balancing these dimensions, we can create a holistic approach to well-being that supports personal and professional growth, resilience, and a meaningful life.

The pursuit of wellness in its various dimensions is integral to effective living. It allows individuals to harness their full potential, overcome challenges, and contribute positively to their communities and the world at large. As we navigate life's complexities, prioritizing wellness can lead to a more balanced, fulfilling, and impactful existence. Fostering each of these dimensions can contribute to an individual's sense of well-being and health, supporting their ability to lead a balanced and fulfilling life. As I think about these wellness dimensions, I see the spiritual, emotional, social, and intellectual dimensions shaping our physical, occupational, financial, and environmental dimensions and therefore how we function in the world.

But fostering each of these wellness areas may produce considerable stress depending on the individual's current situation and context. For example, a person in an abusive situation may not feel physically or emotionally safe in their environment which may also have consequences for financial and occupational security. Such a situation is the kind of context the Brazilian Educator Paulo Freire contemplated.

Personal challenges and overcoming obstacles can lead to greater skills, a sense of purpose, and significant accomplishments, often surpassing those of peers; however, this journey can come with emotional and psychological costs, underscoring the need to balance resilience with self-care. These lessons emphasize the importance of understanding the complex interplay between nature and nurture, the multifaceted purpose of life, and the comprehensive dimensions of wellness in navigating personal and professional challenges. **Table 8-1** showcases various catalysts of transformative learning, including experiential learning and life experiences. These learning pathways illustrate the multifaceted nature of transformative learning and the diverse pathways to achieving transformation enroute to becoming a transformative leader and a more whole and fulfilled person.

Experiential Learning	Cognitive Dissonance	Life Experiences	Dark Knights of The Soul	Aging
• Experimentation and exploration • Travel and recreation • Training / Education programs • Engaging nature • Ropes courses • Testing capacities	• The challenge to mental models, paradigms, belief systems, & a priori assumptions • Discrimination & other major Values conflicts	• Rites of passage • Marriage • Birth of a child • Major new opportunities • Unexpected wealth • New invention	• Psychological and physical trauma • Abuse • Torture • Near-death experience • Loss of job and ability to care for Self and loved ones • Death of loved one • Major illnesses • Homelessness • War • Natural disasters	• Physical and cognitive capacities • Habits and personal traits • Relationships with professional field • Relationships with domain • Generativity

Table 8-1: Transformation Through Intentionality, Synchronistic Event, or Time

Ralph Ellison's *The Invisible Man* exemplifies transformative learning with the line, "When I discover who I am, I'll be free." Ironically, the first time I felt free was when I set foot on Canadian soil in Victoria, British Columbia, in 1992. Two decades later, I made my home in the Pacific Northwest, about a forty-minute drive from the Canadian border. This exemplifies how disparate experiences come together to produce larger, more meaningful experiences later in life.

Conscientization and Transformation

Conscientization is a continuous process of engagement, reflection, and action, leading to a deeper understanding of the world and one's role in it. Freire's work led psychologist Jack Mezirow to define transformative learning, which begins with a disorienting dilemma and progresses towards adopting new perspectives and ways of living. This framework is crucial for navigating significant traumatic events and resolving cognitive dissonance when new information challenges existing beliefs. Mezirow (1991) outlined the ten phases of transformative learning, which are:

1. Disorienting Dilemma

2. Self-examination—may experience feelings of guilt or shame

3. A critical self-assessment of socio-cultural and/or psychic assumptions

4. Recognize discontent and the process of transformation are shared and that others have negotiated a similar change

5. Explore options for new roles, relationships, and actions

6. Plan a course of action

7. Acquire knowledge and skills to implement plans

8. Explore and try out new roles

9. Build competencies and self-confidence in new roles and relationships

10. Integration into one's life on the basis of conditions dictated by one's new perspective

Mezirow's framework is essential for practitioners navigating significant traumatic events and resolving cognitive dissonance. For example, the birth of a child can produce what Tedeschi et al. (2018) called post-ecstatic growth (PEG), forcing parents to make life-altering decisions. Equally significant, disorienting dilemmas that challenge deeply held beliefs based on negative stereotypes can lead to internal battles and lifelong wars. These circumstances can then become precursors to future behaviors that harm others, forcing targets to endure trauma.

The hard part about living is surviving long enough to figure out what's most meaningful and then having time to enjoy it. The path to conscientization and the road to transformation go through discomfort and pain and can lead to growth and wisdom. The goal of fostering conscientization is to enable individuals and communities to perceive social, political, and economic contradictions and to act against the oppressive elements of their reality so all members can thrive.

Freire explains that it's not enough to just go through life accepting things as they are. He believes that to really understand our world, we need to dig deep, question how and why things are the way they are, and see the hidden influences of politics, economics, and social norms. But here's the kicker: once we see these truths, we shouldn't just sit back. Freire says we've got to act, to do something about it. This is what he calls praxis—thinking critically about our world and then jumping in to make a change.

This whole process is about empowering ourselves and those around us. It's about moving from feeling stuck and powerless to realizing we can actually shape our own futures. We start to see ourselves as agents of change, capable of making the world a fairer place. Freire places a big emphasis on dialogue, which means learning from each other in a way that breaks down the traditional teacher-student roles. Everyone has something to teach and something to learn.

A big part of this journey is developing a critique of society, using our own experiences and the experiences of our communities to challenge the status quo. It's about calling out injustice and inequality, not just as a theoretical exercise, but as a step towards dismantling it.

In essence, conscientization is about waking up to the world's realities and realizing we have the power to change them. It's a call to action for anyone who's ever felt that things aren't quite right and believes in the possibility of a better, more just society. Freire's ideas have inspired people all over the world to use education as a tool for real, impactful social change, making his concept of conscientization a powerful guide for anyone looking to make a difference.

What produces the moment conscientization? The moment of conscientization refers to the process of developing a critical awareness of one's social reality through reflection and action. This awareness is often the first step towards transformative change, particularly in the context of social and educational reform. Several factors can contribute to this process:

Conscientization often begins with critical reflection on one's circumstances and the societal structures in place. This involves questioning and analyzing the status quo, rather than accepting it at face value. Exposure to new ideas, education, or learning experiences can provoke critical thinking and a deeper understanding of social injustices and inequalities. Engaging in open discussions with others, especially those from different backgrounds or perspectives, can lead us to greater awareness and understanding of diverse social experiences.

Sometimes, experiential learning occurs through organized events that impact our sense of Self, or through direct experiences of injustice, discrimination, or inequality that can trigger conscientization, as individuals see firsthand the effects of oppressive systems. Witnessing the struggles and injustices faced by others can also be a powerful catalyst for developing critical consciousness and can lead to direct participation in or exposure to social activism and movements to raise awareness of societal issues and the need for change.

Because of such exposures they often include highly charged emotional issues that tend to form lasting impressions and therefore have the potential for leading to direct, vicarious, or secondary traumatic stress as was the case with the birth of our nation, the abolitionist movement leading up to the Civil War, the Underground Railroad, and the 1972 Bloody Sunday March across the Edmund Pettus Bridge. We can also see in public display the lengths people will go to protect their belief systems by looking at mass protests.

Conscientization is an ongoing process of engagement, reflection, and action, leading to a deeper understanding of the world and one's role in it. It is the process of becoming conscious that a change is required to alter status quo conditions and expose the potential for transformative learning and positive change. By integrating these lessons, we can foster a deeper understanding of our social reality, empowering ourselves and others, and actively working towards a more just and equitable society.

Cognitive Dissonance and Change

Disorienting dilemmas produce cognitive dissonance, challenging deeply held belief systems. The more deeply held the beliefs, the harder they are to recognize and address. Disorienting dilemmas offer opportunities to improve our lives or can become burdens that cause psychological harm. Learning about these dilemmas and their potential to foster greater meaning and purpose can inspire perseverance through challenging circumstances.

Shields (2006) identifies critical self-reflection as a precondition for transformative learning and leadership. A disorienting dilemma, as identified by Mezirow, triggers conscientization—a critical awareness of one's social reality through reflection and action. This awareness is the first step toward transformative change.

Factors contributing to conscientization include critical reflection, education and learning, dialogue and discussion, personal experiences, observation of others' experiences, activism and social movements, mentorship and guidance, and cultural and artistic influences. My exposure to Freire was the gateway to my transformation, leading me to this moment and my discussion with you.

The conditions we find ourselves in today offer tremendous possibilities for our collective futures if we can stop the wars being fought in our minds, families, organizations, and societies. We must confront the internal discomfort produced by cognitive dissonance, which occurs when events and circumstances challenge our deeply held beliefs. Conscientization is the gateway to transformation, but the road through transformation can be rough. It requires challenging discomfort, breaking through cognitive dissonance, and confronting our belief systems and frames of reference.

Overcoming cognitive dissonance involves reducing the inconsistency between beliefs, behaviors, or attitudes through several strategies. Recognizing and acknowledging dissonance is crucial for moving forward toward growth. Seeking out more information that aligns with one of the conflicting beliefs can support a more consistent worldview. Modifying behavior to align more closely with beliefs or adjusting attitudes to match behavior also helps resolve dissonance. Acceptance, talking through thoughts and feelings, and seeking reinforcement for new beliefs or behaviors also aid in overcoming cognitive dissonance.

Frames of Reference

Frames of reference are mental structures that shape how we view and interpret the world. These cognitive frameworks, influenced by personal experiences, cultural background, education, beliefs, values, and social environment, determine our understanding of situations and guide decision-making and problem-solving processes. Cultural frames, personal experience frames, professional or disciplinary frames, socioeconomic frames, ethical or moral frames, psychological frames, and ideological or political frames all shape our perspectives.

Understanding frames of reference helps us recognize different interpretations and reactions to the same situation, crucial for effective communication, conflict resolution, and collaboration. This awareness encourages open-mindedness and consideration of diverse perspectives, leading to more inclusive decision-making.

Individuals may be motivated to change their frame of reference due to exposure to different cultures, ideas, or ways of life. Personal growth, higher education, major life changes, workplace adaptation, influential relationships, conflict, recognition of biases, encountering contradictory information, curiosity, empathy, and the availability of diverse viewpoints through the internet and social media all contribute to this motivation.

Changing one's frame of reference involves a deliberate and often challenging process. Actively seeking diverse perspectives, reflecting on personal biases, continuous education, traveling, practicing empathy, regular self-reflection, engaging in conversations, addressing conflicts, cultivating a growth mindset, participating in professional development, engaging in creative thinking, and seeking professional therapy are all strategies that help alter frames of reference.

This continuous process requires openness, effort, and stepping out of one's comfort zone, leading to a more nuanced understanding of the world and improved personal and professional relationships.

Adversity and Its Dual Impact

For those of us who experience adversity as children, we may have an advantage due to the survival skills we develop early on. These skills can provide resilience and adaptability in later life. However, those who escape childhood adversity may find it harder to adjust to difficulties later in life. Yet, their freedom from early trauma allows them to develop more fully in other areas, helping them manage adversity when it arises.

While some adversity can build resilience, too much can lead to negative consequences such as a higher susceptibility to PTSD, especially with significant early trauma exposure. In my case, adversity became personal challenges for me to overcome. Continuously having to overcome greater obstacles than my counterparts allowed me to develop greater skills and accomplish things they failed at, giving me a great sense of purpose and meaning. However, living to a different standard and watching my peers get recognized while I outperformed them took its toll over time.

Reflections on Purpose and Fulfillment

The question of life's purpose is profound and varies across philosophical, spiritual, and individual perspectives. Philosophers often see the purpose of life as finding happiness and fulfillment, as exemplified by Aristotle's concept of eudaimonia, or flourishing. Many religions view life's purpose as fulfilling divine will, achieving spiritual enlightenment, or living according to moral principles. Biologically, life's purpose can be seen as survival and reproduction. On a personal level, people find purpose in their goals and values, such as pursuing passions, achieving career ambitions, nurturing relationships, or contributing to society. Existentialists argue that life inherently lacks purpose, but individuals can create their own meaning through choices and actions. Ultimately, the purpose of life is a personal discovery reflecting our beliefs, values, and experiences. In essence, it reflects every decision we make while alive.

Dark Nights of the Soul

John of the Cross was a Spanish Mystic Theologian (1542-1591) who wrote The Ascent of Mt. Carmel a poem about his creating a spiritual union with God during his time of the dark Nights. The Poem describes the role of Dark Nights of the Soul in our growth toward enlightenment (wisdom) and deeper spirituality.

It is possible for the soul journey to arrive at the point of Spiritual Union without going through the Dark Nights. However, few have the genuine discipline to make the journey without passing through Dark Nights. The Dark Nights result from posttraumatic stress event or loss, severe cognitive dissonance, challenge to self-concept, or the hero's journey. It is a process that produces a journey of the soul that can lead to self-transcendence and spiritual (meta-physical) awakening and new-found enlightenment. In summary, the Dark Nights of the Soul lead the initiate through a process of deep self-exploration to confront their "personal demons" that scare them the most, and by exploring our deepest fears we find our path towards becoming better versions of ourselves, and eventually finding Spiritual Union with God.

- 1st night (self-deprivation) challenges the "lower part of man" for beginners to undergo a period of contemplation of their personal journey.

- 2nd night (faith) is dark and terrible, challenging the higher part of man the road upon which the soul must travel towards awakening.

- 3rd night (end point) wisdom, Spiritual Union, an awakening, and enlightenment (Internet Archives, n.d.).

The Dark Nights are symbolic and not the length of a single night as we know it. From personal experience they can last for many weeks as we navigate our way through them. Everyone experiences Dark Nights at some point in their lifetime. It's been said that the longer it's been since your last Dark Nights experience, the closer you are to the next one. The Dark Nights can be a blessing in disguise and can lead to a fuller and happier life. How we choose to respond to our Dark Nights will determine whether we move beyond what challenges us. The Dark Nights are a solitary journey of the soul so while others can support us as we go through them it is a solitary journey and unfortunately, not everyone survives them by ending their lives through some form of suicide. However, successfully transiting the Dark Nights journey is a fully transformative experience that leads to new ways of finding the meaning of life.

The Dark Night of the Soul has since been broadly used to describe a period of profound spiritual desolation, crisis, and emptiness. This experience is often characterized by a deep sense of loneliness, despair, and the feeling of being lost or abandoned. In spiritual and psychological contexts, it represents a challenging phase of deep inner transformation and self-discovery.

Key aspects of the Dark Night of the Soul include:

- **Spiritual Crisis**: The experience often involves a spiritual crisis, where one's previous sense of religious or spiritual meaning feels inadequate or empty. This can lead to questioning beliefs, values, and one's sense of identity.

- **Emotional Turmoil**: It is typically marked by intense emotional distress, which may include feelings of depression, anxiety, loneliness, and a sense of despair.

- **Sense of Abandonment**: There is often a feeling of being abandoned by God or the divine, or a loss of connection to spiritual or religious sources of comfort and meaning.

- **Inner Conflict**: The Dark Night can involve an intense inner conflict, as the individual grapples with previously held beliefs and their current experience of spiritual emptiness.

- **Transformation and Growth**: Despite its challenges, this period is often seen as an opportunity for deep spiritual growth and transformation. Through enduring the Dark Night, individuals may emerge with a more profound, mature understanding of themselves and their spiritual beliefs.

- **Emergence of New Insights**: Eventually, this phase can lead to new insights, a renewed sense of purpose, and a deeper connection with the Self and the divine or spiritual.

The Dark Nights of the Soul is not just a spiritual or religious concept; it can also be understood psychologically as a period of profound existential crisis or a deep exploration of the subconscious mind. It is important to note that while it shares some characteristics with clinical depression, it is primarily a spiritual and existential crisis and may require different approaches for navigation and resolution. For those experiencing it, support from spiritual guides, counselors, or mental health professionals can be crucial for personal growth and development (see **Table 8-2**).

The PTG Process	Dark Nights Process
• Encounter with a highly challenging seismic event • The challenge to core beliefs	• 1st night (self-deprivation) challenges the "lower part of man" for beginners to undergo a period of contemplation of their personal journey
• Experience with the psychological struggle • Coping with emotional distress • Intrusive rumination	• 2nd night (faith) is dark and terrible, challenges the "higher part of man" the road upon which the soul must travel towards awakening
• Shift to deliberate or effortful rumination about what happened • Experience PTG characteristics • Experience 6 dimensions of well-being	• 3rd night (end point) wisdom, Spiritual Union, an awakening, and enlightenment

Table 8-2: *Aligning Post-Trauma Growth (PTG) With Dark Nights of the Soul (Source: Perry, 2020)*

Faith

Faith is a multifaceted concept that can be understood in various ways, depending on the context. The concept of the *sacred impulse of the divine conscience* can be understood as an inner call or drive within individuals that connects them to a higher moral and ethical standard, often associated with a sense of spirituality or divinity. It's the inner voice or feeling that guides people towards actions and thoughts that are aligned with higher virtues such as compassion, love, justice, and altruism. This concept is deeply personal and varies widely among individuals, depending on their spiritual beliefs, religious backgrounds, and personal philosophies.

In many religious and spiritual traditions, this divine conscience is seen as a connection to the divine or the universe's moral order, encouraging individuals to live in harmony with certain universal principles. It prompts introspection, ethical decision-making, and the pursuit of actions that contribute positively to the well-being of others and the world at large. This divine conscience is often associated with the experience of awe, reverence, and a profound sense of connection to something greater than oneself. It serves not only as a moral compass but also as a source of inspiration and motivation for personal growth, social justice, and the pursuit of peace and harmony in human relations.

The sacred impulse can motivate people to transcend their immediate desires or self-interest for a greater good, guided by a sense of duty to a higher moral law:

Religious Faith

In a religious context, faith typically refers to a strong belief in a supreme being or beings, and the doctrines or teachings of a particular religion. It often involves trust in things not seen and a heartfelt adherence to religious principles and beliefs. This kind of faith is central to many world religions, such as Christianity, Islam, Judaism, Hinduism, and Buddhism.

Personal Faith

On a more individual level, faith can be understood as complete trust or confidence in someone or something. This doesn't necessarily have to be religious. For example, a person might have faith in a friend's honesty or in the reliability of a scientific theory.

Spiritual Faith

Outside of organized religion, faith can also refer to a general spiritual belief or trust in a higher power or the universe, without adherence to a specific religious doctrine. This is often more about a personal sense of spirituality or connection to something greater than oneself.

Secular Faith

In a secular context, faith can simply mean a strong belief in particular principles, ideals, or the potential of humanity, without any spiritual or religious connotations.

In all these variations, faith generally involves a degree of hope, optimism, and a belief in something that cannot be proven empirically but is accepted and trusted by the individual. It plays a significant role in shaping an individual's worldview and guiding their actions and decisions.

Cultivating Wisdom

The essence of wisdom as a multifaceted concept embodies various dimensions of human experience and understanding. At its core, wisdom integrates knowledge, experience, and deep insight, leading to sound judgment and decision-making. It goes beyond merely accumulating facts, reflecting a profound understanding of the meaning and significance of what is known.

True wisdom requires a broad and deep comprehension of the world, encompassing both factual and procedural knowledge. This deep understanding comes from a wealth of experiences, offering varied perspectives and the ability to anticipate possible outcomes or consequences of different actions. Wise individuals are known for their good judgment, making decisions, solving problems, and interacting with others in a manner that is thoughtful, fair, and sensible.

Reflection is another critical dimension of wisdom. It involves self-understanding and an awareness of one's biases, limitations, and strengths. This self-awareness is essential in managing one's behavior and responses. Additionally, wise individuals often exhibit empathy and compassion, demonstrating an understanding of and care for others' feelings and conditions.

Ethical integrity is also integral to wisdom. It is associated with virtues such as honesty, fairness, and benevolence. Wise individuals tend to make choices that benefit not only themselves but also others and society as a whole. Furthermore, wisdom includes the ability to adapt to changing circumstances with an open mind and a learning attitude.

Wisdom is recognized not only in the quality of one's thoughts and judgments but also in their actions and interactions with others, reflecting a deep, integral understanding of life. It is cultivated through a complex interplay of multiple factors over time. Wisdom is not simply acquired; it emerges from ongoing experiences, learning, and introspection.

Life experiences are fundamental to developing wisdom. Exposure to diverse and often challenging life events provides opportunities to learn from success, failure, joy, and hardship, allowing an individual to gain deeper insights into human nature, social dynamics, and the complexities of life. Education and continuous learning expand one's knowledge base and critical thinking skills, which are essential components of wisdom. However, wisdom also involves learning from informal, everyday experiences and interactions.

Critical self-reflection is vital for converting experiences and knowledge into wisdom. Reflecting on one's own beliefs, actions, and their outcomes fosters a deeper understanding of oneself and the world. This reflective process helps individuals learn from their mistakes and successes. The ability to manage one's emotions, especially in challenging situations, enhances judgment and decision-making capabilities. Wisdom involves not only intellectual abilities but also emotional intelligence, which includes understanding and handling one's emotions and empathizing with others.

Interaction with others, particularly wise mentors or peers, can significantly influence the development of wisdom. Feedback from these relationships can provide new perspectives and insights, helping an individual understand complex situations and make better decisions. Cultural values and philosophical beliefs also play a role in shaping what individuals consider wise. Engaging with a wide range of cultural and philosophical ideas can broaden one's understanding and appreciation of different forms of wisdom.

Facing and overcoming adversity is particularly influential in developing wisdom. Challenges often force individuals to adapt and think deeply about life's important questions, fostering resilience and a nuanced understanding of life's impermanence and complexities. Although wisdom is not solely the province of the elderly, aging often contributes to its development through accumulated experiences and the maturation of cognitive and emotional faculties.

In summary, wisdom is created through a lifelong process of experiencing, learning, reflecting, and interacting with others in a meaningful way. It involves both cognitive growth and emotional development, grounded in ethical considerations and enhanced by a commitment to continuous learning and adaptation. Wisdom is not just about acquiring knowledge; it's about shaping how we understand, interact with, and respond to the world, making it a crucial practice for personal and societal growth and development.

Creating a Meaningful Life

Creating a meaningful life is a deeply personal journey that varies significantly from one individual to another. However, there are some common principles and actions that many find helpful in imbuing their lives with purpose and significance. Begin by defining what matters most to you. Identifying your core values, such as love, honesty, creativity, or service, forms the foundation upon which you can build a meaningful life. These values guide your decisions and actions, helping you stay true to what you find important.

Pursuing your passions is essential. Engaging in activities and pursuits that you are passionate about brings joy and fulfillment. Whether it's a career, hobby, or volunteering in a field that resonates with your interests, following your passions can provide a deep sense of purpose. Cultivating strong, healthy relationships is crucial. Invest time and energy in building and maintaining connections with family, friends, and community members. These relationships offer support, love, and a sense of belonging, enriching your life and contributing to its meaning. Helping others and contributing to the community can also provide a profound sense of purpose. Volunteering, mentoring, or simply being a kind and supportive presence in the lives of others fosters a sense of contribution and interconnectedness.

Embrace a mindset of lifelong learning and personal growth. Challenge yourself to grow intellectually, emotionally, and spiritually. This pursuit of personal development continuously expands your horizons and self-awareness, making life more meaningful. Practicing mindfulness helps you live in the moment and appreciate the present. Mindfulness enhances your perception of life's value and meaning by focusing your attention on the here and now, reducing worries about the past or future. Learn to accept and cope with challenges and setbacks with grace. Resilience in the face of adversity deepens your understanding of life and contributes to a stronger, more meaningful existence.

Regularly reflecting on your life, choices, and experiences helps you understand what brings you fulfillment and how you can align your actions with your values. This reflective practice allows you to make informed decisions that enhance your life's meaning. Setting goals that align with your values provides direction and motivation. Establish personal and professional goals that reflect what you find meaningful. These goals guide your choices and help you create a life that resonates with your true Self.

Finally, live authentically. Being true to yourself means acting in ways consistent with your beliefs, values, and desires, rather than conforming to external expectations. Living authentically allows you to lead a life that genuinely reflects who you are. By incorporating these elements into your life, you can build a foundation for a fulfilling and meaningful existence that resonates with your unique personality, values, and aspirations.

Positive Psychology

Positive psychology is a branch of psychology that focuses on the study and promotion of factors that contribute to human happiness and well-being. Unlike traditional psychology, which often emphasizes the treatment of mental illness and dysfunction, positive psychology aims to understand and enhance the positive aspects of human experience.

Positive psychology explores what constitutes happiness and well-being, including subjective well-being (life satisfaction and emotional balance) and psychological well-being (personal growth and purpose in life). Researchers study character strengths and virtues, such as courage, wisdom, compassion, and resilience, identifying and cultivating these strengths to lead a more fulfilling life.

The field examines the role of positive emotions like joy, gratitude, and hope. These emotions contribute to long-term well-being and resilience, extending beyond fleeting states of happiness. Positive psychology also investigates the concept of "flow," a state of deep absorption and engagement in activities that challenge but do not overwhelm an individual, linking flow to greater happiness and productivity.

The quality of relationships is crucial for well-being, and positive psychology looks at how healthy, supportive relationships contribute to happiness and life satisfaction. Finding meaning and purpose in life is another critical area of study, exploring how a sense of purpose can enhance life satisfaction and provide motivation and resilience.

Practices like gratitude journaling and mindfulness meditation are studied for their effects on mental health and well-being. These practices help individuals focus on the present moment and appreciate the positive aspects of life.

Positive psychology principles are applied in various fields. In education, they enhance students' well-being, resilience, and academic performance. In the workplace, they promote employee engagement, job satisfaction, and productivity. Positive psychology interventions are used in therapy to help individuals build on their strengths and cultivate positive emotions and relationships. The principles also promote community well-being and social change, focusing on building supportive and thriving communities.

Creating Your Own Balance

The chapter "Life is What We Choose to Make It" explores the profound idea that our perception and mindset shape the course of our lives. It emphasizes the importance of shifting one's mindset and adopting new perspectives to foster personal growth, resilience, and a more meaningful existence.

Central to this discussion is the concept of "posttraumatic growth," which suggests that individuals can grow and find strength in the aftermath of trauma. The chapter draws from personal experiences and research to illustrate how the way we think about a situation can profoundly affect our emotional and physical responses. For example, a moment of becoming emotionally overwhelmed, or what is known as a "neural hijack" during a physical therapy session taught me how quickly a single thought could change my perception of progress. This idea is extended to suggest that we have the power to alter our experience of life by choosing how we perceive it.

The chapter also emphasizes "authentic leadership," drawing on Kevin Cashman's work, which stresses the importance of self-awareness and self-discovery. By understanding ourselves more deeply, we can align our actions with our core values, leading to more authentic and effective leadership. Cashman also underscores the value of embracing diverse perspectives and connecting to a higher purpose, which allows individuals to transcend personal ambitions and focus on creating a positive impact on others.

Life, the chapter argues, is a solitary journey," where each individual must define what a meaningful life looks like for themselves. While loved ones may offer guidance, it is ultimately up to each person to take responsibility for their beliefs and actions. This journey involves navigating challenges, learning to be kind to oneself, and forgiving past mistakes.

The chapter also touches on the idea that life is largely a product of our imagination, shaped by the meanings we assign to our experiences. Our memories, particularly those charged with strong emotions, influence how we view the world and respond to present challenges. However, by changing our perspective, we can transform negative experiences into opportunities for growth.

Additionally, "willpower" is discussed as a dynamic force shaped by both genetic predisposition and environmental influences. I highlight that willpower can be cultivated through practice, resilience, and intentional effort, allowing individuals to overcome seemingly insurmountable obstacles.

In conclusion, the chapter argues that life is what we choose to make of it. By adopting a growth mindset, embracing resilience, and actively choosing how we respond to adversity, we have the power to shape our lives into meaningful, fulfilling journeys.

WHEN IT MATTERS MOST LEAD WITH COURAGE

Principle 9: *Stand up for your beliefs.*
Know what's worth fighting and dying for.

— My father, Pettis Perry

CHAPTER 9

Seeing Possibilities for Transforming Our Workplaces and Society

My father taught me at a young age that life is about identifying the things that are worth taking a stand to fight for. My goal as a practitioner is to use the best available information to create more effective organizations by fostering kinder, gentler, healthier, and more productive workplaces, organizations, and communities. I believe in achieving better organizational outcomes by shifting from reactive to proactive approaches in addressing incidents, issues, and problem-solving, and by replacing fragmented thinking with holistic, systems-based approaches. My mission is to help individuals and organizations maximize their performance while supporting positive social change, social justice, and peace. By improving the quality of life for all employees and increasing both individual and collective productivity, I aim to reduce attrition and prevent the waste of human energy and financial resources caused by ineffective strategies.

Since completing my dissertation on attrition in 1995, I have dedicated my life to researching and understanding the dynamics that lead to attrition, and to developing strategies to address it. Over the years, I have focused on four key research questions, all centered around keeping my mission in mind: Which strategies can reduce attrition, increase productivity through improved goal behaviors, foster positive and sustainable change, and reduce workplace trauma?

Through this work, I have realized that most corrective strategies aimed at supporting the workforce are often fragmented and reactive, focusing more on isolated events and individual symptoms rather than on the broader system. These approaches are typically *thing-* and *people*-focused, rather than system-oriented, and are aimed at resolving immediate issues, incidents, or perceived conflicts. As a result, these strategies are usually short-lived and fail to produce the desired long-term outcomes.

What emerged was my belief that we needed a whole-systems approach that is specifically designed for supporting the human side of the enterprise. A system in which the leader focus is proactive in nature, system focused, and viewing issues, incidents, perceived conflicts as symptoms and indicators of systemic flaws and breakdowns rather than as events and people to be fixed.

My answer came in 2021, while going through a series of traumatic episodes with my then employer, a large university, I literally had a vision about a system that could help improve working conditions if it was deployed. That vision led to the creation of the *7 Strategies for Organizational Effectiveness*® depicted below in Figure 9-1.

The 7 Strategies for Organizational Effectiveness

The *7 Strategies for Organizational Effectiveness*® is a system with integrity and complimentary elements supporting both organization needs as well as those of individuals within the workforce. The 7 Strategies for Organizational Effectiveness® is a novel approach with elements that are: INTEGRAL implying a sense of indispensability and foundational to integrated and integrative practice without implying the methods or means needed to achieve this goal; INTEGRATED emphasizing the combination of diverse practitioners and their different expertise into one community of practice; and INTEGRATIVE implying offering multiple and diverse interventions—both conventional and complementary using a centralized mode of delivery.

Figure 9-1: *7 Strategies for Organizational Effectiveness*® discussed below is such a whole-systems model that can be easily taught and adopted across organizational systems and types.

Figure 9-1: *7 Strategies for Organizational Effectiveness*®

It is a system that is easily understood and incorporates values that demonstrate commitment to the growth, development, and well-being of the whole person which is sorely lacking in organizations. It frames individual and organizational expectations for learning and problem-solving. It establishes a system for coordinating the allocation of resources to meet emerging and ongoing issues. By shifting to this model, it becomes embedded in the DNA of the organization reshaping the normative behaviors that emerge through a culture of an organized, collaborative community of practice

In 2021, the Society for Human Resource Managers (SHRM) found that employee replacement costs can run between 17% and 200% depending on the position and level in the organization. As I've demonstrated, organizations can reduce attrition by changing their culture and training supervisors and others as leaders. So, there is much more control on the types of leavers causing attrition from the organization than we give ourselves credit for.

We do not do a good job in the United States of teaching people how to learn. Our systems of education are antiquated and built for another time during industrialization. They train people to follow rules, to take tests, and to regurgitate information rather than on the 21st century requirements of an information age which requires much deeper critical thinking, the ability to discern good from bad information, communication skills and the ability to work and communicate cross-culturally, lifelong learning, mental and physical health and wellness.

Strategy 1: Transformative Learning

STRATEGY 1 Transformative Learning is foundational to human growth and development, and it maximizes experience-based and job-specific challenges as opportunities for personal transformation and growth. It is foundational to effective transformative leadership, it supports inside-out learning processes and becomes a pathway to wellness and meaningful life fulfillment.

Taylor and Scyder (2012) suggest that transformative learning is both a cognitive and affective process and it means a fundamental change in our approach to life with outcomes that include transformed thinking and worldviews. This is critical to working through interpersonal and intergroup differences of any kind. It supports navigating seismic events which can lead to transformed hearts and consciousness. It may involve deconstructing knowledge of what is discomforting to tackle such as critical race theory which may help in understanding why conditions are what they are in the United States and globally. What it looks like is unique to each individual and is not a one size fits all approach to growth and development. It acknowledges that transformative learning does not happen in a vacuum. It supports inside-out learning processes, and it can become a pathway to wellness and meaningful life fulfillment.

For those experiencing trauma, transformative learning may also produce meta-physical (spiritual) experiences that can become a catalyst for changes and may involve engagement in trusting relationships. It can result in repositioning of relationships when significant others do not share or may oppose newly formed world views. It also recognizes that transformative learning is a product of others intersecting with triggering personal change (e.g., how we are recognized socially and, in our relationships) (Taylor & Snyder, 2012).

Mezirow (as cited in Taylor & Cranton, 2012) found that transformative learning helps with elaborating on existing frames of reference by expanding the way we look at the world. By learning new frames of reference, we are also learning new ways to look at the world. By transforming points of view through changing our perspectives we are transforming our habits of mind through changing how we think. Transformative learning reflects the idea that life as well as leadership are inside-out processes. By transforming Self, we transform those around us by altering how they respond to us and our behaviors.

Strategy 2: Transformative Leadership

STRATEGY 2 Transformative Leadership is characterized by its activist agenda and its overriding commitment to social justice, equality, and democratic society (van Ord 2013 as cited in Bruce and McKee, 2020). Shields (2016 as cited in Bruce and McKee, 2020) identified the characteristics of transformative leadership as encompassing critical self-reflection (transformative learning), effecting deep and equitable change, deconstructing knowledge frameworks that perpetuate inequity and injustice and reconstructing them in equitable ways, addressing the inequitable distribution of power, emphasizing both private and public (individual and collective) good, focusing on democracy, emancipation, equity, and justice, emphasizing interconnectedness, interdependence, and global awareness, balancing critique with promise, and exhibiting moral courage.

Unlike other leadership styles focused on the outward creation of change by supporting employees in different ways, transformative leadership is an inside out process that achieves results through the leader changing behaviors which then has an external effect to motivate others to do the same. It makes it possible for members in the workforce to feel safe challenging the status quo that might benefit some while harming others and changing toxic work environments because they are inherently unjust and harmful.

Strategy 3: Coaching & Mentoring

STRATEGY 3 Coaching & Mentoring needs to be modernized to a 21st-century model that considers coaching and mentoring over the lifespan rather than simply as interventions. Such a system would:

- View employee development over their lifespans in the organization—emphasizing learning is lifelong

- Focus on developing all employees and policymakers

- Focus on skill development at each level within the organization

- Train all employees in the values and skills of transformative learning, transformative leadership, transformational leadership, servant leadership, and mastery skills (teaching employees to act on growth commitments, create a balanced lifestyle, developing awareness of inner *Being*, expressing Self authentically, finding purpose in work and life pursuits, embracing change and letting go of old patterns of behavior, and shifting from control to trust while serving with the whole heart.

- Ensure upward mobility opportunities are made available for all persons to broaden and extend the talent pool available to fill vacancies

- Enable & encourage employee self-selection into training based on their interests.

- Focus on strengthening intragroup and intergroup relationships

- Focus on whole-systems thinking to identify sources of conflict—work to resolve those systems' flaws

- View Coaching and Mentoring as vehicles for acculturation, building strong and cohesive cultures, and assuring employee longevity

This new approach would replace the current system found in many organizations which has as its focus on selected individuals, Interpersonal relationships, conflict resolution (in some cases), skill development, upward mobility for leaders while others are left out, upward mobility for the most talented (fast-tracking), and mentoring generally for the benefit of younger employees.

Strategy 4: Diversity & Fairness

STRATEGY 4 Diversity & Fairness, which is a more comprehensive approach to insuring inclusion than diversity, equity, and inclusion (DEI) which has come under attack. Shifting the focus to fairness changes the paradigm and broadens what is considered part of the fairness bundle. From a distributive justice perspective equity is but one of three social justice constructs: equity, equality, and needs. By broadening the distributive justice construct to include equality and needs along with equity, more individual needs can be met. Additionally, one of these three principles may be normative for a given situation or circumstance and thus create expectations for what type of distribution will be just (fair). When actual outcomes are congruent with those based on such normative expectations, justice exists.

DEI also does not account for other forms of justice considerations such as inter-actional justice or procedural fairness, which are supremely important in organizations interested in mitigating trauma and toxicity. Interactional justice involves the standards applied to how employees relate to each other at work (e.g., how managers treat their team members and how co-workers and colleagues interact with each other) (Schofield, n.d.). Interactional justice also pertains to the behavior of the leaders and managers as they execute their decisions and authority. It ensures that a high level of respect is shown to all employees and ensures the organization is regarded as a fair and safe workplace. This is important because leaders are responsible for creating positive, productive, and safe work environments which requires interacting in an honest, fair, and respectful way with employees (Schofield, n.d.).

Procedural justice, on the other hand, involves the fairness of procedures involved in decision-making and treatment of people (Hegtvedt, 2010). Such considerations are extremely important because perceptions of fairness are often colored by other such factors as race, biases, and deep-rooted belief systems about the value of one group when compared to another based on some socially categorized process. Gender and racial inequities are prime examples, where women make about 84 cents for every dollar paid to men.

Racialized minorities and other marginalized groups are also treated differentially when compared to White males. Kantor (n.d.) (as cited in Boniello, 2021) found the NFL used *race norming* as part of its concussion protocols where the practice, called race norming resulted in paying players differentially based on their racial categorization. That is, White players received higher concussion compensation rates for injuries than their Black counterparts under the belief that White players were inherently more intelligent than Black players which further illustrates how race alone determines outcomes. This is a clear example of racism according to, a past president of the Florida Society of Neurology, who assessed former NFL players for the settlement program from 2017 to 2019.

Strategy 5: Integrative Cultures

STRATEGY 5 Integrative Cultures allows for efficient use of resources for maximum impact. Integrative Cultures use multiple diverse interventions and solutions coordinated through a centralized delivery vehicle to support the whole person. They provide an organized system for supporting employee retention and other human side of the enterprise outcomes (e.g., fostering collaboration, establishing direction, aligning, motivating, and inspiring people to perform well), and they become mechanisms for maximizing productivity through the efficient and effective use of resources and a focus on improving goal behaviors.

Schein (2010) reminds us that culture formation is always a striving toward patterning and integration, even though in many groups, their actual history of experiences prevents them from ever achieving a clear-cut unambiguous paradigm. The nature of cultural norms shapes how conflicts get resolved: Toxic cultures suppress conflict while healthy cultures embrace conflict as a source of positive changes so how the culture becomes defined matters greatly to organizational performance, and therefore its effectiveness.

Integrative implies offering multiple and diverse interventions–both conventional and complementary using a centralized mode of delivery. Because integrative cultures use multiple and diverse interventions that are both conventional and complementary using a centralized mode of delivery, they offer greater long-term stability, provide greater opportunities for identifying and targeting problems rather than symptoms, maximizing organizational energy and resources with the least amount of waste, and as a result they are more effective and efficient and will produce sustainable results. Integrative cultures offer the promise of 21st century solutions to reduce the volatility during leadership changes by altering the organization's DNA and making it more difficult for a single person to become a destructive force that can destroy the functioning and prosperity of the organization.

Strategy 6: Trauma-informed Communities

STRATEGY 6 Trauma-informed Communities (TICs), a principal theme throughout this guide, provide a broad-based high degree of awareness about the effects of trauma on behaviors and on performance to enable more compassionate interactions facilitating better strategies for maximizing employee performance. Specifically, trauma-informed communities strategies help de-escalate chaos and stress, build social cohesion, and foster community resiliency, all of which create the foundation necessary to maintain community [organizational] development efforts.

Strategy 7: Mental & Physical Wellness

STRATEGY 7 Mental & Physical Wellness is critical to sustaining productivity. Without wellness absenteeism goes up, productivity goes down, conflicts arise, toxicity goes up, and attrition can also rise making this a critical strategy for organizations to manage.

Final Thoughts

It isn't that we do not know what to do, it's a matter of having the leadership and willpower to do it that continues to get lost. The importance of having an organized system to support the human side of the enterprise should be intuitively obvious at this point. Depending on the industry, even when effective leaders make headway, CEOs only stay in place from about three to nine years on average. Each time they are replaced, the organization convulses under the leadership of the new CEO. What if we establish systems first such as the 7 Strategies for Organizational Effectiveness®, and then find the leaders to fit that system? In this case, Strategy 3 Coaching & Mentoring could become the vehicle for growing leaders from within, similarly like sports teams do with farm teams feed their programs.

Using the United States Marine Corps as an example, they are building the culture they want to see from the ground up. The leaders they select believe in the system or they are replaced. Those that are selected train the next groups of recruits and in so doing they feed the system from the source of their traditions. We can do much better!

Food for Additional Thought

Throughout this guide, we have delved into the multifaceted nature of trauma and toxicity within workplaces, social groups, and families. We explored how trauma shapes behaviors, impacts organizational dynamics, and influences interpersonal relationships. We have examined historical and contemporary sources of trauma, including systemic racism, colonization, and personal experiences of violence and loss. The stories shared and the theoretical frameworks discussed highlight the profound and lasting effects of trauma on individuals and communities.

We began by understanding the concept of trauma, recognizing its prevalence, and acknowledging its widespread impact on mental, emotional, and physical well-being. We explored how trauma manifests in various forms, such as developmental trauma, environmental trauma, and systemic trauma, and the importance of creating trauma-informed communities to support healing and resilience. Leadership emerged as a critical factor in shaping organizational culture and mitigating the effects of trauma and toxicity. Effective leaders not only influence workplace dynamics but also play a pivotal role in fostering environments where employees feel valued, supported, and empowered. We discussed the characteristics of both charismatic and humble leaders, recognizing the strengths and potential pitfalls of each leadership style.

We also examined how frames of reference shape thinking patterns and behaviors, influencing how individuals perceive and respond to their environments. Understanding these cognitive frameworks allows leaders, educators, practitioners, and parents to foster more inclusive and empathetic communities.

The journey through trauma and toxicity is complex and often fraught with challenges, but it is also a path toward growth, resilience, and transformation. By understanding the profound impact of trauma on individuals and communities and implementing strategies to address it, we can create healthier, more supportive environments in our workplaces, homes, and social groups.

This guide provides a comprehensive set of processes for navigating these complexities, offering insights and practical recommendations for leaders, parents, practitioners, educators, and all individuals committed to fostering a more compassionate and resilient society. Through collective effort and a commitment to empathy and understanding, we can make a significant difference in the lives of those affected by trauma and build a future where everyone has the opportunity to thrive.

Navigating trauma and toxicity requires a collective effort. By implementing these recommendations, leaders, parents, human service practitioners, educators, and others can create environments that foster resilience, empathy, and well-being. Together, we can build a more supportive and compassionate world, transforming trauma into opportunities for growth and healing.

This guide serves as a resource to help you navigate the complexities of trauma and toxicity. Use the insights and strategies provided here to make a positive impact in your sphere of influence. Your commitment to understanding and addressing these issues will contribute to a brighter future for all. Thank you for embarking on this journey with me.

As we conclude this exploration of trauma and toxicity in the workplace and social groups, including families, it is essential to provide practical recommendations for various stakeholders. Leaders, parents, human service practitioners, educators, and others play crucial roles in navigating and mitigating the impacts of trauma. This final chapter aims to equip you with actionable strategies to foster healthier environments and promote positive social change by embracing transformative leadership in the face of trauma and toxicity. Recognizing that in the United States and globally most of the populations are traumatized, we can better understand the inevitable interpersonal and intergroup conflicts they produce.

Some trauma is inevitable by virtue of being human, but we can greatly reduce its prevalence by mitigating toxic environments contributing to the trauma people experience. By adopting these recommendations, individuals and organizations can create environments that foster resilience, empathy, and well-being. Addressing trauma and toxicity is not only essential for personal growth but also for building healthier, more productive workplaces and communities. Together, through commitment and collective action, we can transform trauma into opportunities for healing and growth, paving the way for a brighter and more compassionate future for all.

By adopting these recommendations, individuals and organizations can create environments that foster resilience, empathy, and well-being. Addressing trauma and toxicity is not only essential for personal growth but also for building healthier, more productive workplaces and communities. Together, through commitment and collective action, we can transform trauma into opportunities for healing and growth, paving the way for a brighter and more compassionate future for all.

Confronting Trauma & Toxicity: Tools for Transformative Leaders and Workforce Warriors, and Community Builders to Foster Resilience and Meaningful Lives explores the pervasive impact of trauma and toxic behaviors within workplace environments, offering insights into how these elements shape individual and organizational dynamics. The guide emphasizes the importance of understanding trauma as a root cause of toxic behaviors, highlighting that trauma experienced in the workplace can significantly influence home and social environments, and vice versa. I use personal anecdotes and research to demonstrate how trauma and toxicity are not only common but are also deeply intertwined within group dynamics, organizational cultures, and leadership behaviors.

The guide underscores the need for a transformative approach to leadership and organizational behavior, suggesting that effective leaders must recognize and address the trauma within their teams to create healthier, more productive environments.

Additionally, it stresses the importance of resilience, optimism, and a growth mindset in navigating the challenges posed by toxic workplaces and broader societal issues.

Addressing trauma and toxicity requires a collective effort. By implementing these recommendations, individuals and organizations can create environments that foster resilience, empathy, and well-being. Together, we can build a more supportive and compassionate world, transforming trauma into opportunities for growth and healing.

This guide serves to help you navigate the complexities of trauma and toxicity. Use the insights and strategies provided here to make a positive impact in your sphere of influence. Your commitment to understanding and addressing these issues will contribute to a brighter future for all. Thank you for embarking on this journey with me. With this conclusion, we underscore the transformative potential within each of us to create meaningful change. By addressing trauma and toxicity, we not only improve our lives but also contribute to a healthier, more empathetic society. This is our collective responsibility and opportunity.

Recommendations for All

Here are recommendations that apply universally to individuals, leaders, and organizations to foster a healthier, more supportive workplace:

1. **Cultivate Empathy and Understanding**

    Practice active listening using a conscious effort to listen to others' perspectives and concerns. This builds mutual respect and fosters a supportive environment. Cultivate a compassionate and empathetic approach in all interactions. Recognize that everyone has their own struggles, and that kindness can significantly impact others' well-being. Acknowledge others' experiences and recognize and validate the experiences and emotions of colleagues, whether they are dealing with stress, trauma, or personal challenges.

2. **Prioritize Mental Health and Well-being**

    Advocate for mental health awareness by actively promoting awareness about mental health and the impact of trauma. Support initiatives that reduce stigma and increase access to mental health resources. Promote mental health awareness through engaging in and supporting initiatives that raise awareness about mental health and reduce stigma. Encourage self-care as an advocate for regular breaks, healthy work habits, and self-care practices to maintain overall well-being. Help increase awareness about trauma and its impacts across all sectors. Provide education and training to help individuals recognize and respond to trauma effectively.

3. Build Cultures of Respect and Inclusivity

Model respectful behavior by treating everyone with respect and kindness, regardless of their position or background. Lead by example in fostering an inclusive environment. Challenge toxicity by actively speaking out against toxic behaviors, such as bullying or discrimination, and encourage others to do the same. Strengthen community ties by participating in local initiatives, supporting community resources, and fostering a sense of belonging and mutual support.

4. Enhance Communication and Transparency

Maintain open communication channels ensuring that there are clear, accessible ways for everyone to express concerns, share feedback, and ask questions. Promote transparency by sharing information openly and honestly, whether in decision-making processes or daily interactions. Transparency builds trust and reduces misunderstandings.

5. Support Personal and Professional Development

Encourage continuous learning by supporting opportunities for professional growth, such as workshops, training, and mentorship programs. Foster a growth mindset and promote the idea that challenges are opportunities for learning and improvement, helping everyone to navigate difficulties constructively. Embrace lifelong learning by continuously seeking knowledge and understanding about trauma, mental health, and human behavior. Stay informed about new research and best practices in your field.

6. Create and Maintain Safe and Inclusive Spaces

Ensure psychological safety by working towards creating an environment where everyone feels safe to express their ideas, concerns, and emotions without fear of judgment or retaliation. Designate areas where employees can take breaks and decompress. Ensure diversity and fairness as integral parts of the organizational strategy, reflecting in hiring practices, team composition, and company policies. Support conflict resolution by providing tools and training for resolving conflicts in a constructive manner, ensuring that disagreements don't escalate into toxic situations.

7. Promote Work-Life Balance

Encourage flexibility and support policies and practices that allow for a healthy balance between work and personal life, such as flexible working hours and remote work options. Respect boundaries encourage everyone to respect each other's time and boundaries, recognizing the importance of time away from work for rest and personal activities.

8. Be an Ally and Advocate

Support colleagues in need by offering support to those who may be struggling with trauma or stress, whether through listening, offering help, advocating on their behalf, or connecting them with resources. Advocate for positive change by taking initiative in advocating for policies and practices that promote a healthier, more inclusive, and supportive work environment.

9. Foster a Collaborative Environment

Encourage teamwork by promoting collaboration and the sharing of ideas, emphasizing the value of diverse perspectives in achieving common goals. Celebrate successes together. Recognize and celebrate the achievements and contributions of individuals and teams, fostering a sense of community and shared purpose.

10. Stay Informed and Adaptive

Keep learning about workplace dynamics and how to improve them. Stay informed about the latest research and best practices in managing workplace trauma and toxicity. Adapt to change by embracing change with a willingness to adapt your behavior, strategies, and policies to better meet the needs of a dynamic workplace environment.

11. Lead by Example

Demonstrate resilience, empathy, and commitment to personal growth in your own life. Inspire others by showing that it is possible to overcome adversity and thrive despite challenges. Address systemic inequities by calling them out. Work towards eliminating systemic inequities that contribute to trauma and toxicity. Advocate for policies and practices that promote social justice, equity, and inclusion. Encourage self-reflection and growth by promoting self-reflection and personal growth as a way of life. Encourage individuals to examine their own biases and behaviors and strive for continuous improvement. Work to implement trauma-informed practices.

Recommendations for Individuals

1. Prioritize self-care by engaging in regular self-care practices such as mindfulness, exercise, and adequate rest to manage stress and maintain mental and physical well-being.

2. Develop personal resilience by cultivating a growth mindset and by viewing challenges as opportunities for learning. Seek out resources that help build emotional resilience, such as counseling or resilience training.

3. Set boundaries and clearly define and maintain personal boundaries at work. This includes managing workloads, saying no when necessary, and ensuring a healthy work-life balance.

4. Seek support when needed whether or not it is provided by the organization. Don't hesitate to reach out to trusted colleagues, mentors, or mental health professionals when dealing with toxic behaviors or traumatic experiences at work.

5. Document and report toxicity. Keep records of any toxic behaviors or incidents of harassment and report them to HR or a trusted authority within the organization. This helps protect your rights and can initiate necessary interventions. If necessary, seek legal advice.

Recommendations for Leaders

1. Become trained yourself and encourage and provide training for all employees on trauma awareness, its effects, and how to support colleagues. Develop policies that recognize and address the impact of trauma on employees. Offer access to mental health services, such as counseling, therapy, and employee assistance programs (EAPs). Promote mental health awareness and reduce stigma through regular workshops and initiatives.

2. Encourage professional development by investing in the growth and development of your team. Offer training in resilience, stress management, and conflict resolution. Empower employees with the tools to navigate when problems arise.

3. Adopt trauma-informed leadership practices by being empathetic when problems arise. Look inward to your role in creating problems that might have produced trauma within your team before looking outward to blame others.

4. Educate yourself on trauma-informed practices and integrate them into your leadership style. This includes being empathetic, supportive, and aware of the signs of trauma in your team members. Cultivate self-awareness and emotional intelligence (EI) to understand your own emotional responses and biases towards members of your team and strive to create a supportive environment. Help team members do the same.

5. Regularly self-reflect and seek feedback that can enhance emotional intelligence and improve decision-making.

6. Model empathy and compassion and demonstrate them in your interactions. Recognize that employees may be dealing with unseen challenges. Your behavior sets the tone for the organization, influencing how others treat their colleagues.

7. Promote work-life balance by acknowledging its importance in reducing stress and burnout.

8. Implement policies that support flexible working hours, remote work options, and adequate time off.

9. Implement support systems through peer support networks, mentorship programs, and employee assistance programs to provide additional layers of support for those experiencing trauma or stress.

10. Foster a Safe Environment: Create an open and inclusive environment where employees feel safe to share their concerns and experiences without fear of retaliation. Promote trauma-informed practices. Implement policies and practices that recognize the impact of trauma on employees. Provide training for staff to identify signs of trauma and offer appropriate support, including access to mental health resources.

11. Foster a trauma-informed culture. Leaders have an obligation to create safe and productive workspaces for all employees and therefore they must understand trauma and its effects on employees. Implement training programs that educate staff about trauma and promote a supportive culture. Encourage open communication and provide resources for mental health support.

12. Promote Transparency and Fairness: Ensure that decision-making processes are transparent and fair. Avoid favoritism and ensure that all employees are treated equitably.

13. Encourage Professional Development: Support the growth and development of your team by offering opportunities for learning and skill-building, which can help them navigate and overcome challenges.

14. Intervene in Toxic Behaviors: Address toxic behaviors immediately. This might involve coaching, setting clear expectations for behavior, or, in severe cases, taking disciplinary action to prevent the spread of toxicity.

Recommendations for Human Service Practitioners

1. Be an advocate for all employees and not just some. Implement trauma-informed care by adopting a trauma-informed approach in your practice. Recognize the signs of trauma, understand its impact, and integrate this knowledge into your interactions with clients.

2. Adopt a holistic approach to problem-solving by recognizing the interconnectedness of physical, emotional, and social well-being in your practice. Address the root causes of trauma and provide comprehensive support. Offer holistic support addressing the diverse needs of clients and others by providing comprehensive support. Collaborate with other professionals to offer services that address physical, emotional, and social aspects of well-being.

3. Stay informed about trauma-informed care. Continuously educate yourself on best practices in trauma-informed care. Attend workshops, seek out new research, and apply these insights to your work.

4. Advocate for systemic change and work towards policy changes that address systemic issuescontributing to trauma, such as poverty, discrimination, and lack of access to healthcare and education.

5. Prioritize self-care and professional support to practitioners who are often at risk of secondary traumatic stress. Prioritize your own well-being by seeking supervision, peer support, and engaging in self-care practices. Promote self-care. Encourage clients to prioritize self-care and develop healthy coping mechanisms. Provide resources and strategies to help them manage stress and build resilience.

6. Empower clients and participants through education. Educate clients about the effects of trauma and the importance of self-care. Provide them with tools and resources to navigate their own healing journeys effectively.

7. Advocate for systemic change by working towards resolving the root causes of trauma and toxicity. Advocate for policies that promote social justice, equity, and access to mental health services.

Recommendations for Educators

1. Recognize the impact of trauma on learning. Monitor personal biases and belief systems that favor some students and harm others. Understand how trauma can affect students' ability to learn and engage in the classroom. Provide accommodations and support to help them succeed.

2. Foster inclusive classrooms. Create inclusive and welcoming environments for all students. Encourage diversity and fairness in your teaching practices and curriculum.

3. Create trauma-informed classrooms by teaching students how to solve problems that arise from difference and diversity. Develop classroom environments that are sensitive to the needs of traumatized students. Implement strategies that promote safety, trust, and emotional regulation.

4. Foster an inclusive learning environment predicated on fairness and respect for others. Encourage respect for diversity and inclusivity in your classroom. Address any discriminatory behaviors and create a culture of acceptance and understanding.

5. Support Social-emotional learning (SEL) by integrating SEL into the curriculum to help students develop essential skills for managing emotions, building relationships, and making responsible decisions. Integrate social-emotional learning (SEL) into your curriculum. Teach students skills such as empathy, self-regulation, and effective communication.

6. Recognize and respond to signs of trauma: Be vigilant in recognizing signs of trauma in students and respond with empathy and appropriate support. Collaborate with school counselors and mental health professionals to provide comprehensive care.

7. Build strong relationships by developing positive relationships with students based on trust and respect. Show genuine interest in their well-being and provide support when needed. A positive connection with a trusted adult can significantly impact a student's ability to cope with trauma and succeed academically.

8. Collaborate with families by engaging with students' families to better understand their needs and provide consistent support. Foster strong home-school partnerships to promote students' overall well-being.

Recommendations for Organizations

1. Conduct regular culture and climate audits by regularly assessing the organizational culture and climate to identify any toxic behaviors or environments. Use these assessments to make data-driven changes that improve workplace dynamics and to implement targeted interventions aimed at improving the overall well-being of employees.

2. Implement clear anti-toxicity policies. Establish and enforce clear policies against harassment, bullying, and any forms of toxicity. Ensure these policies are well-communicated and that there are safe channels for reporting violations.

3. Provide mental health resources that offer accessible mental health resources such as Employee Assistance Programs (EAPs), counseling services, and stress management workshops.

4. Encourage and reward work-life balance. Promote policies that support work-life balance, such as flexible working hours, remote work options, and paid time off. A balanced life reduces the likelihood of burnout and the perpetuation of toxic behaviors.

5. Train managers and HR on trauma and toxicity. Equip HR professionals and managers with the skills to recognize, address, and prevent toxic behaviors and trauma in the workplace. Regular training should be a mandatory part of leadership development.

6. Provide leadership training programs focused on trauma-informed leadership to equip leaders with the tools to recognize and address trauma within their teams, fostering a more supportive work environment.

7. Establish robust support systems, including access to mental health resources, for employees dealing with trauma. This can help mitigate the negative impacts of trauma on workplace dynamics.

8. Foster a culture of open communication where employees feel safe discussing their experiences with trauma and toxicity without fear of retribution.

9. Encourage a growth mindset and resilience among employees by offering workshops and resources that focus on personal development and coping strategies.

10. Regularly review workplace policies to ensure they do not inadvertently contribute to a toxic environment. Policies should promote fairness, inclusion, and psychological safety.

Recommendations for Teams

1. Build Strong Team Cohesion: Engage in team-building activities that foster trust and open communication. A cohesive team is more resilient and better equipped to handle challenges.

2. Encourage Peer Support: Promote a culture of peer support where team members look out for one another, providing help and encouragement during difficult times.

3. Develop Conflict Resolution Skills: Equip teams with conflict resolution skills to manage disagreements constructively, preventing conflicts from escalating into toxic situations.

By implementing these recommendations, all of us can make a difference in our communities. Organizations can begin to mitigate the effects of trauma and toxicity, leading to more positive, productive, and supportive workplaces. By following these recommendations, individuals, leaders, and organizations can work together to create a healthier, more supportive, and pro.

Creating Your Own Balance

The chapter "Transforming the Workplace and Society" presents a vision for reshaping organizations to foster healthier, more productive, and compassionate environments. It starts with the idea of standing up for one's beliefs, inspired by my father, who taught me to identify what is worth fighting for in life. For me that led to my life's work and mission to improve workplaces and communities by shifting from reactive, fragmented approaches to more proactive and holistic systemsbased solutions. His goal is to reduce attrition, enhance productivity, and support positive social change while addressing workplace trauma and promoting social justice.

The chapter introduces the "7 Strategies for Organizational Effectiveness®," a framework I developed after a traumatic experience with a former employer. This system is designed to be integral, integrated, and integrative, meaning it supports both organizational needs and the well-being of individuals in the workforce. The system emphasizes proactive leadership, viewing incidents and conflicts not as isolated problems but as symptoms of broader systemic flaws that need addressing.

The first strategy, "Transformative Learning," is foundational to personal growth and organizational development. It leverages challenges in the workplace as opportunities for personal transformation and wellness. Transformative learning is both cognitive and emotional, encouraging individuals to expand their perspectives, shift their worldviews, and ultimately transform their habits of mind. This process is particularly important for navigating interpersonal and intergroup differences, especially in addressing complex societal issues like race and equity.

The second strategy "Transformative Leadership" focuses on social justice, equality, and creating democratic workplaces. It emphasizes that real change starts from within the leader, who must critically reflect on their own behaviors and beliefs. Transformative leadership creates an environment where employees feel safe challenging the status quo, which is often necessary to dismantle toxic work cultures and foster more equitable, inclusive environments.

The third strategy, "Strategy & Mentoring," proposes a lifelong approach to employee development. Instead of focusing on selected individuals or leadership fast-tracking, this model advocates for the continuous development of all employees throughout their careers. It encourages building strong relationships, enhancing skill development, and promoting upward mobility for everyone, not just a select few.

The fourth strategy, "Diversity & Fairness," expands on the traditional concept of diversity, equity, and inclusion (DEI) by emphasizing fairness in all aspects of organizational life. It suggests that fairness should consider equity, equality, and individual needs, ensuring that all employees are treated justly. I highlight that fairness is not just about equal treatment but about addressing the specific needs and circumstances of individuals to create a truly inclusive environment.

The fifth strategy, "Integrative Cultures," advocates for using diverse interventions and coordinated efforts to support the whole person within an organization. By fostering a culture of collaboration and inclusivity, organizations can maximize productivity while addressing the root causes of conflicts and inefficiencies. Integrative cultures help create a more stable and resilient organization, reducing the impact of leadership changes on the workforce.

The sixth strategy, "Trauma-Informed Communities (TICs)," stresses the importance of understanding how trauma affects behavior and performance in the workplace. By creating trauma-informed workplaces, organizations can reduce stress, build social cohesion, and foster resilience among employees. This approach emphasizes compassion and understanding, creating an environment where people feel supported and valued.

The final strategy, "Mental & Physical Wellness," highlights the critical role wellness plays in sustaining productivity. Without a focus on wellness, organizations are likely to see increased absenteeism, conflicts, and a toxic atmosphere. Ensuring that employees are mentally and physically well is essential to maintaining a positive and productive work environment.

The chapter emphasizes that effective leadership is essential to embedding these strategies within an organization. Leaders must understand trauma, fairness, and wellness to create and sustain supportive and thriving workplaces. I argue that by building systems like the 7 Strategies for Organizational Effectiveness and then finding leaders who align with those systems, organizations can ensure long-term success and stability.

In conclusion, the chapter calls for transforming workplaces into environments that prioritize individual well-being, fairness, and holistic growth. By addressing trauma, promoting social justice, and fostering resilience, organizations can create healthier, more productive workplaces that benefit both employees and society as a whole. The transformation is not only about improving organizational performance but about creating a more compassionate and supportive world.

WILLPOWER CREATES POSSIBILITIES

Principle 10: *The way we perceive and respond to events is deeply influenced by our mindset and perspective, which can either hinder or facilitate personal growth and transformation following traumatic experiences.*

CHAPTER 10

Personal Stories

C hapter 10 offers something special: a collection of deeply personal stories, told in the voices of those who lived them. These narratives bring to light the emotional, psychological, and professional toll of toxic work environments. But they also speak to the enduring strength of the human spirit—the power of resilience, the lessons learned through adversity, and the unwavering belief in creating healthier, more just organizations.

As I read through each contribution, I was struck by the common threads that wove their way through different lives, jobs, and geographies. One of the most prominent themes was workplace toxicity and failed leadership. Many of the storytellers described cultures marked by gaslighting, bullying, and narcissistic behaviors from those in power. The damage was deep. People spoke of emotional exhaustion, anxiety, depression—and a deep disillusionment with organizations that claimed to care about their people but acted otherwise.

Yet, amid the pain, there was also power. The thread of resilience and the will to overcome adversity runs strong throughout the chapter. Contributors shared how they navigated discrimination, workplace injustice, and even personal traumas unrelated to the job itself. Despite these challenges, they held tight to their integrity. They adapted. They survived. Some even found new purpose on the other side.

Taken together, the stories in Chapter 10 reflect not only the harm that toxic systems can cause but also the capacity for individuals to reclaim their power, tell the truth of their experiences, and become forces for healing and transformation.

Janine Crifasi, Board-Eligible Functional Neurologist

Dr. Janine Crifasi, DC, CCST, was born and raised on Long Island, developed a passion for healthcare through personal and family experiences with musculoskeletal, neurological, and infectious diseases. Graduating as the top student in her class in 1995, she pursued chiropractic medicine and became boardcertified. Dr. Crifasi completed advanced studies in clinical neuroscience at the Carrick Institute, becoming Board Eligible in Functional Neurology. She has held leadership roles, including as Executive Clinical Director for several clinics, and currently contributes her expertise to the Arizona Chiropractic Neurology Center. Her work is driven by her deep dedication to her son, her greatest inspiration.

Connections with Toxicity in the Workplace

"Nerves that wire together fire together" — Donald Hebb in 1949.

My first trauma started in utero, as that of a surviving twin; it is understood to have created separation anxiety and validation-seeking behaviors. As someone wired to strive, in childhood I was unaware of a few neurological factors impeding my growth and success. Some of my initial traumas were two concussions before the age of 4 years old from accidental falls, car accidents, parents who smoked, and learning/processing difficulties, to name a few factors. Making and keeping connections with people is what I was taught would support family and work environments.

We all want to be validated and acknowledged for our accomplishments. Who does not want to work where they are appreciated and not tolerated. Let's face it, women tend to be people pleasers inherently. As a woman with my feminine identifying self, I am no different. Having chosen a semi-nontraditional holistic profession, I figured our little herd of black sheep would look after each other. Little did I know, most of them eat their young ... ALIVE!

Both my sister and I were raised in an amazingly loving household with a large extended family and were encouraged to become professionals. Each of our grandmothers had lost their mothers very early in their childhood. Each grandmother was raised by their fathers and families. My mother lost her father in her early adolescence. Attaining self-sufficiency was always touted as the ideal scenario to set us up for success. We were always told by our parents to be independent, but always be available to help others in any way we could. "Do not be a doormat but never burn any bridges" they also said. A dear friend once said that last statement was the best advice and worst advice I could have ever been given. She was right! It coerces my inner *fear* monster (False Evidence Appearing Real) to attach itself like Velcro to circumstances and situations. This FEAR would create doubt in my choices, both in my personal and professional worlds. In efforts to maintain work environments where I would see the toxicity, I often stayed longer than was healthy. Often to sustain the relationship I used my education, training, good business sense, data points etc., to negotiate change, impart sound wisdom of circumstances and share objectifiable observations with solutions to benefit the team. This was not ego driven but rather a role often requested by staff that I take on due to the hostility perceived by the powers that be and my nature of communication. I learned thought that you cannot rationalize with crazy nor help those who do not want it, even if it is negatively impacting productivity, motivation and even the bottom line of revenue. I have come to realize I can only control my actions and business model. Back to suggestion "A" be an independent professional boss, or shall I say Bad Ass Boss Babe!

Never burn any bridges because the professional world shifts and work/life communities will overlap. Being raised in an era where glass ceilings are shattering, today is still a male favored world. Women's roles are poorly defined. Professional women's responsibilities are often dual or triplicate in nature at times. We are expected to fulfill deadlines and prepare dinners, often tending to families. All that needs to be accomplished, we must shift and maintain the assignment of the moment at all times without much notice and with the expectation of doing them all well, and without resistance of exception, which is our never-ending story.

Narcissists tell you what you want to hear. They tell you what they think you want to hear.

Often, they do not present as such initially with a toxic boss or coworker. Those in the work environment will compensate in an effort to understand or rationalize the peculiarities that create anxiety. Anxiety is often masked forms of depression or follow suit of the leader in dishonest manners. Lying, cover ups, poor follow through and fault finding as well as blame and second guessing oneself are results of the toxic environment. If allowed to become pervasive it will have adverse effects on an individual's health, not to mention the company performance.

Many people work in environments where staff is considered a dime a dozen and the boss legit thinks and nitpicks until gaslighting is all that prevails. Egos run high but integrity drops each time that happens.

I have worked under this pattern far too often and hear this much too frequently to know this is not just my personal experience. These individuals berate staff and belittle employees to enhance their Napolean complex or narcissistic, misogynistic egotistical manner to project dominion over another. It is not always an overt display.

Despite the form, we must know and change that which is not acceptable. We all have wounds from traumas. There was one doctor so intimidated by his father that moments after the patriarch passed away his persona softened. Communication improved and staff actually stayed and were invested in the company rather than employed by it. Impaired processing or integration, in what you would see upon assessment would be a lot of chaos or rigidity—those are signs of impaired neural integration processes.

Please realize and do not be ignorant of the fact that this is in all professions. In my second adult professional job the doctor boss was so busy talking about himself and his conquests that he actually let a Multiple Sclerosis patient turn over solo on a narrow table and the poor guy hit the floor. In an everpresent effort to justify as most narcissists do somehow, it was to be deemed the patient's fault. Not to mention the renaming of room 4 in that office to room number fornication. In that very minute I had had more than enough of not being a change in this world and more of a conformist. For the first time I put my learning disabilities to my advantage and not my nemesis. The very next morning I called what is now my alma mater to register. So, despite personal neuro developmental challenges I somehow managed to compensate in the ways I later learned would have been the recommended methods to circumvent the issue.

The research shows that developmental trauma, trauma early in life, blocks the growth of the integrative brain mechanism. Many schools of thought and research suggest patterns may go back generations.

I refuse to be rigid, but I admittedly have not always processed through that which I should have but I took on a lot of personal effort to be mindful as well as hopeful. No matter what choices I have made I always knew I could change them. I tended to tolerate more than motivate myself at times, often feeling locked in through moral obligation or for circumstantial reasons. In reality, they were only fear based excuses.

In terms of functioning, a person who lacks emotional balance can't think clearly under stress. Many do not even realize they are under it. It becomes a drug of choice. When neuroplasticity (the interdependent network firing) of neurons in the brain and its integration is impaired, what you would see in the assessment would be a lot of chaos or rigidity—those are signs of impaired integration. According to research, the earlier in life that occurs the greater chance of developmental trauma. Also, it should be noted that traumatic experiences happen in clusters.

There are therapeutic approaches and neurological reprogramming that I have chosen to dedicate my life to that aids individuals in such areas.

First and foremost, get your rest and stay hydrated. It is essential. Keep your body and mind active as cliche as it sounds. We need oxygen, glucose, gravity and movement for optimum brain function in its most simplistic of needs.

Stress increases cortisol levels and aids in the storage of fat. Stress reduces your hippocampus function (where we store memories for future reference) and decreases neural integration. Adrenaline increases your amygdala firing (the structure that helps rate the significance of memories) allowing proper integration for us to draw upon our experiences and respond appropriately. Staying in stress engrains the feedback loop in a negative way making it harder to discern and express change. Each and every thought, action or behavior that we have is created in our mind; enveloped in a neurotransmitter expressed in a cell, interpreted in the brain and manifested in its action or inaction.

So long chapter short, believe in your perception of the world around you and tune into your personal environment. Do not tolerate what does not suit you. Work where you are appreciated and make it fun. Pursue what you are truly guided to do. Harness all of your energy, passion and fortitude without any distraction into that endeavor. Second guessing is not what your first thought is. Read that again! 2nd guessing is not your 1st thought! If in doubt simply DON'T! Do not let kindness be misinterpreted as foolishness or naivety.

With every sense of my being, I believe people have the ability and the right to change NO MATTER WHAT, if they choose to do so.

Some folks need encouragement, some need new sets of skills, and both need determination to reach their goals. None of those necessary shifts can happen until genuine awareness and desire is present to do so.

One of my mentors shared this with me and reminds me every so often "Crazy people live in an insane world; Sane people are crazy in an insane world." Find your worth. Listen to that little inner voice you hear. It is correct and it is your compass. Walk confidently in the direction of your dreams.

Lucy J. Crowder

Lucy J. Crowder, MBA, PhD, has been a leader, researcher, and consultant for over 25 years. Her focus areas have been higher education, non-profit and organizational evaluation, women's leadership, coaching and mentoring.er consultation work and research is dedicated to supporting leadership selfawareness and employee empowerment within organizations.

My Story

I lost the job that I had, and I did not know it. I continued to work but I suffered for a year and a half under that cloud. They call what I have been through quiet firing. I was quietly fired not for incompetence but rather, competence. A toxic leader wanted to diminish my role and the role of others in the organization due to what appeared to be her ego and insecurities.

Looking back now, I was naïve. I did not believe there was a leader out there who could be this controlling and narcissistic and could do such damage to an organization. I have been the victim of an 18month bullying, gaslighting and misinformation campaign. It has been next to impossible to lead under this cloud and the overt sabotage that accompanied it. It started at biannual organization in person event. I was enthusiastic to attend a meeting and see my colleagues and find new ways to collaborate and I felt like the carpet was pulled out from under me. I learned later that I was not alone.

At this event, my new supervisor said we had to meet and there were things she needed to tell me. When we met it was obvious that she was a pawn to convey messages to me from her supervisor. I was told I needed to be "quieter and less visible" and there was a "perception" that I and others on my team were "doing everything." I asked to participate in a supportive role in a working group that would typically be the responsibility for my area. I was told I could only participate if I had a "quiet voice" in this group. I was confused and I asked for clarification. I calmly asked what I could do to change perceptions, and I was told to "stop taking things personally." As a women leader in the United States today, I could not believe I was being asked (aloud) to be quieter and less visible. It was unbelievable and I was shaken by it.

At this same event there was a group meeting where there was supposed to be an "after party" following a meeting where we could all "relax." I walked in and the upper leader and others at my level were sitting in a circle. She told me to come in and sit down and then continued with her conversation that was filled with veiled threats while mentioning names of people who had been let go. She said they did not fit with "our culture" and "our way of thinking." She was encouraging people to identify others who "did not fit."

And so, it began . . .

What followed was a year and half of removal of my role and responsibilities through reassignment and changing of initiatives. She changed her mind on things in my area that she had previously approved of and vocally supported. When I reached out to discuss, I was ignored. She would not take meetings with me. Email after email went unanswered. When I prepared appropriately or proposed solutions I was disparaged and shut down in meetings. It seemed like the more I tried do my job, the more I was criticized or publicly disparaged. The more I tried to compromise and twist myself in pretzels to work with this leader, nothing worked. I soon realized the treatment was not based on what I was doing or not doing. It was based on who I was, my history in the organization, and the recognition of my competencies by others.

I also realized it was not only me. People from other teams were confused and stressed because similar things were happening to them. She would question people's "critical thinking" when she did not agree with their ideas. Tears became common place. Being a "yes person" without ideas or solutions seemed to be encouraged.

I was baffled. I could not understand why this was happening. After a while, I noticed something. Even though this leader had great power within the organization she seemed to disparage and undermine people who had knowledge and experience in their areas especially those that were mentioned favorably by others. It seemed like she competed with everyone who displayed competence. In most meetings she found ways to brag about herself. If someone else was mentioned favorably she would either take credit for them being there or act offended and say something like "who is she to say that" or "who is she to do that."

Additionally, she seemed to be drawn to risk and wanted to move forward with rash solutions based on reactions and refused to consider data or evaluate outcomes. If anyone challenged these dangerous notions in any subtle way, they were publicly humiliated and disparaged behind their back.

Talking about people and people's skills and job performance in meetings was common as well. It made me extremely uncomfortable. I see now that she was trying to pit people against each other and try to get people to desire to be in her favor.

In a public meeting she brought up an employee who had spoken out about an issue. She said "When I hear things like that I think, why is he here? Why does his office exist" It is important to note that a few months later he was let go and his office was dismantled.

She had been effective in manipulating others. I noticed others going along with decisions that would erode quality and effective practice in the institution. I also noticed them behaving like we had an authoritarian leader who should be adored and mimicked. I saw leaders start speaking like her and disparaging others. My heart breaks for the culture and organization that was. I never realized what one leader can do.

I reached a phase where I felt like I struggled with justified anger for others being mistreated. As I reflect more, I think what I really felt, and feel is grief. Grief for the culture that was. Grief from the previous safe leadership experiences I had. Grief for colleagues who appeared to have lost their moral compass and values under her regime and started to bully their teams and fellow colleagues. Grief because I realized I could not stay if this continued, and I had loved my organization. I loved what we provided to the community and what we represented. I had believed in our mission. It felt like the end of a relationship, and it broke my heart.

Time has passed and things are not so raw. The benefit of this experience is it that has lit my passion and motivated me. I have moved on to my 2.0. I am building my business as an organizational consultant driven to inoculate organizations from the poison of this type of leadership. I want people to be able to take for granted that a workplace is psychologically safe and that there are avenues for keeping cultures safe and supportive.

I want upper leadership to be accountable for creating and maintaining safe environments that support employee well-being.

I was lucky to benefit from the strong support of family and supportive colleagues. I was also lucky to have previously worked with so many leaders who operated with integrity. It helped me find my inner voice that could say "This is really happening, and it is not ok" and then be able to say the same thing to other people suffering in the organization that needed to be seen and heard amidst intense toxicity and trauma.

Alan Faingold

Alan Faingold is a business consultant and academic editor. With forty-plus years in the restaurant industry, he believes that a leader's mission is to connect organizational philosophies and culture to team member values by teaching everyone to deliver exceptional service to all customers. His book, We Are All Customers! *examines organizational culture, team member performance, and service excellence from the customer's vantage point. Alan earned his BA in Business Management, MS in Leader Development, and EdD in Adult Education. He has helped many students actualize their doctorate degrees by editing their dissertations so they would graduate. His website is academiceditinghelp.com*

My Story

S wearing has become an increasingly common and pervasive form of expression in the United States. When asked why they swear, people respond with a variety of reasons like being angry or frustrated, taking a tough stance, drawing attention to their opinion, gaining leverage in a conflict, or cultivating a sense of belonging in certain social situations. Some people have learned to swear as a type of jargon, and it becomes an integral part of their speech patterns. Certainly, we all may have voiced expletives when we inadvertently hurt ourselves or accidentally dropped something on the floor. Is swearing acceptable depending on the circumstances?

The literal meanings of some swear words can be vulgar, with sexual or disgusting representations. When the word's actual meaning is applied, does the speaker have an implicit intent to defame the listener or are the words bombastic rhetoric designed to elicit an emotional reaction or bully someone? George Washington once said, "The foolish and wicked practice of profane cursing and swearing is a vice so mean and low that every person of sense and character detests and despises it." (Brainy Quote, 2024). Antithetically, profane language has become an integral part of movies, music, written literature, and social media, and society continues to become desensitized to swear words.

Courtroom Scrutiny

Lenny Bruce, a popular comedian of the 50s and 60s was arrested for obscenity multiple times because he used vulgar swear words on stage during his live shows. He was convicted of obscenity and sentenced to jail in 1964. Multiple actors and songwriters supported his First Amendment right to freedom of speech and petitioned the government to overturn his conviction. Bruce was released but passed away before his appeal could be heard in court (Biography.com Editors, 2020).

The late 1960s and early 1970s were rampant with social anger and violent unrest resulting in cultural changes in the United States. Swearing out of anger was common for some people at the time; however, swearing was rare in multimedia. Theoretically, the change in attitudes about swearing is traceable to George Carlin's 1972 record album, Class Clown, which included the track *Seven Words You Can Never Say On TV* (Carlin & Hendra, 2009). In 1978, the U.S. Supreme Court deemed the recording indecent because of its intentional and repetitive use of vulgar language. However, the court did not establish a ruling about a punishment for the use of expletives because the plaintiffs argued they were simply words and therefore were First Amendment protected (Nordquist, 2020).

In 2002 and 2003, the U.S. Supreme Court revisited the use of swear words because of vulgarities broadcast on television in two celebrity outbursts. The court decided that the literal definition of a word would apply in public media, regardless of whether the word was used metaphorically. Two of several banned words referred to manure and sex acts. The Federal Communications Commission (FCC) monitored the airwaves to enforce the court's ruling. The enforcement accelerated the growth of subscription cable television channels because those companies were private and did not face the same FCC language restrictions (Nordquist, 2020). The media's perpetuation of swearing to its audience plays a role in its desensitization and challenges leaders to control its use in professional business and academic settings.

Enforcing Company Policy

A positive organizational culture was the goal of every company I worked for during my restaurant management career. During our quarterly corporate-led manager meetings at two high-profile national brands, our top corporate leaders reviewed the policy manual as standard practice. One of the rules was that swearing, cursing, and the use of vulgar language were not allowed at any time in the restaurants because every customer and team member had to be treated with dignity and respect. At the conclusion of the manual presentation, we all had to commit to following and enforcing all the rules, with all the people, all the time. This statement was made each quarter because of the lack of consistent enforcement by managers as the leaders of the restaurants who sometimes allowed non-company policy behaviors to occur.

Scott (2004) said, "As a leader, you get what you tolerate" (p. 60). Her statement applies to interactive experiential relationships. For example, parents' guidance and discipline of children during their formative years have positive or negative effects on their values, vision, attitudes, and behaviors. Children's life experiences and emotions also influence them positively or negatively, especially if they have resisted authority, acted in anti-social ways, or faced traumatic events that caused stress and anxiety. Trauma, social media influences, and previously learned behaviors become ingrained and migrate with children as they mature to adulthood often shaping their personalities, worldviews, and behaviors.

When entering the workforce, people bring their values, beliefs, attitudes, behaviors, and ways they cope with trauma and stress into the work environment. Therefore, if swearing goes unchallenged during their lives, the new team members carry that tendency into the job. Team members' diverse experiences and backgrounds may cause them to act in an individualistic manner and create a personal agenda in their minds. Their individualistic actions reflect only their desires and goals as opposed to those of the organization (Faingold & Kronon, 2020). When team members begin work on their first day, leaders become immediately responsible for ensuring that the actions, behaviors, and communication of everyone comply and align with every company policy.

Organizational Culture is a Shared Experience

Sometime in our lives, we may have seen or been victims of another team member's individualistic behaviors. Some examples are quests for power, gaining favor or popularity with supervisors, and ruthless competitiveness with an intent to intimidate or bully colleagues. Faingold and Kronon (2020) pointed out "Organizational culture brings vision and business planning into the real world through the attitudes, actions, and behaviors of all team members who star center-stage in every customer experience. Executive leaders and in-house managers are responsible for ensuring that every person on their team believes in the organization's customer service philosophy" (p. 6). Leadership expectations include being a role model who reinforces professional team member behaviors and reinforces the standard of all the rules, all the people, all the time.

With multiple stakeholder responsibilities designed to achieve the organization's expectations and outcomes, culture is a shared experience. Individual agendas interfere with the total buy-in necessary to optimize all stakeholder outcomes. The business model of a restaurant involves several essential stakeholders. Owners and administrators who create the mission and fund the organization, managers (internal customers) who operate the company, customers (external customers) who patronize and sustain the company, and team members (internal customers) who provide the products and services to the customers who are sustaining the company. The job responsibilities differ for each group, yet their objective is shared, earn customer loyalty to ensure repeat patronage so the organization survives (Faingold and Kronon, 2020). Individualistic actions allowed by some leaders set the framework and essentially encourage toxic behaviors at work, directly in contrast with the shared culture expected by an organization. Throughout my career, I have yet to see swearing included in the responsibilities of any stakeholder or designated as a unifying action in any of my employer's policy manuals!

Workplace Experiences

Examples from two restaurants I worked in for the same company illustrate my resolve to eliminate swearing. I worked on a four-manager team at the first restaurant for six months. By setting the example of professional language, I explained to our team members why swearing was unacceptable. The entire management team supported the effort to enforce company standards, demonstrating care for the team, and the atmosphere in the restaurant. The positive attitudes and morale helped team members achieve better financial success and resulted in measurably improved operations. In the corporate report, which ranked 350 restaurants' sales increase percentage and employee turnover, we improved from number 280 to number 7. It was a team effort and a fantastic achievement. My supervisor recognized my ability to influence the team and transferred me to a different location that needed leadership help. At the end of my last shift, some of the team members got together and requested that I say a swear word so they would know I was 'human.' I laughed and refused, saying that I would not compromise my standards.

On my first day working at the struggling restaurant, I observed that swearing was out of control. The team members swore for many reasons like, they were overwhelmed, a guest asked for something, or they thought their tip was insufficient. The other managers took a laissez-faire approach to the swearing policy, giving the behavior tacit approval. Laissez-faire leadership means not interfering with the status quo. By not correcting the swearing problem, the management team tacitly signaled it was acceptable. I insisted that no cursing occurs on my shifts, but the fact that other managers allowed it caused animosity. Negativity and anger continued to infect the restaurant and swearing exacerbated the problems. The restaurant's performance never improved. Although I was never harmed by the three other managers' refusal to follow company policy, it impacted the restaurant negatively and caused customer complaints because the customer experience suffered. In the fast-paced pressure-packed restaurant environment, enforcing the no-swearing rule affected employee morale and retention due to a positive or negative shift in culture brought about by shared team member behaviors. In the first restaurant, team members complied with and embraced the no-swearing policy. In the second restaurant, the team members were angry that I enforced it. How can leaders inspire changes in non-compliant team members' behavior and reduce swearing in the workplace?

Transformative Change Using Positive Leadership

Today's educational resources include public, private, and in-home schooling, in-person and online learning from early grades through college, and trade schools, as options for learners. Yet education does not occur only in academic settings, learning in the workplace, television and music, video gaming, social media, life lessons from experience, and street learning, influence people's ability to communicate professionally. The insidious nature of negativity caused by swearing leads to poor attitudes and behaviors, which contributes to the development of toxic work environments.

Employers have no guarantee that every team member knows how to communicate effectively with customers. Customers expect to be valued by an organization and the people serving them. As a customer loyalty coach, my company values align with my beliefs about how internal and external customers should be treated, with care, respect, fairness, grace, and integrity. Although leaders cannot change team members' educational backgrounds, they can institute onboarding systems and training programs that hold team members accountable for their behaviors. Communicating professionally and respectfully with customers and team members is a policy of most organizations. Leaders who allow swearing to affect their workplace undermine the organizational culture they were hired to lead and protect. Leaders can transform team members' understanding of why swearing is unacceptable, negative, and leads to a toxic environment in the workplace. It starts with challenging swearing, explaining why swearing contributes to toxicity, and gaining buy-in from the team to be part of a shared positive culture that benefits every internal and external customer.

Customer Loyalty Concepts Company Values

We Believe Every Customer to be Treated with:

- **Care:** The genuine desire to provide help and support.

- **Respect:** Recognition that every customer has unique life experiences, thoughts, and emotions.

- **Fairness:** Equal treatment at all times, every time for everyone.

- **Grace:** With appreciation that your organization has been granted the honor to serve.

- **Integrity:** Honest and transparent customer engagement that promotes loyalty.

References

Biography.com Editors. (2020). *Lenny Bruce biography*. https://www.biography.com/celebrities/lennybruce

Brainy Quote (2024). *Swearing quotes*. https://www.brainyquote.com/topics/swearing-quotes Carlin, G., & Hendra, T. (2009). *Last words*. Simon & Schuster.

Faingold, A., & Kronon, E. (2020). *We are all customers! Earning and keeping our loyalty*. Book Baby Publishing.

Nordquist, R. (2020, March 9). *What are swear words and what are they used for?* https://www.thoughtco.com/swear-word-term-1691888

Scott, S. (2004). *Fierce conversations: Achieving success at work and in life, one conversation at a time*. Berkley Books.

Karen Linyard

Dr. Karen Linyard received her Doctor of Business Administration with a focus in consulting from Walden University. Her doctoral study is titled "Strategies Nonprofit Organization Leaders Use to Increase Human and Financial Resources. She received her Master of Business Administration and Bachelor of Science in Healthcare Administration from ECPI University.

She currently works as a project manager at Atrium Health. In this position, she has successfully managed multiple projects in the ambulatory setting, executing process improvement projects designed to deliver quality patient care, improve patient outcomes, and improve operational efficiency. She focuses on working with leaders to collect and analyze data to identify gaps in performance and institute solutions to improve efficiency and achieve strategic goals.

My Story

In 2011, I worked in a full-time clinical position in an ambulatory healthcare facility. Approximately 40 employees were working in this facility, including approximately nine physicians. I was assigned to assist a physician most in the office considered challenging to work with. I was determined to work hard and consistently in the role given to me to ensure I provided quality patient care daily. After four years of working at the facility, my manager shared that a clinical leadership position was available, and I was in consideration for the position. I was delighted to hear of this opportunity and believe I was an excellent fit for the position. In the weeks following this conversation, my manager told me I would not be chosen to receive the promotion. My manager told me I was not promoted because she did not want to find anyone else to work with the physician I was assigned because everyone thought he was hard to work with. When I questioned the rationale for her decision, she admitted that her decision had nothing to do with my leadership or clinical skills but because she did not want to make any changes that might upset the physician, I worked with she had chosen someone else for the position. As a result, another clinical teammate with less experience and seniority than me was promoted to the clinical leadership position. This experience further emphasized the toxic work environment I was suffering through daily. After careful consideration, I applied for a new clinical position in a different facility.

After my manager learned I accepted a new clinical position in a different facility, she immediately stopped communicating with me. She would not acknowledge me and avoided interactions with me. Bothered by her actions, I requested to meet with her to discuss what was taking place. During our discussion, my manager told me that I would never get ahead in my career and that she would not support my decision to transfer to another position. She did not give a reasonable explanation for her statement, and our conversation ended. During my remaining time at the facility, my manager and I did not communicate at her request. I left the facility hurt and disappointed after working diligently to care for our patients and manage the tasks and responsibilities assigned to me during my four years there.

As I reflected on this toxic work environment, it became clear that my manager at the time lacked respect for me and was not concerned about my career goals. She created a hostile environment that would stay with me for quite a while. Since experiencing this negativity, I have learned how to quickly recognize the toxic traits that could affect my confidence and mental and emotional well-being. My health is a priority, and I am committed to protecting myself by not working in a hostile and toxic work environment as I continue in my career.

Peterson Mirville

Dr. Pete Mirville, a U.S. Army Veteran, holds a Doctorate in Business Administration (DBA) with a leadership focus from Walden University and a Master's in Healthcare Administration from American Public University. With over 30 years of healthcare experience, he currently operates a 179-bed nursing home as its administrator. Dr. Pete is dedicated to guiding leaders and helping others achieve their personal goals. Known for his high standards, he has led teams to national quality awards and improved federal survey outcomes. He also teaches at Concordia University and mentors' leaders through social media platforms like YouTube and LinkedIn.

My Trauma

When I think about trauma, I think about any disruption to homeostasis, whether physical, mental, or spiritual. Many can relate to trauma when it comes to physical being. Many are comfortable and feel safe sharing their physical trauma experience. However, when it comes to mental or spiritual trauma, most hide it in their inner being to be never shared with others. This secret that we hide from others eats at us, and there's an internal cry out from our inner being, longing to share that trauma.

The earliest form of trauma that I can recall involves how I was treated as a child. My father is a West Indian native. There are distinct differences between rearing a child in the West Indies and America. As a child, my dad would call me names. I can particularly remember that he would tell me in his native tongue that "a jackass like you will never amount to anything." So, I grew up with the idea that I was worthless. However, I don't think that his harsh words penetrated by itself, per se. It was more of the collective repeated insults at home and in elementary school that would create trauma that I would carry in the military. As an army soldier, I was ridiculed and bullied. The constant barrage of insults from my childhood at home, at school, and in the military created an insecure man. An insecure man who was timid and always felt like he was not good enough.

This timidity and unworthiness contributed to my failed marriage. In 1994, I married a woman I only dated for a month. I met her through my sister while I was stationed at an Army post in Kansas. One summer I visited home, and there she was. She was stunning. The crazy thing was that she took an interest in me. I thought to myself, there was no way someone so beautiful would be interested in someone like me. Someone that my dad said would never amount to anything. After two weeks of visiting, I returned to Kansas and began our long-distance relationship. On my next visit home, I proposed, and after a year of our long-distance relationship, we were married. To add insult to injury, after just a year, she expressed that she married me to get out of the house. She would periodically repeat that sentiment throughout our nine-year marriage and several deployments. I proposed to her on our ninth anniversary to renew our vows. That same year, the day I returned after a vasectomy procedure, she asked for a divorce. She cited that while I was a good man and father, "she didn't love me like that." How's that for trauma?

So, you see, sometimes it's not just one trauma that will shape the course of your life, but the repetition and the compiling of several traumas that compound on each other. The constant barrage of these little traumas profoundly impacts how you view people in the world and process information. I like to refer to it as the lens of trauma because your thoughts must travel through that lens, creating a false and toxic perspective that is crippling. Viewing the world through this lens alters one's perception and interaction with one's environment. In addition, it's not just the compounded trauma but the overlapping traumatic experiences that reinforce each other, deepening the impact on our cognitive and emotional responses. These traumas alter our perception of our ability to effectively process information, disrupt how we regulate our emotions, and cause us to go into survival mode. In this survival mode, we develop strategies that are often disruptive. These strategies could include avoidance, withdrawal, and or aggression. I am certainly guilty of avoidance, but I was quite withdrawn in many situations.

What I have mentioned represents a fraction of my 53 years on this earth. We won't discuss the trauma of divorce, the death of my two-year-old grandson, and an injury at 40 that almost left me crippled.

Nonetheless, after therapy and practicing mindfulness, I was able to cope with the traumas of my past. There was one thing that truly helped me cope and overcome my trauma, and that was becoming a martial artist. Taekwondo training gave me the confidence that I needed to overcome the trauma caused by bullying in the Army. The simple task of breaking a board with different techniques creates a sense of confidence and knowing that you are not as weak as others makes you think. Couple that with my faith and a supportive network of friends and family, and you will have a winning solution.

Ann M. Morgan

Ann M. Morgan, PhD, is board-certified coach and appreciative inquiry expert with more than 20 years of experience in higher education. As a teacher, leadership coach, and consultant, Ann leverages positive education frameworks, transformational learning theory, and systems thinking to co-create an inspiring vision, goals, and culture. Clients and colleagues' express gratitude for her creativity, energy, deep listening, respect for the mission and core values of institutions and individuals, and care for the well-being of all people.

Ann teaches as a professor of human behavior, emotional intelligence, and lifespan development. She researches, publishes, and presents on mentoring, positive leadership, inclusive engagement and assessment, and applied appreciative inquiry work. She lives with her family in the Twin Cities of Minnesota.

My Story

In my career, I have been exposed to leaders and organizational cultures that have been healthy and safe and others that have been harmful, toxic, and even traumatic. I started some writing that aimed to reach back to my earlier career experiences that I now know were dangerous and unhealthy for me. It is clear, looking back, that I had a trauma response throughout much of that time that has resulted in my forgetting most of the details. I remember basic contextual clues and the resulting pain, tears, anger, frustration, confusion, and times I lied or sneaked around situations so I wouldn't call attention to or create issues with the toxic leader. I remember feeling like that toxic leader (from a job I had in my mid to late 30s) was feeding on and learning from a toxic culture and I had nowhere to go with my concerns.

I remember the way I felt but I cannot remember the specific behaviors or events that resulted in those feelings. I can see particular scenes, but I have a lot of trouble articulating what was happening, and I could not recreate the specific image of him or his behaviors for this writing.

The memory lives in me though. So, in the past decade (in my late 40s), when I was working at a different educational institution, and I had a boss that made me feel safe and seen and valued—I felt deeply grateful and at peace. I was energized by the challenges in my work, proud of my team's successes, capable and supported for innovating and creating positive change . . . and safe from abuses, manipulation, political acrimony, and sabotage.

Just about two years into my work at the organization under this realistically imperfect but phenomenal, safe boss, he resigned. I was inexplicably sad. I embarrassingly and seemingly dramatically cried at his going-away party. I felt in my bones the fear of losing the workplace safety I'd found with him.

During the transition, and while a new Provost/Chief Academic Officer (hereinafter CAO) was being sought, I reported to the University President and worked to continue serving my team and nurturing the momentum we had. I experienced less interaction, knowledge/awareness, and time from a supervisor during the transition, but I was confident the team and I would settle in and benefit from a new leader when one was named.

Not long after a new CAO was put in place and reporting lines were shuffled, team members (from the wider academic affairs team) were jockeying for positioning, alignment, attention, and favor of the new CAO. This could be considered normal behavior, but the way the CAO let it happen—even encouraged it was very uncomfortable for me. My body knew very quickly that the new CAO would not be a safe leader for me. Looking back is clearer cognitively for me, but I responded at the time in three phases based on what I was feeling:

1. I doubted my instincts and persevered hopefully. This included forgiving irrational or inappropriate behavior of the new CAO and her followers, and even making excuses for it.

2. I believed my instincts but thought I could work through it. During this phase, I tried to maintain my own integrity, gave almost all my energy to my team, and actively sought safe or trustworthy people in the organization for my team and me. I stopped taking things personally and stopped caring about things in the same way. (Notably, during the 2020+ Pandemic, there was a lot of talk of "quiet quitting," which resonated for me.)

3. I realized I could not be aligned with my integrity in the situation any longer. I made an exit plan to keep myself safe (though I still didn't know if it was just a "me" issue).

If I knew then that it would be dangerous for others, I wish to think I would have been braver and louder in my leaving. I was afraid to tamper with anyone else's views or loyalties, and I hesitated to share the true reason for my leaving with anyone.

One of the most memorable moments with the new CAO was at a summit-style meeting where tech strategies and tools were being evaluated for future planning. In the meeting, I mentioned a tool that was in place (though new and yet unknown by many), and the new leader had a very visible visceral response. Her face turned red, and her voice got louder and full of fury when she said there were better options that should have been pursued. I explained that we did look at the option to which she was referring, but it didn't have all the features our faculty indicated they needed and hoped for when we had worked with focus groups. I do not remember her full response, but I remember that her eyes welled up with angry tears, and she let the group know we'd be taking a break in the meeting, and she asked me to take a walk with her around the office. On our walk, she spoke in a loud whisper as she told me that the recently former CFO exerted power and made decisions, he had no right to make. (This was news to me and didn't seem logical). "He had no f-ing right to make that call." She let me know it was not a done deal and left me feeling very uncomfortable because it was an in-progress, fully approved venture for the university that had already taken a great deal of time, money, and people resources. I knew at this point that there was a great deal she didn't know about the work that went into the decision and the work that was ongoing with the building of the tool, the number of teams involved, and the success it was having with faculty. While the exchange was weird and was an introduction to the kind of behavior I could expect to see from this new leader, I let it go with the knowledge that I would need to tread carefully around this topic and seek to earn her trust on it and make her a believer over time.

NO HELP NEEDED

In another very early interaction with the new CAO as she oriented herself to the office and to the staff when I joined her in person for our regular 1to1 meeting, she talked about one of the office staff members saying "Well, it's obvious some people just need to be needed." She was talking about administrative support team members—who were needed! However, the new academic leader made clear from the very beginning that she did not want anyone managing or even accessing her calendar, her travel plans, or meeting agendas. This was alarming to me on so many levels.

THE INNER CIRCLE OF TRUST

Talking about others was one way that the CAO showed you were in the *inner circle of trust*. Of course, no one stayed there. You could be there for one part of one meeting, but it was still made to be a coveted place to be. One way people knew they were part of the inner circle is that in front of you, the CAO talked disparagingly or full of pity about people who were not in the inner circle. At one point, I joined a meeting where the academic leader was talking to her direct reports, and I heard her finish what she was saying, ". . . she is used to having the authority to make decisions . . . going to have to get used to not . . ." The details don't matter as much as the tone and mean-girl behavior. It was very uncomfortable for me. It could have been *about* me, in fact. And, it could have been about the person I was now reporting to (after continued reorganization of the organizational charts). I continued to observe her talking about people who were not in the room in a critical way in small or large-group meetings. It was always uncomfortable, but regrettably, I never felt positioned or equipped to stop it.

ONLY ROOM FOR ONE ON TOP

With the reorganization of organizational charts, it felt clear to me pretty early that any person or department that had reported to or created something with the former chief academic officer was subject to demotion, defunding of programming, or deception and undermining that would eventually take away power and energy or momentum from the project or department. This included my team. Regular proactive communication with the faculty and activity that was on behalf of the center that I directed needed to be stopped. There was to be no center "branding" or anything that made the center stand out as anything but part of a "one university" approach. Saying this now, it feels like nationalism.

The CAO told me to make changes in the way my team worked because one of the other executive leaders (to whom she reported) did not care for the center and did not see the value in it. The CAO told me that she was trying to protect me and my team, and so to work with her, we should get quiet, stop making new moves or introducing new programming (unless it was something she asked us to do), and stick to training and development of faculty (the very basics of what the team did). What I was being asked to do was relatively unclear, it was difficult to pull apart the service of training and development from communication with faculty and academic leaders. I did not trust what she was saying about the source of the message, but I did trust the message. Without letting my team know of my concern about the CAO's behavior and beliefs, I worked to communicate and initiate a modified strategic plan that would back-burner several projects and refocus the team's communication and work for a smaller and more pointed audience. We would, in essence, continue to build and work for faculty but we would be less visible to the rest of the university.

This shift felt inauthentic and uncomfortable. I knew I could not lead in this way. I also knew that more conversations about moving members off my team and renaming and reconfiguring the objectives of the team were inevitable. So, I did exactly what I am sure she'd hoped. I resigned from my position.

MORE "IN-CROWD" / FIRST-TEAM BULLSHIT

My role was not opened for application. The CAO named a former team member of hers (which was occurring at a rapid pace across the academic department), and I stayed on long enough to transition work, try to make solid introductions of the team for her, and prepare her for what was to come. It was my hope that she would come in and authentically lead under the direction and vision of the CAO—something I know I could not do for the team.

ORG CHART DISORGANIZATION

When I resigned, I asked to move into a faculty role, but the CAO and her team asked me to join a new team of academic researchers that would be defined for me later. I was told I could teach 50% of my role and research the other 50%, and that seemed to be my only option if I wanted to remain fulltime. The team that was put together to do this work was a strong but relatively vocal group of employees. We called ourselves the "misfits" for a while, but nothing about it felt safe or right. It was a holding place for people who would potentially be hard to fire, helpful to retain, and important for the new CAO to *contain*.

BECAUSE I SAID SO.

From this new role, I observed leaders were making decisions because the CAO mandated something, not because there was data to show a need or because there was a call from faculty or students to do something. One of my direct experiences with this was a call from the CAO to decrease the requirement for turn-around time on grading and feedback. The CAO made the mandate and set a deadline. She made clear that it was something she had "promised" to her executive leaders (the board or CEO). I saw it as my job, then, to ensure there was buy-in at every level; data to show it was needed, possible, and beneficial; and to figure out how this responsibility fit my new role in research. There is not need here to go into detail about how that was done, but for all the mandates the CAO made from the time she began in her role, I will note that not every leader had the time or wherewithal to manage the mandates in a way that didn't completely harm individuals or departments or processes in the organization. Her "visionary" mandates were doing true damage to the institution. After wrapping up that project, I left fulltime work for the university entirely. I was physically, emotionally, and mentally exhausted; negative; and heartbroken for myself and others.

Frederick Douglass Perry

Frederick Douglass Perry spent 40 years in the entertainment industry, transitioning from TV to theater and film. His career began in 1971 with a year-long training program at KQED TV, learning to become a producer and engineer. After a brief period in TV, he worked in local theaters and the San Francisco Opera before helping create the first TV station at Howard University, a historically African American institution. Returning to the Bay Area, he freelanced at three TV stations, including ABC, and worked in Silicon Valley as a stage manager, producer-director, and technician. For the last decade of his career, he worked in digital master control at San Francisco's PBS station. Active in union roles, he served in NABET and the DGA. Now retired, he enjoys reading, photography, and a peaceful life.

My Story

T he War Memorial Opera House in San Francisco is a landmark, known for its grandeur and towering stage sets. While audiences marvel at the spectacular performances, few realize the behind-thescenes work that brings the opera to life. As a young man in my mid-twenties, I became a part of the crews responsible for this magic, working as a freelance stagehand and a member of the International Alliance of Theatrical and Stage Employees (IATSE-Local 16).

My journey began in smaller theaters around San Francisco, where I honed my skills, but I longed to work in the bustling, grand environment of the San Francisco Opera House. Finally, I got the call to report to the War Memorial Opera House. With tools strapped around my waist, I stepped through the stage door, eager to immerse myself in the world of grand opera.

The scale of the opera house was overwhelming—vast corridors, towering sets, and a labyrinth of staging areas buzzing with activity. As a newcomer, I felt a mixture of excitement and trepidation. This was a world where experience and expertise reigned supreme. I was determined to prove myself, but uncertainty lingered—would I be hired for just a day's work, or would I stay for the entire season?

As the season wore on, I found myself fully immersed in the opera's backstage life. I worked alongside crews in various departments: grips constructing massive set pieces, electricians crafting dazzling lighting effects, and wardrobe and makeup artists creating the characters that brought the opera to life. The prop department, where I was based, became my second home. We were responsible for the intricate details that made the opera's world believable—from ornate furnishings to weapons and immense ground cloths that covered the stage. The work was demanding but fueled by a shared passion for the craft.

However, being the only Black man in this predominantly white environment came with its challenges. From the moment I set foot in the opera house, I sensed the subtle glances and exclusion from conversations. At first, the bias was subtle—a dismissive glance here, a snide remark there. But over time, it escalated. One day, a member of the grip crew "accidentally" bumped into me, muttering a derogatory remark under his breath. What might have been considered traditional hazing for new hires took on a sharper, more racially charged edge in my case.

As the weeks went by, the hostility became more overt. I was often passed over for opportunities, and my colleagues were given more responsibility while I remained sidelined. The stage crew at the time was only beginning to integrate, and old attitudes were hard to change. Tension grew until it boiled over into a physical altercation during one particularly stressful setup, where shoving matches broke out between myself and a fellow biracial colleague and members of the grip crew. It was hard to distinguish between the normal hazing of newcomers and racially motivated animus, but the impact was clear—each day felt like a battle to prove I deserved to be there.

Yet, every setback only strengthened my resolve. I realized that while I couldn't control others' prejudices, I could control how I responded to them. Instead of letting their hostility define me, I focused on mastering my craft. I took pride in even the simplest tasks, such as tracking down ground cloths or placing props on the stage, letting my work speak for itself. I believed that excellence was the best way to fight back, and slowly, my efforts began to pay off.

The more I focused on my work, the more I earned the respect of some of my colleagues. Allies began to emerge—individuals who recognized my talent and dedication regardless of the color of my skin. These allies helped create a more inclusive environment and challenged outdated attitudes within the workplace. It wasn't an immediate victory, but through persistence and resilience, I began to break through the barriers that had once held me back.

Navigating discrimination in the workplace meant confronting it head-on while remaining committed to my craft. I understood that actions spoke louder than words, so I made it my mission to excel in everything I did, regardless of the obstacles in my path. As the curtain rose on each performance, I stood backstage, surrounded by the fruits of my labor. The audience, unaware of the challenges I faced, marveled at the spectacle unfolding before them, and I took great pride in knowing that I had contributed to that magic.

Throughout my time at the opera, I refused to let prejudice dictate my success. Instead, I let my actions and the quality of my work define me. As I gained more experience, I was entrusted with increasingly complex tasks, and my confidence grew alongside my reputation. In doing so, I began to gather more allies and supporters—people who stood by my side, offering solidarity in the face of discrimination.

For me, the Opera House became more than just a workplace—it became a symbol of triumph and a testament to the power of perseverance. Overcoming bias wasn't easy, but it was a battle worth fighting. By staying focused and leading by example, I helped create a more equitable and inclusive environment for future generations of stagehands and technicians.

My experience at the San Francisco Opera House taught me valuable lessons about adaptability and perseverance. Stagecraft is a fast-paced, collaborative, and unpredictable field, and success depends on being able to pivot when necessary while remaining steadfast in your goals. Every project, every challenge, and every setback taught me to roll with the punches but never lose sight of the bigger picture.

As my career progressed, I moved beyond the opera house and into other areas of the entertainment industry, including broadcast television, industrial television, documentaries, and major sporting events. With each new role, I carried with me the lessons I had learned about resilience and adaptability. I had the great opportunity at one point to help launch the first television station owned and operated by a historically African American university at Howard University. Where I got the chance to pass on my perspective on succeeding in the industry.

I also took on leadership positions within unions, such as the National Association of Broadcast Employees and Technicians (NABET) and the Directors Guild of America (DGA), where I advocated for fair treatment, diversity, and inclusion. Taking part in negotiating several contracts.

Mentorship became an important part of my later career. I was committed to sharing my knowledge and experience with younger generations of stagehands and technicians, particularly those from underrepresented backgrounds. By guiding and supporting them, I hoped to help future generations navigate the challenges of the industry, just as I had. Encouraging diversity within the industry became a key focus, and I worked to create more inclusive environments where talent and creativity could thrive, regardless of background.

One of the most important lessons I learned throughout my career is that the world is constantly changing, and we are always going to face obstacles—some of which are beyond our control. But if we can adapt to the challenges we face while staying determined to overcome them, we can find success, even in the most difficult circumstances. That's the lesson I carry with me to this day, and it's one I impart to those I mentor: stay adaptable, stay resilient, and success will come, even if the path isn't always the one you expected.

Overcoming bias required perseverance, self-confidence, and building strong relationships with those who believed in my potential. Here's how I approached it:

1. **Excellence and Mastery of My Craft:** From the beginning, I understood that the best way to combat bias was to excel in my work. Whether in television, theater, or film, I dedicated myself to mastering my skills, staying up-to-date with the latest technologies, and delivering high-quality work. Over time, this earned me the respect of my colleagues, making it harder for them to dismiss me based on prejudice alone.

2. **Resilience and Focus:** Racial bias, whether subtle or overt, could have been deeply discouraging. Early in my career, I encountered dismissive attitudes and racially charged remarks. Instead of letting these experiences bring me down, I used them as fuel to push forward. My resilience helped me stay focused on my long-term goals, refusing to let others' biases define my path.

3. **Finding Allies and Building Networks:** Throughout my career, I sought out allies who recognized my talent and dedication. Building relationships with colleagues, mentors, and industry veterans not only gave me professional support but also created a network of advocates who could vouch for me when I faced bias. Their encouragement and solidarity were crucial in overcoming obstacles.

4. **Navigating Bias with Professionalism:** When confronted with discrimination, I chose to address these situations with professionalism. I often weighed whether it was more effective to confront the bias directly or let my work speak for itself. In some cases, I stood my ground, calling out unfair treatment respectfully. At other times, I focused on excelling in my craft, knowing that excellence could be the most powerful response to bias.

5. **Union Involvement and Advocacy:** Being active in union leadership roles allowed me to fight back against bias on a broader scale. As part of NABET and DGA, I advocated for fair treatment, diversity, and inclusion in the industry. By negotiating fair contracts and pushing for representation, I worked to create a more equitable environment for everyone facing similar challenges.

6. **Mentoring the Next Generation:** As my career advanced, I made it a priority to mentor younger stagehands and technicians, especially those from underrepresented backgrounds. Guiding and supporting them became one of the most rewarding aspects of my career, as I helped future generations avoid some of the biases I had faced.

7. **Staying True to Myself:** Perhaps the most important part of overcoming bias was staying true to who I was. I never let others' biases diminish my sense of worth or belief in my abilities. Holding on to that inner strength gave me the confidence to navigate difficult situations and continue progressing in my career.

In the end, I overcame bias by excelling in my work, building strong relationships, and staying committed to creating a more inclusive industry. These efforts not only helped break down the barriers I faced but also paved the way for others to follow in my footsteps.

A Final Highlight

One last highlight of my career in the entertainment industry came toward the end of my career when I worked as a master control engineer at San Francisco's PBS station in the digital master control room. After decades of working across TV, theater, and film, this role represented a culmination of all the knowledge, experience, and perseverance that I had built throughout my career. I had begun my career as a trainee at KQED in a program designed to give minorities and women a well-rounded idea of the intricacies of TV production and engineering.

Why was it a highlight?

1. **Mastering the Digital Shift:** By this time, the industry had fully transitioned from analog to digital, and I had successfully adapted to the technological changes, despite starting my career in the analog era. Working in digital master control at PBS was a testament to my ability to continually learn and stay relevant in an evolving industry.

2. **Seeing It All Come Together:** This role required me to oversee the entire broadcast process, ensuring the quality and seamless transmission of content. It felt like everything I had worked on in my career—technical expertise, problem-solving, leadership—had come full circle. It was deeply satisfying to know I could handle such a complex, high-stakes role with confidence.

3. **The Culmination of Perseverance:** Having faced numerous challenges, including racial discrimination and navigating a predominantly white industry, reaching this position felt like a personal and professional triumph. I had proven to myself and others that I could overcome adversity and still reach the top of my field.

4. **Legacy and Contribution:** Working for PBS, a network that provides educational and cultural content to millions, allowed me to feel that I was contributing to something greater—helping deliver meaningful programming that makes a positive impact on society. It aligned with the values I had developed over the years, and knowing that my work was part of something so valuable made me incredibly proud.

That moment, standing in the digital control room, reflecting on how far I had come, was the highlight of a career built on resilience, adaptability, and hard work.

Dr. Pettis Perry

Dr. Perry is an organizational effectiveness thought leader, consultant, educator, and author with more than six decades of field experience as a practitioner. He is the principal consultant with Perry Organizational Effectiveness Consulting, (Perry OEC) LLC, a Washington state consulting firm. When opportunities present themselves, he serves as a professor of transformative leadership and organizational effectiveness. His mission and vision are to improve individual and organizational performance; and to foster kinder, gentler, healthier organizations and communities by promoting positive social change, social justice, and peace.

His personal story is one of significant accomplishments in the face of great adversity. The story you are about to read may seem fantastical, but it is true. Unfortunately, it is also a story told some 250,000 times each year. Likewise, his story is one of hope and encouragement for anyone living in a post trauma state of being.

Convicted Without Trial by a Christian Organization

Since 1998, I've known I would share my story one day. It was only a matter of time, and that time is now. That year changed my life forever because of a lie that led to my abandonment and betrayal by the organization I'd devoted my life to serving and loved so much. I am sharing my version of the events because if it can happen to me, it can happen to anyone.

Ironically, less than a decade earlier, in 1990 my therapist at the time identified abandonment and betrayal as a lifetime pattern. Little did I know how many more times the pattern would appear over the length of my career. In this case, I think it is important to name the organization because it is essential to understand that even the most well-respected organizations have dark personalities and horrific stories to hide. However, corporate cover-ups harm innocent people and therefore sharing my story as someone who has been deeply harmed in the workplace may help others.

To fully appreciate my story, I need to start at the beginning. My mom determined my two brothers, and I would grow up as healthy children despite our living in the shadow of my father's volatile political activism during Jim Crow, the McCarthy era, and the fight for Civil Rights. I walked my first picket line in the third grade, participated in multicultural Bazaars, learned folk songs, ate foods from around the world, and attended some of my father's meetings, where he worked to organize people to advocate for civil rights. He even worked behind the scenes to help organize the 1963 March on Washington for Civil Rights. These experiences had a profound impact on the person I would later become.

We had our issues as a blended, multiracial, multiethnic family that complicated our family dynamics. Still, my parents did their best to ensure we had what we needed under the circumstances within which we lived. My mom did whatever she needed to do, including working in the kitchen so that we could attend a Woodcraft Rangers family resident camp. She also ensured we learned to swim at the local YMCA in Los Angeles. I have fond memories of one particular YMCA counselor who lived without feet and hands, likely from a congenital disability, I learned much later.

By nineteen, I was elected to the South Berkeley Model Cities Board where we fought for and completed senior housing projects. I met a girl at a party whose dad was a senior leader for the YMCA in Berkeley, California, where I lived. I was looking for work, and he suggested volunteering at the YMCA in my area in South Berkeley, about three blocks from my home, which I did. A few months later, a parttime position opened up. I was hired as a Youth Leader to develop sports programs for the kids in the neighborhood which was a great fit because I was a local athlete who played football at Berkeley High School and, at the time, Laney College in Oakland, California. I also picked up some additional work at the YMCA as a custodian. Little did I know that work would come in handy decades later when I became a senior YMCA executive leader.

At the age of twenty-three, I moved to program director at the YMCA in East Oakland, California. Once I graduated with my bachelor's degree at twenty-six, I was eligible to become an executive director with a job opportunity in front of me. My supervisor at the time told me she was stepping down to move on with her career as a mental health therapist. I was disappointed to hear she would be leaving because she had done so much to help me begin to understand the inner journey, we all must take if we want to grow and evolve as people.

We talked a lot about life issues, so she knew some of the details of my own personal trail of tears, and we became great friends (which I find has happened with select people who remain friends for decades). She gave me a poster by Virginia Satir titled *I am Me, I am Okay*, which still hangs near my front door to this day. My ritual was to read it aloud every day before leaving home and again when I returned home. Over the days, weeks, months, and years, my life changed in remarkable ways with the positive affirmations that I was not the terrible monster my teachers, coaches, and others were making me out to be.

During my junior year in college, I encountered Jane Elliott's Blue Eye-Brown Eye experiments that illustrated the power of self-fulfilling prophecies. Such perceptions led me to further explore human dynamics through transactional analysis, which examines relationships based on roles and behaviors. By analyzing these interactions, we can determine whether individuals act as Parents, Adults, or Children. Ideally, adults should engage with each other as adults, having mature, adult conversations. If one person takes on the role of a Parent and the other a Child, their behaviors will be reflected in these roles, and they become self-fulfilling prophecies. When this occurs, the task is to get the parties to shift towards adult-adult conversations. I gave the course text to my mom to read, and I found that it strengthened our relationship because we became better at adult-adult conversations.

During that same period, I enrolled in other subjects that expanded my perspectives on human behavior and, most importantly, myself. Once I graduated with my undergraduate degree in social science (research), I was faced with making a career path decision to either coach or become a professional YMCA executive director. I chose the YMCA because of the positive impact I knew I was having working with the young people in our inner-city programs.

Shortly after accepting the executive director role, another executive vacancy occurred at the crosstown YMCA branch in West Oakland. It was another struggling branch that nobody wanted to lead. After assessing the situation from my new vantage point of view, I approached my supervisor, the director of operations, to consolidate the two branch operations under my leadership. He responded with; "*you know if you fail, you'll be out of a job!*" I let him know that I was clear about that fact. I then asked him for some advice about Board development, and he responded with, "*I don't know how to work with you [Black] people.*" He was the director of operations in Oakland, California and he was so willfully ignorant that he did not understand that Black people are like other people, and my question was about Board development and not about Black people. I believe that had I been White he would have been able to tell me how to work with Boards of Directors.

When I made the proposal, I did not experience fear because I had a clear vision of what needed to happen. I got a standing ovation from the West Oakland Board of Managers after giving a slide presentation of what we were accomplishing at the East Oakland Branch YMCA, and most importantly, I believed in the people at both branches and that with their help, we would succeed. We consolidated the branches and became very successful for the first time in many years. The experience taught me that leadership, rather than management, determines the success or failure of two identical organizations. This belief has been consistently reinforced over time.

Thanks to my mom's commitment to always helping develop children, I grew up in the YMCA from childhood in Los Angeles into executive leadership in Oakland. After completing a three-year 360-hour intensive Career Development Program (CDP), I was certified as a YMCA Senior Director. I also became part of the YMCA National Training Faculty, teaching other YMCA professionals how to develop, manage, and evaluate programs and training others on segments of the CDP. At one point, many of the employees I knew called me *Mr. YMCA* because I lived and breathed the YMCA. I loved the nature of my work delivering programs and services to local urban, suburban, and rural communities throughout California.

During my tenure, I was a member of the YMCAs Serving Disadvantaged Communities (YSDAC) working group that met and trained interested YMCA program and executive professional directors serving mostly inner-city YMCA to become more skilled as practitioners. I worked at five branch YMCAs before becoming the Executive Director/CEO of the California YMCA Model Legislature & Court program, the most extensive model government program in the United States. One of our most unique characteristics was that we got to use the Governor's Office, both legislative chambers, and the Supreme Court facilities for our programs, and we were the only program allowed to do so. As such we lived by a very strict code of conduct and zero tolerance policies because one slipup and everything could be taken away from us. Consequently, we practiced idealism in our behaviors to protect what we had for future generations.

In July 1990, I was the fourth candidate offered the job and I jumped at the chance because it was a great program, and the Governing Board wanted to grow the program and increase the minority representation in the process. The downside was that it took me away from my two-month-old son for extended periods because it involved extensive travel and time away from home.

Before accepting the position, I called one of the CEOs I knew to ask him for his thoughts. His response was, "it's a career-ender"! I wasn't overly concerned because the YMCA culture identified particular career paths for those seeking upward mobility to CEO levels or other corporate-level leader roles. My path was already atypical, and I never saw myself as the CEO of a large corporate YMCA. It never dawned on me that my career would end by treachery and palace intrigue—a warning my mother had been giving me for more than a decade telling me to get away from the YMCA before they hurt me—but I loved my work too much to let go prematurely.

At the time I accepted the position, the program was forty-two years old with highly standardized policies and practices. It was staffed by a small team of paid staff who relied on more than three hundred volunteers to operate successfully. Between July 1990 and February 1998, I delivered executive leadership to the statewide Board of Directors and committees. My job was to organize conferences for local YMCAs who wanted to participate in the program. While they participated in our program the behaviors of participants were governed by our rules but managed by their own delegation of adult leaders. There was a very clear delineation and separation of powers defined by the YMCA of the USA and locally incorporated YMCAs which meant that I supported local YMCAs while local YMCAs governed themselves. All YMCA leaders know this organizational structure and live within their respective boundaries—at least until they feign ignorance when inconvenient truths manifest as in what happened in my case.

Based on the established jointly agreed Board policies and staff strategies, my role as the executive leader was to formulate multi-year strategies and tactical plans to achieve desired goals, objectives, and outcomes which were defined as growing the program in both numbers and ethnic minority representation. I engineered growth and managed the most extensive state government simulation program in the United States including budgeting, staffing, financial development, program development and evaluation, advisor training and certification, policy formation, conflict management, and facilities management. I also managed liaison relationships with the Governor of California, cabinet members, state legislators, the California National Guard, corporate leaders, and public officials in more than 100 communities throughout California. Some of our accomplishments under my leadership included:

- Expanding services to constituents from 1,000 to more than 2,500 participants, and from 50 to more than 100 remote YMCA program sites distributed from Sacramento to San Diego.

- Increasing ethnic minority participation by 7% and at the same time expanding services to new communities.

- Increasing organizational revenues from $250,000 to more than $1,000,000.

- Generating approximately $500,000 in revenue for the State of California.

- Driving roughly $10,000,000 in revenue for hospitality and transportation industries supporting our program.

- Creating an Advisor Certification Academy for 300+ volunteers annually. With input from program area specialists, I wrote the curriculum and training protocols and evaluated the Academy's success in outcomes.

- Boosting annual support fundraising from $50,000 to $187,000 annually and endowment revenue from $550,000 to $1,000,000+.

- Organizing and hosting four large conferences per year for more than 2,500 participants with the involvement of advisors and other volunteers and organized entertainment activities for participants.

- Recruiting high-level speakers such as the Governor, Speaker of the House, and other leaders to speak with our participants and to respond to unedited questions.

- Organizing and leading cross-country trips for our delegate groups to compete in the YMCA Conference on National Affairs debates where our delegates formed and debated ideas with participants from around the country. The California YMCA Model Legislature & Court program became the gold standard for the conference.

By 1998, I was one of only a half dozen Black YMCA executive leaders on the West Coast and the only one with a Master of Nonprofit Administration degree as well as a doctorate in Organization and Leadership. I developed a reputation as an innovative turnaround and growth-oriented executive leader who took underperforming operations and revitalized them. As we prepared for our annual February Model Legislature & Court session, we met as customary for our January final pre-training mid-state conference at Camp Roberts, which at the time was the largest active artillery base west of the Mississippi. It has a proud history of being a major training facility for all sorts of military units, which is all I will say about it. We were very fortunate to be allowed to use their facilities because it was the only place big enough at the time to house us as we grew larger, and it was centrally located.

This year was a very special year because it marked our 50th Anniversary, so everyone was especially excited. In each of the previous years when I arrived at Camp Roberts, I met with the garrison commander to learn about any conditions that might interfere with our normal operations, and he would designate my point of contact while on post. But for some reason, the new garrison commander was too busy to meet with me. I knew most of the personnel because it was our location for seven of my eight years as director.

But this year, for the first time the garrison also had two different military units arrive for training and there was a security alert in place with delineated off-limit areas restricting some of our movements. Muddling matters even more because the garrison commander did not have our usual meeting, the coordination between groups became messy and there was intermingling between groups which further complicated matters. I began receiving reports of harassment of high school students by military personnel who had been drinking.

Around eleven pm I received a call on my radio that a group from one of our largest delegations had vandalized military property. We went through our standard procedures and after reviewing the facts the decision was made to send them home for violating our zero tolerance policies. After returning to my office about a week later I received a call from one of the parents asking me to reconsider my decision. I explained what happened and that the delegates violated our zero-tolerance policies and code of conduct, so my decision was final. He responded with, *"oh yeah, we'll see about that."* A few days later I received a letter stating that I used military-type tactics to torture kids.

The next week the local YMCA executive director called me to ask me whether the claims were true, and I told him they were absolutely not true and if they were I would be in jail. The next thing I knew, I got to my hotel in Sacramento and secured my hotel room. My Board chair met me and told me I could not be at the conference because a decision was made to allow the delegates who were sent home to attend the conference. I could not be there. It was unbelievable! Eight years of working my fingers to the bone, missing time with my son, planning and creating what was to be an epic conference, and I did not get to participate. The lead advisor for that delegation, who happened to also be one of my staff volunteers, was also sent home. On my way home, all I could think of was, *"mom, you were right!"*

In the end, I learned a false document was placed in my personnel file. It was supposed to be a complaint to Child Protective Services who assured me that if such a report had been filed, I would have heard about it, letting me know it too was a lie. The Western Regional Director never spoke to me about the issue, but he hired two investigators. I learned later they were former police officers he'd used before.

When I met with the investigator to review my version of events, I did not realize at the time that everything I stated refuting the events was scrubbed from the report. I learned later that more people than those who were witnesses to the events were included in the report from the other side, and I was never given an opportunity to include people who could have clarified the events, policies, and longstanding practices including attorneys who managed our Court program and who were present during the conference, as well as a judge who was on my Board. I also learned the delegates came from exceptionally wealthy families living in one of the wealthiest communities in the country and whose parents were donors to the local YMCA capital campaign. As I understood it at the time, they threatened to withhold their donations if their children were not allowed to attend the conference. The three of them were allowed to attend: two did, one was sent home, and one accepted his punishment.

There was never any internal investigation by some of the most capable attorneys in the country who understood the policies and practices of the organization and who could have added to the investigation into the events creating a more complete picture. But that was not the intention, because the YMCA of the USA did not want to risk losing donors for a local YMCA capital campaign. In my opinion, it had nothing to do with facts or truth but was a way to sweep an ugly event under the carpet regardless of the outcomes for a dedicated employee with nearly thirty years of achievement where others failed.

No one cared about what would happen to my then eight-year-old son or the long-term psychological and financial harm done to me; someone who devoted their life to actualizing a stated Christian purpose and was then made the sacrificial lamb to protect a local YMCA from its failure to manage the behaviors of its own delegates. As a result, I became the fall guy when the local YMCA did not own their failed leadership which led to their delegates being sent home.

My attorneys fought to get me a hearing at the YMCA of the USA headquarters in Chicago. I was not allowed to have an attorney present, and I could not ask questions of the regional director or anyone else. I was allowed to state my case and that was it. The rules were explained to me at the start of the meeting making preparation impossible. I was allowed a representative to participate in private discussions on my behalf. For my representative, I selected a fellow statewide director who happened to be the former speaker of his state's house of representatives. After meeting with the organizing group, he called me and apologized for refusing to represent me because there was no fairness in the process, and I could not win. He was right!

On the morning of the hearing meeting, I flew into Chicago and when exiting the shuttle the driver, who happened to be Black, said "*have a great day, brother.*" I responded with, "*brother I am heading into a lynching.*" He said, "*God be with you brother.*" I found the building's lavatory and changed into my suit. When the people walked into the meeting even those I knew, wouldn't look at me although a couple shook my hand. The Western Regional Director who orchestrated my removal stuck out his hand and smiled, and I ignored him.

During the hearing, I did my best to state a case and the hearing committee was kind enough to hear me out, but it was an impossible case to make when you have already been found guilty and have to prove your innocence, complaints are lies, the reports had been sanitized, and the complainants are major donors to a local YMCA in a capital campaign. It was a fait accompli.

My attorneys were able to maneuver my case into federal court. I was required to attend a meeting with a federal magistrate to determine whether a pre-trial settlement could be reached. As we walked into the magistrate's office my attorneys were in front of me, and when I hit the threshold to enter the magistrate's chambers, the magistrate said, "*well, my estimation of you went up a hundred-fold.*" When hearing that, one of my attorney's asked, "*why is that your honor?*" The magistrate said, "*he could have made this a race-based case, and he didn't.*" My attorney said, "*we know your honor, we tried to get him to do that, but we believe we can win this case on its merits.*" The magistrate said, "*I have to tell you that you cannot win your case because six months ago the California Supreme Court changed the law indicating that any company accepting a third-party report in good faith, whether it was factually true or not, can no longer be held liable. I know because my wife works for the Supreme Court.*" He then asked me how much I spent thus far, and when I responded with "*about $30,000,*" he asked my attorneys whether my estimate was accurate, and they confirmed it was. He asked, "*have your attorneys told you how much it would cost to take your case to federal court?*" When I said "*no,*" he responded with, "*at least $100,000.*" He then capped the discussion by saying "*you cannot win your case because of the change in the law and if you bring it to my court I will be pissed!*"

My case ended at that moment. I was out of about $30,000, a single parent, out of money, out of work, no home, and with no ability to make my case in court to defend myself even though my case was one of the law firm's top cases. Left to defend myself and my career for the rest of my life, my attorneys were compassionate enough to waive any balance of fees owed to them. That day, my mom's prophecy that my career would end by treachery and palace intrigue came true and, in my opinion, it was manipulated by the then Western Regional Director.

By then, I learned through the grapevine, that he had his hands in ending the careers of two other Black executives: One director brought a new state-of-the-art YMCA facility to Watts serving the SouthCentral area of Los Angeles. He too was on the YMCA of the USA national training faculty and chair of the YSDAC. The other was one of the most creative directors I know who was the first to introduce hypertension and wellness clinics through the YMCA serving the largely Black population in SouthCentral Los Angeles; and when he became executive director of one of the San Francisco Metropolitan YMCA's inner-city branches, he pioneered the first computer center in a YMCA (as well as in the country), and his summer youth employment program offered jobs and labor market orientation training to more than four-hundred inner-city youth. Together we designed a dynamic and robust training program that became one of the best in the city.

He was introduced to my brother who worked in television and together they produced a wonderful broadcast-quality video for the upcoming Martin Luther King Jr. Day celebration. He was so proud of the project as he should have been, but it produced a racial backlash internally and he became perceived as a radical, effectively ending his career not long after at the hands of the corporate HR director who would later become the Western Regional Director.

In addition to the three of us being fraternal brothers committed to serving among the most impoverished communities in California, there is another common thread to the intersectionality of our career paths. In my opinion, a single HR professional eliminated three Black executive leaders. He singlehandedly destroyed the careers of three highly successful, committed, and loyal Black YMCA executive leaders, causing great harm to them and their respective families illustrating how trauma and toxicity migrate from the workplace into homes.

Without a doubt, wrongful terminations can have lasting and devastating long-term impacts. In my case, it not only produced immediate and substantial economic harm when I lost my home and had to tap my retirement prematurely just to survive, but it produced a substantial amount of psychological harm as well because of the false accusations that could have landed me in jail, and it ended my dynamic and strong career.

My fears were fully justified because there is a long history of Blacks and other people of color being falsely accused by Whites and suffering because of it. He also refused to allow me to resign ensuring the greatest harm would be inflicted. Ironically, I had spoken to my Board chair during the fall of 1997, letting him know that I was exhausted and would look to transition to another job after the 50th anniversary was over. However, the abrupt termination did not leave me with any capacity to create a soft landing so I could continue my life less harmed.

Unfortunately, my case was not unique. Wrongful terminations profoundly impact about 250,000 people and their families annually according to the Armstrong Law Firm (2017). These impacts can be both immediate and long-term. For example, today, I continue without the ability to recover financially from the catastrophic harm caused by the Western Regional Director and the YMCA of the USA. I will also never be able to recover from the trauma caused by my former employer because of their wrongful termination and corrupt fact-finding efforts they undertook.

In the end, I experienced the very real impact of losing my job abruptly. Aside from the trauma impacts, it cost me more than $25,000 of additional interest on my school loans because I could no longer pay off my loans after being ahead of the payment schedule by paying off 40% of my loans before things fell apart. So rather than paying off my loans in about ten years, it took me more than twice that long because of accumulated interest. Additionally, using a portion of my retirement funds produced a 40% tax liability for early withdrawal.

It also set in motion a 25-year fear of what was going to happen when I needed to retire one day in the future. The lingering psychological effects have compounded because when I need my retirement funds most today, which has come this year, a large part of it is long gone. The cost to me today is the loss of roughly $50,000 annually for the rest of my life thereby greatly diminishing my quality of life in retirement. What would have been a wonderful retirement well-funded from my career, instead produced the conditions I find myself struggling in today just to make my economic ends meet.

The psychological harm also remains with me and will for the rest of my life, it was that devastating, and it added to my previous traumas and those that followed. For twenty-five years I've lived in dread of the day I would have to retire, and that day has now arrived. As I write this story, I've been in tears because of the losses I've incurred through my retirement account, but also from the losses in other workplaces where I encountered toxic supervisors who attacked me, stole my work, forced me to do their work, and passed me over more than a dozen times for promotions restricting the amount of money, I've been able to earn over the life of my career.

My destiny turned on a dime in one day. People who did not care about the zero-tolerance policy and procedures we all agreed to live by as members of our program abused their wealth to override what we were teaching their children about truth, living with honor, and adjusting to life consequences when poor decisions are made. In my opinion, the YMCA of the USA for its part failed to live up to the Christian principles it espouses. It failed to seek truth and instead sold its corporate soul for a lie to protect an independent corporate YMCA from accusations of dereliction of duty for improperly managing its delegation.

Instead, they destroyed my career, kicked me to the curb, and inflicted major trauma in how they managed the process to cover up a lie that could have caused me to be arrested. Nothing, however, compares to what happened to my son in the process who went through my trauma with me. My example illustrates that there is a huge price paid by the 250,000 people wrongfully terminated annually, particularly when it happens to people without deep pockets. Those with deep pockets get special treatment as is evident in the political arena today.

In addition, the Western Regional Director cost the YMCA three highly creative executives who took on projects others did not want to do in communities where the YMCA raises millions of dollars and routinely uses the plight of the people in these communities to make their fundraising case statements. I recall a conversation with another senior executive who admitted that the YMCA does well with affluent and middle-income people, but not so much with low-income people where the three of us excelled. As I've reflected on my YMCA experiences, I am proud of the tens of thousands of people I helped during my career, the array of communities that benefited from my work, and proving that leadership and not management produce greatness in others when it is allowed to flourish.

The pain runs deep, I'm bloodied, exhausted but unbowed. I choose to stand tall rather than grovel in pity on my knees in front of those who've harmed me. What I've accomplished over the course of my lifetime is guided by a deep desire to minimize the needless suffering of so many people globally. There are wars involving bombs and missiles and there are hidden psychological wars occurring in the minds of 70% to 90% of people including those in the United States, where the population is highly traumatized.

My story is important to let people know that no matter how hard you work to create initiatives that bring goodness into your world there are always people who will want to stop you. If you stand up for what's right, expect blowback from smaller minds not able to see your vision. It does not matter whether you work in a small, medium, or large-scale organization, the distribution of toxic people means that they exist in every organization. This is true for government, for-profit as well as non-profit organizations.

The actions of the YMCA of the USA, Western Regional Director directly led to twenty-five more years of suffering that I've had to turn into personal growth through projects like this one. I'd lived a life filled with trauma prior to going to work for the YMCA. I've never known life without trauma, so I was traumatized as a child joining their programs and as a staff person working my way through my career. The fact that trauma is additive means that it would become further compounded after my ordeal with the YMCA of the USA when I encountered five more highly toxic supervisors and several other people who made my life miserable before the end of my career.

Of all the trauma I have endured, and there have been a number of very substantial life altering experiences, the cowardice of my beloved YMCA to seek convenience rather than truth and to intentionally inflict such trauma that it thrust me into near homelessness is unconscionable. I would have been homeless had it not been for an Army National Guard family I met in Paso Robles, California while working for the California YMCA Model Legislature & Court program who took me in. They were at Camp Roberts when the events happened, so they knew the truth about my circumstances.

The perspective that *I don't know how to work with you people* belief system repeated itself many times over my career in varying forms including, *only you people can do diversity work*. I also live with the echo of words spoken to me by a friend I invited to sit in on my dissertation in 1995, who said as we were leaving my successful defense, "*remember, you will never be anything more than a Nigger with a doctorate!*" He too was right!

With the advantage of hindsight, I can now see that my plight during my career was actually a matter of struggling to have adult-adult conversations with toxic supervisors, some I believe to be racists, who in some cases were also incompetent and unable to do their jobs effectively. The fact that I had to work harder than others to succeed meant my skills also increased. However, no matter how hard I worked, how good my work products may have been throughout my career, after leaving the YMCA of the USA the trauma and toxicity in the workplaces where I was hired continued elsewhere, including academia where I spent twenty-five years.

But what the YMCA (and others) could not take from me are the wonderful memories I have of the great work I was able to do, and they cannot take my training and expertise. They also cannot take the lessons I've learned that sometimes there are those few good leaders who will support you and there are many more who will attack you and try to stop you from doing what you were born to do because their egos will not let you thrive for whatever personal reasons they might have. In those, the lessons come from learning *how to not be*. Find joy in your life's work and enjoy every moment of it while you can because someday it will end with the only things to be determined being how and when.

My research demonstrates that trauma is prevalent in society and that prevalence leads to toxicity in the majority of our workplaces, and by extension our other groups. My story is not unique by any stretch of the imagination. There are people who have been falsely accused of crimes who found themselves incarcerated, in some cases, for decades. Former Alabama Governor Don Siegelman, who I had the pleasure of interviewing for the *Be Bold America* radio show on KSQD 90.7FM, serving Santa Cruz and the California Central Coast, spoke candidly about how he was incarcerated on bogus charges to move him out of the way of a presidential election; that is what is so scary and makes the trauma so real.

Remember always, that those who walk point in combat generally get shot at, first. It comes with the territory when you choose to make a difference. Be clear about the potential personal cost that can come from challenging the status quo or from racial and other differences when speaking up. Consider the discomfort that will undoubtedly come with making difficult decisions that could lead to a brighter future. Be humble enough to never think that you cannot be touched by people who wish to do you harm. But remember that whatever happens along your path, as long as you've got breath in your body a better tomorrow is possible when making tough decisions today.

Remember too, smiles can be deceiving so you never know how much pain lies behind them. My photo was taken when I was living with friends because I did not have a home to call my own. They showed up without my asking to save me from a more difficult fate. In the process they bought me a year to dig my way out of the morass I found myself in at the time. What I found was that my faith in people became stronger while I became ever humbler. At a metaphysical level I changed inside and as those changes took hold things began to materialize, and what was once confusing became clearer. In many ways, my self-transcendence became more complete as I worked through the significant disorienting dilemmas that turned my world upside down, starting the moment my destiny turned on a dime because of a lie. So, remember, when it comes to creating a meaningful life, where you start is less important than where you end up. I wish you peace and success on your journey and the best outcomes for your life!

René Pratt

René is a former educator having spent almost twenty years teaching in inner city schools in the Midwest. She received her undergraduate, English as a Second Language endorsement and a master's degree in reading from the University of Nebraska. Currently, she resides in Western Washington where she enjoys hiking, biking, and traveling.

My Story

In December of 1993, I sat in a large hall at the University of Nebraska with about 200 teacher candidates as we gathered in excitement to move forward in our final phase of getting an undergraduate degree in elementary education.

Our supervisor, DM told us all the things we needed to know. One thing she said stuck with me. She said, not everyone will have a positive experience, and she would be there to get us through whatever was happening.

The next week, I was given my student teaching assignment. I would be teaching 6th grade at Field Club Elementary in midtown Omaha, NE.

I was excited and nervous as I went to meet my cooperating teacher, DB. I recently purchased a new wardrobe suitable for teaching. I showed up at her classroom on a day without students. She looked down her nose at me, not saying much. I felt she didn't approve of what I was wearing. I really don't even remember what I had on.

The university has a strongly suggested timeline of how each subject should be released to the student teacher to teach the class. Mrs. B. had her own timeline and as she told me what her expectations were of me, my heart sank. She was not going to give me the proper time to teach the class. In sixth grade, the teacher was responsible for teaching all subjects, except art, music, and PE.

When I showed up on my first official day, I found a very small student desk butted up to her desk. My knees hit the top and I had no room for supplies and materials.

I was introduced to the class and spent the day watching Mrs. Bradley teach and interact with the students. Her style of teaching was lecture style and could see her students bored and uncaring I spent two weeks observing before I was allowed to walk with them to lunch and specials. I learned their names and always addressed them by name.

After 2 more weeks, I was given the responsibility of teaching spelling. I prepared interactive games and activities rather than the usual sentence writing and "copy the word ten times." The students loved it, but she did not.

Four weeks into the sixteen-week program, I was one week behind the university's timeline.

Meanwhile, Mrs. B. is doing her best to glare and stare at me. It seemed she was hoping to turn the students against me. In the teacher's room or hallway, other teachers made comments about how she is with student teachers. They all said the same thing, "hang in there."

The next subject released to me was social studies. I love social studies. The students were learning about Mexico. I borrowed a bunch of books from Mexico to put them in the classroom library. At this point, there were no additional resources. Only the basal, which was quite old. I also used nonfiction to teach the objectives. She made it clear, she didn't approve and even said, they better pass the end of the chapter test.

I was working at a steak house at the time and was surprised to see the principal of the building there for dinner. He told me he knew I was struggling and if I ever needed help, to let him know.

At about week 7, she gave the students a math test. I was surprised to see students lining up at her desk for help. I'm thinking, if she taught them the concepts, why are they asking for help on a test and why is she allowing it?

At one point, she told some students to come to me for help. Well, first of all, math is not my strong suit and I hadn't been teaching math yet.

I paused and hesitated to guide the students through the process without giving them any answers.

Then it happened. She ordered the students in my line back to their seats; told me I didn't know math and gave me the test to take. What the hell! I lost all credibility in that minute. I did not take the test.

After taking them to art, I walked into the principal's office and broke down in tears. He picked up the phone, dialed a number, and handed me the phone. On the other end was my university supervisor.

She advised me to continue the day, go home, and act like I would be back the next day. I walked out of the building hoping to never see her again.

The next day, I met with DM and listed everything I had left behind. The plan was to gather my things and more importantly, find me another place to student teach. In a different district. Halfway through the semester.

I didn't get a teaching contract that the first year of being out of university. I subbed in many buildings [working] with all grade levels.

Towards the end of that first year, I was called into Marrs Middle and Elementary. There were a few buildings that had [the] kindergarten through 7th model.

It was on a Friday, and I was called to teach a rambunctious 5th class. I was the third sub that week. Their teacher was having health problems and none of the subs stuck around to finish the assignment. I was called into the principal's office and was asked if I could stay indefinitely. I said sure! The students and I were figuring each other out and I started to shape them up.

It was probably the next week when I was taking them to the library when Mrs. B. and I crossed paths. She had taken a position on the middle school side as a gifted teacher. We didn't exchange any words, but the media specialist DP (whom I became very good friends with) noticed and made a comment to me. I told her I had a difficult time in her classroom. DP said yeah, she is known for being difficult. Word had it, Mrs. Bradley said I would never be a good teacher.

My assignment was a five-week success, and I was given a contract to teach 2nd grade in that building.

When we passed in the hall, I held my head high.

Over the next few years, I worked on my ESL endorsement which ked to getting a master's degree in teaching Reading. I was hired by the district for several literacy-based projects and was made the writing coach at the building.

Mrs. B. went to another building at the end of my first year.

One of the projects I worked on was formatting our reading basal end-of-story comprehension assessments to reflect the district-wide test each third grader had to take.

During our fall district-wide workshops, I was asked to present my process and how to make it work.

I remember looking at my room assignment and noticing I was scheduled in the same room as Mrs. B. would be presenting after her presentation.

Oh boy! I put on a suit and high heels and did my makeup and hair perfectly.

I strolled into the room with 20 minutes left of her presentation. I wore heels on purpose. I wanted to make a self-confident statement as I sat in an empty seat in the front row. I never took my eyes off her. have to say, that my time spent teaching made me a confident person.

Lara Raggon

Lara Raggon holds an MBA with a focus on Supply Chain and Logistics, and she works in public procurement for a city in Oregon, focusing on strategic sourcing and contract management. She appreciates the positive, collaborative work environment that makes her role both rewarding and enjoyable, even during challenging projects. Outside of work, Lara likes to travel, explore the outdoors, listen to music, and spend time with her husband and their pets. As an active Rotary member, she is also committed to community service and personal growth.

My Story

Trauma and the lingering impact of toxic work environments are subjects that often remain unspoken and underappreciated, but the trauma produced by toxic work environments can have impacts on our lives that we may not fully realize; the impacts may even stick with us for a long time after leaving those toxic environments. I'm going to share some long-lasting effects of such an environment as a reminder of the importance of ensuring work environments are healthy and to illustrate that it takes time and, sometimes, professional help to overcome the shadows left by traumatic workplace experiences.

I left a toxic work environment, and I am now in a healthy and professional working environment, but I'm still dealing with wounds that haven't fully healed. The scars left by a toxic work environment are like hidden injuries, surfacing when least expected. Sometimes we don't even realize the wound is still there until something causes us to notice it.

A recent conversation with my husband, Mark, has caused me to do some self-reflection about the last few years, delving into the impact of recent professional changes. I'm currently planning a party to celebrate our 10-year wedding anniversary. We aren't usually the kind of people to throw large gettogethers, but in addition to this being a special milestone, I have felt a strong desire to reconnect with friends and family after a long period of solitude and exhaustion. This feeling is what led to the conversation.

I told my Mark that I was looking forward to our anniversary party and that I was eager for more opportunities to host more events at our home with friends and family. I have been longing to connect more with the important people in our lives. I addressed this void with him. "We don't get together with friends very often," I said.

Mark responded with a perceptive observation, "Yeah, but you haven't had the energy the last few years to do much on the weekends." He tactfully addressed the energy drain that had become an inherent part of our lives over the past couple of years, stemming from the mental and emotional exhaustion caused by my work.

And my goodness, that resonated deeply with me. I had not realized that since leaving the company I resigned from that I had more capacity for other people. As an introvert, I do need downtime away from people to re-energize, but in the last few years, I sometimes needed full weekends of rest away from people and activities. Some nights I would tell Mark, "Today was too people-y," and he knew that meant I needed time alone to recover from a particularly draining day.

It wasn't simply that my job was stressful and had a substantial demand for my energy and dedication. I was immersed in one of the most toxic workplace environments I had ever experienced, where more unrelenting harmful and abusive situations led me to find myself completely depleted of all energy and emotional bandwidth by the end of the day, especially at the end of the week. The psychological toll was immense. I was often required to console employees who also endured the toxicity and trauma. Additionally, I was frequently compelled to wear a facade, concealing the turmoil within so as not to unsettle my subordinates and coworkers. To say it was emotionally and mentally draining is an understatement, and its true impact was not obvious to me until several months following my resignation.

My former boss, whom I'll refer to as Ted, initially presented himself as a charismatic and charming person when I first joined the company. He wasted no time in expressing his satisfaction with my hire, professing a strong belief in my abilities and the value I brought to the company. The praise and the flattery were undoubtedly gratifying, even though Ted had scarcely interacted with me long enough to form such opinions. Astonishingly, within the initial days of my tenure at the company, Ted unveiled his grand vision to restructure the organization. He boldly predicted that, should all go according to his plans, I would ascend to the esteemed position of Chief Financial Officer. The sheer audacity of this goal was apparent, considering I possessed a mere two years of experience in financial roles. My academic focus during my MBA was supply chain, not finance or accounting, and I had only recently embarked on this journey with the company. Nevertheless, I felt a potent mixture of flattery and hope, envisioning myself rising to meet the challenge. In my optimism, I also naturally assumed that adequate training would be extended to me.

In the initial weeks at the company, I was granted a glimpse behind the metaphorical curtain, casting a new light on the inner machinations. It was then that I began to question whether the charm and charisma that Ted exuded were merely a facade.

Ted asked me how much experience I had working with specific software, a linchpin of the company's accounting operations. I told him forthrightly I had no prior experience with it but expressed my eagerness to acquire proficiency. I knew it would be an integral part of my job, and I was happy to learn it. He told me I should talk to Phil or Marcia for access so I could start getting some hands-on experience.

My request to Phil and Marcia echoed Ted's directive, seeking access to the software. Marcia kindly helped me with getting my account and log-in set up, and away I went with trying to master the software, fueled by the desire to demonstrate my rapid adaptability and soon make a substantial contribution to the team. I was feeling nervous, but I'd learned other such programs before without too much trouble.

However, this seemingly small event transformed into a disheartening episode. I was soon faced with a crying and upset Marcia, upset due to a storm that erupted after Ted learned of her assistance to me. He chastised her, asserting that my inexperience could potentially compromise critical data. He astonishingly feigned amnesia regarding his prior instruction and reproached Marcia for her giving me access to the program. I felt horrible and this incident weighed heavily on my conscience. I genuinely questioned whether I had misconstrued our interactions. I sought to make amends and apologized to Marcia, and I asked if I could do anything to help. She absolved me of any culpability, though, and explained that this was simply the norm with Ted. I hadn't misunderstood anything. He'd definitely told me to reach out to Phil or Marcia to get access. Why was he so upset?

It soon became patently clear that Ted harbored a profound distrust and apathy toward Marcia. His descriptions of her portrayed her as incompetent, duplicitous, and untrustworthy. I began to see that, regardless of Marcia's actions, Ted was poised to find reasons to chastise her. This realization was underscored when, shortly after the software incident, Marcia resigned from the company. Ted, undeterred, boldly declared that he would have terminated her employment if she hadn't opted to leave of her own accord.

This one incident left such an impression on me. I had to grapple with a range of emotions from self-blame and confusion to complete empathy for Marcia. I know that Marcia likely would have left anyway, whether her decision or not, but I couldn't help but feel terrible. I had a desire to change the working environment for the better, but this was the beginning of the anxiety I experienced at the company and the beginning of the distrust I had in Ted going forward. His abrupt shift in attitude was now apparent, and while I don't think I was completely conscious of it, I knew I could be on the receiving end of this kind of irrational and unpredictable behavior.

Within a few weeks of Marcia leaving, the company was restructured, and I was promoted to CFO, a part of the executive level of the company. I was the only non-owner member of this inner circle. Part of my new duties included tasks that Marcia had done. I now can't help but wonder if, when I'd been hired about five months before, Ted had already planned on ousting Marcia and giving me some of her responsibilities. Because other areas were restructured, and not everything I took on had been hers, it's hard for me to know for sure, but the timing was interesting, to say the least.

As time passed, Ted became increasingly at ease discussing individuals he harbored reservations about, particularly those long-serving employees who had been with the company prior to his and his partners' acquisition. In the company of fellow owners and executive leaders, he would disparage certain employees behind closed doors while maintaining a facade of appreciating their contributions in their presence. Initially, this behavior appeared to be typical office gossip, the sort one encounters in most workplaces. I, unfamiliar with these individuals, had no grounds to disbelieve Ted's portrayal of them as inept, obstinate, or problematic employees. What concerned me most was that some of these individuals were slated to be my direct reports, prompting me to think, "I've got quite a challenge ahead."

However, as I gradually got to know these employees, I found myself increasingly taking Ted's descriptions with a large grain of salt. Each member of my team demonstrated their worth through valuable contributions. Many had served the company for so long that their earlier careers were a distant memory, and this company was their only professional home. They had been instrumental in keeping the company afloat during tough times under the old ownership, and they had navigated the myriad challenges of the transition to new ownership. They genuinely cared for their colleagues and embraced my leadership as their team leader.

This isn't to suggest that we never encountered disagreements or the need for corrective actions; like any other humans, we made mistakes. Yet, I had seldom worked with such dedicated and proficient professionals. It was mind-boggling that Ted failed to see their value. I thought to myself, "He just doesn't know them as I do. I'll need to demonstrate their worth to him."

The challenge of caring for my direct reports and shielding them from a boss who failed to appreciate their worth as individuals came with the burden of absorbing the brunt of his anger and frustration. My earnest desire was to see my team thrive, find happiness, or at least experience contentment and comfort in their roles. When Ted vented his anger over a mistake or when another owner disparaged a team member for taking sick leave, I shielded my team from such negativity. I firmly believed in their exceptional abilities and understood that errors are a natural part of any work environment and that people have lives outside of the office. I aimed to be the kind of leader I would want for myself, reserving corrective actions only when absolutely necessary.

The defense of my team didn't solely stem from loyalty; it was rooted in the reality that they were, for the most part, diligent, highly motivated, and ethically sound employees. Nonetheless, acknowledging that nobody is infallible, my mission became twofold: to proactively prevent mistakes wherever possible and rectify them before they could come to Ted's attention. A typo in an accounting entry? I rectified it the moment I spotted it. A task overlooked? I pushed to have it completed before Ted had a chance to realize it was unfinished.

My approach had extended beyond diligent oversight; it had become an obsession with every conceivable issue that might arise, and my aim was to preemptively address or rectify them before they could become ammunition for an outburst from a boss who could shatter my team's morale when my guard was down. My days were consumed with fretting over the emotions, reactions, and behaviors of a grown man who, when unbridled, had the potential to wreak havoc on my team's well-being.

The original purpose of my job, which primarily revolved around managing finances, had been overshadowed by this new mission. I functioned merely as a means to ensure my team's daily survival with as little drama as possible. Most of my other responsibilities took a backseat.

Whenever Ted assigned me a task, no matter how small, I found myself consumed by anxiety. I fretted over anything he might have visibility of. I obsessively reviewed each email or message multiple times before hitting "send." A rush of adrenaline coursed through me upon sending, and I winced at the mere sight of a response, even before reading it. I often sought the interpretations of others regarding his requests to ensure I met his expectations, often too intimidated to ask him directly. This state of affairs hadn't been my starting point, but gradually, as I witnessed him belittling others seeking clarifications, or heard him proclaiming that he would "just do it" himself when faced with questions, I grew uncomfortable asking him anything.

My team was genuinely grateful and expressed their thanks for my role as a buffer. This was especially true for those who had previously been the target of Ted's wrath on numerous occasions. They recognized that I shielded them from his outbursts and effectively kept them out of his firing line.

Every time I received a message or call from Ted, my stomach churned. I couldn't help but wonder: Who had provoked his anger today? Had someone committed another typographical error that we would need to discuss as if it were a criminal offense? Would he once again threaten someone's job security?

In the midst of this toxic job, I started finding myself navigating a mental landscape littered with forgotten details and overlooked commitments. While it's normal to have occasional lapses of memory, the frequency of my forgetfulness was disconcerting. I misplaced everyday items, lost track of essential tasks, and, in one regrettable instance, even failed to meet up with a friend.

The incident that stands out vividly in my memory occurred on a Sunday morning. Work had become an incessant source of stress and emotional exhaustion, pushing my anxiety levels to their zenith. I was struggling to find some semblance of peace and reprieve. Fortunately, the prior night had granted me a rare, restful slumber.

As I sipped my coffee at home, attempting to hold onto my sense of presence and calm, I noticed a text from a friend. The message was simple: "I hope you're okay." In an instant, it hit me—I was supposed to be meeting my friend for coffee that very morning. In the blink of an eye, I realized my oversight.

Regrettably, my moment of clarity came too late. My friend had waited for my arrival at the coffee shop, growing concerned about my well-being. She waited there by herself, tried reaching out to me, and ultimately, she left the coffee shop, not knowing what had happened to me.

I felt an overwhelming sense of guilt and remorse. I had unintentionally abandoned my friend, an act inconceivable to me in the past. It pained me to realize that the mounting pressures and demands of my job were transforming me into the kind of person who let down friends due to the strain of work. It was a stark reminder of how important it is to find a balance and regain control of my life amidst the chaos of my career.

It was less than a month later that I made the decision to leave the company, making just how allconsuming and taxing the toxic environment had become more apparent.

Since leaving my previous company and beginning a new job, one of the most revealing aspects of my journey has been my reactions to my new boss. In this new professional environment, I've been met with nothing but professionalism and kindness, yet an inexplicable unease still lingers. The mere prospect of a meeting request from her sends my mind into a frenzy, and an unannounced visit to my desk triggers an overwhelming sense of discomfort.

While it's typical for people to feel nervous when starting a new job, my level of unease goes beyond the ordinary. Overhearing the pronouns "she" and "her" said in the distance instantly leads me to believe that I'm the subject of conversation and that a reprimand or discussion is imminent. Instead of having a default stance of respect and deference for my new boss, I find myself trapped in a cycle of fear and anxiety.

I worry continually about what might be transpiring behind closed doors and, even more significantly, how those deliberations might affect those around me. To date, there hasn't been a single unreasonable action taken by the leadership in my new organization. This persistent fear, I've come to realize, is no longer rational or justified.

In recognition of the toll this irrational anxiety is taking on my well-being, I've decided to take a proactive step. I'm planning to seek counseling to address and manage this recurring automatic anxiety that's affecting my work life. I've landed in an organization that is a far better fit for me, one that has welcomed me with open arms, and I'm determined to be in a better mental and emotional state to fully contribute and be my best self. It doesn't have to be this way, and I'm committed to regaining a sense of confidence and peace in my new professional environment.

I'm also in the process of releasing the anger I've held towards my old company and, in particular, Ted. It's become apparent to me that Ted might be struggling with his mental well-being, and while this doesn't excuse his behavior toward employees, it allows me to view him with a degree of empathy.

Despite the lingering effects of trauma and anxiety that I'm still working through, my life has undeniably improved and continues to do so since I made the decision to move on. My relationship with my husband has been reinvigorated, and I find myself spending more quality time with friends. I've regained the energy to pursue outside interests, prioritizing self-care. I exercise more, maintain a healthier diet, and enjoy more restful sleep.

I've always been intrinsically motivated to excel at work, but being in an environment that not only failed to nurture my growth but also left me afraid to make any imperfections due to the threat of humiliation and degradation was deeply demoralizing. I lost all sense of pride in my work. My primary focus shifted towards preserving the well-being of my staff and myself, leaving little room to dedicate the time and energy I would have liked to creative solutions, new innovations, or self-improvement.

At every turn, I was haunted by the fear that any attempt to pursue something different or new, without flawless execution, would result in chastisement. Consequently, I stopped trying. During my final months as CFO, I restricted myself to the bare minimum. Despite harboring ideas for improvement and a desire to contribute more to both my own growth and the betterment of the company, I found myself plagued by exhaustion stemming from adrenal fatigue and a deep-seated fear. As an intrinsically motivated individual, this brought me more shame and anguish than anything external forces could inflict. I've always been someone who goes above and beyond, not one who rests on their laurels, but my ability to take risks or push myself had dwindled.

As I grapple with shame, PTSD, and anxiety, I look forward most to rediscovering my ability to push myself and reembrace the role of the employee, team member, and leader I've always known myself to be. I recognize my strengths as a problem solver, an advocate for my team, a hard worker, and a motivated contributor. Now that I've liberated myself from the toxic work environment, I'm once again certain that this is the person I can be. I've also known myself to be a good partner and friend, and now that I'm not consumed by work-related anxiety, I'm determined to continue nurturing these facets of my identity.

Dawn De Palma Ross

Dawn Ross is the Head Teacher and owner of Mayday Educational Services (MES). She brings over three decades of teaching experience in US schools. She has a B.S. in Education from the University of Detroit Mercy and an M.A. in Educational Administration from Wayne State University. She is a founding member and writer for the English Curriculum, Building Exceptional Students for Tomorrow (BEST). This is an interactive curriculum for teaching English to all levels of learners.

Navigating Gender and Professional Challenges

The first time I realized I was treated differently as a female, I was about 12, walking down the street with a friend when we heard a catcall. Confused, I realized it was directed at us. That was the first time I felt uncomfortable being seen more as a woman than a girl. This uncomfortable feeling followed me throughout my life, as women often face objectification and lack of respect, especially from men of various ages.

As a cheerleader in high school and college, I received unwanted attention. Even though I didn't seek it, being a college cheerleader exposed me to more harassment, especially from college athletes.

After graduating, I became a teacher, thinking my professional status would shield me from such treatment. I found out I was pregnant shortly after I was hired. I was afraid to tell my school because it was my first year. My advising teacher suggested waiting as long as possible to announce it. Thankfully, my principal was supportive when I finally did. However, the undertone of sexual harassment persisted.

I remember one incident in the teacher's lounge where someone wrote "Debbie does Dallas" on the board, along with comments questioning my baby's paternity. It was demeaning and made me feel like I was still seen as a sex object despite my professional achievements. For three days, I watched to see who would erase it, but no one did. Eventually, I erased it myself.

Determined to address the issue, I decided to speak with my principal at the start of the next school year. Although I wasn't tenured, I felt it was important. The women at a year-end party encouraged me to speak up, as many had faced similar issues. When I finally spoke to my principal, he was visibly shocked and immediately called an emergency meeting. This led to the introduction of a mandatory sexual harassment training program in our district.

Later, in my current district, I faced similar issues. My experience and education were initially recognized, and I was placed in the administrative academy. However, I encountered resistance from male colleagues. One male teacher even sent a nasty email about me. I confronted him directly, using assertive language to earn his respect. While it improved our relationship, it was disappointing that I had to resort to aggression to be taken seriously.

Sexual harassment training is mandatory in all public schools. Inappropriate comments and behaviors still continued until the late 2010s. When I reported a colleague's email, the principal dismissed it, instead commenting on my appearance and suggesting I'd face difficulties due to my looks and intelligence.

In my current district, while there is less verbal harassment, opportunities for advancement are limited. Despite my qualifications and experience, I've been overlooked for administrative positions in favor of less qualified men or more passive women.

Reflecting on my experiences, I've realized that both men and women can be barriers to professional growth for women. Women sometimes feel threatened by strong, assertive colleagues. Despite these challenges, I remain assertive and vocal, thanks to my childhood experiences of being bullied and the strong support from my family. I believe in having courageous conversations and accepting constructive criticism, traits that have helped me navigate a career filled with both gender-based challenges and professional accomplishments.

Jealousy and stigma are often attached to being a PE teacher. When financial cuts led to the reduction of PE, I was reassigned to teach biology despite having a successful career in PE. I had been a curriculum leader and was nominated PE Teacher of the Year. However, the stigma of being a PE teacher followed me into the biology department.

In my new role, I sought help but was often met with resistance and unfriendly colleagues. This was especially challenging as I had never taught biology before. The transition highlighted the stark differences in how PE teachers are perceived compared to other educators.

Despite the challenges, I maintained my commitment to my students and my profession. My principal acknowledged the dysfunction within the biology department and appreciated my efforts to improve it. The department's toxic environment, marked by catty behavior and lack of collaboration, was a stark contrast to the supportive and unified PE department I had come from.

I faced verbal attacks in meetings and persistent undermining by certain colleagues. One passive teacher, who had been bullied herself, initially seemed relieved when the focus shifted to me. However, I confronted her directly, addressing her behavior and asserting my stance.

Throughout my career, I noticed that personal insecurities and egos often impacted professional dynamics. In one notable incident, a male colleague sent a derogatory email about my biology class. When this issue was addressed in a meeting, I received support from other colleagues who were tired of the toxic behavior. Their backing was crucial in confronting the bullying culture within the department.

Reflecting on my experiences, I recognize the impact of my upbringing and early bullying on my assertiveness. Growing up in a loving but passive family, I developed a strong sense of justice and a willingness to stand up for what is right. My feisty Italian grandparents were role models who influenced my assertive nature.

Despite the challenges, I continued to advocate for positive change in my professional environment. When PE programs were cut, I organized a comprehensive research project to expose the inaccuracies presented by the administration. This effort highlighted the importance of standing up for the truth and the value of PE in education.

These experiences have shaped my resilience and determination. I have consistently stood up for myself and others, navigating professional challenges with integrity and courage. My journey underscores the importance of perseverance, advocacy, and the willingness to confront systemic issues for the betterment of the educational environment.

Heather Timmons, BSN, RN, MSL

Growing up in Southern Oregon, Heather has been a nurse since 1992, with 20 years in Critical Care before transitioning to the Emergency Department, where she focused on staff education and critical care competencies. Later, she became a Trauma Program Coordinator, taking on leadership roles at local, regional, and state levels. After 26 years at one facility, she moved into travel nursing during the COVID-19 pandemic in 2021. She earned a Master of Science in Leadership degree in 2022, driven by her passion for supportive workplace cultures. She currently lives in Western North Carolina with her partner Ed and their rescue dog Zoe.

Cool

It's a funny thing when you experience a situation where you realize despite your wisdom, education, and, most importantly, intuition, you end up thinking, "How did *I* end up *here*? It's safe to say that no one takes a job thinking, "I hope my boss is toxic and horrible." We laugh during the movie "Horrible Bosses," confident in *our* assessment of spotting bad bosses and negative situations. Like others, I felt certain I possessed the appropriate skills and knowledge to identify the bad apple quickly; however, like choosing apples in the produce section, sometimes the shiny, perfect-looking apple is mushy, gross, and disappointing when the insides are revealed. My story probably parallels many others who experienced a negative workplace with a hostile boss. Yet, after working through my anger and bitterness, I've tried to turn my experience into a learning and growth opportunity, which required patience and selfreflection. But it wasn't easy.

I worked at a hospital where I had started as a New Graduate nurse twenty-six years prior. I worked in Critical Care and the Emergency Department and then managed the hospital's Trauma Program. I networked and often collaborated with the Trauma Program Coordinator from the other local hospital, Brand X, which raised eyebrows from some. Historically, the relationship between the two hospitals was competitive and, at times, contentious. Yet, my colleague, JD, and I saw our collaborative relationship as positively influential, modeling teamwork and community partnership. A few years later, JD invited me to join the trauma team at Brand X, requiring me to leave the comfort zone of what I've known my entire nursing career. JD claimed that we would be "equals" although she moved into the Trauma Program Manager role, leaving her now vacated Trauma Program Coordinator position for me; thus, JD was my boss. My decision to leave took much courage and soul-searching, yet this chance for professional growth and joining an effective team (or so I thought) piqued my curiosity and gave me hope for a shiny new professional journey. I was excited to start my new job, and JD was delighted to have me on the team. Looking back, I saw a few warning signs regarding the depth of JD's leadership skills, emotions, and decisions, but I trusted her vision of our partnership and shrugged off any doubt I had.

My first year at Brand X went well, and I welcomed working for a new hospital and system. I wasn't used to being the new girl, but I was open to learning, and JD helped show me around and introduced me to staff and leadership. I observed JD manage our trauma program, organize meetings, plan trauma classes, and essentially do everything. I followed along, letting her take the lead; however, after the first year, I asked for a check-in, how-are-things-going meeting. I started our meeting by thanking her for helping me and taking me under her guidance for the past year. I then asked for more responsibility and growth opportunities and explained that coming from managing the trauma program at my previous hospital, I was used to the autonomy, creativity, and responsibility of making decisions rather than just wading through chart reviews. I was ready for more responsibility. JD listened, and I felt a flicker of tension start to burn. Managing conflicts isn't a strong skill of mine, and I nervously kept trying to explain my position, thinking it was my fault she didn't understand me. "What do you mean?" JD finally asked while crossing her arms.

"I need my own lane," I said. "It's been great following you on the track this past year, but I need my own lane to run in" (my runner's mind helped with the metaphor). JD crossed one leg over the other and steadily bounced her foot. "Cool," she replied, the flicker of tension building into a small flame. She sighed and stated she would look at our list of responsibilities and activities and delegate some to me. There was no eye contact or other communication. I felt dismissed. I left her office feeling uncomfortable and guilty, like asking for my lane was offensive and I was being ungrateful, but that was my perception. After that conversation, things felt weird and slightly tense. She acted differently towards me. I shrugged it off and jumped into my new lane of responsibilities. I kept her apprised of my activities and asked for her opinions and feedback, yet the pilot light of tension stayed lit.

Over the next few years, it was apparent that JD was defensive and annoyed whenever I disagreed with her, asked questions, or suggested alternative solutions. Interestingly, our Director (JD's boss *and close friend*) asked my teammates and me to participate in JD's annual evaluation. I spent a week writing and editing my evaluation, wanting to be positive, supportive, fair, and honest. Although organized and efficient, JD was a new manager, and I felt she could benefit from coaching and support in learning leadership skills and communication techniques. My teammates responded with similar feedback, and we submitted our forms to our Director. The following week, JD called the team into her office and proceeded to tearfully inform us that she'd received her evaluation and that our feedback hurt her feelings. She was angry and sat behind her desk with her arms and legs crossed, her foot fiercely bouncing. We sat in stunned silence. The flicker of tension was now a blazing campfire.

I considered my role as a follower, knowing I played a part in our professional relationship. Leaders wanted followers who were motivated, inspired, loyal, and trusting; I felt anything but that. I sought out a colleague in the Professional Development department for personal coaching and assembled a plan to improve my relationship with JD. The tension was unpleasant between us, and I felt increased anxiety and mistrust; I hated feeling that way. I studied JD's leadership and communication style and developed my strategy for handling her reactive and defensive management style. Despite my attempts at establishing a better follower-leader relationship, I failed or felt like I had failed. And then Covid hit. Our office went home to work, and I welcomed the reprieve from the daily face-to-face tension, yet our relationship remained strained.

While working from home, I embarked on a personal journey to learn more about self-awareness, emotional intelligence, professional growth, and how to be an effective and supportive leader. Our return to the office in August 2020 coincided with my acceptance to a Master of Science in Leadership program. Bad boss, strained work environment, and Covid pandemic be damned! I excitedly shared my news with JD in the spirit of transparency and wanting to hit the reset button. She leaned against her office door frame, crossed her arms, and said, "Cool," without emotion, and asked, "What're you getting a master's in?" "Leadership," I said, "I've always been intrigued about relationships and connections with others, which is essentially the foundation of leadership." Again, she responded with "cool." I felt judged and exposed. Oh shit. My intuition punched me in the gut again. I realized I didn't trust JD, and I never would. I pondered her reaction, trying to understand her perspective. She was an associate degree nurse starting a BSN program, a degree required for her job; I thought about how I might feel in her position.

September 8, 2020 (the second day of my master's program), brought a horrific wildfire to our beautiful Southern Oregon valley. My house was a few blocks from where the fire started, and I planned to go home to pack a go-bag and retrieve my animals; however, my neighborhood was closed to traffic as the firefighters fought the flames. Our office watched live coverage of the fire and realized that the warm Santa Ana winds grabbed the fire and changed its direction to the North, towards a denser population and our hospital. We started to get nervous, and JD released us to leave for the rest of the day. I drove to my Dad and Stepmom's house, and we watched the massive plume of smoke in the sky grow closer. Eventually, they were evacuated and went to a safety center at the local county fairgrounds. My Dad was 84 years old, healthy, and mobile, but I worried about their home and how long until they could return, if ever. I returned to the hospital to help as they prepared for a possible evacuation. Around midnight, I drove home through an apocalyptic scenario, realizing the magnitude of devastation left by the fire, which was still actively burning. I cried as I saw huge flames engulf trees and homes and wondered if my family's homes had burned. Thankfully, my house and pets were safe, and I arranged for my Dad, stepmom, my ex-husband, his Dad, and caregiver, and two dogs to stay with me, as they were all evacuated and unsure if their homes were safe. Everyone was exhausted, and we anxiously wondered what the next day would reveal.

I spent the next day taking care of my family. The cell coverage was spotty, and there was no WiFi. I got a text to our team via a work text platform, checked in, and gave updates. My teammates opted to stay home in case the fire changed course again, requiring more evacuations, and I did the same. I cooked meals, did laundry, and cared for my family. I was grateful we were safe and together. A few days later, they received the all-clear and returned to their homes. Thankfully, their homes were spared; however, my sister's home burned to the ground.

Our team returned to work on Monday, and we spent the first hour debriefing about our experiences. We talked about some hospital employees, friends, and loved ones who lost their homes and businesses. The fire was devastating for our community, and we shared our anxiety and stress about this tragedy. JD went to her office and closed her door. Shortly after, she called me into her office, where she had a typed paper in front of her, moving it towards me across the desk. As I reached for it, she said, "I *have to* give you an unexcused absence. You didn't notify me about taking the day off after the fire." I stared at her, and my body went numb. I was speechless and emotionally hijacked. Everything happened in slow motion as I explained my family's evacuation situation. They needed me, and I *had* to be home. JD nodded slightly and looked at me with a little smile, "But Heather, *your house* didn't burn down. Other people lost their homes." I was stunned, and my mind went blank. I had to leave and blindly went for the door. JD quickly handed me the unexcused absence form, "You need to sign this." I bolted out of her office, through the hospital lobby, and made it outside just as the angry tears flowed. That was the catalyst that forever changed everything. I knew I would never trust her and couldn't stay at that job.

I'm not claiming that I reacted perfectly or always went above and beyond to improve things with JD. But I tried, I *really* did. I realized that once I'd lost trust in her, I would never feel safe, secure, or supported, no matter how many times we hit the reset button. I worked for her for five more months while I quietly sought other job opportunities, and once I secured my next move as a travel nurse, I submitted my notice. JD's muted reaction told me she was somewhat relieved. As was I.

Time can be an effective healer, allowing us to process and reflect on significant and impactful events, especially traumatic matters. Ironically, I used my master's program homework, materials, classmate feedback, and professor guidance to move through my hurt and anger to a place of acceptance and understanding. I frequently used my experience with JD as a writing prompt, applying my developing awareness and lessons learned to something new and exciting that I could grow from. I realized I needed to change the narrative; I couldn't shift JD's behavior, but I could change mine. I was determined to reclaim the energy and power I had given her; thus, I changed my negative thinking and committed myself to accepting a positive perspective. I admit it was challenging and took a while, but I'm in a much healthier place and learned some valuable lessons. I realized that JD's lesson was how *not* to act as a leader, providing me with a definitive bar; I knew I didn't want to be *that*.

I recently ran into JD at a conference. We hadn't talked to or seen each other for three years since I left. Our greeting was cordial and flat, exchanging minimal pleasantries. She had been let go from her Trauma Program Manager job and was in a leadership role at a pain clinic facility. I had a pang of compassion for her staff. I listened as she described how great she was at her job. She was the best boss, and everyone thought she was amazing. I smiled and turned to walk away.

I looked back over my shoulder, "Cool," I said. And I kept walking.

Collective Contributor Story Themes

Based on the document, several recurring themes emerge from the personal stories shared by various individuals. These include:

1. Workplace Toxicity and Leadership Failures: Many stories highlight experiences of toxic leadership, with employees being subjected to gaslighting, bullying, and narcissistic behaviors by superiors. Several narratives describe how toxic environments led to severe emotional and psychological distress, and how poor leadership undermined organizational success and personal well-being.

2. Resilience and Overcoming Adversity: A recurring theme is the ability to persevere despite difficult circumstances. Several individuals reflect on overcoming discrimination, workplace injustice, and personal traumas. Their stories convey the importance of resilience, adaptability, and maintaining integrity in the face of adversity.

3. The Impact of Trauma: Trauma, both personal and professional, plays a significant role in shaping the experiences shared. Some describe trauma from childhood or military experiences, while others reflect on the emotional toll of being undervalued or mistreated in the workplace. The longterm effects of trauma and the journey toward healing are central to their reflections.

4. Navigating Racial and Gender Bias: Several stories touch on the challenges of navigating racial and gender discrimination in professional environments. Individuals recount how bias, both overt and subtle, affected their career progression, relationships with colleagues, and overall experience in the workplace.

5. The Importance of Mentorship and Support: Many narratives emphasize the value of mentorship and support systems, both in overcoming challenges and in personal growth. Whether through family, mentors, or colleagues, having a supportive network is depicted as crucial to resilience and success.

6. Personal Growth and Transformation: A consistent theme is the journey of personal growth, selfawareness, and transformation. Individuals discuss how they learned from difficult experiences, became stronger, and, in many cases, transitioned into roles where they can help others avoid similar pitfalls.

These themes collectively highlight the personal and professional struggles of navigating toxic work environments, the strength found in resilience, and the importance of advocating for positive organizational cultures.

Creating Your Own Balance

In Chapter 10 of "Personal Stories," various experiences of workplace and personal trauma are shared, emphasizing the profound impact toxic environments and leadership can have on individuals. The stories highlight themes of resilience, growth, and the transformation that comes from adversity. For example, one individual faced a toxic work environment where their energy was depleted, affecting their personal life and relationships. Others describe navigating professional challenges, such as being undermined by supervisors or struggling with strained professional relationships. Despite the hardship, each story offers insights into overcoming adversity, demonstrating the importance of self-awareness, resilience, and the eventual reclaiming of personal power and positivity. These stories reflect how adversity can foster personal growth and wisdom when approached with determination and self-reflection.

APPENDIX 1

AI Model Predicting outcomes for Autocratic v Laissez-faire Leadership styles over 100 years.

Predicting outcomes for AUTOCRATIC v DEMOCRACY leadership styles over 100 years. I used AI to produce the outcomes for a thought experiment predicting 2 futures 10, 25, 50, and 100 years with Autocratic and Laissez-faire leaders: 1 with Autocratic leaders in charge of all countries and 1 with Laissez-faire leaders in charge of all countries. The outcomes are below.

	AI PREDICTED AUTOCRATIC LEADERSHIP STYLE	AI PREDICTED LAISSEZ-FAIRE LEADERSHIP STYLE
	OUTCOMES	OUTCOMES
	Predicting the impact of Autocratic Leadership and laissez-faire Leadership styles globally over extended periods involves considering various social, economic, and political factors. Here's a broad overview of potential outcomes at different time intervals:	
10 Years	In the initial 10 years, centralized decision-making might stabilize some countries, but political repression and censorship would likely increase. While some countries might see short-term economic growth due to streamlined decision-making, others could suffer from corruption and mismanagement. Social dynamics would feature increased human rights abuses despite some improvements in social programs. Internationally, conflicts could rise, and global cooperation might decrease.	Under laissez-faire leadership, the initial period would likely see a mixed set of outcomes. In organizations or countries with highly selfmotivated and competent individuals or teams, productivity and innovation might flourish due to the autonomy granted. However, in environments lacking such inherent motivation or where clear direction is needed, there could be significant issues with disorganization, inefficiency, and lack of accountability. Critical decisions might be delayed, and problems could fester without proactive management. Employees or citizens might feel unsupported and uncertain about their roles and responsibilities, potentially leading to decreased morale and engagement.
25 Years	Power structures would become entrenched, with potential for dynastic rule and increased resistance. Economic stagnation might set in, innovation could decline, and social inequality could grow. Alliances among autocratic states might form, leading to a divided global landscape.	Over a quarter-century, the impact of laissez-faire leadership would become more pronounced. In environments that initially thrived, the absence of consistent leadership might begin to take its toll as cohesive strategy and long-term planning falter. Innovation could stagnate without direction and support. In less proactive settings, the lack of oversight could lead to systemic issues such as corruption, poor performance, and significant inequalities. Organizational or societal structures might become fragmented, with clear disparities between those who can navigate the lack of direction and those who cannot. There could be an increase in internal conflicts and a decline in overall effectiveness and efficiency.
50 Years	Deeply entrenched regimes might face significant challenges, potential revolutions, or civil wars. Economic inefficiencies and corruption could cause widespread decline, with some states becoming isolated. Social repression would be pervasive, and human rights abuses rampant. International relations would likely see large-scale conflicts as autocratic states vie for resources.	Laissez-faire leadership would likely result in deeply entrenched issues. Without strong leadership to address and mitigate challenges, many organizations or countries might experience severe inefficiencies and widespread disarray. The gaps between different groups—those thriving on autonomy and those struggling without guidance—would become more pronounced. In many cases, the lack of strategic direction could lead to significant economic and social problems, including stagnation, increasing inequality, and potential unrest. Without proactive management, innovation would likely suffer, and the ability to adapt to changing circumstances could be severely compromised.
100 Years	Many autocratic regimes might collapse due to unsustainable governance, potentially giving rise to new political systems. Economies could face long-term devastation, with some reverting to feudal-like systems. Societal scars from prolonged repression would be deep, possibly sparking democratic or alternative movements. Global order might be fractured, with ongoing conflicts and instability. Autocratic governance, while potentially offering short-term stability, often leads to long-term negative consequences such as economic inefficiency, social repression, and increased potential for conflict. The resilience and adaptability of human societies, however, suggest that new forms of governance and social structures would likely emerge over time, seeking to address the failures of prolonged autocracy.	The long-term consequences of Laissez-faire Leadership would be fully realized. Successful areas might still exist, driven by exceptionally self-motivated and competent individuals, but these would likely be the exception rather than the rule. Most environments would suffer from chronic issues related to lack of leadership, including deep systemic inefficiencies, widespread inequality, and potential social fragmentation. The absence of cohesive strategy and proactive problem-solving could lead to significant societal or organizational decline. There might be a shift towards more structured forms of governance as a reaction to the failures of laissez-faire leadership, with new systems emerging to address the long-standing issues created by decades of minimal oversight and direction.

APPENDIX 2

AI Model Predicting outcomes for Democratic Leadership v Transformative Leadership styles over 100 years.

Predicting outcomes for DEMOCRATIC v TRANSFORMATIVE leadership styles over 100 years. I used AI to produce the outcomes for a thought experiment predicting 4 futures 10, 25, 50, and 100 years with Autocratic and Democratic leaders: #3 with Democratic leaders in charge of all countries and #4 with Transformative leaders in charge of all countries. The outcomes are below.

	AI PREDICTED DEMOCRATIC LEADERSHIP STYLE OUTCOMES	AI PREDICTED TRANSFORMATIVE LEADERSHIP STYLE OUTCOMES
	Predicting the outcomes of global democratic leadership over extended periods involves various factors such as political stability, economic growth, and social progress. Here's a broad overview of potential outcomes at different time intervals:	
10 Years	Democratic Leadership would increase political stability and transparency, with greater citizen participation in governance. Economic growth would be driven by innovation and accountability, and social dynamics would see enhanced human rights and social justice. International relations would strengthen through cooperation and diplomacy.	Under transformative leadership, as defined by Carolyn Shields (2010/2016), significant positive changes would be observed. Transformative Leaders focus on equity, social justice, and organizational change that empowers individuals and groups. Initially, there would be an emphasis on building trust, fostering inclusive practices, and creating a shared vision. The leader's commitment to dialogue and reflective practice would help identify and begin addressing systemic inequities. As a result, organizational culture would become more collaborative, innovative, and inclusive, leading to improved morale and increased engagement among all members.
25 Year	Mature democratic institutions with strong checks and balances would foster civic engagement. Sustainable economic development would focus on reducing inequality and advancing technology. Social progress in justice, diversity, and inclusion would continue, with a strong emphasis on environmental sustainability. Global order would stabilize with effective multilateral organizations addressing common challenges.	The impact of Transformative Leadership would be deeply rooted within the organization or community. Policies and practices promoting equity and social justice would be well established. The environment would be characterized by high levels of mutual respect and collaboration. Long-term strategic goals focusing on sustainable development and continuous improvement would likely have been implemented. The commitment to reflective practice and ongoing dialogue would ensure that the organization remains adaptable and responsive to emerging challenges. There would be a noticeable improvement in outcomes related to diversity, equity, and inclusion, and the organization would likely be seen as a leader in these areas.
50 Years	Highly developed democratic institutions would adapt governance mechanisms, promoting global leadership in democratic values. Economic prosperity would be widespread, reducing poverty and inequality, with high standards of living. Social dynamics would see a deeply ingrained culture of democracy and human rights. International alliances would be strong and stable, addressing transnational issues effectively.	Transformative Leadership would have resulted in profound and lasting changes. The principles of equity, social justice, and inclusivity would be deeply ingrained in the organizational DNA. There would be a strong sense of community and shared purpose, with all members feeling valued and empowered to contribute. The organization would be characterized by high levels of innovation and adaptability, as continuous improvement and reflective practice are core elements of its culture. The successes achieved in social justice and equity would likely inspire other organizations or communities to adopt similar transformative approaches. Additionally, the organization's ability to adapt and thrive in the face of challenges would ensure its long-term sustainability and success.
100 Years	Democratic systems would show resilience and adaptability, potentially evolving to address contemporary challenges. Economies would be highly advanced, with equitable resource distribution and continuous innovation. Societal harmony would be profound, with deeply rooted principles of justice and inclusion. The international community would be cohesive, effectively collaborating to address global challenges and maintaining peace through diplomacy. Democratic leadership is likely to foster political stability, economic prosperity, and social progress. Democratic systems promote accountability, transparency, and inclusiveness, leading to sustainable development and enhanced well-being. Despite challenges like political polarization, democratic systems' resilience and adaptability can address these issues effectively, contributing to a more peaceful and stable global order.	Transformative Leadership would be monumental. The organization or community would have evolved into a model of equity, social justice, and sustainable development. The deeply embedded practices of dialogue, reflection, and continuous improvement would have created a resilient and adaptive system capable of navigating future challenges. The long-term focus on empowerment and inclusivity would result in an environment where every individual has the opportunity to reach their full potential. The organization's sustained success in promoting social justice and equity would serve as a blueprint for others, influencing broader societal change. The transformative leadership approach would have fundamentally reshaped the culture, values, and practices, ensuring a legacy of positive impact and continuous growth.

Bibliography

Alexander, M. (2010). The New Jim Crow: Mass Incarceration in the Age of Colorblindness. The New Press.

American Psychological Association. (2013). Diagnostic and Statistical Manual of Mental Disorders (5th ed.). Washington, DC.

American Psychological Association. (n.d.). Toxic workplaces leave employees sick, scared, and looking for an exit. https://www.apa.org/topics/healthy-workplaces/toxic-workplace

Arakawa, D., & Greenberg, M. (2007). Optimistic managers and their influence on productivity and employee engagement in a technology organization: Implications for coaching psychologists. International Coaching Psychology Review, 2(1), 78-89.

Aquino, K., Grover, S. L., Bradfield, M., & Allen, D. G. (1999). The effects of negative affectivity, hierarchical status, and self-determination on workplace victimization. Academy of Management Journal, 42(3), 260-272.

Aquino, K., Lewis, M. U., & Bradfield, M. (1999). Justice constructs, negative affectivity, and employee deviance: A proposed model and empirical test. Journal of Organizational Behavior, 20(7), 10731091.

Aquino, K., Tripp, T. M., & Bies, R. J. (2001). How employees respond to personal offense: The effects of blame attribution, victim status, and offender status on revenge and reconciliation in the workplace. Journal of Applied Psychology, 86(1), 52-59. https://doi.org/10.1037/00219010.86.1.52

Baldwin, D. S., Waldman, S., & Allgulander, C. (2011). Evidence-based pharmacological treatment of generalized anxiety disorder. International Journal of Neuropsychopharmacology, 14(5), 697-710.

Bandura, A. (1977). Social Learning Theory. Englewood Cliffs, NJ: Prentice-Hall.

Bar-On, D. (1995). Fear and Hope: Three Generations of the Holocaust. Harvard University Press.

Baron, R. A., & Neuman, J. H. (1996). Workplace violence and workplace aggression: Evidence on their relative frequency and potential causes. Aggressive Behavior: Official Journal of the International Society for Research on Aggression, 22(3), 161-173.

Bass, B. M. (1990). From Transactional to Transformational Leadership: Learning to share the vision. Organizational Dynamics, 18(3), 19-31.

Bass, B. M., & Bass, R. (2008). The Bass Handbook of Leadership: Theory, Research, and Managerial Applications. Free Press.

Bass, B. M., & Riggio, R. E. (2006). Transformational Leadership. (2nd ed.). Lawrence Erlbaum Associates.

Bazerman, M. H., & Moore, D. A. (2012). Judgment in Managerial Decision Making. Wiley.

Beck, J. S. (2011). Cognitive Behavior Therapy: Basics and Beyond. Guilford Press.

Benjet C., Bromet E., Karam, E.G., Kessler R.C., McLaughlin KA, Ruscio AM, Shahly V, Stein DJ, Petukhova, M., Hill E, Alonso J, Atwoli L, Bunting B, Bruffaerts R, Caldas-de-Almeida JM, de Girolamo G, Florescu S, Gureje O, Huang Y, Lepine JP, Kawakami N, Kovess-Masfety V, Medina-Mora ME, Navarro-Mateu F, Piazza M, Posada-Villa J, Scott KM, Shalev A, Slade T, ten Have M, Torres Y, Viana MC, Zarkov Z, Koenen KC. (2023, June). The epidemiology of traumatic event exposure worldwide: results from the World Mental Health Survey Consortium. Psychol Med. 2016 Jan;46(2):327-43. doi: 10.1017/S0033291715001981. Epub 2015 Oct 29. PMID: 26511595; PMCID: PMC4869975.

Bies, R. J., & Tripp, T. M. (1996). Beyond distrust: "Getting even" and the need for revenge. In R. M. Kramer & T. R. Tyler (Eds.). Trust in organizations: Frontiers of theory and research (pp. 246260). Sage Publications.

Blanchard, K., Zigarmi, P., & Zigarmi, D. (1985). Leadership and the One Minute Manager: Increasing Effectiveness through Situational Leadership. William Morrow & Co.

Boddy, C. R. (2023). The Corporate Psychopaths Theory of the Global Financial Crisis. Journal of Business Ethics, 102, 255-259. https://doi.org/10.1007/s10551-011-0810-4

Bracha, H. S. (2004). Freeze, flight, fight, fright, faint: Adaptationist perspectives on the acute stress response spectrum. CNS Spectrums, 9(9), 679-685.

Bracken, D. W., Rose, D. S., & Church, A. H. (2016). The Evolution and Devolution of 360° Feedback. Industrial and Organizational Psychology, 9(4), 761-794.

Brave Heart, M. Y. H., & DeBruyn, L. M. (1998). The American Indian Holocaust: Healing historical unresolved grief. American Indian and Alaska Native Mental Health Research, 8(2), 60-82.

Braveman, P., Egerter, S., & Williams, D. R. (2011). The social determinants of health: Coming of age. Annual Review of Public Health, 32, 381-398.

Brutus, S., London, M., & Martineau, J. (1999). The impact of 360-degree feedback on planning for career development. Journal of Management Development, 18(8), 676-693.

Burns, J. M. (1978). Leadership. Harper & Row.

Cameron, K. S. (2012). Positive leadership: Strategies for extraordinary performance (2nd ed.). BerrettKoehler Publishers.

Calhoun, L. G., & Tedeschi, R. G. (2006). The foundations of posttraumatic growth: An expanded framework. In L. G. Calhoun & R. G. Tedeschi (Eds.), Handbook of posttraumatic growth: Research and practice (pp. 1–23). Mahwah, NJ: Lawrence Erlbaum Associates.

Cannon, W. B. (1915). Bodily Changes in Pain, Hunger, Fear, and Rage. Appleton and Company.

Carnegie, D. (1936). How to Win Friends and Influence People. New York: Simon and Schuster.

Casey, B.J., Somerville, L.H., Gotlib, I.H., Ayduk, O., Franklin, N.T., Askren, M.K., Jonides, J., Berman, M.G., Wilson, N.L., Teslovich, T., Glover, G., Zayas, V., Mishcel, W., & Shoda, Y. (2011). Behavioral and neural correlates of delay of gratification 40 years later. Proceedings of the National Academy of Sciences, 108(36), 14998-15003.

Cashman, K. (2008). *Leadership from the Inside Out: Becoming a Leader for Life* (2nd ed.). BerrettKoehler Publishers.

CDC (2024, April 25). Facts about suicide. CDC [Suicide prevention]. https://www.cdc.gov/suicide/facts/index.html#:~:text=Suicide%20is%20a%20serious%20public,one%20death%20every%2011%20minutes.&text=The%20number%20of%20people%20who,att empt%20suicide%20is%20even%20higher.

Clark, D. A., & Beck, A. T. (2010). Cognitive Therapy of Anxiety Disorders: Science and Practice. Guilford Press.

Clark, D. M., & Wells, A. (1995). A cognitive model of social phobia. In R. G. Heimberg, M. R. Liebowitz, D. A. Hope, & F. R. Schneier (Eds.), Social Phobia: Diagnosis, Assessment, and Treatment (pp. 69-93). Guilford Press.

Collins, J. (2001). Good to Great: Why Some Companies Make the Leap and Others Don't. New York: HarperCollins.

Collins, J. (2005). Level 5 Leadership: The Triumph of Humility and Fierce Resolve. Harvard Business Review, 83(7/8), 136-146.

Cortina, L. M., & Magley, V. J. (2003). Raising voice, risking retaliation: Events following interpersonal mistreatment in the workplace. Journal of Occupational Health Psychology, 8(4), 247-265.

Covey, Stephen R. (1989). *The 7 Habits of Highly Effective People: Powerful Lessons in Personal Change*. Free Press.

Deci, E. L., & Ryan, R. M. (2000). The "What" and "Why" of Goal Pursuits: Human Needs and the SelfDetermination of Behavior. Psychological Inquiry, 11(4), 227-268.

Denchak, M. (2024, April 16). Flint Water Crisis: Everything You Need to Know. NRDC. https://www.nrdc.org/stories/flint-water-crisis-everything-you-need-know#summary

Dirks, K. T., & Ferrin, D. L. (2002). Trust in leadership: Meta-analytic findings and implications for research and practice. Journal of Applied Psychology, 87(4), 611-628.

Dixon, W. (1962). You can't judge a book by the cover [Song recorded by Bo Diddley]. On Bo Diddley. Checker. Chicago, Illinois.

Duckworth, A. L., & Seligman, M. E. (2005). Self-discipline outdoes IQ in predicting academic performance of adolescents. Psychological Science, 16(12), 939-944.

Dweck, C. S. (2006). Mindset: The New Psychology of Success. Random House Publishing Group.

Eagly, A. H., Johannesen-Schmidt, M. C., & Van Engen, M. L. (2003). Transformational, transactional, and laissez-faire leadership styles: A meta-analysis comparing women and men. Psychological Bulletin, 129(4), 569-591.

Edmonds, W. M. (2021). Intoxicating Followership: in the Jonestown Massacre. Emerald Publishing Limited. Kindle Edition.

Edmondson, A. C. (2003). Speaking up in the operating room: How team leaders promote learning in interdisciplinary action teams. Journal of Management Studies, 40(6), 1419-1452.

Ehring, T., & Watkins, E. R. (2008). Repetitive Negative Thinking as a Transdiagnostic Process. International Journal of Cognitive Therapy, 1(3), 192-205.

Einarsen, S., Aasland, M. S., & Skogstad, A. (2007). Destructive leadership behavior: A definition and conceptual model. The Leadership Quarterly, 18(3), 207-216.

Eliot, T. S. (1949). The Cocktail Party. Harcourt, Brace.

Engel, G. L. (1977). The Need for a New Medical Model: A Challenge for Biomedicine. Science, 196(4286). 129-136.

Fayol, H. (1949). General and Industrial Management. [C. Storrs, Trans.]. Pitman Publishing. (Original work published 1916).

Feiler, B. (2020). Life Is in Transitions: Mastering Change at Any Age. Penguin Publishing Group. Kindle Edition.

Fiske, S. T. (2004). Social Beings: Core Motives in Social Psychology. New York: Wiley.

Foa, E. B., & Kozak, M. J. (1986). Emotional processing of fear: Exposure to corrective information. Psychological Bulletin, 99(1), 20.

Foucault, M. (1975). Discipline and Punish: The Birth of the Prison. Vintage Books.

Fox, S., Spector, P. E., & Miles, D. (2001). Counterproductive work behavior (CWB) in response to job stressors and organizational justice: Some mediator and moderator tests for autonomy and emotions. Journal of Vocational Behavior, 59(3), 291-309.

Fredrickson, B. L. (2001). The Role of Positive Emotions in Positive Psychology: The Broaden-and-Build Theory of Positive Emotions. American Psychologist, 56(3), 218-226.

Freire, P. (1970). Pedagogy of the Oppressed. Rowman & Littlefield Publishers, Inc.

Gallup. (2007). The business benefits of positive leadership. https://www.gallup.com/business-benefits-positive-leadership

Getzels, J. W., & Thelen, H. A. (1960). The Classroom Group as a Unique Social System. In N. B. Henry (Ed.), The Dynamics of Instructional Groups: Sociopsychological Aspects of Teaching and Learning. (pp. 53-82). University of Chicago Press.

Goldman, A. (2006). Personality Disorders in Leaders: Implications of a Psychodynamic Perspective for Consulting Psychologists. Consulting Psychology Journal: Practice and Research, 58(4), 252-268. https://doi.org/10.1037/1065-9293.58.4.252

Goleman, D., Boyatzis, R., & McKee, A. (2013). Primal Leadership: Unleashing the Power of Emotional Intelligence. Harvard Business Review Press.

Gramsci, A. (1971). Selections from the Prison Notebooks. International Publishers.

Greenberg, M., & Arakawa, D. (n.d.). The business benefits of positive leadership. Gallup. Retrieved from https://www.gallup.com

Gundlach, M. J., Douglas, S. C., & Martinko, M. J. (2003). The decision to blow the whistle: A social information processing framework. Academy of Management Review, 28(1), 107-123.

Hare, R. D. (1993). Without Conscience: The Disturbing World of the Psychopaths Among Us. New York: The Guilford Press.

Hare, R. D. (2006). Snakes in Suits: When Psychopaths Go to Work. New York: HarperCollins Publishers.

Hartmann, T. (2021). The Hidden History of American Healthcare: Why Sickness Bankrupts You and Makes Others Insanely Rich. Berrett-Koehler Publishers.

Hegtvedt, K. A. (2010). Social psychological perspectives on justice. Springer.

Heifetz, R., & Linsky, M. (2002). Leadership on the Line: Staying Alive through the Dangers of Leading. Harvard Business Review Press.

Herman, J. L. (1992). Trauma and Recovery: The Aftermath of Violence—from Domestic Abuse to Political Terror. Basic Books.

Hersey, P., & Blanchard, K. H. (1985). Management of organizational behavior: Utilizing human resources. (5th ed.). Prentice Hall.

Hill, L., & Artiga, S. (2022, August 22). COVID-19 cases and deaths by race/ethnicity: Current data and changes over time. KFF. https://www.kff.org/racial-equity-and-health-policy/issue-brief/covid-19-cases-and-deaths-by-race-ethnicity-current-data-and-changes-over-time/

Hinkin, T. R., & Schriesheim, C. A. (2008). An examination of "non-leadership": From laissez-faire leadership to leader reward omission and punishment omission. Journal of Applied Psychology, 93(6), 1234-1248.

Hitlin, S. (2003). Values as the Core of Personal Identity: Drawing Links between Two Theories of Self. Social Psychology Quarterly, 66(2), 118-137.

Hofstede, G. (1980). Culture's Consequences: International Differences in Work-Related Values. Sage Publications.

Hovannisian, R. G. (1992). The Armenian Genocide: History, Politics, Ethics. St. Martin's Press.

Ibarra, H., Carter, N. M., & Silva, C. (2010). Why do men still get more promotions than women? Harvard Business Review, 88(9), 80-85.

Inwood, B. (2007). *Seneca: Selected Philosophical Letters*. [Translated]. Oxford University Press. N.Y. ISBN:978-0-19-823894-2.

Jones, J. H. (1981). Bad Blood: The Tuskegee Syphilis Experiment. Free Press.

Kabat-Zinn, J. (1994). Wherever You Go, There You Are: Mindfulness Meditation in Everyday Life. Hyperion.

Karunathilake, I. & Witharana, C. (2020). Take-Home: Communication skills can be taught. Effective Medical Communication: The A, B, C, D, E of it, 257-266. www.//doi.org/10.1007/978-981-153409-6_25.

Kilpatrick, D. G., Resnick, H. S., Milanak, M. E., Miller, M. W., Keyes, K. M., & Friedman, M. J. (2013). National Estimates of Exposure to Traumatic Events and PTSD Prevalence Using DSM-IV and DSM-5 Criteria. Journal of Traumatic Stress, 26(5), 537-547. https://doi.org/10.1002/jts.21848.

Kishimi, I., & Koga, F. (2019). The Courage to Be Disliked: The Japanese Phenomenon That Shows You How to Change Your Life and Achieve Real Happiness. Atria Books.

Lazarus, R.S., & Folkman, S. (1984). Stress, Appraisal, and Coping. New York: Springer Publishing Company.

LeDoux, J. E. (1996). The Emotional Brain: The Mysterious Underpinnings of Emotional Life. Simon & Schuster.

Lewin, K. (1936). Principles of Topological Psychology. McGraw-Hill.

Lewin, K. (1939). Experiments in Social Space. Harvard Educational Review, 9(3), 270-277.

Lewin, K. (1943). Defining the Field at a Given Time. Psychological Review, 50(3), 292-310.

Lewin, K. (1947). Frontiers in Group Dynamics: Concept, Method, and Reality in Social Science; Social Equilibria and Social Change. *Human Relations*, 1(1), 5-41.

Liden, R. C., Wayne, S. J., & Sparrowe, R. T. (2000). An examination of the mediating role of psychological empowerment on the relations between the job, interpersonal relationships, and work outcomes. Journal of Applied Psychology, 85(3), 407-416.

Lipman-Blumen, J. (2004). *The Allure of Toxic Leaders: Why We Follow Destructive Bosses and Corrupt Politicians—and How We Can Survive Them.* Oxford University Press.

Locke, E. A., & Latham, G. P. (2002). Building a Practically Useful Theory of Goal Setting and Task Motivation. American Psychologist, 57(9), 705-717.

Luthans, F., & Youssef, C. M. (2007). Emerging Positive Organizational Behavior. Journal of Management, 33(3), 321-349.

Maren, S. (2001). Neurobiology of Pavlovian fear conditioning. Annual Review of Neuroscience, 24(1), 897-931.

Marx, K. (1867). Capital: Critique of Political Economy. Penguin Classics.

Mass Shooting Tracker. (2023, December 31). U.S. Mass Shootings in the United States. https://www.massshootingtracker.site

Mathieu, C. (2014). Employee Well-Being Under Corporate Psychopath Leaders. In Corporate Psychopathy: Investigating Destructive Personalities in the Workplace. Springer.

Mathieu, C. (2021). Dark Personalities in the Workplace. Academic Press.

McCombs, B. L., & Miller, L. (2006). Learner-Centered Psychological Principles: A Framework for School Reform and Redesign. Washington, DC: American Psychological Association.

McCombs, B. L., & Miller, L. (2007). Learner-centered classroom practices and assessments: Maximizing student motivation, learning, and achievement. Corwin Press.

McGaugh, J. L. (2004). The amygdala modulates the consolidation of memories of emotionally arousing experiences. Annual Review of Neuroscience, 27, 1-28.

McGovern, M. (2022, November 22).. Employees don't trust HR! Here's why – and 4 things you can do now. HRMorning. https://www.hrmorning.com/articles/employees-dont-trust/

McGregor, D. (1960). The Human Side of Enterprise. McGraw-Hill.

Mezirow, J. (1991). Transformative Dimensions of Adult learning. Jossey-Bass.

Milad, M. R., & Quirk, G. J. (2012). Fear extinction as a model for translational neuroscience: Ten years of progress. Annual Review of Psychology, 63, 129-151.

Moffitt, T. E., Arseneault, L., Belsky, D., Dickson, N., Hancox, R. J., Harrington, H., Houts, R., Poulton, R., Roberts, B.W., Ross, S., Sears, M.R., Thompson, W.M, & Caspi, A. (2011). A gradient of childhood self-control predicts health, wealth, and public safety. Proceedings of the National Academy of Sciences, 108(7), 2693-2698. https://doi.org/10.1073/pnas.1010076108

Monroe, S. M., & Simons, A. D. (1991). Diathesis-stress theories in the context of life stress research: Implications for the depressive disorders. Psychological Bulletin, 110(3), 406-425.

Montuori, A. & Stephenson, H. (2010). Creativity, cultural contact, and diversity. Routledge. https://doi.org/10.1080/02604021003680503

Montuori, A., & Donnelly, G. (2017). Transformative Leadership. Routledge.

Near, J. P., & Miceli, M. P. (1996). Whistle-blowing: Myth and reality. Journal of Management, 22(3), 507-526.

Nolen-Hoeksema, S., Wisco, B. E., & Lyubomirsky, S. (2008). Rethinking Rumination. Perspectives on Psychological Science, 3(5), 400-424.

Northouse, P. G. (2018). Leadership: Theory and Practice. (8th ed.). Sage Publications.

Oyez. (n.d.). Thomas v. Chicago Park District. Cornell University Legal Information Institute, Justia, and Chicago-Kent College of Law. https://www.oyez.org/cases/2001/00-1249

Perry P. (1995). Attrition in United States YMCAs. [9721829]. University of San Francisco. Proquest. https://www.proquest.com/pqdtglobal1/dissertationstheses/attrition-united-states-ymcas/docview/304283402/sem-2?accountid=14674

Reverby, S. M. (2009). Examining Tuskegee: The Infamous Syphilis Study and Its Legacy. [Presidential Apology: The White House Office of the Press Secretary (1997).] University of North Carolina Press.

Robinson, S. L. (1996). Trust and breach of the psychological contract. Administrative Science Quarterly, 41(4), 574-599.

Rokeach, M. (1973). The Nature of Human Values. New York: Free Press.

Saad, M., de Medeiros, R., & Mosini, A. C. (2017). Are We Ready for a True Biopsychosocial–Spiritual Model? The Many Meanings of "Spiritual." Medicines, 4(4), 79. https://doi.org/10.3390/medicines4040079. https://www.mdpi.com/journal/medicines

Sapolsky, R. M., Romero, L. M., & Munck, A. U. (2000). How do glucocorticoids influence stress responses? Integrating permissive, suppressive, stimulatory, and preparative actions. Endocrine Reviews, 21(1), 55-89.

Schein, E. H. (2010). Organizational Culture and Leadership. Jossey-Bass.

Schneider, B. (1990). (ed). Organizational Climate and Culture. Jossey-Bass

Schwartz, S. H. (1992). Universals in the Content and Structure of Values: Theoretical Advances and Empirical Tests in 20 Countries. Advances in Experimental Social Psychology, 25, 1-65.

Sherwood, J., & Smith, L. (2021). The impact of toxic leadership on workplace culture and employee well-being. Journal of Organizational Behavior, 42(3), 271-290.

Shields, C. M. (2010). Transformative leadership: Working for equity in diverse contexts. Educational Administration Quarterly, 46(4), 558-589.

Shields, C. M. (2011). Transformative Leadership: A Reader. Peter Lang Publishing.

Sinek, S. (2009). Start with Why: How Great Leaders Inspire Everyone to Take Action. Portfolio.

Skarlicki, D. P., & Folger, R. (1997). Retaliation in the workplace: The roles of distributive, procedural, and interactional justice. Journal of Applied Psychology, 82(3), 434-443.

Skogstad, A., Einarsen, S., Torsheim, T., Aasland, M. S., & Hetland, H. (2007). The destructiveness of laissez-faire leadership behavior. Journal of Occupational Health Psychology, 12(1), 80–92. https://doi.org/10.1037/1076-8998.12.1.80

Smedley, B.D., Stith, A.Y., & Nelson, A.R. (2003). (Eds.) Unequal Treatment: Confronting Racial and Ethnic Disparities in Health Care Institute of Medicine (US) Committee on Understanding and Eliminating Racial and Ethnic Disparities in Health Care. National Academies Press: Washington, DC. https://doi.org/10.17226/12875

Smith, S. (2016, February 16). Fewer than half of U.S. employers offer support following workplace trauma. EHS Today. https://www.ehstoday.com/health/fewer-half-us-employersoffer-support-following-workplace-trauma

Society for Human Resource Management. (2019). The High Cost of a Toxic Workplace Culture: How Culture Impacts the Workforce—and the Bottom Line. https://www.shrm.org/content/dam/en/shrm/research/SHRM-Culture-Report_2019.pdf

Soosalu, G.& Oka, M. (2012). mBraining: Using Your Multiple Brains to Do Cool Stuff. Balboa Press.

Stogdill, R.M. (1974). Handbook of Leadership: A survey of theory and leadership. The Free Press.

Stover, E., & Weinstein, H. M. (Eds.). (2004). My Neighbor, My Enemy: Justice and Community in the Aftermath of Mass Atrocity. Cambridge University Press.

Swedo, E. A., Aslam, M. V., Dahlberg, L. L., Niolon, PH., Guinn, A.S., Simon, T.R., & Mercy, J.A. (2023, June 30). Prevalence of Adverse Childhood Experiences Among U.S. Adults — Behavioral Risk Factor Surveillance System, 2011–2020. PubMed. 72(26);707–715

Tannenbaum, R., & Schmidt, W. H. (1958). How to choose a leadership pattern. Harvard Business Review, 36(2), 95-101.

Taylor, S. N., & Snyder, C. R. (2012). Positive psychology and leadership development. In S. J. Zaccaro, S. M. Banks (Eds.), Leader development for transforming organizations: Growing leaders for tomorrow (pp. 43-66). Routledge.

Tedeschi, R. G., & Moore, B. A. (2016). The posttraumatic growth workbook: Coming through trauma wiser, stronger, and more resilient. New Harbinger Publications.

Tedeschi, R. G., Shakespeare-Finch, J., Taku, K., & Calhoun, L. G. (2018). Posttraumatic Growth: Theory, Research, and Applications. Routledge.

Tepper, B. J., Duffy, M. K., & Shaw, J. D. (2001). Personality moderators of the relationship between abusive supervision and subordinates' resistance. Journal of Applied Psychology, 86(5), 974-983.

The Armstrong Law Firm (2017, May 12). 250,000 workers are wrongfully terminated annually. [Blog]. https://www.thearmstronglawfirm.com/blog/2017/05/250000-workers-are-wrongfullyterminated-annually/

University of Sussex. (2023). The business impact of positive leadership. https://www.sussex.ac.uk/research/business-impact-positive-leadership.

Van der Kolk, B. (2014). The Body Keeps the Score: Brain, Mind, and Body in the Healing of Trauma. Viking.

Wajngarten, M. (2023, July 12). Lessons From the Longest Study on Happiness. MedScape. https://www.medscape.com/viewarticle/994286?form=fpf

Walker, S. M., & Watkins, D. V. (2023). Toxic Leadership: Research and Cases. Routledge.

Watkins, D. V., & Walker, S. M. (2021). Victims in the Dark Shadows: A Model of Toxic Leadership. Journal of Organizational Psychology, 21(2), 10-20. Available at [commons.erau.edu] (https://commons.erau.edu/publication/1715/).

Westen, D. (1998). The scientific status of unconscious processes: Is Freud really dead? Journal of the American Psychoanalytic Association, 46(4), 1061–1106. https://doi.org/10.1177/000306519804600403

Wilkinson, R., & Pickett, K. (2009). The spirit level: Why more equal societies almost always do better. Allen Lane.

YMCA of the USA. (2023). https://www.ymca.org/who-we-are/our-impact/

Zhang, Y., & Peterson, S. J. (2019). Toxic leadership behaviors and their impact on the workforce: A review. The Leadership Quarterly, 30(5), 697- 709. https: //doi.org/10.1016/j.leaqua.2019.101313

About The Author

Dr. Pettis Perry is a transformative leader, educator, consultant, author, and thought leader in organizational effectiveness, with nearly six decades of hands-on experience. His life and work are grounded in an unwavering commitment to healing, fairness, and both personal and systemic transformation.

He lives with Complex Posttraumatic Stress Disorder (CPTSD), but rather than allowing trauma to define his story, Dr. Perry chose to make it a catalyst for change. Over the decades, he has navigated harm and healing, ultimately forging a path toward a meaningful life for himself and his family, one built on purpose, growth, and the radical act of self-empowerment.

Dr. Perry's lived experiences now form the foundation of his mission to help others create more meaningful lives for themselves and support leaders in building trauma-informed, inclusive, and high-performing communities. Through teaching, writing, and consulting, he advocates for safer workplaces and institutions that have kinder, healthier, and more just cultures producing environments where people are empowered to reach their full potential.

His latest work, *Confronting Trauma & Toxicity: Tools for Transformative Leaders, Workplace Warriors, and Community Builders to Foster Resilience and Meaningful Lives*, is a powerful illustration of how to convert personal pain into purposeful impact, while inspiring others to do the same.

Index